THE GUINNESS BOOK OF
WINNERS AND CHAMPIONS

FAWLTY TOWERS

MODESTY BLAISE
by PETER O'DONNELL

MODESTY BEGINS A CIRCUIT OF THE GROUND FLOOR...

ARE THOSE TEAR-GAS BOMBS YOU'RE SCATTERING?

JUST LITTLE SMOKE BOMBS

Key—see page 4

THE GUINNESS BOOK OF
WINNERS AND CHAMPIONS

CHRIS COOK

Sports Editor
Peter Matthews

Guinness Superlatives Limited
2 Cecil Court, London Road, Enfield, Middlesex

Editor: Anne Smith

© Chris Cook, Peter Matthews and Guinness Superlatives Limited

ISBN 0 85112 201 9

British Library Cataloguing in Publication Data
Cook, Chris
    The Guinness book of winners and champions.
    1. Competitions – Dictionaries
    I. Title   II. Matthews, Peter, *b. 1945*
    790.13′4   GV11
    ISBN 0–85112–201–9

Published by
Guinness Superlatives Limited
2 Cecil Court, London Road
Enfield, Middlesex

Guinness is a registered trademark of Guinness Superlatives Limited

Design and layout: David Roberts

Illustration research: Melanie Georgi, Valerie Greenhill, Anne Smith, Beverley Waites

Jacket artwork: Pat Gibbon

Printed and bound in Great Britain by Redwood Burn Limited, Trowbridge & Esher

Key to frontispiece (left to right, from top to bottom):
A scene from 'The Onedin Line' (*see* Television); John Cleese in 'Fawlty Towers' (*see* Television); Mr Universe 1978 (*see* p. 63); Modesty Blaise cartoon (*see* p. 70); Miss World 1978 (*see* p. 59); Miss Piggy, The Muppet Show (*see* Television); Ove Fundin (*see* Speedway, p. 227); 1978 World Custard Pie Championship (*see* p. 95); Tom Conti in a scene from 'Whose Life Is It Anyway?' (*see* Theatre); Tom Courtenay and Felicity Kendal in a scene from 'The Norman Conquests' (*see* Theatre); 'Star Wars' (*see* Cinema); Jack Nicklaus (*see* Golf, p. 122)

Contents

Acknowledgements

This new work of reference would never have appeared without the help and co-operation of many scores of people. Countless information officers and secretaries of a host of organisations, many of them replying voluntarily in their spare time, provided much of the information contained in this book. The list of organisations cited at the end of this book can only hint at the value of the co-operation they have so generously given. A special debt is due to the staffs of the BBC and ITV for many hours of research. Eric Morley gave very generously of his time in providing details of the Miss World and other beauty competitions. Peter Matthews contributed greatly by compiling all sport sections.

Among the colleagues and friends who have provided me with ideas and inspiration are Stephen Brooks, Tommy Godfrey, Chris Hoyland, Margaret Kennard, Peter Morgan, Keith Reader, Will Richardson, Hilary Rubinstein, Pat Smith and John Stevenson. Nat and Dolly Conn provided conditions admirably suited to research. Richard Gordon, Graham Hatton and Peter Humphries provided convivial support when work on the book was at its most tiring.

For their secretarial help I owe my largest debt to Jean Ali, who was ably helped by Dianne Adams, Hilary Alexander, Kim Gale, Sandra Joyce and Barbara Williams.

At Guinness Superlatives I must thank Melanie Georgi and Peter Matthews for making the production of this book so pleasant a process, but most of all my thanks are due to Anne Smith whose work on this book went far beyond the call of duty.

Finally, I owe my deepest debt to Philip Jones who not only undertook the crucial research needed to produce this book but who proved the most loyal of friends.

Preface

The ranks of champions and winners are almost without limit. Not only in the many areas of sport, but also in music, show business and the arts the number of competitions has multiplied enormously in recent years. No book can ever hope to include the winners of every competition, but in this new *Guinness Book of Winners and Champions* the publishers have tried to include as many widely varied and representative events as possible—from Miss World and the Football League Championship through the many literary and musical prizes to such more specialised (if, perhaps, less scholarly) events as the annual custard pie throwing contest or the 'Super Sunflower' champion. Whether one is searching for details of the Pulitzer Prizes, the Nobel Prizes or Pet of the Year, Beer of the Year, or indeed Mr Universe, this book provides the answer.

Each competition is arranged under a main heading (eg all the film awards are under Cinema) but the comprehensive index at the end of the book should be consulted if in any doubt. Nationalities of individuals are included, where appropriate, in brackets after the name, using a system of the first three letters of the country.

The editor would welcome suggestions for additional entries and would be grateful for any information concerning updated entries to include in any future edition of this book.

ACCOUNTANCY

The Institute of Actuaries Gold and Silver Medals

In 1919 it was decided to institute a Gold Medal. In 1963 the Council revised the regulations and the award of Gold and Silver Medals is now to be made in accordance with the following rules:

A Silver Medal is to be given only in recognition of services which are of especial importance to the actuarial profession in furtherance of one or more of the various objects as set out in the Royal Charter.

A Gold Medal is to be given only in honour of work which is of pre-eminent importance, either in originality, or content, or consequence, in the actuarial field.

So far as published work is relevant, it may be considered for the purpose of making an award, even if it did not appear in the Institute's own Journal.

Gold Medals have been presented to the following:

1927 George King, FIA, FFA, FAS, in recognition of long and distinguished service rendered to the Institute of Actuaries and actuarial science.

1929 George James Lidstone, LLD, FIA, FFA, FRSE, a past President of the Faculty, jointly by the Institute and the Faculty of Actuaries in recognition of his unique services to actuarial science.

1937 Sir William Palin Elderton, KBE, FIA, FFA, a past President of the Institute, in recognition of his distinguished services to actuarial science.

Under the revised regulations, awards in honour of actuarial work of pre-eminent importance have been made to:

1964 Wilfred Perks, FIA
1964 William Phillips, OBE, FIA

1968 Frank Mitchell Redington, MA, FIA, a past President of the Institute

1975 Professor Bernard Benjamin, BSc, PhD, FIA, FIS, FSS, a past President of the Institute

Silver Medals have been presented to the following:

1966 Robert James Kirton, CBE, MA, FIA
1966 Maurice Edward Ogborn, FIA
1967 Herbert Weston Haycocks, BSc(Econ), FIA (posthumously)
1972 Robert Eric Beard, OBE, FIA, ASA
1975 Peter Richmond Cox, CB, FIA
1975 Professor Alfred Hurlstone Pollard, MSc, MSc (Econ), PhD, FIA, ASA, FSS, FAASS

Institute of Chartered Accountants Business Game for Sixth Formers

Launched in 1967–68 with the co-operation of International Computers Ltd, the competition involves over 300 schools each year. The winners are as follows:

1968 Downside School
1969 Cheltenham College
1970 Cranbrook School
1971 Stowe School
1972 The King's School, Canterbury
1973 St Edmund's College

1974 Taunton School
1975 The John Fisher School
1976 Sir John Leman High School
1977 South East Essex Sixth Form College
1978 South East Essex Sixth Form College
1979 Simon Laughton Grammar School for Boys, Canterbury

The National Management Game

Organised since 1970 by the Institute of Chartered Accountants, the *Financial Times* and International Computers Ltd in association with the Confederation of British Industry and the Institute of Directors. The prizes are worth over £5000. The winners are as follows:

1970 Industrial and Commercial Finance Corporation
1971 Rolls-Royce (1971) Ltd
1972 Essex County Council (Treasurer's Department)
1973 The Norwich Union Insurance Group
1974 'Honeylips' (private entry)

1975 The Littlewoods Organisation
1976 Rank Xerox Ltd
1977 Rank Xerox Ltd
1978 Shell UK
1979 Rank Xerox Ltd

Rt. Hon. Edward Heath presenting the awards at the 1975 National Management Game Finals

ADVERTISING

There are a bewildering number of schemes for awards in advertising, at both national and international levels. The awards honour the advertising agents, the featured product and firm or sponsoring organisation, the film makers, and the graphic designers or illustrators.

Full lists of award winners are published each year in *Campaign* magazine, and the following are just a few of the main awards.

British Direct Mail Marketing Association Awards

Examples of advertisements and campaigns are submitted for competition, and in 1978 the scope of the contest was widened to include media other than direct mail – press, television, radio and household distribution. An additional trophy rewarded successful exploitation of the computer's power to segment and personalise.

In recent years the following companies have gained distinction for one or more of the available awards:

Automobile Association	Mirror Group Newspapers	Schering Chemicals
British Aluminium Company	Mobil Oil Company	Shelter
Ciba-Geigy (UK) Ltd	Muscular Dystrophy Group	The Spastics Society
Financial Times	Osram (GEC) Ltd	Terrapin International
Ford Motor Company	Philips Hi-Fi	Thames Board Mills Ltd
Four Square Catering Ltd	John Pinches Medallist Ltd	Time Life Books
Hoechst Pharmaceuticals	Polaroid UK	Unirose Ltd
Imperial Chemical Industries Ltd	Rank Xerox Ltd	Uniroyal Ltd
Institute of Ophthalmology	Reed Paper Group	Westland Aircraft Ltd
Inveresk Paper Company Ltd	Reckitt & Colman Ltd	Wiggins Teape Ltd
IPC Magazines Ltd	Royal Commonwealth Society	Wolf Electrical Tools
Lansing Bagnall Ltd	for the Blind	

THE 1978 AWARDS AND WINNERS

The Five Major Awards
All entries must be submitted for one of the Specific Award categories. The Judges will choose winners for the five Major Awards from the whole field of entries.

The BDMMA Design Award
For a single piece of direct mail design. Entries are considered from every aspect: copy, design, implementation and results.
Winner: McCorkell Sidaway and Wright
Campaign: Elliott Stores

The Chairman's Award
For a multi-media campaign in which direct mail played the prime role.
Winner: Amherst Direct Mail
Campaign: Dunn and Bradstreet

The Post Office Consumer Award
For any customer mailing or direct marketing campaign in which direct mail played a significant role.
Winner: Delaney-Hazard
Campaign: Wilkinson Sword

The Post Office Industrial Award
For any industrial, commercial or professional mailing or campaign in which direct mail played the prime role.
Winner: Fletcher Shelton Delaney
Campaign: Kimberley-Clark

The Wunderman International Innovation Award
For the innovative use of any mailing component which clearly and effectively breaks new ground and which is measurably successful.
Winner: No award
Campaign: No award

The 17 Specific Awards
(Each entry must be submitted for one of these)

Computer Mailing Award
Presented by Ogilvy, Benson and Mather.
For outstanding use of the segmentation and personalisation power of the computer.
Winner: McCorkell Sidaway and Wright
Campaign: British Mail Order Corporation

Financial Award
For outstanding work in any medium where financial services were promoted using direct response techniques.
Winner: Amherst Direct Mail
Campaign: Dunn and Bradstreet Commercial Collection Service

Direct Response: Press Advertising
For an advertisement combining the best of direct response creativity with proven cost-effective performance.
Winner: SJIP
Campaign: Scotcade
Merit: SJIP
Campaign: Fios Group

Direct Response: TV and Radio
For excellence in use and proven response in the electronic mass media.
Winner: McCorkell Sidaway and Wright
Campaign: Encyclopaedia Britannica

Export: The Kemps Directory Award
For export promotion by direct mail.
Winner: Magnesium Elektron

Medical: The Medical Mailing Award
For a direct mail campaign of not less than three mailings to members of the medical or allied professions.
Winner: Smith Kline and French Laboratories
Merit: Zyma (UK)

Charity: The Vernon's Charity Award
For a fund-raising mailing or campaign in which direct mail played the prime role.
Winner: The Spastics Society ('Save a Baby' campaign)

Public Service: The Post Office Workers' Union Award
For a mailing campaign by a non-profit organisation, in which direct mail played the prime role.
Winner: House of Planet Direct Mail
Campaign: Clwyd County Council

Overseas Entries: The American Express Award
For a mailing produced and mailed by an overseas entrant. (Translation is not necessary but would be appreciated.)
Winner: No award
Campaign: No award

Copy: The Cope Martin Award
For a single piece of direct mail copy.
Winner: Fletcher Shelton Delaney
Campaign: Kimberley-Clark

Envelope Design: The Wiggins Teape Envelope Award
For a direct mail envelope.
Winner: No award
Campaign: No award

Letterhead Design: The Wiggins Teape Letterhead Award
For a direct mail letterhead.
Winner: No award
Campaign: No award

Direct Mail Letter: The Domtar–Howard Smith Award
For a single mail letter, eg copy, letterhead design, quality, layout.
Winner: McCorkell Sidaway and Wright
Merit: Ogilvy Benson and Mather
Campaign: American Express Company card division
Merit: Wunderman International
Campaign: Book Club Associates

Series Mailing: The Arthur Chadwick Award
Presented by Customer Loyalty Campaigns Ltd
For a direct mail campaign of not less than three mailings to the same list.
Winner: Mailplan International
Campaign: British Road Services

Low Budget: The Inveresk Economy Award
For a direct mail piece or campaign whose success relied
on concept rather than cost.
Winner: Primary Contact
Campaign: Bonusplan

First Time Entrants: The Denis Jarrett Award
For a direct mail piece or campaign submitted by a can-
didate who has never before entered for any BDMMA
Award.

Winner: Delaney-Hazard
Campaign: Wilkinson Sword
Merit: The Birmingham Mint Collection

Household Distribution: The Hector Jones Award
For a direct response promotion delivered other than by
posted mail.
Winner: Ogilvy Benson and Mather
Campaign: Leisure Circle

British Press Advertising Awards

The premier awards for advertising in Britain, organised by *Campaign* magazine, were instituted in 1974. The most recent awards include:

NEWSPAPER COLOUR/Gold Award
1977–78   Barclaycard by Collett Dickenson Pearce

NEWSPAPER BLACK AND WHITE/Gold Award
1977–78   Metropolitan Police recruitment by Collett
Dickenson Pearce

MAGAZINE BLACK AND WHITE
1977–78   British Lego by TBWA

MAGAZINE COLOUR
1977–78   Knitmaster by Collett Dickenson Pearce

TRADE AND TECHNICAL
1977–78   Hestair by Boase Massimi Pollitt Univas

DIRECT RESPONSE
1977–78   Scotcade by Samuels Jones Isaacson Page

Cannes Festival Awards 1978

The details listed include the film-makers, the name of the advertisement, the product, and
the advertising agents.

Grand Prix Cinema
Franco American Films: La Copieuse, Waterman Pens,
Benton and Bowles

Grand Prix Television
Boase Massimi Pollitt Univas: French Lesson, Coty,
Hudson Films

Gold Lions Cinema
Benton and Bowles: Ticket, British Leyland, Bussmann
Llewellyn
Citeca Productions: L'Homme aux 250 Grandes
Marques, Darty, Havas Conseil
Telema: SOS Bretagne, Croix Rouge Française

Gold Lions Television
Vernon Howe Films: Train, Schweppes, Saatchi and
Saatchi Garland-Compton
Spots Film Services: Headmistress, Cadbury, Leo
Burnett
Dick McNeil Associates: Park Bench, Pascalls, Leo
Burnett
Gomes Loew: Campaign – Ladle, Truck, Store, Milk
Truck, Kraft Foods, Dairy Div. Richard K. Manoff
Citeca Productions: Campaign – Le Restaurant, Les
Pecheurs, Collective du Roquefort, Havas Conseil
Spots Film Services: Loosen Your Belt, H. J. Heinz,
Doyle Dane Bernbach
The Producers Film Co: Loes, Steradent, Ogilvy and
Mather

Julienne Castillon Productions: Campaign – Waterfall,
Big Jump, Flip, Fiat, Ally and Gargango (New York)
SSC and B Lintas Brasil Comunicacoes: Bicycle Boy, Co
Int. de Seguros, Blow Up Producoes Cinemat
Young and Rubicam: Conway/Auto Loan, Manufac-
turers Hanover Trust, Gomes Loew
Foote Cone and Belding: Agatha, Associated News-
papers, Ruck Ryan Linsell
Wasey Campbell-Ewald: What Do We Do? COI, The
Garrett Group
Franco American Films: Campaign – Skateboard, Les
Amies, Stand Sandwiches, Ministère de la Santé,
CFRP
Estudio Borras: Anuncios, Ministerio Bienestar y
Cultura, MMLB y Ricardo Perez
Tandem: Unmarried Mother, Ministerio de Cultura,
Tre's Films

Silver Lions Cinema
Sid Roberson Productions: Brinkhoff No. 1, Dort-
munder Union Bräuerei
Young and Rubicam: Sorry, Gilbey's Gin

Silver Lions TV
Spots Film Services: Zoo Keeper – Hofmeister Lager:
Gas Masks – Tefal
Cotswold Management: Bitter Bitter – Schweppes:
Walkies – Health Education Council

Foote Cone and Belding: The Perfect Dunking Biscuit –
Associated Biscuits: Churchill Commandos – Asso-
ciated Newspapers: Fly the Tube – London Transport
Brooks Fulford Cramer Seresin: The Swing, Cadbury
Pascall Marshmallows
Dorland Advertising: Dance, Poem, Irish Cheddar
McCann-Erickson: Spring/Summer Can-Can, Spring/
Summer Tango – Eggs Authority: Connie Francis 20
Greatest Hits – Polydor Records
Jennie and Co: Edwards Speech, The Letter, Kellogg's
Rice Krispies

Boase Massimi Pollitt Univas: Stay, Ambre Solaire
Wasey Campbell Ewald: Eggs, Goodyear Tyres
Davidson Pearce Berry and Spottiswoode: Nothing Like
It, IWS
Ayer Barker Hegemann: Ustinov's Thirst, Ustinov's
Timekeeping, Ustinov's Secret: Irish Tourist Board
Picture Palace Productions: Beauty, Lee Harvey Oswald,
Unions, *Sunday Times*
Joe Film Producers: Classified, Associated Newspapers
Arks Advertising: Island, Guinness

Creative Circle Awards

In 1978, there were nine awards, of which five went to Collett Dickenson Pearce for advertise-
ments on Parker Pens, Clark's Shoes, Rawlings' Mixer Drinks, Hamlet Cigars, and Fiat Cars.
Saatchi and Saatchi Garland–Compton won three prizes for advertisements on Dunlop
Products, and the Health Education Council. Doyle Dane Bernbach won a prize for their
COI Nurses' Recruitment campaign, and McCaan Erickson for Levi Jeans. Samuels Jones
Isaacson Page won the President's Award for its direct response advertisements for Scotcade.

Dada Awards

The Design and Art Direction awards are given each year by the charity of that name for the
best examples of work in the advertising industry.

These awards are divided into 28 categories, together with special craft awards and an ITV
award for the best commercial of the year whose winner in 1978 was: 'Three Little Girls',
EMI Records, The Supremes, Vernon Howe Films, Collett Dickenson Pearce.

GOLD AWARDS 1979
TV design and programme identity
'The South Bank Show', London Weekend Television,
dir: Pat Gavin, des: Pat Gavin, set des: Michael Turney,
prod. co: LWT and Jerry Hibbert Productions.

Film advertising
'Swimming Pool', Benson and Hedges, Gallaher, dir:
Hugh Hudson, c/w: Mike Cozens. Art dir: Alan Waldie,
set des: Geoffrey Kirkland, agency prod: Judy Hurst,
editor: Stuart Taylor, music: Lol Creme, Kevin Godley,
lighting cameraman: Mike Molloy, ad manager: Peter
Wilson, agency: Collett Dickenson Pearce.

SILVER AWARDS 1979
Arts programme title
'The South Bank Show', London Weekend Television,
dir: Pat Gavin, des: Pat Gavin, set des: Michael Turney,
prod. co: LWT and Jerry Hibbert Productions.

Best cinema advertisement
'Swimming Pool', Benson and Hedges, Gallaher, dir:
Hugh Hudson, c/w: Mike Cozens, art dir: Alan Waldie,
set des: Geoffrey Kirkland, agency prod: Judy Hurst,
editor: Stuart Taylor, music: Lol Creme: Kevin Godley,
lighting cameraman: Mike Molloy, ad manager: Peter
Wilson, agency: Collett Dickenson Pearce.

Best use of music
'Swimming Pool', Benson and Hedges, Gallaher, dir:
Hugh Hudson, c/w: Mike Cozens, art dir: Alan Waldie,
set des: Geoffrey Kirkland, agency prod: Judy Hurst,
editor: Stuart Taylor, music: Lol Creme, Kevin Godley,
lighting cameraman: Mike Molloy, ad manager: Peter
Wilson, agency: Collett Dickenson Pearce.

Best direction
'Swimming Pool', Benson and Hedges, Gallaher, dir:
Hugh Hudson, c/w: Mike Cozens, art dir: Alan Waldie,
set des: Geoffrey Kirkland, agency prod: Judy Hurst,
editor: Stuart Taylor, music: Lol Creme, Kevin Godley,
lighting cameraman: Mike Molloy, ad manager: Peter
Wilson, agency: Collett Dickenson Pearce.

Colour consumer magazine advertisement
'Why doesn't the Renault 14 have a wheel at each
corner?', Renault, art dir: Gordon Smith, c/w: Patrick
Woodward, phot: Graham Ford, Geoff Senior, typo:
Ed Church, ad manager: Alan Dakers, agency: Boase
Massimi Pollitt Univas.

Best advertisement copy
'How long can these men survive without food?', Abott
Mead Davies and Vickers, c/w: David Abbott, art dir:
Ron Brown, phot: Martin Reavley, typo: Joe Hoza,
agency: Abbott Mead Davies and Vickers.

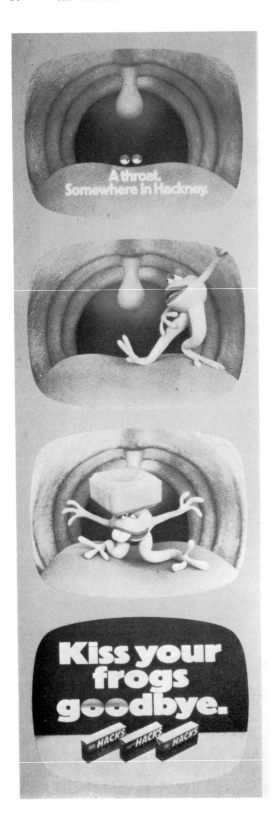

Advertisement colour photograph

'Is it so shameless to be so sure of something so expensive?', Audemars Piguet, phot: Rolph Gobits, art dir: David Owen, c/w: Helen Barley, typo: Bob Fryer, ad manager: Graham Brooks, agency: Colman and Partners.

Photography campaign (see illustrations in colour section)

'When a luxury becomes a necessity', Clark Son and Morland, phot: John Claridge, art dir: Graham Cornthwaite, c/w: Geoffrey Seymour, marketing dir: Joe Morland, agency: Cherry, Hedger & Seymour.

Public service poster

'Grave', Scottish Health Education Unit, art dir: Jim Downie, des: Jim Downie, c/w: Tony Cox, phot: Tony May, typo: Jim Downie, ad manager: David Player, agency: Hall Advertising.

Best poster

'Headless Man', Victory-V, Barker and Dobson, art dir: Derrick Hass, c/w: David Trott, illus: Larry Learmont, ad manager: Tony Sharpe, agency: Boase Massimi Pollitt Univas.

Poster photography

'Pyramids', Benson and Hedges, Gallaher, phot: Jimmy Wormser, art dir: Neil Godfrey, c/w: Tony Brignull, marketing manager: Peter Wilson, agency: Collett Dickenson Pearce.

Best poster campaign

'Double Scotch', 'Scotch and Ginger', 'Neat Scotch', 'Scotch on the Rocks', White Horse Distillers, art dir: Graeme Norways, c/w: Nick Hazzard, phot: Lester Bookbinder, typo: Graeme Norways, ad manager: Alan Ramsay, agency: French Cruttenden Osborn.

Range of packaging

Crabtree and Evelyn, art dir: Peter Windett, des: Peter Windett, illus: Ron Lampitt, des group: Peter Windett and Associates, ad manager: Cy Harvey.

Best stationery

Des: Nicholas Wurr, des. group: Wurr and Wurr.

Best window display

The Italian State Tourist Board, art dir: Marcello Minale, Brian Tattersfield, typo: Paul Browton, des. group: Minale Tattersfield and Partners.

Best radio commercial

'Major Fawcett Mildew', Camping Gaz (GB), concept creators: Iain Dunn, Mark Ready, agency prod: Celestine Parsons, ad manager: David Plume, agency: Colman and Partners.

Best animation

'The Power', Jovan, dir: Richard Williams, c/w: Bill Pittman, art dir: Mary Aries, editor: Richard Williams, music arrangement: Don Piestrup, agency: J. Walter Thompson, Chicago.

Best set design

'Barbershop', Manikin cigars, Gallaher, dir: Dick

MIDDLE TAR
H.M. Government Health Departments WARNING: CIGARETTES CAN SERIOUSLY DAMAGE YOUR HEALTH

McNeil, c/w: Geoff Horne, John Wood, art dir: John Wood, set des: Tony Noble, agency prod: Sandy Watson, editor: Tom Morrish, lighting cameraman: David MacDonald, prod. co: Dick McNeil Associates, ad manager: Michael Ashdown, agency: KMP Partnership.

Film photography
'French Lesson', L'Oreal, dir: Hugh Hudson, c/w: Sue Trott, art dir: John Webster, agency prod: Peter Valentine, editor: Stuart Taylor, music: Library Music, lighting cameraman: Peter Suschitzky, prod. co: Hudson Film, ad manager: Roy Stevens, agency: Boase Massimi Pollitt Univas.

Best 30-second TV advertisement
'Singing Frog', Hacks, Barker and Dobson, dir: Denis Russo, Ken Turner, c/w: Graham Rose, art dir: David Christensen, set des: Denis Russo, editor: John Farrow, music: Joe Campbell, lighting cameraman: Terry Permane, prod. co: Clearwater Films, ad manager: Tony Shape, agency: Boase Massimi Pollitt Univas.

Best 45-second TV advertisement
'Stay', Ambre Solaire, L'Oreal, dir: Tony Scott, c/w: John Webster, art dir: John Webster, agency prod: Roger Shipley, editor: Roger Wilson, music: Billy Gray, lighting cameraman: Derek Van Lindt, prod. co: RSA Productions, ad manager: Franklin Berebi, agency: Boase Massimi Pollitt Univas.

Best TV campaign
'Comparison', 'Alfie Binns', 'Poet', 'Conversation', 'Fishing', Courage Brewing, dir: Peter Webb, c/w: John Webster, art dir: John Webster, agency prod: Roger Shipley, editor: Peter Beston, music: Library Music, lighting cameraman: Ian MacMillan, prod. co: Park Village Productions, ad manager: Frank Cockayne, agency: Boase Massimi Pollitt Univas.

Best documentary title
'Horizon', BBC Television, dir: Roger Kennedy, des:

Far left: **'The Singing Frog'. Winner of the 1979 Dada Award for the best 30-second TV advertisement**

Above: **'Pyramids'. Winner of the 1979 Dada Award for the poster photography and a special mention for overall design of a complete unit of advertising**

Roger Kennedy, agency prod: Tony Edwards, lighting cameraman: Peter Chapman, laser co: Holoco, prod. co: BBC television.

Drama programme title
'My Son, My Son', BBC television, dir: Stefan Pstrowski, des: Stefan Pstrowski, sculptor: John Friedlander, prod: Keith Williams, lighting cameraman: Doug Adamson, prod. co: BBC TV.

Entertainment programme title
'The Pink Medicine Show', London Weekend Television, dir: Paul Smith, des: Tony Oldfield, animator: Ted Rockley, comp: Max Marris, lyrics: Chris Beetles, Rob Buckman, rostrum camera: Ian Lett, prod. co: Rock-steady Rostrums.

Irish Advertising Awards

Awards made in 1978 were as follows:
TELEVISION
Grand Prix British National Award: Frank Sinatra 'Animals'; EMI; Collett Dickenson Pearce.
Irish Grand Prix: Zip Firelighters 'Party'; Reckitts Ireland; McConnells Advertising Service.
Cinema Grand Prix: Waterman Pencils 'Love Story'; Waterman; Benton and Bowles, Paris.
Palme d'Or (for production company): Brooks Fulford Cramer.
Worldwinner 78: L'Aimant 'French Lesson'; Coty; BMP Univas.
National Award for Entries from Australia: Ever Ready Dolphin Lantern 'Dolphin'; Union Carbide Australia; J. Walter Thompson.

IRISH SECTION

Delegates Prize: Zip Firelighters 'Party'; Reckitts Ireland; McConnells Advertising Service.

Alcoholic Drinks: Bass Ale 'The Dubliners'; Beamish and Crawford; O'Connor O'Sullivan.

Non-Alcoholic Drinks: Sugar Free Seven-Up 'Redundant Calorie'; Seven-Up; Young Advertising.

Food: Sunrose 'Rising Cakes'; Kraft Foods; J. Walter Thompson.

Confectionery: Bolands Cream Crackers 'Cracker and Jam Movement'; Irish Biscuits; Hunter Advertising.

Household Maintenance: Zip Firelighters 'Party'; Reckitts Ireland; McConnells Advertising Service.

INTERNATIONAL SECTION

Alcoholic Drinks: Campari 'Bogey'; Findlater Matta Agency; J. Walter Thompson.

Non-Alcoholic Drinks: Indian Tonic Water 'Trade Secret'; Rawlings; Collett Dickenson Pearce.

Food: Wall's Sausages 'Airport'; Wall's Meat Company; Collett Dickenson Pearce.

Confectionery: Hanky Panky 'Park Bench'; Pascals; Leo Burnett.

Household Maintenance: Insecticide 'That's all Bugs'; Laboratorios Anakol; Young and Rubicam Brazil.

Cosmetics: Tri-Ply Tissues 'Bridge', Bowater Scott; Lintas.

Automotive: Fiat 128 'Dirty Weekend'; Fiat; Collett Dickenson Pearce.

Publications: *Evening News* 'Classified'; Associated Newspapers; Saatchi and Saatchi.

Services: Ireland 'Thirst'; Irish Tourist Board; Ayer Barker Hegemann.

Public Service: Anti-Drink and Drive 'What Shall We Do?'; Central Office of Information; Wasey-Campbell-Ewald.

Miscellaneous: Hamlet Cigars 'Robot'; Gallaher; Collett Dickenson Pearce.

International Series: Vitamalz Drinks; Brauerie Thier; GGK Dusseldorf.

Low Budget Commercials: Gelomatic G360 'Department Store'; Pereira Lopes Ibesa Brazil; MPM Casabranca Prop SP.

International Cinema: National Westminster Bank 'Splash'; National Westminster Bank; J. Walter Thompson.

INTERNATIONAL RADIO

Thirty Seconds and Under: Campbells Soups 'Silent Soups'; Campbells Soups; The Marcom Group.

Over Thirty Seconds: Jus-Rol 'Tea Party'; Clayton Love Distributors; Wilson Hartnell Advertising and Marketing.

London Television Advertising Awards

These awards are divided into 28 categories, together with special craft awards and an ITV award for the best commercial of the year whose winner in 1978 was: 'Three Little Girls', EMI Records, The Supremes, Vernon Howe Films, Collett Dickenson Pearce.

The Gold Medal winners in 1978 were:

Canned, frozen and dried food: Made for it II, Heinz, Salad Cream, Park Village Production, Doyle Dane Bernbach.

Soft drinks: Mr Rawlings, Rawlings Ginger Ale, Brooks Fulford Cramer Seresin, Collett Dickenson Pearce.

Automotive Products: James Hunt Number 2 – Eric and Ernie, Texaco Petrol, The Alan Parker Film Company, Collett Dickenson Pearce.

Consumer Services: Corporate, Dunlop Products, Park Village Productions, Saatchi and Saatchi Garland-Compton.

Public Services: Ageing Man, Health Education Council, Personal Health, The Cotswold Management, Saatchi and Saatchi.

Entertainments: Three Little Girls, EMI Records, The Supremes, Vernon Howe Films, Collett Dickenson Pearce.

Series: Neighbours, and Home from the Office, Cadbury Typhoo's Smash, Brooks Fulford Cramer Seresin, Boase Massimi Pollitt Univas.

The Mackintosh Medal

This is the highest award from the advertising business made annually by the Advertising Association for personal and public service to advertising. It is not a recognition of business success, technical achievement or monetary donation, but takes the form of a Silver Medal. Inaugurated at the International Advertising Conference held in London in 1951, the award perpetuates the name of the Advertising Association's then president, the late Lord Mackintosh of Halifax. The awards committee consists of representatives from the Advertising Association and its constituent organisations, namely:

Association of Independent Radio Contractors Ltd, Association of Multi-Media Proprietors Ltd, British Direct Mail Marketing Association, British Printing Industries

Federation, Communication, Advertising and Marketing Education Foundation, Direct Mail Producers Association, Graphic Reproduction Federation, Incorporated Advertising Management Association, International Advertising Association United Kingdom Chapter Ltd, Incorporated Society of British Advertisers Ltd, Independent Television Companies Association Ltd, Institute of Practitioners in Advertising, Newspaper Publishers Association, Newspaper Society, Outdoor Advertising Council, Periodical Publishers Association Ltd, Proprietary Association of Great Britain, Screen Advertising Association Ltd, and the Publicity Federation.

1951	The Rt Hon Viscount Mackintosh of Halifax, DL, LLD	1965	A. Charles Buck
1952	The Rt Hon Lord Thomas, DFC, MIMechE, MSAE	1966	Tom Gardner Moore
		1967	E. Glanvill Benn
		1968	H. G. L. Lazell, FCIS
1953	Sir George Reginald Pope	1969	R. C. Sykes, MA, FIPA
1954	Hubert A. Oughton, OBE, FIPA	1970	The Rt Hon Lord Robens of Woldingham, PC, DCL, LLD
1955	Norman Moore, MA, FIPA		
1956	Andrew Milne	1971	W. J. Ambrose, OBE
1957	Major George Harrison, MC, FIPA	1972	John W. Hobson, CBE, MA, FRSA, FIPA
1958	Leslie W. Needham, MC	1973	Sir Alex McKay, KBE
1959	W. H. Hamp-Hamilton, JP, FIPR	1974	Archie Graham, OBE
1960	The Rt Hon Lord Luke of Pavenham, TD, DL	1975	J. S. Williams, OBE, BCom, MCAM
1961	Sinclair Wood, OBE, FIPA	1976	The Rt Hon Lord Cole, GBE
1962	Ivor Cooper	1977	Patricia Mann, MCAM, FIPA
1963	Miss K. M. Murphy, BA, FIL	1978	James O'Connor, OBE, FCIS, M.CAM, FIPA
1964	Brian F. MacCabe, MC, FIPA		

Radio Campaign Awards

First organised by *Campaign* magazine in 1976, these are now an annual event. The awards honour the best in advertising on commercial radio. The 1978 winners of the 'Silver Microphone' were:

Travel
Silver Microphone: Saatchi and Saatchi Garland-Compton; Advertiser: British Caledonian; 'Pound Note Collector'; 30 seconds; C/W: Jeff Stark; Prod: Joanna Kemp; v/o: Barry Ingham, Gary Watson, John Shrapnel; Aud Eng: Cameron; Std: Molinare.

Financial
Silver Microphone: Spikins Paul & Young; Advertiser: London & Manchester Assurance; 'Stolen TV'; Prod. Co: Leeward Sound Recording Studios; 30 seconds; C/W: D. Young; Dir: F. Spikins; v/o: Warren Mitchell, Miriam Margoyles; Aud. Eng: Lloyd Billing; Std: Leeward Sound Recording Studios.

Drink
Silver Microphone: The Radio Operators; Advertiser: Youngers Tartan Special; 'The Answer'; 60 seconds; C/W: Tony Hertz; Mus. Dir: Mike McNaught; Mus. Comp: Offenbach, Tony Hertz; Prod: Peter Perrin; Dir: Tony Hertz; Aud. Eng.: Andre Jacquemin; Std: Redwood.

Consumer Durables
Silver Microphone: Colman & Partners; Advertiser: Camping Gaz; 'Indian Bus Conductor'; Prod. Co: Molinare; 60 seconds; C/W: Iain Dunn; Prod: Celestine Parsons; Dir: Iain Dunn; v/o: Peter Sellers; Aud. Eng/Std: Molinare.

Food
Silver Microphone: Little Strodl Advertising; Advertiser: Outspan Oranges; 'Diver'; 30 seconds; C/W: David Little; Prod: Sally Sawders; Dir: David Little; v/o: Bob Baker; Aud. Eng.: Derek French; Std: John Wood.

Entertainment and Media
Silver Microphone: Leo Burnett; Advertiser: *The Times*; 'Caesar'; 30 seconds; C/W: Stuart Cooper; Library Music; Prod: Alec Ovens; v/o: Hannah Gordon, Dinsdale Landen, Hugh Burden; Aud. Eng./Std: Leeward Sound Recording Studios.

Best Use of Humour
Silver Microphone: Colman & Partners; Advertiser: Camping Gaz; 'Major'; Prod. Co: Molinare; 60 seconds; C/W: Iain Dunn; Prod: Celestine Parsons; Dir: Iain Dunn; v/o: Peter Sellers; Aud. Eng/Std: Molinare.

Best Use of Music
Silver Microphone: Collett Dickenson Pearce & Partners; Advertiser: Cinzano UK; 'Blindfold'; 45 seconds; C/W: Ron Collins; Mus. Dir: Air-Edel; Mus. Comp: Don Partridge; Prod: Linda Downs; v/o: Max Wall.

Best Campaign
Silver Microphone: Grey Advertising; Advertiser:

Crosse & Blackwell-Ready to Serve Soup; 'Tutty-Tut-Tut', 'Wowee'; 60 seconds, 45 seconds; C/W: Ian Mason, Roger Barson; Mus. Comp: John Lewis, Electrophon; Prod: T. J. Fry; v/o: Peter Hawkins; Aud. Eng: Dave Hodge; Std: Molinare.

Cosmetics and Toiletries
Judges decision – no award.

Public Service Announcements
Silver Microphone: The Radio Operators; Advertiser: Scottish Health Education – Anti-Smoking; 'Suicide

Department'; Agency: Halls, Edinburgh; 45 seconds; C/W: Tony Hertz, Tony Cox; Prod: Maggie Dimambro; Dir: Tony Hertz; Aud. Eng: John Rowland, Andre Jackquemin; Std: The Barge, Redwood.

Others
Silver Microphone: NSW Partners; Advertiser: NSW Partners; 'Phone-In'; 90 seconds; C/W: Chris Munds; Mus. Dir: Ronnie Bond; Mus. Comp: Ronnie Bond; Prod: Amanda Robinson; Dir: NSW Partners; v/o: Chris Munds, Sara Munds; Aud. Eng: Tony Fossard; Std: SAY.

AERONAUTICS

The Royal Aeronautical Society's Gold Medal

This is the highest honour the Society can confer for work of an outstanding nature in aeronautics.

Gold Medallists of the Society

1909	The Wright brothers
1910	Professor O. Chanute
1915	Professor G. H. Bryan
1915	E. T. Busk
1926	Dr F. W. Lanchester
1927	Professor L. Prandtl (*Honorary Fellow*)
1933	Sir Richard Glazebrook
1937	Senor Juan de la Cierva (posthumously)
1945	Air Commodore F. Whittle (*Fellow*)
1946	Professor L. Bairstow (*Honorary Fellow*)
1947	Sir B. Melvill Jones (*Fellow*)
1950	Sir Geoffrey de Haviland (*Fellow*)
1951	W. G. A. Perring (*Fellow*) (posthumously)
1952	Dr Theodore von Kármán (*Honorary Fellow*)
1953	E. F. Relf (*Fellow*)
1954	Sir Geoffrey Taylor (*Honorary Fellow*)
1955	Lord Hives (*Honorary Fellow*)
1956	Sir William S. Farren (*Fellow*)
1957	Professor J. C. Hunsaker (*Honorary Fellow*)
1958	Sir Sydney Camm (*Fellow*)
1959	Marcel Dassault
1960	Sir Frederick Handley Page (*Honorary Fellow*)
1962	Sir Arnold Hall (*Fellow*)
1963	H. Constant (*Fellow*)
1964	R. E. Bishop (*Fellow*)
1965	Professor M. J. Lighthill (*Fellow*)
1966	Professor A. R. Collar (*Fellow*)
1967	Dr S. G. Hooker (*Fellow*)
1968	A. A. Rubbra (*Fellow*)
1969	Dr D. Küchemann (*Fellow*)
1970	W. Tye (*Fellow*)
1971	Sir Morien Morgan (*Fellow*)
1972	Professor A. D. Young (*Fellow*)
1973	Handel Davies (*Fellow*)
1974	F. W. Page (*Fellow*)
1975	Professor D. Keith-Lucas (*Fellow*)
1976	Dr W. J. Strang (*Fellow*)
1977	Sir Clifford Cornford (*Fellow*)
1978	Dr Ludwig Bolköw

The Royal Aeronautical Society's British Gold Medal For Aeronautics

This is awarded for outstanding practical achievement leading to advancement in aeronautics. The British Gold Medal was founded by the Royal Aeronautical Society in 1933 following a request from Lord Amulree, then Secretary of State for Air, that an award be given for outstanding feats in aviation. The Medal commemorates Sir George Caylay and his first model aeroplane of 1804.

British Gold Medallists

1934	Captain G. de Haviland (*Fellow*)
1936	Dr H. Eckener
1937	A. Gouge (*Fellow*)
1948	E. W. Hives (*Fellow*)
1949	S. Camm (*Fellow*)
1950	Major F. B. Halford (*Fellow*)
1951	A. E. Russell (*Fellow*)
1952	G. R. Edwards (*Fellow*)
1953	R. E. Bishop (*Fellow*)
1954	A. G. Elliott (*Fellow*)
1955	G. H. Dowty (*Fellow*)
1956	J. Smith (*Fellow*) (posthumously)

1957	R. L. Lickley (*Fellow*)
1958	S. D. Davies (*Fellow*)
1959	R. S. Stafford (*Fellow*)
1960	B. E. Stephenson (*Fellow*)
1961	Dr S. G. Hooker (*Fellow*)
1962	F. W. Page (*Fellow*)
1963	A. C. Lovesey (*Fellow*)
1964	G. C. I. Gardiner (*Fellow*)
1965	A. A. Lombard (*Fellow*)
1966	R. M. Clarkson (*Fellow*)
1967	H. H. Gardner (*Fellow*)
1968	G. L. Wilde (*Fellow*)

1969	G. R. Jefferson (*Fellow*)
1970	P. A. Hufton (*Fellow*)
1971	L. Haworth (*Fellow*)
1972	Dr G. S. Hislop (*Fellow*)
1973	F. W. W. Morley (*Fellow*)
1974	P. F. Foreman (*Fellow*)
1975	R. P. Probert (*Fellow*)
1976	J. T. Stamper (*Fellow*)
1977	Dr B. J. O'Kane
1978	G. M. Lewis (*Fellow*)

AGRICULTURE

Massey-Ferguson National Award

This is given for services to UK agriculture, and is open to farmers and others engaged in non-commercial support to agriculture. The silver trophy and prize money of £1000 is awarded annually.

Names of potential candidates are submitted to a selection committee from a variety of sources within agriculture and the committee then makes a selection of a winner who has made a 'proven practical and outstanding contribution to the advancement of agriculture in the UK or to a significant section thereof'. The award is, however, not made for the best contribution in the year in question but is more a recognition of services rendered over a period of time.

Winners are selected by a committee of leading agriculturists under the chairmanship of the Marquess of Abergavenny. Previous winners of the Massey-Ferguson National Award are:

1964	Howell Evans, MBE – Cow Cubicles	1973	Dr G. D. H. Bell, CBE, FRSE – Services to Plant Breeding
1965	Rex Paterson, OBE – Milk from Grass	1974	The Duke of Northumberland, KG, PC, TD – National Services to Agriculture
1966	Leslie Aylward, OBE – Farm Machinery Syndicates	1975	W. H. Cashmore, CBE, BA, NDA – Services to Farm Mechanisation
1967	Trevor Ensor – Floor Drying of Cereals	1976	Sir Nigel Strutt, TD, DL, FRAgS – National Services to Agriculture
1969	Lord Netherthorpe – Shaping Agricultural Policy while President of the NFU	1977	Sir Kenneth Blaxter, FRS – Services to Animal Nutrition
1970	Professor M. McG. Cooper, CBE – Advancing Knowledge of Grassland and Grazing Animals	1978	Dr Norman H. Pizer, CBE, PhD, FRIC – Services to Horticulture and Agriculture through his work on soil structure, and soil mechanics
1971	Sir Richard Trehane – Services to the Dairy Industry		
1972	Cadzow Brothers – Development of the Luing Breed		

National Dairy Council's Dairy Queen

Inaugurated in 1956 by the National Dairy Council, the title is awarded for personality, good looks and knowledge of the dairy industry. The winner in 1979 received a Chrysler car, a trip to North America, clothes, and a modelling and grooming course at the London Academy of Modelling. The winners, since 1956, are as follows:

1956	Evelyn Clegg, Coulsdon, Surrey	1968	Joan Harland, Thirsk, North Yorkshire
1957	Mona Griffiths, Denbigh, Clwyd	1969	Mary Vincent, Wymondham, Norfolk
1958	Eirlys Morgan, Llanelli, Dyfed	1970	Julia Greenleaf, Colchester, Essex
1959	Marjorie Watson, Howden, East Yorks	1971	Josephine Ayre, South Molton, North Devon
1960	Eirian Evans, Holt, nr. Wrexham, Clwyd	1972	Karen Langstaff, RAF Coltishall, Norfolk
1961	Jean Walling, Kendal, Cumbria	1973	Helen Richardson, Bedale, Yorkshire
1962	Heather Bomford, Kidderminster, Worcestershire	1974	Rachael Reddaway, Crediton, Devon
1963	Rosemary Manister, Ipswich, Suffolk	1975	Janet Barnett, Wheatley Hill, Co. Durham
1964	Christine Hewitt, nr. Norwich, Norfolk	1976	Diana Tibbs, Stanton Drew, Bristol
1965	Mary Llewellin, Dyfed	1977	Angela Watkins, South Wales
1966	Pamela Cox, Buxton, Derbyshire	1978	Sabrina Jones, Garthmyl, Powys
1967	Christine Ginns, Bury, Lancashire	1979	Fiona Pooler, Dorridge, Solihull

AMERICAN FOOTBALL

The American Professional Football Association was formed in 1920. Its name was changed in 1922 to the National Football League. Winners from 1921 to 1932 were as follows:

1921	Chicago Bears	1927	New York Giants
1922	Canton Bulldogs	1928	Providence Steamrollers
1923	Canton Bulldogs	1929	Green Bay Packers
1924	Cleveland Bulldogs	1930	Green Bay Packers
1925	Chicago Cardinals	1931	Green Bay Packers
1926	Frankford Yellow Jackets	1932	Chicago Bears

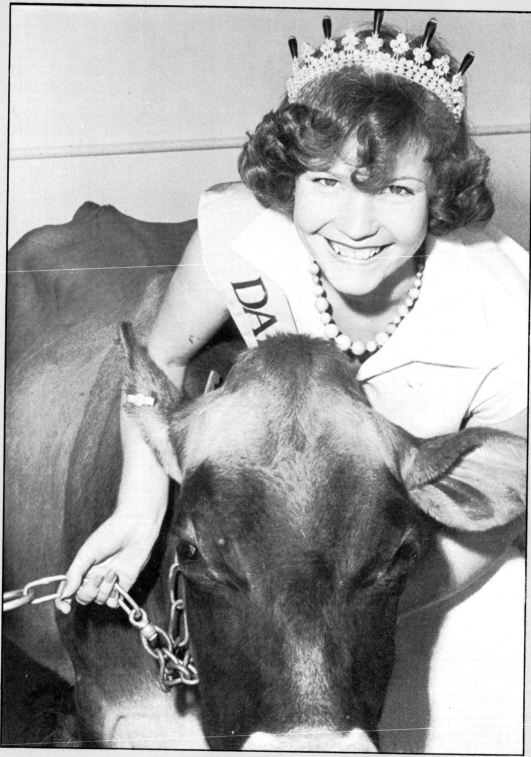

Diana Tibbs, the 1976 Dairy Council's Dairy Queen

In 1933 the National Football League (NFL) was divided into two divisions – Eastern and Western, with the winners of each division meeting in the championship play-off. From 1950 to 1952 the two divisions were named American and National, before reverting to Eastern and Western from 1953 to 1970.

Meanwhile in 1960 the American Football League (AFL) was formed and from 1970 under the umbrella of the National Football League there was a re-organisation of teams. From then there were two conferences, the National Conference and the American Conference, each containing three divisions.

National Football Conference (NFL until 1969) Winners

1933	Chicago Bears
1934	New York Giants
1935	Detroit Lions
1936	Green Bay Packers
1937	Washington Redskins
1938	New York Giants
1939	Green Bay Packers
1940	Chicago Bears
1941	Chicago Bears
1942	Washington Redskins
1943	Chicago Bears
1944	Green Bay Packers
1945	Cleveland Rams
1946	Chicago Bears
1947	Chicago Cardinals
1948	Philadelphia Eagles
1949	Philadelphia Eagles
1950	Cleveland Browns
1951	Los Angeles Rams
1952	Detroit Lions
1953	Detroit Lions
1954	Cleveland Browns
1955	Cleveland Browns
1956	New York Giants
1957	Detroit Lions
1958	Baltimore Colts
1959	Baltimore Colts
1960	Philadelphia Eagles
1961	Green Bay Packers
1962	Green Bay Packers
1963	Chicago Bears
1964	Cleveland Browns
1965	Green Bay Packers
1966	Green Bay Packers
1967	Green Bay Packers
1968	Baltimore Colts
1969	Minnesota Vikings
1970	Dallas Cowboys
1971	Dallas Cowboys
1972	Washington Redskins
1973	Minnesota Vikings
1974	Minnesota Vikings
1975	Dallas Cowboys
1976	Minnesota Vikings
1977	Dallas Cowboys
1978	Dallas Cowboys

One of the all-time greats in American Football, O. J. Simpson, of the Buffalo Bills, sets a season record of 23 touchdowns in 1975 (*Popperfoto*)

American Football Conference (AFL until 1969) Winners

1960	Houston Oilers
1961	Houston Oilers
1962	Dallas Texans
1963	San Diego Chargers
1964	Buffalo Bills
1965	Buffalo Bills
1966	Kansas City Chiefs
1967	Oakland Raiders
1968	New York Jets
1969	Kansas City Chiefs
1970	Baltimore Colts
1971	Miami Dolphins
1972	Miami Dolphins
1973	Miami Dolphins
1974	Pittsburgh Steelers
1975	Pittsburgh Steelers
1976	Oakland Raiders
1977	Denver Broncos
1978	Pittsburgh Steelers

SUPER BOWL WINNERS

At the end of each season the winners of each Conference meet in the Super Bowl. The game is played in mid-January. Results have been:

1967	Green Bay (NFL)	35	Kansas City (AFL)	10
1968	Green Bay (NFL)	33	Oakland (AFL)	14
1969	New York (AFL)	16	Baltimore (NFL)	7
1970	Kansas City (AFL)	23	Minnesota (NFL)	7
1971	Baltimore (AFC)	16	Dallas (NFC)	13
1972	Dallas (NFC)	24	Miami (AFC)	3
1973	Miami (AFC)	14	Washington (NFC)	7
1974	Miami (AFC)	24	Minnesota (NFC)	7
1975	Pittsburgh (AFC)	16	Minnesota (NFC)	6
1976	Pittsburgh (AFC)	21	Dallas (NFC)	17
1977	Oakland (AFC)	32	Minnesota (NFC)	14
1978	Dallas (NFC)	27	Denver (AFC)	10
1979	Pittsburgh (AFC)	35	Dallas (NFC)	31

AMERICANS

The Hall of Fame for Great Americans

The Hall of Fame for Great Americans was founded in 1900 by Dr Henry Mitchell MacCracken, Chancellor of New York University, with funds donated by Mrs Helen Gould Shepard. It honours persons whose outstanding achievements have influenced the culture and course of the nation. Formerly administered by New York University, the Hall of Fame became a separately incorporated educational institution in 1974, maintaining joint affiliation with New York University and the City University of New York. The Americans honoured to date are:

1900 John Adams
John James Audubon
Henry Ward Beecher
William Ellery Channing
Henry Clay
Peter Cooper
Jonathan Edwards
Ralph Waldo Emerson
David Glasgow Farragut
Benjamin Franklin
Robert Fulton
Ulysses Simpson Grant
Asa Gray
Nathaniel Hawthorne
Washington Irving
Thomas Jefferson
James Kent
Robert Edward Lee
Abraham Lincoln
Henry Wadsworth Longfellow
Horace Mann
John Marshall
Samuel Finley Breese Morse
George Peabody
Joseph Story
Gilbert Charles Stuart
George Washington

Daniel Webster
Eli Whitney

1905 John Quincy Adams
James Russell Lowell
Mary Lyon
James Madison
Maria Mitchell
William Tecumseh Sherman
John Greenleaf Whittier
Emma Willard

1910 George Bancroft
Phillips Brooks
William Cullen Bryant
James Fennimore Cooper
Oliver Wendell Holmes
Andrew Jackson
John Lothrop Motley
Edgar Allan Poe
Harriet Beecher Stowe
Frances Elizabeth Willard

1915 Louis Agassiz
Daniel Boone
Rufus Choate

Charlotte Saunders Cushman
Alexander Hamilton
Joseph Henry
Mark Hopkins
Elias Howe
Francis Parkman

1920   Samuel Langhorne Clements (Mark Twain)
James Buchanan Eads
Patrick Henry
William Thomas Green Morton
Alice Freeman Palmer
Augustus Saint-Gaudens
Roger Williams

1925   Edwin Booth
John Paul Jones

1930   Matthew Fontaine Maury
James Monroe
James Abbott McNeil Whistler
Walt Whitman

1935   Grover Cleveland
Simon Newcomb
William Penn

1940   Stephen Collins Foster

1945   Sidney Lanier
Thomas Paine
Walter Reed
Booker T. Washington

1950   Susan B. Anthony
Alexander Graham Bell
Josiah Willard Gibbs
William Crawford Gorgas
Theodore Roosevelt
Woodrow Wilson

1955   Thomas Jonathan Jackson
George Westinghouse
Wilbur Wright

1960   Thomas A. Edison
Edward A. MacDowell
Henry David Thoreau

1965   Jane Addams
Oliver Wendell Holmes Jr
Sylvanus Thayer
Orville Wright

1970   Albert Abraham Michelson
Lillian D. Wald

1973   Louis Dembitz Brandeis
George Washington Carver
Franklin Delano Roosevelt
John Philip Sousa

1976   Clara Barton
Luther Burbank
Andrew Carnegie

ANGLING

World Champions

World Championships have been held annually since 1957, following European Championships which started in 1953.

Team winners		Individual winners	
1957	Italy	1964	Fontanet (Fra)
1958	Belgium	1965	Robert Tesse (Fra)
1959	France	1966	H. Guiheneuf (Fra)
1960	Belgium	1967	Isenbaert (Bel)
1961	GDR	1968	G. Grebenstein (Ger)
1962	Italy	1969	Robin Harris (Eng)
1963	France	1970	M. Van den Eynde (Bel)
1964	France	1971	Dino Bassi (Ita)
1965	Romania	1972	Hubert Levels (Hol)
1966	France	1973	P. Michiels (Bel)
1967	Belgium	1974	A. Richter (Ger)
1968	France	1975	Ian Heaps (Eng)
1969	Holland	1976	Dino Bassi (Ita)
1970	Belgium	1977	Jean Mainil (Bel)
1971	Italy	1978	Jean-Pierre Fouquet (Fra)
1972	France		
1973	Belgium		
1974	France		
1975	France		
1976	Italy		
1977	Luxembourg		
1978	France		

Individual winners	
1957	Mandeli (Ita)
1958	Garroit (Bel)
1959	Robert Tesse (Fra)
1960	Robert Tesse (Fra)
1961	Legogue (Fra)
1962	Tedesco (Ita)
1963	William Lane (Eng)

Jim Bazley, winner of the 1909 English National Federation of Anglers' Championship (see p. 24) (*Angling News Services*)

(see p. 24)

English National Federation of Anglers' Championship

First held in 1906. Winners are as follows:

1906	F. Beales (Boston)	1948	W. Thompson (Leeds)
1907	A. Croft (Sheffield)	1949	R. Woodhall (Whit. Reans)
1908	J. Mason (Sheffield)	1950	W. Rockley (Peterborough)
1909	J. H. R. Bazley (Leeds)	1951	S. Buxton (Doncaster)
1910	A. Blackman (Hull)	1952	H. Seed (Leeds)
1911	W. Lowe (Sheffield)	1953	N. N. Hazelwood (Camb)
1912	G. Beales (Boston)	1954	R. Lye (Notts/Fed)
1913	W. Gough (Nottingham)	1955	J. Carr (Sheffield Amal.)
1914	A. Skerratt (Derby)	1956	C. R. Lusby (Lincoln)
1919	T. Hill (Derby)	1957	H. Storey (Notts AA)
1920	R. Barlow (Hull)	1958	W. Hughes (Northern Anglers)
1921	J. Wakesfield (Derby)	1959	J. Sharp (Bedford)
1922	B. Hobday (Lincoln)	1960	K. Smith (Norwich)
1923	J. W. Couldwell (Sheffield)	1961	J. Blakey (Saltaire)
1924	W. T. Willcocks (London)	1962	V. A. Baker (Derby Railways)
1925	G. Allen (Provincial)	1963	R. Sims (N Som and W Wilts)
1926	A. Fletcher (Boston)	1964	G. Burch (Essex County)
1927	J. H. R. Bazley (Leeds)	1965	D. Burr (Rugby)
1928	W. Tetley (Leeds)	1966	R. Jarvis (Boston)
1929	J. Sykes (Boston)	1967	E. Townsin (Cambridge FP)
1930	C. Muddimer (Leicester)	1968	D. Groom (Leighton Buzzard)
1931	W. Daddy (Hull)	1969	R. Else (Lincoln)
1932	H. Sallis (Long Eaton)	1970	B. Lakey (Cambridge)
1933	E. Dabill (Sheffield)	1971	R. Harris (Peterborough)
1934	H. Smith (Sheffield)	1972	P. Coles (Leicester)
1935	A. Kellett (Doncaster)	1973	A. Wright (Derby Railways)
1936	A. E. Bryant (Buckingham)	1974	P. Anderson (Cambridge)
1937	H. Jones (Co. Palatine)	1975	M. Hoad-Reddick (Rotherham)
1938	G. Bright (Bristol)	1976	N. Wells (Newark)
1945	M. T. Cotterill (Worksop)	1977	R. Foster (Rotherham)
1946	G. Laybourne (York)	1978	D. Harris (Bradford)
1947	W. Edwards (Rotherham)		

ARCHAEOLOGY

Rescue: British Archaeological Trust Awards

The 1978 awards were presented by Prince Charles at the British Museum. The *Illustrated London News* sponsored an award for the best presentation to the public of an archaeological excavation or fieldwork. The joint winners in 1978 were: Dover Roman Painted House and Norton Priory Museum, Runcorn.

The BBC Chronicle Archaeological Awards

These are given for the best 'rescue' project by a group of amateur archaeologists. In effect, this means digs of archaeological sites or the recording of above-ground remains that are unlikely to be dealt with by professionals and which are threatened with destruction. The 44 entries submitted in the first two years of the competition included surveys of 14th-century standing buildings in Sussex, tombstones in Welsh churchyards, burial mounds on military firing ranges and standing stones on Scottish islands; surveys from the air of all archaeological sites in the Severn and Avon valleys, and digs on Hampstead Heath.

A wall panel showing the restored Roman painting at the Dover Roman Painted House – joint winner of the 1978 British Archaeology Trust Award

The crystal goblet, engraved with the 'Chronicle' insignia, which is presented to winners of the BBC Chronicle Archaeological Award

The winners receive a crystal goblet engraved with the 'Chronicle' insignia and a cheque for £250.

The winner of the 1977 competition was the Manchester University Extramural Group for their survey of the major Anglo-Saxon monument of Offa's Dyke which revealed the fact that, despite its being scheduled as an Ancient Monument, several miles of the length had already been recently destroyed or was still under threat.

The winner of the 1978 competition was the Alice Holt Survey Group who won the award for their total historical and archaeological survey of the ancient forest of Alice Holt, near Farnham in Hampshire, which uncovered one of the largest Roman pottery industries in Britain.

ARCHERY

World Champions

World Championships were first held in 1931, and were held annually from 1931 to 1939 and 1946 to 1950. From 1959 they have been held every other year, while they were also held in 1952, 1953, 1955, 1957 and 1958. Since 1957 both team and individual competitions have been held with competitors shooting Double FITA (Fédération Internationale de Tir à l'Arc) rounds. That is 72 arrows each, at four different distances.

Winners since 1957 of Target Archery championships:

	Men's Individual	Women's Individual
1957	O. K. Smathers (USA) 2231	Carole Meinhart (USA) 2120
1958	S. Thysell (Swe) 2101	Sigrid Johansson (Swe) 2053
1959	James Caspers (USA) 2247	Ann Weber Corby (USA) 2023
1961	Joseph Thornton (USA) 2310	Nancy Vonderheide (USA) 2173
1963	Charles Sandlin (USA) 2332	Victoria Cook (USA) 2253
1965	Matti Haikonen (Fin) 2313	Maire Lindholm (Fin) 2214
1967	Ray Rogers (USA) 2298	Maria Mazynska (Pol) 2240
1969	Hardy Ward (USA) 2423	Dorothy Lidstone (Can) 2361
1971	John Williams (USA) 2445	Emma Gapchenko (USSR) 2380
1973	Viktor Sidoruk (USSR) 2185	Linda Myers (USA) 2204
1975	Darrell Pace (USA) 2548	Zebiniso Rustamova (USSR) 2465
1977	Richard McKinney (USA) 2501	Luann Ryon (USA) 2515
1979	Darrell Pace (USA) 2474	Jin-Ho Kim (S Kor) 2507

Team Competitions

	Men	Women		Men	Women
1957	USA 6591	USA 6187	1969	USA 7194	USSR 6897
1959	USA 6634	USA 5847	1971	USA 7050	Poland 6907
1961	USA 6601	USA 6376	1973	USA 6400	USSR 6389
1963	USA 6887	USA 6508	1975	USA 7444	USSR 7252
1965	USA 6792	USA 6358	1977	USA 7444	USA 7379
1967	USA 6816	Poland 6686	1979	USA 7409	S Korea 7314

Olympic Champions

Archery was included in the Olympic Games of 1900, 1904, 1908 and 1920 and re-introduced in 1972 and 1976 when the winners were:

	Men	Women
1972	John Williams (USA) 2528	Doreen Wilbur (USA) 2424
1976	Darrell Pace (USA) 2571	Luann Ryon (USA) 2499

World and Olympic champion Darrell Pace on his way to a world archery record in 1975 (*Keystone*)

ARCHITECTURE

Department of the Environment Awards

National competitions are held each year, and the list of winners may be obtained from the Department.

The *Financial Times* Industrial Architecture Award

The award is open to all, both architects and engineers, concerned with the design of industrial works which can bring to either town or country an outstanding contribution in encouraging a better industrial environment. The assessment panel comprises two architects, selected for their eminence in practice and their interest in the industrial landscape, appointed with the co-operation of the Royal Institute of British Architects, together with one lay assessor. The award has been presented to the following:

1967 Reliance Controls Ltd, Swindon
Architects: N. Foster, W. Foster and R. Rogers
(Foster Associates)

1968 Engineering Research Station for the Northern Gas Board, Killingworth, Newcastle upon Tyne
Architects: Ryder & Yates & Partners

1969 Wallace Arnold Quality Tested Used Car Factory, York Road, Leeds
      Architects: Derek Walker & Partners
1970 Chemical and Administration Building, Treatment Plant for Bradford Water Supply, Chellow Heights, Bradford
      Architects: Whicheloe & Macfarlane
1971 Lee Abbey Farm, Lynton, North Devon
      Architect: John Burkett of Scarlett Burkett Associates
1972 IBM Havant Plant for IBM United Kingdom
      Architects: Arup Associates
1973 Horizon Project, Nottingham for John Player and Sons
      Architects: Arup Associates

1974 Warehouse and office for Modern Art Glass Company, Thamesmead Industrial Estate
      Architects: N. Foster, W. Foster and R. Rogers (Foster Associates)
1975 Carlsberg Brewery, Northampton
      Architect: Knud Munk
1976 PATS Centre, Industrial Research Laboratory, Melbourn, Herts
      Architects: Piano and Rogers
1977 Furniture Factory for Herman Miller Ltd, Bath, Avon
      Architects: Farrell/Grimshaw Partnership
1978- Solid Wastes Rail Transfer Station, Brentford
      Architects: GLC Department of Architects and Civil Design

Royal Gold Medallists of the Royal Institute of British Architects

The Royal Gold Medal for the promotion of architecture, instituted by Her Majesty Queen Victoria in 1848, is conferred annually by the Sovereign on some distinguished architect, or group of architects, for work of high merit, or on some distinguished person or group whose work has promoted either directly or indirectly the advancement of architecture. The following is a complete roll of recipients:

1848 Chas. Robt. Cockerell, RA
1849 Luigi Canina, Italy
1850 Sir Charles Barry, RA
1851 Thomas L. Donaldson
1852 Leo von Klenze, Austria
1853 Sir Robert Smirke, RA
1854 Phillip Hardwick, RA
1855 J. I. Hittorff, France
1856 Sir William Tite
1857 Owen Jones
1858 August Stuler, Germany
1859 Sir G. Gilbert Scott, RA
1860 Sydney Smirke, RA
1861 J. B. Lesueur, France
1862 Rev. Robert Willis
1863 Anthony Salvin
1864 E. Voillet-le-Duc, France
1865 Sir James Pennethorne
1866 Sir M. Digby Wyatt
1867 Charles Texier, France
1868 Sir Henry Layard
1869 C. R. Lepsius, Germany
1870 Benjamin Ferrey
1871 James Fergusson
1872 Baron von Schmidt, Austria
1873 Thomas Henry Wyatt
1874 Geo. Edmund Street, RA
1875 Edmund Sharpe
1876 Joseph Louis Duc, France
1877 Charles Barry
1878 Alfred Waterhouse, RA
1879 Marquis de Vogue, France
1880 John L. Pearson, RA
1881 George Godwin
1882 Baron von Ferstel, Austria
1883 Fras. Cranmer Penrose
1884 William Butterfield
1885 H. Schliemann, Germany

1886 Charles Garnier, France
1887 Ewan Christian
1888 Baron von Hansen, Austria
1889 Sir Charles T. Newton
1890 John Gibson
1891 Sir Arthur Blomfield, ARA
1892 Cesar Daly, France
1893 Rich. Morris Hunt, USA
1894 Lord Leighton, RA
1895 James Brooks
1896 Sir Ernest George, RA
1897 Dr P. J. H. Cuypers, Holland
1898 George Aitchison, RA
1899 George Fredk. Bodley, RA
1900 Professor Rodolfo Amadeo Lanciani, Italy
1901 (Not awarded, owing to the death of Queen Victoria)
1902 Thos. Edward Collcutt
1903 Chas. F. McKim, USA
1904 Auguste Choisy, France
1905 Sir Aston Webb, PPRA
1906 Sir L. Alma-Tadema, RA
1907 John Belcher, RA
1908 Honore Daumet, France
1909 Sir Arthur John Evans, DLitt, MA(Oxon), FRS, FSA
1910 Sir Thomas Graham Jackson, Bart, BA
1911 Wilhelm Dorpfeld, Germany
1912 Basil Champneys
1913 Sir Reginald Blomfield, MA(Oxon), LittD (L'pool), RA, FSA
1914 Jean Louis Pascal, France
1915 Frank Darling, Canada
1916 Sir Robert Rowand Anderson
1917 Henri Paul Nenot, Membre de l'Institut, France
1918 Ernest Newton, RA
1919 Leonard Stokes

1920	Charles Louis Girault, Membre de l'Institut, France
1921	Sir Edwin Landseer Lutyens, OM, KCIE, LLD, RA, FAS
1922	Thomas Hastings, USA
1923	Sir John James Burnett, RA, RSA
1924	Not awarded
1925	Sir Giles Gilbert Scott, OM, DCL, LLD(L'pool), LLD(Cantab), RA
1926	Professor Ragnar Ostberg, Sweden
1927	Sir Herbert Baker, KCIE, RA
1928	Sir Guy Dawber, RA, FSA
1929	Victor Alexandre Frederic Laloux, France
1930	Sir Percy Scott Worthington, MA(Oxon), LittD, FSA
1931	Sir Edwin Cooper, RA
1932	Dr Hendrik Petrus Berlage, Holland
1933	Sir Charles Reed Peers, CBE, MA(Cantab), PPSA
1934	Henry Vaughan Lanchester, LittD(Leeds), PPTPI
1935	Willem Marinus Dudok, Holland
1936	Charles Henry Holden, DLitt(Lond), LittD (Mancr), MTPI
1937	Sir Raymond Unwin, LLD(Mancr), DA (Harvard)
1938	Professor Ivar Tengbom, Sweden
1939	Sir Percy Thomas, OBE, LLD(Wales), DL, JP, MTPI
1940	Charles Francis Annesley Voysey
1941	Frank Lloyd Wright, USA
1942	William Curtis Green, RA
1943	Professor Sir Charles Herbert Reilly, OBE, LLD
1944	Sir Edward Maufe, RA, LLD(Belfast), MA
1945	Victor Vesnin, USSR
1946	Professor Sir Patrick Abercombie, MA, DLitt, LLD, DSc, FSA, PPTPI, FILA
1947	Professor Sir Albert Edward Richardson, RA, MA, FSA
1948	Augustus Perret, France
1949	Sir Howard Robertson, MC, ARA, SADG
1950	Eliel Saarinen, USA
1951	Emanuel Vincent Harris, OBE, RA
1952	George Grey Wornum
1953	Le Corbusier (C. E. Jeanneret), France
1954	Sir Arthur George Stephenson, CMG, AMTPI, Australia
1955	John Murray Easton
1956	Dr Walter Adolf Georg Gropius, USA
1957	Hugo Alvar Henrik Aalto, Finland
1958	Robert Schofield Morris, BArch (McGill), FRAIC, Canada
1959	Professor Ludwig Mies van der Rohe, USA
1960	Professor Pier Luigi Nervi, Italy
1961	Lewis Mumford, USA
1962	Professor Sven Gottfrid Markelius, Sweden
1963	The Lord Holford, LLD(L'pool), ARA, MA (L'pool), PPTPI, FILA
1964	E. Maxwell Fry, CBE
1965	Professor Kenzo Tange, Japan
1966	Ove Arup, CBE, MICE, MIStructE
1967	Sir Nikolaus Pevsner, CBE, FBA, FSA, MA, PhD, HonARIBA
1968	Dr Richard Buckminster Fuller, FRSA, HonAIA, USA
1969	Jack Antonio Coia, CBE, BArch (Strathclyde), RSA, AMTPI
1970	Professor Sir Robert Matthew, CBE, ARSA, LLD, MA
1971	Hubert de Cronin Hastings
1972	Louis I. Kahn
1973	Sir Leslie Martin, MA, PhD, LLD
1974	Powell & Moya
1975	Michael Scott
1976	Sir John Summerson, CBE, FBA, FSA
1977	Sir Denys Lasdun, CBE
1978	John Utzon, Australia and Denmark
1979	Charles & Ray Eames Office

The Royal Institute of British Architects also organises other award schemes, for which there are numerous winners each year. In 1970 there were 370 entries, and eleven buildings were chosen for awards as outstanding examples of current architecture. In 1976 there were eight major prize winners.

In 1968 Gillespie, Kidd and Coea, Glasgow, became the first architects' company to receive an RIBA award for three years in succession.

ART

John Moores Liverpool Exhibition

These biennial exhibitions are jointly sponsored by the Walker Art Gallery and John Moores, of Littlewoods Football Pools. The 1978 exhibition, open to all living artists working in the UK, concentrated on painting rather than comprehensively embracing all new developments in art.

There is a top prize, £6000 in 1978, which has been awarded to:

1957	Jack Smith	1963	Roger Hilton	1969	Richard Hamilton	1974	Myles Murphy
1959	Patrick Heron	1965	Michael Tyzack		Mary Martin	1976	John Walker
1961	Henry Mundy	1967	David Hockney	1972	Euan Uglow	1978	Noel Forster

THE ARTS

National Annual Awards for Business Sponsorship

Inaugurated in 1978, the awards are presented by the Association for Business Sponsorship of the Arts and the *Daily Telegraph*.

They are designed to focus attention on the growing contribution the business world is now making to help the nation's arts organisations, and also stimulate further business involvement.

Best Single Event Sponsorship
1978   Benson & Hedges, Festival at Snape Maltings, Suffolk
Crown Wall Coverings, Contemporary Art Association's exhibition, 'Interior Motives'
Midland Bank, Midland Bank Proms at the Royal Opera House

Best Corporate Programme
1978   Provincial Insurance Company, Kendal; Bank of Scotland; John Harvey and Sons

Best First Time Sponsor
1978   Bryant and May, 'The Matchmaker' by the Cambridge Theatre Company
Hallmarks Cards, Royal Shakespeare Company

Sponsorship giving Most Encouragement to Young Performers and Young Audiences
1978   Ciba–Geigy (UK) Ltd, Manchester Youth Theatre
Lloyds Bank, National Youth Orchestra of Great Britain

ASSOCIATION FOOTBALL

World Cup

First held in 1930 in Uruguay. Held every four years.

1930	Uruguay	1950	Uruguay	1962	Brazil	1974	West Germany
1934	Italy	1954	West Germany	1966	England	1978	Argentina
1938	Italy	1958	Brazil	1970	Brazil		

European Football Championship

First contested as the Nations Cup between 1958 and 1960, the European Football Championship is played every four years over a two-year period.

1960	USSR		
1964	Spain	1972	West Germany
1968	Italy	1976	Czechoslovakia

European Champion Clubs Cup (European Cup)

Contested annually since the 1955–56 season by the champion clubs of each member of the European Union (UEFA) together with the previous winner.

1955–56	Real Madrid	1963–64	Inter Milan	1971–72	Ajax (Amsterdam)
1956–57	Real Madrid	1964–65	Inter Milan	1972–73	Ajax (Amsterdam)
1957–58	Real Madrid	1965–66	Real Madrid	1973–74	Bayern Munich
1958–59	Real Madrid	1966–67	Celtic (Glasgow)	1974–75	Bayern Munich
1959–60	Real Madrid	1967–68	Manchester United	1975–76	Bayern Munich
1960–61	Benfica	1968–69	A C Milan	1976–77	Liverpool
1961–62	Benfica	1969–70	Feyenoord	1977–78	Liverpool
1962–63	A C Milan	1970–71	Ajax (Amsterdam)	1978–79	Nottingham Forest

European Cup Winners' Cup

Contested annually since the 1960–61 season by the winners of national cup competitions (or the runners-up, if the winners contest the European Cup).

1960–61	Florentina	1966–67	Bayern Munich	1972–73	A C Milan
1961–62	Atletico Madrid	1967–68	A C Milan	1973–74	Magdeburg
1962–63	Tottenham Hotspur	1968–69	Slovan Bratislava	1974–75	Dynamo Kiev
1963–64	Sporting Lisbon	1969–70	Manchester City	1975–76	Anderlecht
1964–65	West Ham United	1970–71	Chelsea	1976–77	SV Hamburg
1965–66	Borussia Dortmund	1971–72	Rangers (Glasgow)	1977–78	Anderlecht
				1978–79	Barcelona

UEFA Cup (Fairs Cup)

First contested over a three-year period 1955–58 as the Inter-City Fairs Cup. Now held annually and known since the 1971–72 season as the UEFA (Union of European Football Associations) Cup.

1955–58	Barcelona	1965–66	Barcelona	1972–73	Liverpool
1958–60	Barcelona	1966–67	Dynamo Zagreb	1973–74	Feyenoord
1960–61	A S Roma	1967–68	Leeds United	1974–75	Borussia Mönchengladbach
1961–62	Valencia	1968–69	Newcastle United	1975–76	Liverpool
1962–63	Valencia	1969–70	Arsenal	1976–77	Juventus
1963–64	Real Zaragossa	1970–71	Leeds United	1977–78	PSV Eindhoven
1964–65	Ferencvaros	1971–72	Tottenham Hotspur	1978–79	Borussia Mönchengladbach

European Super Cup

Held annually since 1972 between the winners of the European Champion Clubs Cup and the European Cup Winners' Cup.

1972	Ajax (Amsterdam)
1974	Ajax (Amsterdam)
1975	Dynamo Kiev
1976	Anderlecht
1977	Liverpool
1978	Anderlecht

European Footballer of the Year

Elected annually since 1956 in a poll organised by *France Football* by journalists from all over Europe.

1956	Stanley Matthews (Blackpool & England)	1969	Gianni Rivera (A C Milan & Italy)
1957	Alfredo Di Stefano (Real Madrid & Spain)	1970	Gerd Müller (Bayern Munich & W. Germany)
1958	Raymond Kopa (Real Madrid & France)	1971	Johann Cruyff (Ajax & Holland)
1959	Alfredo Di Stefano (Real Madrid & Spain)	1972	Franz Beckenbauer (Bayern Munich & W. Germany)
1960	Luis Suarez (Barcelona & Spain)	1973	Johann Cruyff (Barcelona & Holland)
1961	Omar Sivori (Juventus & Italy)	1974	Johann Cruyff (Barcelona & Holland)
1962	Josef Masopust (Dukla, Prague & Czechoslovakia)	1975	Oleg Blokhin (Dynamo Kiev & USSR)
1963	Lev Yashin (Moscow Dynamo & USSR)	1976	Franz Beckenbauer (Bayern Munich & W. Germany)
1964	Denis Law (Manchester Utd & Scotland)	1977	Allan Simonsen (Borussia Mönchengladbach & Denmark)
1965	Eusebio (Benfica & Portugal)	1978	Kevin Keegan (SV Hamburg & England)
1966	Bobby Charlton (Manchester Utd & England)		
1967	Florian Albert (Ferencvaros & Hungary)		
1968	George Best (Manchester Utd & N. Ireland)		

Kevin Keegan after scoring his 13th goal for England versus Scotland in May 1979. English Footballer of the Year in 1975–76 when with Liverpool he was voted European Footballer of the Year in 1978 after joining SV Hamburg (*Syndication Int.*)

Johann Cruyff, European Footballer of the Year, both with Ajax in Holland and Barcelona in Spain (*Associated Press*)

Stanley Matthews, (*right*) was aged 38 when he won his first F.A. Cup winners medal in 1953 with Blackpool, whose Captain Harry Johnston holds the cup (*Keystone*)

World Club Cup

Contested by the winners of the European Cup and the Copa Libertadores de America, the South American Club Cup, since 1960.

1960	Real Madrid (Spa)		1969	A C Milan (Ita)
1961	Penarol (Uru)		1970	Feyenoord (Hol)
1962	Santos (Bra)		1971	Nacional (Uru)
1963	Santos (Bra)		1972	Ajax (Hol)
1964	Inter-Milan (Ita)		1973	Independiente (Arg)
1965	Inter-Milan (Ita)		1974	Atletico Madrid (Spa)
1966	Penarol (Uru)		1975	Not held
1967	Racing Club (Arg)		1976	Bayern Munich (Ger)
1968	Estudiantes (Arg)		1977	Boca Juniors (Arg)

Olympic Games

Winners of the Olympic Games soccer competition have been:

1908	Great Britain	1932	Not held	1960	Yugoslavia
1912	Great Britain	1936	Italy	1964	Hungary
1920	Belgium	1948	Sweden	1968	Hungary
1924	Uruguay	1952	Hungary	1972	Poland
1928	Uruguay	1956	USSR	1976	GDR

F.A. Cup

First held in the 1871–72 season. Finals since 1923 have been held at Wembley.

1872	Wanderers	1903	Bury	1938	Preston North End
1873	Wanderers	1904	Manchester City	1939	Portsmouth
1874	Oxford University	1905	Aston Villa	1946	Derby County
1875	Royal Engineers	1906	Everton	1947	Charlton Athletic
1876	Wanderers	1907	Sheffield Wednesday	1948	Manchester United
1877	Wanderers	1908	Wolverhampton Wanderers	1949	Wolverhampton Wanderers
1878	Wanderers	1909	Manchester United	1950	Arsenal
1879	Old Etonians	1910	Newcastle United	1951	Newcastle United
1880	Clapham Rovers	1911	Bradford City	1952	Newcastle United
1881	Old Carthusians	1912	Barnsley	1953	Blackpool
1882	Old Etonians	1913	Aston Villa	1954	West Bromwich Albion
1883	Blackburn Olympic	1914	Burnley	1955	Newcastle United
1884	Blackburn Rovers	1915	Sheffield United	1956	Manchester City
1885	Blackburn Rovers	1920	Aston Villa	1957	Aston Villa
1886	Blackburn Rovers	1921	Tottenham Hotspur	1958	Bolton Wanderers
1887	Aston Villa	1922	Huddersfield Town	1959	Nottingham Forest
1888	West Bromwich Albion	1923	Bolton Wanderers	1960	Wolverhampton Wanderers
1889	Preston North End	1924	Newcastle United	1961	Tottenham Hotspur
1890	Blackburn Rovers	1925	Sheffield United	1962	Tottenham Hotspur
1891	Blackburn Rovers	1926	Bolton Wanderers	1963	Manchester United
1892	West Bromwich Albion	1927	Cardiff City	1964	West Ham United
1893	Wolverhampton Wanderers	1928	Blackburn Rovers	1965	Liverpool
1894	Notts County	1929	Bolton Wanderers	1966	Everton
1895	Aston Villa	1930	Arsenal	1967	Tottenham Hotspur
1896	Sheffield Wednesday	1931	West Bromwich Albion	1968	West Bromwich Albion
1897	Aston Villa	1932	Newcastle United	1969	Manchester City
1898	Nottingham Forest	1933	Everton	1970	Chelsea
1899	Sheffield United	1934	Manchester City	1971	Arsenal
1900	Bury	1935	Sheffield Wednesday	1972	Leeds United
1901	Tottenham Hotspur	1936	Arsenal	1973	Sunderland
1902	Sheffield United	1937	Sunderland	1974	Liverpool

| 1975 | West Ham United | 1977 | Manchester United | 1979 | Arsenal |
| 1976 | Southampton | 1978 | Ipswich Town | | |

Football League Champions

1888–89	Preston North End	1919–20	West Bromwich Albion	1952–53	Arsenal
1889–90	Preston North End	1920–21	Burnley	1953–54	Wolverhampton Wanderers
1890–91	Everton	1921–22	Liverpool	1954–55	Chelsea
1891–92	Sunderland	1922–23	Liverpool	1955–56	Manchester United
1892–93	Sunderland	1923–24	Huddersfield Town	1956–57	Manchester United
1893–94	Aston Villa	1924–25	Huddersfield Town	1957–58	Wolverhampton Wanderers
1894–95	Sunderland	1925–26	Huddersfield Town	1958–59	Wolverhampton Wanderers
1895–96	Aston Villa	1926–27	Newcastle United	1959–60	Burnley
1896–97	Aston Villa	1927–28	Everton	1960–61	Tottenham Hotspur
1897–98	Sheffield United	1928–29	Sheffield Wednesday	1961–62	Ipswich Town
1898–99	Aston Villa	1929–30	Sheffield Wednesday	1962–63	Everton
1899–1900	Aston Villa	1930–31	Arsenal	1963–64	Liverpool
1900–01	Liverpool	1931–32	Everton	1964–65	Manchester United
1901–02	Sunderland	1932–33	Arsenal	1965–66	Liverpool
1902–03	Sheffield Wednesday	1933–34	Arsenal	1966–67	Manchester United
1903–04	Sheffield Wednesday	1934–35	Arsenal	1967–68	Manchester City
1904–05	Newcastle United	1935–36	Sunderland	1968–69	Leeds United
1905–06	Liverpool	1936–37	Manchester City	1969–70	Everton
1906–07	Newcastle United	1937–38	Arsenal	1970–71	Arsenal
1907–08	Manchester United	1938–39	Everton	1971–72	Derby County
1908–09	Newcastle United	1946–47	Liverpool	1972–73	Liverpool
1909–10	Aston Villa	1947–48	Arsenal	1973–74	Leeds United
1910–11	Manchester United	1948–49	Portsmouth	1974–75	Derby County
1911–12	Blackburn Rovers	1949–50	Portsmouth	1975–76	Liverpool
1912–13	Sunderland	1950–51	Tottenham Hotspur	1976–77	Liverpool
1913–14	Blackburn Rovers	1951–52	Manchester United	1977–78	Nottingham Forest
1914–15	Everton			1978–79	Liverpool

Footballer of the Year

Elected annually since 1947–48 by the Football Writers' Association.

1947–48	Stanley Matthews	1963–64	Bobby Moore
1948–49	Johnny Carey	1964–65	Bobby Collins
1949–50	Joe Mercer	1965–66	Bobby Charlton
1950–51	Harry Johnston	1966–67	Jackie Charlton
1951–52	Billy Wright	1967–68	George Best
1952–53	Nat Lofthouse	1968–69	Dave Mackay and Tony Book
1953–54	Tom Finney	1969–70	Billy Bremner
1954–55	Don Revie	1970–71	Frank McLintock
1955–56	Bert Trautmann	1971–72	Gordon Banks
1956–57	Tom Finney	1972–73	Pat Jennings
1957–58	Danny Blanchflower	1973–74	Ian Callaghan
1958–59	Sid Owens	1974–75	Alan Mullery
1959–60	Bill Slater	1975–76	Kevin Keegan
1960–61	Danny Blanchflower	1976–77	Emlyn Hughes
1961–62	Jimmy Adamson	1977–78	Kenny Burns
1962–63	Stanley Matthews	1978–79	Kenny Dalglish

Scottish Cup

First contested in the 1873–74 season. Held on a knock-out basis. Summarised table of winners (years shown are second half of season in which the club won the Cup):

Queens Park   1874, 1875, 1876, 1880, 1881, 1882, 1884, 1886, 1890, 1893
Vale of Leven   1877, 1878, 1879
Dumbarton   1883
Renton   1885, 1888
Hibernian   1887, 1902
Third Lanark   1889, 1905
Heart of Midlothian   1891, 1896, 1901, 1906, 1956
Celtic   1892, 1899, 1900, 1904, 1907, 1908, 1911, 1912, 1914, 1923, 1925, 1927, 1931, 1933, 1937, 1951, 1954, 1965, 1967, 1969, 1971, 1972, 1974, 1975, 1977
Rangers   1894, 1897, 1898, 1903, 1928, 1930, 1932, 1934, 1935, 1936, 1948, 1949, 1950, 1953, 1960, 1962, 1963, 1964, 1966, 1973, 1976, 1978, 1979

St Bernards   1895
Dundee   1910
Kilmarnock   1920, 1929
Partick Thistle   1921
Morton   1922
Airdrieonians   1924
St Mirren   1926, 1959
East Fife   1938
Clyde   1939, 1955, 1958
Aberdeen   1947, 1970
Motherwell   1952
Falkirk   1913, 1957
Dunfermline   1961, 1968

Scottish League

Formed in the 1890–91 season. The second division was formed in 1893, but was suspended from 1915 to 1921. A third division was included from 1925–27 and 1946–55. In 1975 the League was reformed into Premier, First and Second Divisions. Summarised winners of the First Division from 1891 to 1975 (years shown are for second half of winning season):

Dumbarton   1891 (shared), 1892
Rangers   1891 (shared), 1899, 1900, 1901, 1902, 1911, 1912, 1913, 1918, 1920, 1921, 1923, 1924, 1925, 1927, 1928, 1929, 1930, 1913, 1933, 1934, 1935, 1937, 1939, 1947, 1949, 1950, 1953, 1956, 1957, 1959, 1961, 1963, 1964, 1975
Celtic   1893, 1894, 1896, 1898, 1905, 1906, 1907, 1908, 1909, 1910, 1914, 1915, 1916, 1917, 1919, 1922, 1926, 1936, 1938, 1954, 1966, 1967, 1968, 1969, 1970, 1971, 1972, 1973, 1974

Heart of Midlothian   1895, 1897, 1958, 1960
Hibernian   1903, 1948, 1951, 1952
Third Lanark   1904
Motherwell   1932
Aberdeen   1955
Dundee   1962
Kilmarnock   1965

Premier Division Champions

1976	Rangers	1978	Rangers
1977	Celtic	1979	Celtic

Scottish League Cup

First contested in the 1945–46 season. Summarised list of winners:

Aberdeen   1946, 1956, 1977
Rangers   1947, 1949, 1961, 1962, 1964, 1965, 1971, 1976, 1978, 1979
East Fife   1948, 1950, 1954
Motherwell   1951

Dundee   1952, 1953, 1974
Heart of Midlothian   1955, 1959, 1960, 1963
Celtic   1957, 1958, 1966, 1967, 1968, 1969, 1970, 1975
Partick Thistle   1972

Football League Cup

First contested in the 1960–61 season. Winners:

1961	Aston Villa	1965	Chelsea	1969	Swindon Town
1962	Norwich City	1966	West Bromwich Albion	1970	Manchester City
1963	Birmingham City	1967	Queen's Park Rangers	1971	Tottenham Hotspur
1964	Leicester City	1968	Leeds United	1972	Stoke City
				1973	Tottenham Hotspur

| 1974 | Wolverhampton Wanderers | 1976 | Manchester City | 1978 | Nottingham Forest |
| 1975 | Aston Villa | 1977 | Aston Villa | 1979 | Nottingham Forest |

ASTRONOMY

British Interplanetary Society

The Bronze and Gold Medals are awarded for contributions and advances in space research and technology and for an outstanding current event by an individual. Established in 1954, they are awarded as merited. Recipients include:

Gold Medals
1961   Uri Gagarin
       Wernher von Braun
1964   Valentina Tereschkova
1970   Neil Armstrong
       Edwin E. Aldrin, Jr
       Michael Collins

Bronze (Pioneer) Medals
1962   Karel J. Bossart
       S. Fred Singer
       Andrew G. Haley
1970   George W. Hoover
       John P. Stapp
       H. E. Ross
       Ernst Stuhlinger
1972   Arnold W. Frutkin
       W. H. Stephens
       S. Hoffman
1979   R. F. Freitag

GOLOVINE AWARD
This is given for outstanding contributions to and advances in space research and technology. Recipients include:
1967   R. C. Speiser
       G. Sohl
1968   P. Bono
1970   G. A. Flandro

HONORARY FELLOWSHIP
For contributions and advances in space research and technology, and for pioneering achievements in the field. Recipients include:
1943   Herman Oberth
1949   P. E. Cleator
       R. Esnault-Pelterie
       E. Sanger
       Wernher von Braun
       Ing. von Pirquet
1962   A. V. Cleaver
       Hugh L. Dryden
       L. R. Shepherd
1967   Arthur C. Clarke
1969   G. E. Mueller
       William Pickering
1970   Charles Stark Draper

SILVER PLAQUE
For contributions to, and advances in, space research and technology. To an organisation. Established 1954. Awarded as merited. Silver trophy. Recipients include:
1961   NASA
1965   Jet Propulsion Laboratory
1966   USSR Academy of Sciences
1968   USSR Academy of Sciences
1969   NASA
1970   NASA

ATHLETICS

Olympic Champions

The first Olympics of the modern age were held in 1896 in Athens. They are still very much the pinnacle of athletics success, although World Championships have been announced by the IAAF for 1983, and for certain non-Olympic events at earlier dates.

Most Olympic titles: 10 Ray Ewry (Standing High, Long & Triple Jumps 1900–1908).

Olympic champions since 1948 have been:

MEN
100 Metres
1948   Harrison Dillard (USA) 10.3
1952   Lindy Remigino (USA) 10.4
1956   Bobby-Joe Morrow (USA) 10.5
1960   Armin Hary (Ger) 10.2
1964   Robert Hayes (USA) 10.05
1968   James Hines (USA) 9.95
1972   Valeriy Borzov (USSR) 10.14
1976   Hasely Crawford (Tri) 10.06

200 Metres
1948   Melvin Patton (USA) 21.1
1952   Andrew Stanfield (USA) 20.7
1956   Bobby-Joe Morrow (USA) 20.6
1960   Livio Berrutti (Ita) 20.2
1964   Henry Carr (USA) 20.36
1968   Tommie Smith (USA) 19.83
1972   Valeriy Borzov (USSR) 20.00
1976   Donald Quarrie (Jam) 20.23

400 Metres
1948   Arthur Wint (Jam) 46.2
1952   George Rhoden (Jam) 45.9
1956   Charles Jenkins (USA) 46.7
1960   Otis Davis (USA) 44.9
1964   Michael Larrabee (USA) 45.15
1968   Lee Evans (USA) 43.86
1972   Vincent Matthews (USA) 44.66
1976   Alberto Juantorena (Cub) 44.26

800 Metres
1948   Malvin Whitfield (USA) 1:49.2
1952   Malvin Whitfield (USA) 1:49.2
1956   Thomas Courtney (USA) 1:47.7
1960   Peter Snell (NZ) 1:46.3
1964   Peter Snell (NZ) 1:45.1
1968   Ralph Doubell (Aus) 1:44.3
1972   David Wottle (USA) 1:44.9
1976   Alberto Juantorena (Cub) 1:43.5

1500 Metres
1948   Henry Eriksson (Swe) 3:49.8
1952   Josef Barthel (Lux) 3:45.1
1956   Ron Delany (Ire) 3:41.2
1960   Herbert Elliott (Aus) 3:35.6
1964   Peter Snell (NZ) 3:38.1
1968   Kipchoge Keino (Ken) 3:34.9
1972   Pekka Vasala (Fin) 3:36.3
1976   John Walker (NZ) 3:39.2

5000 Metres
1948   Gaston Reiff (Bel) 14:17.6
1952   Emil Zatopek (Cze) 14:06.6
1956   Vladimir Kuts (USSR) 13:39.6
1960   Murray Halberg (NZ) 13:43.4
1964   Robert Schul (USA) 13:48.8
1968   Mohamed Gammoudi (Tun) 14:05.0
1972   Lasse Viren (Fin) 13:26.4
1976   Lasse Viren (Fin) 13:24.8

10 000 Metres
1948   Emil Zatopek (Cze) 29:59.6
1952   Emil Zatopek (Cze) 29:17.0
1956   Vladimir Kuts (USSR) 28:45.6
1960   Pyotr Bolotnikov (USSR) 28:32.2
1964   William Mills (USA) 28:24.4
1968   Naftali Temu (Ken) 29:27.4
1972   Lasse Viren (Fin) 27:38.4
1976   Lasse Viren (Fin) 27:40.4

Marathon
1948   Delfo Cabrera (Arg) 2:34:51.6
1952   Emil Zatopek (Cze) 2:23:03.2
1956   Alain Mimoun (Fra) 2:25:00.0
1960   Abebe Bikila (Eth) 2:15:16.2
1964   Abebe Bikila (Eth) 2:12:11.2
1968   Mamo Wolde (Eth) 2:20:26.4
1972   Frank Shorter (USA) 2:12:19.8
1976   Waldemar Cierpinski (GDR) 2:09:55.0

4 × 100 Metres Relay
1948   USA 40.6
1952   USA 40.1
1956   USA 39.5
1960   Germany 39.5

1964   USA 39.06
1968   USA 38.23
1972   USA 38.19
1976   USA 38.33

4 × 400 Metres Relay
1948   USA 3:10.4
1952   Jamaica 3:03.9
1956   USA 3:04.8
1960   USA 3:02.2
1964   USA 3:00.7
1968   USA 2:56.1
1972   Kenya 2:59.8
1976   USA 2:58.7

110 Metres Hurdles
1948   William Porter (USA) 13.9
1952   Harrison Dillard (USA) 13.7
1956   Lee Calhoun (USA) 13.5
1960   Lee Calhoun (USA) 13.8
1964   Hayes Jones (USA) 13.67
1968   Willie Davenport (USA) 13.33
1972   Rodney Milburn (USA) 13.24
1976   Guy Drut (Fra) 13.30

400 Metres Hurdles
1948   Roy Cochran (USA) 51.1
1952   Charles Moore (USA) 50.8
1956   Glenn Davis (USA) 50.1
1960   Glenn Davis (USA) 49.3
1964   Warren 'Rex' Cawley (USA) 49.69
1968   David Hemery (GB) 48.12
1972   John Akii-Bua (Uga) 47.82
1976   Edwin Moses (USA) 47.64

3000 Metres Steeplechase
1948   Tore Sjöstrand (Swe) 9:04.6
1952   Horace Ashenfelter (USA) 8:45.4
1956   Christopher Brasher (GB) 8:41.2
1960   Zdzislaw Krzyszkowiak (Pol) 8:34.2
1964   Gaston Roelants (Bel) 8:30.8
1968   Amos Biwott (Ken) 8:51.0
1972   Kipchoge Keino (Ken) 8:23.6
1976   Anders Garderud (Swe) 8:08.0

10 000 Metres Walk
1948   John Mikaelsson (Swe) 45:13.2
1952   John Mikaelsson (Swe) 45:02.8

20 000 Metres Walk
1956   Leonid Spirin (USSR) 1:31:27.4
1960   Vladimir Golubnichiy (USSR) 1:34:07.2
1964   Kenneth Matthews (GB) 1:29:34.0
1968   Vladimir Golubnichiy (USSR) 1:33:58.4
1972   Peter Frenkel (GDR) 1:26:424
1976   Daniel Bautista (Mex) 1:24:40.6

50 000 Metres Walk
1948   John Ljunggren (Swe) 4:41:52.0
1952   Giuseppe Dordoni (Ita) 4:28:07.8
1956   Norman Read (NZ) 4:30:42.8
1960   Don Thompson (GB) 4:25:30.0
1964   Abdon Pamich (Ita) 4:11:12.4

1968 Christophe Höhne (GDR) 4:20:13.6
1972 Bernd Kannenberg (GDR) 3:56:11.6
1976 Not held

High Jump
1948 John Winter (Aus) 1.98
1952 Walter Davis (USA) 2.04
1956 Charles Dumas (USA) 2.12
1960 Robert Shavlakadze (USSR) 2.16
1964 Valeriy Brumel (USSR) 2.18
1968 Richard Fosbury (USA) 2.24
1972 Yuriy Tarmak (USSR) 2.23
1976 Jacek Wszola (Pol) 2.25

Pole Vault
1948 Guinn Smith (USA) 4.30
1952 Robert Richards (USA) 4.55
1956 Robert Richards (USA) 4.56
1960 Donald Bragg (USA) 4.70
1964 Frederick Hansen (USA) 5.10
1968 Robert Seagren (USA) 5.40
1972 Wolfgang Nordwig (GDR) 5.50
1976 Tadeusz Slusarski (Pol) 5.50

Long Jump
1948 William Steele (USA) 7.82
1952 Jerome Biffle (USA) 7.57
1956 Gregory Bell (USA) 7.83
1960 Ralph Boston (USA) 8.12
1964 Lynn Davies (GB) 8.07
1968 Robert Beamon (USA) 8.90
1972 Randy Williams (USA) 8.24
1976 Arnie Robinson (USA) 8.35

Triple Jump
1948 Arne Ahman (Swe) 15.40
1952 Adhemar Ferreira da Silva (Bra) 16.22
1956 Adhemar Ferreira da Silva (Bra) 16.35
1960 Jozef Schmidt (Pol) 16.81
1964 Jozef Schmidt (Pol) 16.85
1968 Viktor Saneyev (USSR) 17.39
1972 Viktor Saneyev (USSR) 17.35
1976 Viktor Saneyev (USSR) 17.29

Shot
1948 Wilbur Thompson (USA) 17.12
1952 Parry O'Brien (USA) 17.41
1956 Parry O'Brien (USA) 18.57
1960 William Nieder (USA) 19.68
1964 Dallas Long (USA) 20.33
1968 Randel Matson (USA) 20.54
1972 Wladyslaw Komar (Pol) 21.18
1976 Udo Beyer (GDR) 21.05

Discus
1948 Adolfo Consolini (Ita) 52.78
1952 Sim Iness (USA) 55.03
1956 Alfred Oerter (USA) 56.36
1960 Alfred Oerter (USA) 59.18
1964 Alfred Oerter (USA) 61.00
1968 Alfred Oerter (USA) 64.78
1972 Ludvik Danek (Cze) 64.40
1976 Mac Wilkins (USA) 67.50

Hammer
1948 Imre Nemeth (Hun) 56.07
1952 Jozsef Csermak (Hun) 60.34
1956 Harold Connolly (USA) 63.19
1960 Vasiliy Rudenkov (USSR) 67.10
1964 Romuald Klim (USSR) 69.74
1968 Gyula Zsivotzky (Hun) 73.36
1972 Anatoliy Bondarchuk (USSR) 75.50
1976 Yuriy Syedikh (USSR) 77.52

Javelin
1948 Tapio Rautavaara (Fin) 69.77
1952 Cyrus Young (USA) 73.78
1956 Egil Danielsen (Nor) 85.71
1960 Viktor Tsibulenko (USSR) 84.64
1964 Pauli Nevala (Fin) 82.66
1968 Janis Lusis (USSR) 90.10
1972 Klaus Wolfermann (Ger) 90.48
1976 Mikos Nemeth (Hun) 94.58

Decathlon
1948 Robert Mathias (USA) 6825
1952 Robert Mathias (USA) 7731
1956 Milton Campbell (USA) 7708
1960 Rafer Johnson (USA) 8001
1964 Willi Holdorf (Ger) 7887
1968 William Toomey (USA) 8193
1972 Nikolai Avilov (USSR) 8454
1976 Bruce Jenner (USA) 8618

WOMEN
100 Metres
1948 Fanny Blankers-Koen (Hol) 11.9
1952 Marjorie Jackson (Aus) 11.5
1956 Betty Cuthbert (Aus) 11.5
1960 Wilma Rudolph (USA) 11.0
1964 Wyomia Tyus (USA) 11.49
1968 Wyomia Tyus (USA) 11.07
1972 Renate Stecher (GDR) 11.07
1976 Annegret Richter (Ger) 11.08

200 Metres
1948 Fanny Blankers-Koen (Hol) 24.4
1952 Marjorie Jackson (Aus) 23.7
1956 Betty Cuthbert (Aus) 23.4
1960 Wilma Rudolph (USA) 24.0
1964 Edith Maguire (USA) 23.05
1968 Irena Szewinska (Pol) 22.58
1972 Renate Stecher (GDR) 22.40
1976 Barbel Eckert (GDR) 22.37

400 Metres
1964 Betty Cuthbert (Aus) 52.01
1968 Colette Besson (Fra) 52.03
1972 Monika Zehrt (GDR) 51.08
1976 Irena Szewinska (Pol) 49.29

800 Metres
1960 Lyudmila Shevtsova (USSR) 2:04.3
1964 Ann Packer (GB) 2:01.1
1968 Madeline Manning (USA) 2:00.9
1972 Hildegard Falck (Ger) 1:58.6
1976 Tatyana Kazankina (USSR) 1:54.9

1500 Metres
1972   Lyudmila Bragina (USSR) 4:01.4
1976   Tatyana Kazankina (USSR) 4:05.5

80 Metres Hurdles
1948   Fanny Blankers-Koen (Hol) 11.2
1952   Shirley Strickland (Aus) 10.9
1956   Shirley Strickland (Aus) 10.7
1960   Irina Press (USSR) 10.8
1964   Karin Balzer (GDR) 10.5
1968   Maureen Caird (Aus) 10.3

100 Metres Hurdles
1972   Annelie Ehrhardt (GDR) 12.59
1976   Johanna Schaller (GDR) 12.77

4 × 100 Metres Relay
1948   Netherlands 47.5
1952   USA 45.9
1956   Australia 44.5
1960   USA 44.5
1964   Poland 43.69
1968   USA 42.87
1972   W. Germany 42.81
1976   GDR 42.55

4 × 400 Metres Relay
1972   GDR 3:23.0
1976   GDR 3:19.2

High Jump
1948   Alice Coachman (USA) 1.68
1952   Esther Brand (SA) 1.67
1956   Mildred McDaniel (USA) 1.76
1960   Iolanda Balas (Rom) 1.85
1964   Iolanda Balas (Rom) 1.90
1968   Miloslava Rezkova (Cze) 1.82
1972   Ulrike Meyfarth (Ger) 1.92
1976   Rosi Ackermann (GDR) 1.93

Long Jump
1948   Olga Gyarmati (Hun) 5.69
1952   Yvette Williams (NZ) 6.24
1956   Elzbieta Krzesinska (Pol) 6.35
1960   Vyera Krepkina (USSR) 6.37

1964   Mary Rand (GB) 6.76
1968   Viorica Viscopoleanu (Rom) 6.82
1972   Heide Rosendahl (Ger) 6.78
1976   Angela Voigt (GDR) 6.72

Shot
1948   Micheline Ostermeyer (Fra) 13.75
1952   Galina Zybina (USSR) 15.28
1956   Tamara Tishkyevich (USSR) 16.59
1960   Tamara Press (USSR) 17.32
1964   Tamara Press (USSR) 18.14
1968   Margitta Gummel (GDR) 19.61
1972   Nadyezhda Chizhova (USSR) 21.03
1976   Ivanka Khristova (Bul) 21.16

Discus
1948   Micheline Ostermeyer (Fra) 41.92
1952   Nina Ponomaryeva (USSR) 51.42
1956   Olga Fikotova (Cze) 53.68
1960   Nina Ponomaryeva (USSR) 55.10
1964   Tamara Press (USSR) 57.26
1968   Lia Manoliu (Rom) 58.28
1972   Faina Melnik (USSR) 66.62
1976   Evelin Schlaak (now Jahl) (GDR) 69.00

Javelin
1948   Herma Bouma (Aut) 45.56
1952   Dana Zatopkova (Cze) 50.46
1956   Inese Jaunzeme (USSR) 53.86
1960   Elvira Ozolina (USSR) 55.98
1964   Mihaela Penes (Rom) 60.54
1968   Angela Nemeth (Hun) 60.36
1972   Ruth Fuchs (GDR) 63.88
1976   Ruth Fuchs (GDR) 65.94

Pentathlon
80m hurdles, Shot, High Jump, Long Jump, 200m
1964–68: 100m hurdles replaced 80mh 1972 and 800
metres replaced 200m in 1976.

1964   Irina Press (USSR) 4702
1968   Ingrid Becker (Ger) 4559
1972   Mary Peters (GB) 4801
1976   Sigrun Siegl (GDR) 4745
(1964 and 1968 scores re-totalled on current scoring
tables)

World Championships

Announced by the IAAF as due to be held for all regular events in 1983, the first official world
championship was held for 50 000 Metres Walk in 1976, after that event had been omitted
from the Olympic programme. Winner: Venyamin Soldatenko (USSR) 3:54:40.

World Cup

First contested by eight men's and eight women's teams in 1976.

Men
1977   GDR

Women
1977   Europe select

Fanny Blankers-Koen (Hol) leading Maureen Gardner (GB) in the 1948 Olympics 80 Metres Hurdles final at Wembley. This was the second of her record four athletics Gold Medals (*Syndication Int.*)

Emil Zatopek who set 18 world records in his distance running career as well as winning four Olympic and three European Gold Medals, leads from Gordon Pirie, who five times set world records, and Ken Norris, National Cross-country champion in 1956 (*E. D. Lacey*)

European Cup

First held in 1965, the European Cup is now contested biennially.

Men				Women			
		1973	USSR			1973	GDR
1965	USSR	1975	GDR	1965	USSR	1975	GDR
1967	USSR	1977	GDR	1967	USSR	1977	GDR
1970	GDR	1979	GDR	1970	GDR	1979	GDR

European Championships

First held in 1934 (men) and 1938 (women). The European Championships are now contested over a full range of events every four years. Winners of three or more Gold Medals at one event have been:

4 Janis Lusis (USSR): Javelin 1962, 1966, 1969, 1971
4 Nadyezhda Chizhova (USSR): Women's Shot 1966, 1969, 1971, 1974
3 Adolfo Consolini (Ita): Discus 1946, 1950, 1954
3 Vasiliy Kuznyetsov (USSR): Decathlon 1954, 1958, 1962
3 Igor Ter-Ovanesyan (USSR): Long Jump 1958, 1962, 1969

3 Karin Balzer (GDR): Women's 80mh 1966; 100mh 1969, 1971
3 Wolfgang Nordwig (GDR): Pole Vault 1966, 1969, 1971
3 Valeriy Borzov (USSR): 100m 1969, 1971, 1974

Most Gold Medals in all: 5 Fanny Blankers-Koen (Hol) – 80mh and 4 × 100m Relay 1946, 100m, 200m, 80m Hurdles 1950.

Commonwealth Games

First held in 1930. Athletics events are contested over a full range of events every four years. Winners of three or more Gold Medals at one event:

3 Valerie Sloper/Young (NZ): Shot 1958, 1962, 1966
3 Pam Kilborn/Ryan (Aus): Women's 80mh 1962, 1966; 100mh 1970
3 Don Quarrie (Jam): 100m 1970, 1974, 1978
3 Howard Payne (Eng): Hammer 1962, 1966, 1970

Most Gold Medals in all: 7 Marjorie Jackson/Nelson (Aus) – 4 in 1950 and 3 in 1954.

British Athletics League

First held in 1969. Contested by British men's teams.

1969	Birchfield Harriers	1975	Wolverhampton & Bilston AC
1970	Thames Valley Harriers	1976	Wolverhampton & Bilston AC
1971	Thames Valley Harriers	1977	Wolverhampton & Bilston AC
1972	Cardiff AAC	1978	Wolverhampton & Bilston AC
1973	Cardiff AAC	1979	Wolverhampton & Bilston AC
1974	Cardiff AAC		

British Athletics Cups

Knock-out inter-club competitions for both men and women. The Men's Cup was first contested in 1973, from 1974 to 1976 it was the Pye Gold Cup and from 1977 to date the GRE Gold Cup. The Women's Cup was first contested in 1974 and from 1977 has been the GRE Jubilee Cup. Winners:

Men		**Women**	
1973	Wolverhampton & Bilston AC	1974	Mitcham AC
1974	Cardiff AAC	1975	Edinburgh Southern Harriers
1975	Edinburgh Southern Harriers	1976	Stretford AC
1976	Wolverhampton & Bilston AC	1977	Stretford AC
1977	Wolverhampton & Bilston AC	1978	Stretford AC
1978	Shaftesbury Harriers		

AAA Championships

The AAA (Amateur Athletic Association) championships were first held in 1880, and thus their centenary is being celebrated in 1980. Although, strictly speaking, they are the national championships for England, for many years they have been a major international event on the athletics calendar, and indeed in the early part of the century were regarded as virtually world championships.

Most individual titles have been won by:

14 McDonald Bailey: 100 yards 1946–47, 1949–53; 220 yards 1946–47, 1949–53
13 Dennis Horgan: Shot 1893–99, 1904–05, 1908–10, 1912
11 Harry Whittle: 220 yards hurdles 1953; 440 yards hurdles 1947–53; Long Jump 1947, 1949; Decathlon 1950
10 Alfred Shrubb: 1 mile 1903–04; 4 miles 1901–04; 10 miles 1901–04
10 Ken Matthews: 2 miles walk 1959, 1961–64; 7 miles walk 1959–61, 1963–64

In addition to the above, winners 7 or more times at one event have been:

8 Donald Finlay: 120 yards hurdles 1932–38, 1949
8 Maurice Herriott: 3000 metres steeplechase 1959, 1961–67
8 Roger Mills: 3000 metres walk 1969, 1972–79
7 Albert Cooper: 2 miles walk 1932–38
7 Bill Tancred: Discus 1966–70, 1972–73
7 David Travis: Javelin 1965, 1968, 1970–74
7 Tom Ray: Pole Vault 1881–82, 1884–88
7 Geoff Capes: Shot 1972–73, 1975–79

AUNT SALLY

An English pub game almost entirely confined to Oxfordshire, although it has many distant relations among the games of the South West and Midlands. The 'summer season' extends from mid April to September, when there is a heavy programme of league fixtures.

The game is one of the oldest and simplest forms of skittles.

The winners: Oxford and District Aunt Sally Finals.

1976   Singles title: Monty Greenaway, British Legion, Littlemore – winner for the fourth time in six years
Pairs title: Monty Greenaway and C. Green
Hall Cup: British Legion, Littlemore
League championship: Royal British Legion A, Littlemore
Landlords' Trophy: Ken Warmington, Royal Greenjackets

1977   Singles title: Monty Greenaway
Pairs title: Dennis Sellar and Eddie Butler, The Black Swan
Halls Cup: The George, Littlemore
League championship: The Black Swan A
Landlords' Trophy: Jim Adams, The George

1978   Singles title: Laurie Woods, British Legion, Littlemore
Pairs title: M. Greenaway and Norman Evans
Halls Cup: British Legion A, Littlemore
League championship: British Legion A, Littlemore
Landlords' Trophy: T. Rose, Isis

BABIES

Point of Sale Photographic Competition

Arranged annually by Kodak Limited and Robinson's Baby Foods to find the best 'candid camera' shot of a baby born since 1 October of the previous year.

The 1978 prize included camera equipment and materials valued to £100, plus a cheque for £50, plus a photograph taken by entertainer Rolf Harris of the winning baby.

1975   Andrew Boothman (Goole, N. Humberside), one year old
His parents won a Kodak 'Carousel' projector and a professional portrait of Andrew each year for the first five years of his life. Plus a generous supply of Robinson's Baby Food Two and two Robinson's cuddly toys – Susie Squirrel and Betsy Bunny.

1976   Lyndsey Heys (Blackpool), eight months
Her parents won £150 retail value of Kodak equipment plus a generous supply of Robinson's baby food. Also professional portrait of Lyndsey, each year for next five years.

1977   (Also Jubilee Birthday Competition)
Joanne Astrup (Moorland, Nr. Bridgwater, Somerset)
Her parents won £200 Kodak photographic equipment, £100 in cash and photographs by Patrick Lichfield, plus a generous supply of Robinson's Baby Food.

1978   Jonathan Rodgers (Lancaster)
His parents won £100 Kodak photographic equipment, £50 cash, photograph of Jonathan taken by Rolf Harris plus a supply of Robinson's Baby Food.

Ten-month-old Jonathan Rodgers captured in a serious mood by his father, David Rodgers. This photograph won the Robinsons Baby Food and Kodak 'candid camera' shot award for 1978

BADMINTON

Thomas Cup

First held in 1948–49, the Thomas Cup is the international men's team championship, and is contested every three years.

1948–49	Malaya	1960–61	Indonesia	1969–70	Indonesia
1951–52	Malaya	1963–64	Indonesia	1972–73	Indonesia
1954–55	Malaya	1966–67	Malaysia	1975–76	Indonesia
1957–58	Indonesia				

Uber Cup

First held in 1956–57, the Uber Cup is the international women's team championship, and is held every three years.

1956–57	USA	1968–69	Japan
1959–60	USA	1971–72	Japan
1962–63	USA	1974–75	Indonesia
1965–66	Japan	1977–78	Japan

World Championships

The first ever world championships were held in 1977 and are intended to be held every three years. Winners were:

Men's Singles: Flemming Delfs (Den)
Women's Singles: Lene Köppen (Den)

Men's Doubles: Johan Wahjudi & Tjun-Tjun (Ind)
Women's Doubles: Etsuko Tuganoo & Emiko Ueno (Jap)
Mixed Doubles: Steen Skovgaard & Lene Köppen (Den)

Rudy Hartono won the All-England Badminton men's singles title a record 8 times. He also helped Indonesia to three successive Thomas Cup wins (*Associated Press*)

All-England Championships

First held in 1899, and, until the advent of the World Championships, the premier tournament in the world. Singles winners since 1947:

MEN

1947	Conny Jepsen (Swe)	1969	Rudy Hartono (Ind)	1957	Judy Devlin (USA)
1948	Jorn Skaarup (Den)	1970	Rudy Hartono (Ind)	1958	Judy Devlin (USA)
1949	David Freeman (USA)	1971	Rudy Hartono (Ind)	1959	Heather Ward (Eng)
1950	Wong Peng Soon (Mal)	1972	Rudy Hartono (Ind)	1960	Judy Devlin (USA)
1951	Wong Peng Soon (Mal)	1973	Rudy Hartono (Ind)	1961	Judy Hashman (Devlin) (USA)
1952	Wong Peng Soon (Mal)	1974	Rudy Hartono (Ind)	1962	Judy Hashman (USA)
1953	Eddie Choong (Mal)	1975	Svend Pri (Den)	1963	Judy Hashman (USA)
1954	Eddie Choong (Mal)	1976	Rudy Hartono (Ind)	1964	Judy Hashman (USA)
1955	Wong Peng Soon (Mal)	1977	Flemming Delfs (Den)	1965	Ursula Smith (Eng)
1956	Eddie Choong (Mal)	1978	Liem Swie King (Ind)	1966	Judy Hashman (USA)
1957	Eddie Choong (Mal)	1979	Liem Swie King (Ind)	1967	Judy Hashman (USA)
1958	Erland Kops (Den)			1968	Eva Twedberg (Swe)
1959	Tan Joe Hok (Ind)	**WOMEN**		1969	Hiroe Yuki (Jap)
1960	Erland Kops (Den)	1947	Marie Ussing (Den)	1970	Etsuko Takenaka (Jap)
1961	Erland Kops (Den)	1948	Kirsten Thorndahl (Den)	1971	Eva Twedberg (Swe)
1962	Erland Kops (Den)	1949	Aase Schiött Jacobsen (Den)	1972	Noriko Nakayama (Jap)
1963	Erland Kops (Den)	1950	Tonny Ahm (Den)	1973	Margaret Beck (Eng)
1964	Knud Nielsen (Den)	1951	Aase Schiött Jacobsen (Den)	1974	Hiroe Yuki (Jap)
1965	Erland Kops (Den)	1952	Tonny Ahm (Den)	1975	Hiroe Yuki (Jap)
1966	Tan Aik Huang (Mal)	1953	Marie Ussing (Den)	1976	Gillian Gilks (Eng)
1967	Erland Kops (Den)	1954	Judy Devlin (USA)	1977	Hiroe Yuki (Jap)
1968	Rudy Hartono (Ind)	1955	Margaret Varner (USA)	1978	Gillian Gilks (Eng)
		1956	Margaret Varner (USA)	1979	Lene Köppen (Den)

BALLET

The Queen Elizabeth II Coronation Award

This is presented annually in recognition of outstanding services to the Art of Ballet by the Royal Academy of Dancing.

1954	Dame Ninette de Valois, DBE, DMus, FRAD	1966	Serge Grigorieff and Lubov Tchernicheva
1955	Madame Tamara Karsavina	1967	Madame Lydia Sokolova
1956	Dame Marie Rambert, DBE, FRAD	1968	Stanislas Idzikowski
1957	Phyllis Bedells, FRAD	1969	John Hart
1958	Anton Dolin	1970	John Gilpin
1959	Sir Frederick Ashton, OM, CH, CBE	1971	Louise Browne, OBE, FRAD
1960	Sir Robert Helpman, CBE	1972	Ruth French, FRAD
1961	Ursula Moreton	1973	Norman Morrice
1962	Cyril Beaumont, CBE	1974	Brian Shaw
1963	P. J. S. Richardson, OBE (deceased)	1975	Robin Howard
	Dame Alicia Markova, DBE, DMus	1976	Pamela May
1964	Kathleen Gordon	1977	Winifred Edwards
1965	Dame Peggy Van Praagh, DBE	1978	Kenneth MacMillan

The Royal Academy of Dancing Adeline Genée Medal Awards

This is a competition for ballet dancers, initiated by Dame Adeline Genée (founder and president of the Royal Academy of Dancing) in 1931. It is designed to test the professional potential of young dancers. All candidates must hold either the Intermediate or Advanced Certificates, passed at Highly Commended or Honours level, and the competition is held every year. There are six medals – Gold, Silver, and Bronze for girls and for male dancers, which are only awarded if the standard is sufficiently high.

Over the years many distinguished dancers have won Gold Medals – Bryan Ashbridge, David Drew, John Gilpin, Maria Guerrero, John Hart, Rowena Jackson, Brenda Last, Diana Vere and Doreen Wells, to name but a few.

Adeline Genée Medal Award winners since 1973 are as follows:

	Gold Medal	*Silver Medal*	*Bronze Medal*
1973	Jane Devine	Angailika MacArthur	Sheila Styles
1974	Nicola Katrak	Amanda Wilkinson	Nicola MacLaurin
	Nigel Jones	Kenneth Burke	
1975	Summer Rhatigan	Flora Cheong-Leen	
1976	Jill Taylor	Deborah Kinsey	Sharon Hamilton
1977	Sharon McGorian	Samira Saidi	Julie Mitchell
1978	Ravenna Tucker	Alison Townsend	Kim Miller
	Roland Price		
1979	Madonna Benjamin	Madeleine Sheehan	Karen Donovan

The Royal Academy of Dancing Adeline Genée Medal Awards for 1979. Gold: Madonna Benjamin (*left*)**, Silver: Madeleine Sheehan** (*centre*)**, Bronze: Karen Donovan** (*right*)

BALLOONS

The annual grand release of all the gas-filled balloons in the Beefeater Gin Balloon Race. The furthest travelled balloon is the winner

Beefeater Gin Balloon Race

Entry forms are on neck collars around bottles of Beefeater Gin. The 1978–79 entry forms featured two drawings of a London Transport bus. There are a certain number of differences between the two drawings and contestants decide whether the total number of differences is 6, 8, 10, 12, and then put a tick in the appropriate box next to that number.

Provided you get this part of it correct, a gas-filled balloon is released, and the one that travels furthest is the winner. The 1979 winner received £2000 in prizes.

The names of the winners of the first prizes are as follows:

1969–70 William Shelton	1972–73 Mr Ripley	1976–77 Gordon Vann
1970–71 Mr Perryman	1973–74 Barrington Tucker	1977–78 H. Cross
1971–72 James Hartly	1975–76 Albert Woodroofe	1978–79 D. Davis

BANDS

The Dysart & Dundonald Pipe Band displaying all their trophies. They won the World Pipe Band Championships in both 1977 and 1978

'Fanfare': BBC Radio Scotland's Brass Band Contest

Winners of this annual contest are as follows:

1974 Whitburn Burgh Band Conductor: George Thomson	1977 CWS (Glasgow) Band Conductor: Nigel Boddice
1975 Kirkintilloch Silver Band Conductor: David James	1978 CWS (Glasgow) Band Conductor: Nigel Boddice
1976 Kirkintilloch Silver Band Conductor: David James	

Rothmans Brass in Concert Championship

Now an annual event, held at Darlington, the Championship is established as one of the major brass band competitions to take place in the UK. The bands compete for a first prize of £1000.

1977 Grimethorpe Colliery Band, Yorkshire
1978 Hammonds Sauce Works Band, Shipley, Yorkshire

Tobacco Workers' Union Trophy

Presented to the best featured soloist in the Rothmans Brass In Concert Championship.

1978   Bobby Millar (Wingates Temperance Band), for
his euphonium performance of Bladon Races

World Pipe Band Championships

Bands from around the world compete annually and each year sees representatives from Canada, USA, Australia, New Zealand, Eire, Scandinavia, Netherlands, Denmark, France and, of course, bands from HM and Commonwealth Forces.

	Band	*Venue*	*Pipe-Major*
1947	Bowhill Colliery	Edinburgh	C. Sutherland
1948	Shotts & Dykehead Caledonia	Glasgow	T. McAllister, Sen., BEM
1949	Glasgow Police	Edinburgh	J. MacDonald
1950	Edinburgh Police	Dundee	D. S. Ramsay
1951	Glasgow Police	Edinburgh	J. MacDonald
1952	Shotts & Dykehead Caledonia	Ayr	T. McAllister, Sen., BEM
1953	Clan MacRae	Edinburgh	A. MacLeod
1954	Edinburgh Police	Aberdeen	D. S. Ramsay
1955	Muirhead & Sons	Stirling	J. Smith
1956	Muirhead & Sons	Belfast	J. Smith
1957	Shotts & Dykehead Caledonia	Paisley	J. K. MacAllister
1958	Shotts & Dykehead Caledonia	Aberdeen	J. K. MacAllister
1959	Shotts & Dykehead Caledonia	Kirkcaldy	J. K. MacAllister
1960	Shotts & Dykehead Caledonia	Inverness	J. K. MacAllister
1961	Muirhead & Sons	Edinburgh	J. Smith
1962	277 (A & SH), Regt., RA(TA)	Belfast	J. Weatherstone, MBE, BEM
1963	Edinburgh Police	Dumfries	I. McLeod
1964	Edinburgh Police	Ayr	I. McLeod
1965	Muirhead & Sons	Forfar	R. Hardie
1966	Muirhead & Sons	Inverness	R. Hardie
1967	Muirhead & Sons	Oban	R. Hardie
1968	Muirhead & Sons	Grangemouth	R. Hardie
1969	Muirhead & Sons	Perth	R. Hardie
1970	Shotts & Dykehead Caledonia	Aberdeen	T. McAllister, Jr
1971	Edinburgh Police	Lanark	I. McLeod
1972	Edinburgh Police	Hawick	I. McLeod
1973	Shotts & Dykehead Caledonia	Ayr	T. McAllister, Jr
1974	Shotts & Dykehead Caledonia	Stirling	T. McAllister, Jr
1975	Edinburgh City Police	Corby	I. McLeod
1976	Strathclyde Police	Hawick	I. McLellan
1977	Dysart & Dundonald	Aberdeen	R. Shepherd
1978	Dysart & Dundonald	Lanark	R. Shepherd
1979	Strathclyde Police	Nottingham	I. McLellan

BASEBALL

National League American League

The National League was founded in 1876 and the American League in 1901. In 1903 and each season since 1905 the winners of these two leagues have met in the World Series.

Winners of these major leagues since 1901, with the World Series winners identified by (WS) have been:

National League		American League	National League		American League
1901	Pittsburgh Pirates	Chicago White Sox	1903	Pittsburgh Pirates	Boston Red Sox (WS)
1902	Pittsburgh Pirates	Philadelphia Athletics	1904	New York Giants	Boston Red Sox

National League	American League		National League	American League
1905 New York Giants (WS)	Philadelphia Athletics	1942	St Louis Cardinals (WS)	New York Yankees
1906 Chicago Cubs	Chicago White Sox (WS)	1943	St Louis Cardinals	New York Yankees (WS)
1907 Chicago Cubs (WS)	Detroit Tigers	1944	St Louis Cardinals (WS)	St Louis Browns
1908 Chicago Cubs (WS)	Detroit Tigers (WS)	1945	Chicago Cubs	Detroit Tigers
1909 Pittsburgh Pirates (WS)	Detroit Tigers	1946	St Louis Cardinals (WS)	Boston Red Sox
1910 Chicago Cubs	Philadelphia Athletics (WS)	1947	Brooklyn Dodgers	New York Yankees (WS)
1911 New York Giants	Philadelphia Athletics (WS)	1948	Boston Braves	Cleveland Indians (WS)
1912 New York Giants	Boston Red Sox (WS)	1949	Brooklyn Dodgers	New York Yankees (WS)
1913 New York Giants	Philadelphia Athletics (WS)	1950	Philadelphia Phillies	New York Yankees (WS)
1914 Boston (WS)	Philadelphia Athletics	1951	New York Giants	New York Yankees (WS)
1915 Philadelphia	Boston Red Sox (WS)	1952	Brooklyn Dodgers	New York Yankees (WS)
1916 Brooklyn	Boston Red Sox (WS)	1953	Brooklyn Dodgers	New York Yankees (WS)
1917 New York Giants	Chicago White Sox (WS)	1954	New York Giants (WS)	Cleveland Indians
1918 Chicago Cubs	Boston Red Sox (WS)	1955	Brooklyn Dodgers (WS)	New York Yankees
1919 Cincinnati (WS)	Chicago White Sox	1956	Brooklyn Dodgers	New York Yankees (WS)
1920 Brooklyn	Cleveland Indians (WS)	1957	Milwaukee Braves (WS)	New York Yankees
1921 New York Giants (WS)	New York Yankees	1958	Milwaukee Braves	New York Yankees (WS)
1922 New York Giants (WS)	New York Yankees	1959	Los Angeles Dodgers (WS)	Chicago White Sox
1923 New York Giants	New York Yankees (WS)	1960	Pittsburgh Pirates (WS)	New York Yankees
1924 New York Giants	Washington (WS)	1961	Cincinnati Reds	New York Yankees (WS)
1925 Pittsburgh Pirates (WS)	Washington	1962	San Francisco Giants	New York Yankees (WS)
1926 St Louis Cardinals (WS)	New York Yankees	1963	Los Angeles Dodgers (WS)	New York Yankees
1927 Pittsburgh Pirates	New York Yankees (WS)	1964	St Louis Cardinals (WS)	New York Yankees
1928 St Louis Cardinals	New York Yankees (WS)	1965	Los Angeles Dodgers (WS)	Minnesota Twins
1929 Chicago Cubs	Philadelphia Athletics (WS)	1966	Los Angeles Dodgers	Baltimore Orioles (WS)
1930 St Louis Cardinals	Philadelphia Athletics (WS)	1967	St Louis Cardinals (WS)	Boston Red Sox
1931 St Louis Cardinals (WS)	Philadelphia Athletics	1968	St Louis Cardinals	Detroit Tigers (WS)
1932 Chicago Cubs	New York Yankees (WS)	1969	New York Mets (WS)	Baltimore Orioles
1933 New York Giants (WS)	Washington	1970	Cincinnati Reds	Baltimore Orioles (WS)
1934 St Louis Cardinals (WS)	Detroit Tigers	1971	Pittsburgh Pirates (WS)	Baltimore Orioles
1935 Chicago Cubs	Detroit Tigers (WS)	1972	Cincinnati Reds	Oakland Athletics (WS)
1936 New York Giants	New York Yankees (WS)	1973	New York Mets	Oakland Athletics (WS)
1937 New York Giants	New York Yankees (WS)	1974	Los Angeles Dodgers	Oakland Athletics (WS)
1938 Chicago Cubs	New York Yankees (WS)	1975	Cincinnati Reds (WS)	Boston Red Sox
1939 Cincinnati Reds	New York Yankees (WS)	1976	Cincinnati Reds (WS)	New York Yankees
1940 Cincinnati Reds (WS)	Detroit Tigers	1977	Los Angeles Dodgers	New York Yankees (WS)
1941 Brooklyn Dodgers	New York Yankees (WS)	1978	Los Angeles Dodgers	New York Yankees (WS)

Most Valuable Player

Each season the 'most valuable player' in each of the major leagues is elected by the Baseball Writers' Association of America. Four men have won three awards: Jimmy Foxx, Stan Musial, Roy Campanella, and Mickey Mantle. Winners since 1970:

	National League	American League		National League	American League
1970	Johnny Bench (Cincinnati)	John Powell (Baltimore)	1974	Steve Garvey (Los Angeles)	Jeff Burroughs (Texas)
1971	Joseph Torre (St Louis)	Vida Blue (Oakland)	1975	Joe Morgan (Cincinnati)	Fred Lynn (Boston)
1972	Johnny Bench (Cincinnati)	Richard Allen (Chicago)	1976	Joe Morgan (Cincinnati)	Thurman Munson (New York)
1973	Pete Rose (Cincinnati)	Reggie Jackson (Oakland)	1977	George Foster (Cincinnati)	Rod Carew (Minnesota)
			1978	Dave Parker (Pittsburgh)	Jim Rice (Boston)

BASKETBALL

World Championships

First held in 1950, the World Championships for men are held between Olympic Games. Contested by amateur teams.

1950	Argentina	1959	Brazil	1967	USSR	1974	USSR
1954	USA	1963	Brazil	1970	Yugoslavia	1978	Yugoslavia

Women's World Championships were first held in 1953.

1953	USA	1959	USSR	1967	USSR	1975	USSR
1957	USA	1964	USSR	1971	USSR	1979	Canada

Olympic Champions

Men

1936	USA	1956	USA	1968	USA
1948	USA	1960	USA	1972	USSR
1952	USA	1964	USA	1976	USA

NCAA Championship

The most important amateur basketball competition in the USA is the National Collegiate Athletic Association Championship. Winners since 1965 have been:

1965	UCLA	1969	UCLA	1973	UCLA	1976	Indiana
1966	Texas Western	1970	UCLA	1974	North Carolina	1977	Marquette
1967	UCLA	1971	UCLA		State	1978	Kentucky
1968	UCLA	1972	UCLA	1975	UCLA	1979	Michigan State

(UCLA = University of California at Los Angeles)

NBA Champions

The major American professional competition is under the auspices of the National Basketball Association (NBA), which was formed in 1946 by a merger of the Basketball Association of America and the National Basketball League. In 1976 the American Basketball Association merged with the NBA. The teams are currently divided into four divisions, Atlantic and Central in the East and Midwest and Pacific in the West. Winners of the Championships play-off since 1965:

1965	Boston	1970	New York	1975	Golden State
1966	Boston	1971	Milwaukee	1976	Boston
1967	Philadelphia	1972	Los Angeles	1977	Portland
1968	Boston	1973	New York	1978	Washington
1969	Boston	1974	Boston	1979	Seattle

BATTLES

Winners of a Hundred Famous Battles

Abraham, Plains of	13 Sep 1759	British Conquest of Canada	5000 British under Wolfe defeated 4500 French under Montcalm to capture Quebec
Actium	2 Sep 31 BC	Wars of the Second Triumvirate	400 Roman vessels under Octavian defeated 480-strong Roman–Egyptian fleet under Mark Antony and Cleopatra
Adowa	1 Mar 1896	Italian–Ethiopian War	80 000 Ethiopians under King Menelik II defeated 20 000 Italians under General Baratieri
Adrianople	9 Aug 378	Gothic invasions of the Roman Empire	A Gothic army under Fritigern defeated 60 000 Romans under Emperor Valens
Agincourt	25 Oct 1415	Hundred Years' War	9000 English under Henry V defeated 30 000 French under the Constable of France

Napoleon I who led 73 000 French on 2 Dec 1805 at the Battle of Austerlitz, defeating 85 000 Austrians and Russians under Kutusov (*Courtesy of Musées Nationaux*)

The Battle of Bunker's Hill took place on 17 June 1775 during the War of American Independence. The British suffered heavy losses but drove the Americans from their entrenchments

Arbela-Gaugamela	1 Oct 331 BC	Macedonian Conquests	47 000 Macedonians under Alexander the Great defeated 250 000 Persians under King Darius III
Ardennes Offensive	16 Dec 1944–16 Jan 1945	Second World War	Allied forces under Eisenhower and Montgomery defeated a German offensive under Field Marshal von Rundstedt
Arnhem	17–25 Sep 1944	Second World War	German forces defeated the attempt by the British 1st Airborne Division to take control of the bridge at Arnhem
Atlantic	1940–1944	Second World War	Allied air and sea forces defeated the campaign by German U-boats and surface vessels to cut vital allied supply lines
Austerlitz	2 Dec 1805	Napoleonic Wars	73 000 French under Napoleon defeated 85 000 Austrians and Russians under Kutusov
Balaclava	25 Oct 1854	Crimean War	British forces under Lord Raglan repulsed a Russian attack under Prince Menshikov, the battle ending with the famous 'Charge of the Light Brigade'
Bannockburn	4 Jun 1314	English–Scottish Wars	8500 Scots under Robert the Bruce defeated 15 000 English under Edward II
Battle of Britain	8 Aug–30 Oct 1940	Second World War	Royal Air Force (Fighter Command under Sir Hugh Dowding) defeated attacks by Goering's Luftwaffe aimed at winning aerial supremacy prior to invasion of Britain
Blenheim	13 Aug 1704	War of the Spanish Succession	56 000 British, Austrians and allies under Marlborough and Eugène defeated 60 000 French and Bavarians under Marshal Tallard and the Elector of Bavaria
Borodino	7 Sep 1812	Napoleonic Wars	133 000 French and allies under Napoleon defeated 120 000 Russians under Kutusov

Bosworth Field	22 Aug 1485	Wars of the Roses	5000 men under Henry Tudor defeated 10 000 under Richard III after much of this force had changed sides
Boyne	1 Jul 1690	War of the English Succession	An Anglo-Dutch army of 36 000 under William III defeated a 25 000-strong Irish–French army under James II
Bull Run	21 Jul 1861	American Civil War	29 000 Confederates under General Beauregard defeated 35 000 Federal troops under General McDowell
Bunker's Hill	17 Jun 1775	War of American Independence	2500 British under General Howe suffered heavy losses but drove the Americans under Colonel Prescott from their entrenchments
Cambrai	20 Nov–3 Dec 1917	First World War	The British Third Army under General Byng attacked General von der Marwitz's German Second Army; the initial tank assault was successful, but counter-attacks forced a partial British withdrawal
Cannae	2 Aug 216 BC	Second Punic War	50 000 Carthaginians under Hannibal defeated 85 000 Romans under Consuls Varro and Paulus
Cape St Vincent	14 Feb 1797	French Revolutionary Wars	15 British ships under Sir John Jervis defeated 27 Spanish ships under Don Juan de Langara
Caporetto	24 Oct–12 Nov 1917	First World War	Austro-German forces under General von Below broke through the Italian front inflicting 40 000 casualties and taking 275 000 prisoners
Chalons	20 Jun 451	Wars of the Western Roman Empire	A Roman army with their Visigoth and Alan allies under Flavius Aetius and King Theodoric defeated the Huns and their allies under Attila
Crecy	26 Aug 1346	Hundred Years' War	10 000 English under Edward III defeated 12 000 French under Philip VI
Culloden	16 Apr 1746	Jacobite Rebellion	9000 Royalists under the Duke of Cumberland defeated 5000 Jacobites under Prince Charles Edward
D-Day	6 Jun 1944	Second World War	Allied forces under General Eisenhower successfully accomplished the greatest amphibious assault in history to breach Hitler's 'Atlantic Wall' on the Normandy beaches
Dien Bien Phu	13 Mar–7 May 1954	Indo-China War	70 000 Vietminh under General Giap defeated 15 000 French under Colonel de Castries
El Alamein	23 Oct–4 Nov 1942	Second World War	The British Eighth Army under Montgomery defeated Rommel's German and Italian forces
Flodden	9 Sep 1513	English–Scottish Wars	25 000 English under the Earl of Surrey defeated 50 000 Scots under James IV
Fontenoy	11 May 1745	War of the Austrian Succession	52 000 French under Marshal de Saxe defeated 46 000 English and allies under the Duke of Cumberland
Gallipoli Peninsula	25 Apr 1915–9 Jan 1916	First World War	Allied forces under Hamilton (succeeded by Monro) failed to overcome the resistance of the Turks under General Liman von Sanders, and were forced to evacuate the peninsula
Gettysburg	1–3 Jul 1863	American Civil War	88 000 Federal troops under General Meade defeated 75 000 Confederates under Robert E. Lee
Guadalcanal	7 Aug 1942–7 Feb 1943	Second World War	After a prolonged period of land and sea conflict the Americans forced the Japanese to evacuate the island

Hastings	14 Oct 1066	Norman Conquest of England	7000 Normans under William defeated a similar number of Saxons under King Harold
Hattin	4 Jul 1187	Crusades	20 000 Moslems under Saladin defeated a similar number of Crusaders under King Guy of Jerusalem
Inchon Landings	15–25 Sep 1950	Korean War	The US X Corps under Maj-Gen Almond successfully landed at Inchon, recaptured Seoul and broke the North Korean invasion of the South
Inkerman	5 Nov 1854	Crimean War	Anglo-French forces under Lord Raglan and General Pélissier repulsed a Russian sortie from Sebastopol under Prince Menshikov
Isandhlwana	22 Jan 1879	Zulu War	10 000 Zulus under Cetewayo defeated 1600 British and 2500 natives
Jena	14 Oct 1806	Napoleonic Wars	96 000 French under Napoleon defeated 53 000 Prussians and Saxons under Hohenlohe
Jutland	31 May–1 Jun 1916	First World War	Naval engagement between the British Grand Fleet under Jellicoe and the German High Seas Fleet under Scheer which was tactically indecisive, but resulted in the German fleet withdrawing to base for the remainder of the war
Kursk	5–13 Jul 1943	Second World War	In the greatest tank battle of the war the Russians defeated an offensive by the Germans under Manstein against the Kursk salient
Leipzig	16–19 Oct 1813	Napoleonic Wars	365 000 Russians, Austrians, Prussians and allies under Schwarzenberg defeated 195 000 French and allies under Napoleon
Leuthen	5 Dec 1757	Seven Years' War	43 000 Prussians under Frederick the Great defeated 72 000 Austrians under Prince Charles and Marshal Count von Daun
Leyte Gulf	23–26 Oct 1944	Second World War	In the greatest naval battle of the war the US navy under Admiral Halsey defeated the Japanese navy
Little Big Horn	25 Jun 1876	Sioux Wars	Indian warriors under Chief Crazy Horse wiped out 211 soldiers of the US 7th Cavalry under Lieutenant Colonel Custer
Loos	25 Sep–14 Oct 1915	First World War	A British offensive under Sir John French failed to break the German line
Malplaquet	11 Sep 1709	War of the Spanish Succession	90 000 English and allies under Marlborough and Eugène defeated a similar number of French under Marshal Villars
Marathon	12 Sep 490 BC	Persian–Greek Wars	11 000 Greeks under Callimachus and Miltiades defeated 15 000 Persians under Artaphrenes and Datis
Marengo	14 Jun 1800	Napoleonic Wars	28 000 French under Napoleon defeated 31 000 Austrians under Melas
Marne	5–10 Sep 1914	First World War	French and British attacks led to a retreat by the German army under von Moltke and the final abandonment of the Schlieffen Plan for the defeat of France
Marston Moor	2 Jul 1644	English Civil War	27 000 Parliamentarians under the Earl of Manchester defeated 18 000 Royalists under Prince Rupert
Midway	4–6 Jun 1942	Second World War	US Fleet under Admirals Fletcher and Spruance decisively defeated a Japanese force under Admirals Yamamoto, Nagumo and Kondo
Minden	1 Aug 1759	Seven Years' War	43 000 British and allies under Ferdinand of Brunswick defeated 54 000 French under Marquis de Contades

Mons	23 Aug 1914	First World War	The British Expeditionary Force under Sir John French held up the advance of von Kluck's First German Army but withdrew during the night
Naseby	14 Jun 1645	English Civil War	13 000 Parliamentarians under Fairfax defeated 9000 Royalists under Prince Rupert
Navarino	20 Oct 1827	War of Greek Independence	27 British, French and Russian ships under Admirals Codrington, de Rigny and Heiden defeated a Turkish–Egyptian fleet of 89 vessels under Tahir Pasha
New Orleans	8 Jan 1815	War of 1812	4500 Americans under General Jackson defeated 5300 British under General Pakenham
Nile	1 Aug 1798	French Revolutionary Wars	14 British ships under Nelson defeated 13 French ships under Brueys
Omdurman	2 Sep 1898	British Conquest of the Sudan	26 000 British and Egyptian troops under Kitchener defeated some 40 000 Sudanese under Kalifa Abdullah
Oudenarde	11 Jul 1708	War of the Spanish Succession	80 000 English and allies under Marlborough and Eugène defeated 85 000 under the Dukes of Burgundy and Vendôme
Passchendaele	31 Jul–11 Oct 1917	First World War	Allied offensive which gained little ground at enormous human cost in the mud of Flanders
Pavia	21 Feb 1525	French Wars in Italy	Imperial army of 20 000 under Duke Charles de Bourbon and Marquis de Pescara defeated a similar number of French under Francis I
Pearl Harbor	7 Dec 1941	Second World War	Surprise attack by 360 planes of the Japanese First Air Fleet under Vice-Admiral Nagumo crippled the US Pacific Fleet
Philippi	27 Oct 42 BC	Wars of the Second Triumvirate	100 000 men under Antony and Octavian defeated a similar number under Brutus and Cassius
Plassey	23 Jun 1757	British Conquest of India	3000 British and Indian allies under Clive defeated 60 000 Indians under Siraj-ud-Daula
Poitiers	17 Sep 1356	Hundred Years' War	7000 English under the Black Prince defeated 16 000 French under King John II
Pultava	8 Jul 1709	Great Northern War	50 000 Russians under Peter the Great defeated 20 000 Swedes under Charles XII
Pyramids	21 Jul 1798	French expedition to Egypt	25 000 French under Bonaparte defeated 60 000 Egyptians under Murad Bey
Quiberon Bay	20 Nov 1759	Seven Years' War	23 British ships under Admiral Hawke defeated 21 French ships under Marshal de Conflans
Ramillies	23 May 1706	War of the Spanish Succession	60 000 British and allies under Marlborough defeated a similar number under Marshal Villeroi
Rorke's Drift	22–23 Jan 1879	Zulu War	140 British troops repelled attacks by 4000 Zulus under Cetewayo
Rossbach	5 Nov 1759	Seven Years' War	21 000 Prussians under Frederick the Great defeated 41 000 French and Imperial troops under the Prince de Soubise and the Prince of Saxe-Hildburghausen
Sadowa	3 Jul 1866	Austro-Prussian War	220 000 Prussians under von Moltke defeated a similar size Austrian and Saxon force under von Benedek
The Saints	12 Apr 1782	War of American Independence	36 British ships under Admiral Rodney defeated 34 French ships under Comte de Grasse
Salamanca	22 July 1812	Peninsular War	48 000 British and allies under Wellington defeated 50 000 French under Marmont

A gun crew at Trafalgar. On 21 October 1805, 27 British ships under Nelson defeated a Franco–Spanish fleet of 33 ships under Villeneuve

Salamis	23 Sep 480 BC	Persian–Greek Wars	366 Greek vessels under Themistocles defeated 600 Persian ships under Xerxes
Saratoga	13 Sep–17 Oct 1777	American War of Independence	General Burgoyne surrendered with over 5000 British and German troops to the Americans under General Gates
Sedan	1 Sep 1870	Franco-Prussian War	200 000 Prussians under von Moltke defeated 100 000 French under Louis Napoleon and Generals MacMahon, Ducrot and de Wimpffen
Six-Day War	5–10 Jun 1967	Arab–Israeli Wars	In a war fought on three fronts Israel's forces defeated its Arab enemies and captured Sinai, the Golan Heights and old Jerusalem
Solferino	24 Jun 1859	Italian Wars of Independence	A Franco-Piedmontese army of 100 000 men under Louis Napoleon and Victor Emmanuel defeated a similar number of Austrians under Emperor Franz Josef
Somme	1 Jul–13 Nov 1916	First World War	Major offensive by British and French forces which failed to achieve the expected breakthrough and advanced the allied line by less than 10 miles
Spanish Armada	19–29 Jul 1588	English–Spanish Wars	121 English ships under Lord Howard of Effingham defeated 130 Spanish ships under the Duke of Medina Sidonia in a running battle in the Channel
Stalingrad	24 Aug 1942– 2 Feb 1943	Second World War	German Sixth Army under General Paulus failed to take the city and was forced to surrender to the Russians under Zhukov
Talavera	28 Jul 1809	Peninsular War	55 000 British and Spanish under Wellesley defeated 46 000 French under King Joseph and Marshal Victor
Tannenberg	26–31 Aug 1914	First World War	Germans under Generals von Hindenburg and Ludendorff defeated the Russian Second Army under Samsonov
Tet Offensive	30 Jan–24 Feb 1968	Vietnam War	Major Viet Cong assaults on South Vietnamese cities resulted in a military defeat but a political victory in terms of influencing American policy

Thermopylae	Aug 480 BC	Persian–Greek Wars	100 000 Persians under Xerxes defeated 5000 Greeks under Leonidas
Tours	Oct 732	Moslem Invasion of France	Army of Franks under Charles Martel defeated 60 000 Moslems under Abd-er-Rahman, halting tide of Moslem conquests
Trafalgar	21 Oct 1805	Napoleonic Wars	27 British ships under Nelson defeated a Franco-Spanish fleet of 33 ships under Villeneuve
Ulm	7–17 Oct 1805	Napoleonic Wars	Napoleon's Grand Army forced the surrender of 30 000 Austrians under General Mack
Ushant	1 Jun 1794	French Revolutionary Wars	25 British ships under Admiral Howe defeated 26 French ships under Admiral Villaret-Joyeuse
Valmy	20 Sep 1792	French Revolutionary Wars	59 000 French under Dumouriez and Kellermann defeated 35 000 Prussians under Brunswick
Verdun	21 Feb–18 Dec 1916	First World War	French under Pétain withstood major assaults by the Fifth German Army and mounted successful counter-attacks
Vimeiro	21 Aug 1808	Peninsular War	17 000 British under Wellesley defeated 13 000 French under Junot
Vitoria	21 Jun 1813	Peninsular War	79 000 British and allies under Wellington defeated 66 000 French troops under King Joseph
Wagram	5–6 Jul 1809	Napoleonic Wars	170 000 French under Napoleon defeated 146 000 Austrians under Archduke Charles
Waterloo	18 Jun 1815	Napoleonic Wars	67 000 British and allies with 53 000 Prussians under Wellington and Blücher defeated 72 000 French under Napoleon
Worcester	3 Sep 1651	English Civil War	28 000 Parliamentarians under Cromwell defeated 12 000 Royalists under Charles II
Zama	202 BC	Second Punic War	43 000 Romans under Scipio defeated 48 000 Carthaginians under Hannibal

BEAUTY

Large is Lovely Competition

The three winners of the 1978 Large is Lovely Competition are standing in front of the dias. *Left to right:* Helen Ager (3rd), Denise Manning (2nd), Joan Shannon (1st)

Sponsored by *Woman's Weekly* and BBC television's Nationwide, the contest was for the country's most glamorous larger ladies. The first prize was clothes vouchers to the value of £500. The twelve finalists were invited to London and appeared on television. Contestants are judged for their fashion sense, grooming and poise. Swimming costumes are definitely not on in this contest. The 1978 winner was Joan Shannon.

Miss Britain

This contest began in 1961 and is held to choose a representative to compete in Miss International held in Tokyo. A Mecca contest organised by JEM International Ltd, the winners have twice won the Miss International title (in 1969 and 1972). The first Miss Britain in 1961 was Nicky Allen and winners since 1968 have been:

1968	Gloria Best	1971	Christine Owen	1974	Joanna Booth	1977	Sian Adey-Jones
1969	Valerie Holmes	1972	Linda Hooks	1975	Sharon Jermyn	1978	Sarah Long
1970	Jackie Molloy	1973	Zoe Spink	1976	Janet Withey	1979	Beverley Isherwood

'Miss Great Britain' National Bathing Beauty Contest

This was inaugurated in 1945 by the then Morecambe and Heysham Borough Council, and since local government reorganisation in 1974 Lancaster City Council promotes the contest in association with Pontin's holidays. National heats throughout the country are followed by regional finals which produce contestants for the semi-final. During the summer, seasonal heats are held in Morecambe and the winners also qualify for the semi-final, which takes place in September. The winners from this stage are then joined by the winners of various television heats, sponsored by the ITV regional companies, for the grand final, also in September. The prizes are valued at more than £10 000. Previous winners are:

1945   Lydia Reed, Morecambe and Heysham
1946   June Rivers, Manchester
1947   June Mitchel, Birmingham
1948   Pamela Bayliss, Northern Ireland
1949   Elaine Price, Bolton
1950   Anne Heywood, Birmingham
1951   Marlene Dee, Henley on Thames
1952   Doreen Dawne, London
1953   Brenda Mee, Derby
1954   Patricia Butler, Hoylake
1955   Jennifer Chimes, Royal Leamington Spa
1956   Iris Waller, Gateshead
1957   Leila Williams, Walsall
1958   Christina Mayo, Abergele
1959   Valerie Martin, Blackburn
1960   Eileen Sheridan, Walton on Thames
1961   Libby Walker, BSc, Blackpool
1962   Joy Black, Dumfries
1963   Gillian Taylor, Cheadle
1964   Carol Redhead, Poulton le Fylde
1965   Diane Westbury, Altrincham
1966   Carole Fletcher, Southport
1967   Jennifer Gurley, Sale
1968   Yvonne Ormes, Nantwich
1969   Wendy Ann George, Derby
1970   Kathleen Winstanley, Wigan
1971   Carolyn Moore, Nantwich
1972   Elizabeth Robinson, Nottingham
1973   Gay Spink, Halifax
1974   Marilyn Ward, New Milton
1975   Susan Anne Cuff, Manchester
1976   Dinah May, Little Neston, Wirral
1977   Susan Marcelle Hempel, Bispham
1978   Patricia Morgan, Whitley Bay

Miss Great Britain 1978: Patricia Morgan

Miss England, Miss Scotland and Miss Wales

These national competitions are held annually to choose representatives from the three countries to compete in the Miss Universe Beauty Pageant which originated in Long Beach, California, in 1952, and is now held in different parts of the world each year. First prizes for the contests total £5000 each. All of the contests are sponsored by Mecca and organised by JEM International Ltd.

Miss England winners since 1963 have been:

1963	Susan Pratt	1972	Jenny McAdam
1964	Brenda Blackler	1973	Veronica Cross
1965	Jennifer Gurley	1974	Kathy Anders
1966	Janice Whiteman	1975	Vicki Harris
1967	Jennifer Lewis	1976	Pauline Davies
1968	Jennifer Summers	1977	Sarah Long
1969	Myra Van Heck	1978	Beverley Isherwood
1970	Yvonne Ormes	1979	Carolyn Seaward
1971	Marilyn Ward		

Miss Scotland winners since 1966 have been:

1966	Linda Lees	1975	Marie Kirkwood
1967	Lena McGarvie	1976	Carol Grant
1968	Helen Davidson	1977	Sandra Bell
1969	Sheena Drummond	1978	Angela MacLeod
1970	Lee Hamilton-Marshall	1979	Lorraine Davidson
1971	Libus Montgomery		
1972	Liz Stevely		
1973	Caroline Meade		
1974	Catherine Robertson		

Miss Wales winners since 1970 have been:

1970	Sandra Cater	1974	Helen Morgan	1977	Christine Murphy
1971	Dawn Cater	1975	Gina Kerler	1978	Ann Jones
1972	Eileen Darroch	1976	Sian Adey-Jones	1979	Beverley Neils
1973	Deirdre Greenland				

Miss United Kingdom

This competition has been held annually since 1958 in Blackpool and the first prize now totals £7500 with the winner gaining automatic entry into the Miss World contest. Miss United Kingdom is a Mecca contest organised by JEM International Ltd.

1958	Eileen Sheridan, Walton-on-Thames
1959	Anne Thelwell, Heswall
1960	Hilda Fairclough, Lancaster
1961	Rosemarie Frankland, Lancaster
1962	Jackie White, Alvaston
1963	Diane Westbury, Ilkeston
1964	Ann Sidney, Parkstone
1965	Lesley Langley, London
1966	Jennifer Lowe, Warrington
1967	Jennifer Lewis, Leicester
1968	Kathleen Winstanley, Wigan
1969	Sheena Drummond, Tullibody
1970	Yvonne Ormes, Nantwich
1971	Marilyn Ward, New Milton
1972	Jenny McAdam, London
1973	Veronica Cross, London
1974	Helen Morgan, Barry
1975	Vicki Harris, London
1976	Carol Grant, Glasgow
1977	Madeleine Stringer, North Shields
1978	Ann Jones, Welshpool

Miss United Kingdom 1978: Ann Jones

Miss World

Founded in 1951 by Eric D. Morley and sponsored by the Mecca Organisation, the contest is held annually in London. Originally a 'one off' event to publicise the Festival of Britain, it became an annual fund raising charitable event, with the entire proceeds going to the Variety Club of Great Britain's children's charities.

The Miss World line-up at the Waldorf Hotel prior to the Miss World 1978 contest at the Royal Albert Hall on 16 November. The winner, Silvana Suarez from Argentina, is on the far left of the front row (*Popperfoto*)

1951	Kiki Haakonson (Sweden)	1966	Reita Faria (India)
1952	May Louise Flodin (Sweden)	1967	Madeleine Hartog-Bel (Peru)
1953	Denise Perrier (France)	1968	Penny Plummer (Australia)
1954	Antigone Costanda (Egypt)	1969	Eva Rueber-Staier (Austria)
1955	Carmen Susana Duijm (Venezuela)	1970	Jennifer Hosten (Grenada)
1956	Petra Schurmann (West Germany)	1971	Lucia Petterle (Brazil)
1957	Marita Lindahl (Finland)	1972	Belinda Green (Australia)
1958	Penny Coelen (South Africa)	1973	Marji Wallace (USA)
1959	Corine Rottschafer (Holland)	1974	Helen Morgan (United Kingdom) (resigned)
1960	Norma Cappegli (Argentina)		Anneline Kriel (South Africa)
1961	Rosemarie Frankland (United Kingdom)	1975	Wilnelia Merced (Puerto Rico)
1962	Rina Lodders (Holland)	1976	Cindy Breakspeare (Jamaica)
1963	Carole Crawford (Jamaica)	1977	Mary Stavin (Sweden)
1964	Ann Sidney (United Kingdom)	1978	Silvana Suarez (Argentina)
1965	Lesley Langley (United Kingdom)		

Miss World of Talent

During the run-up to the 1978 Miss World competition, BBC television's Nationwide featured a contest between the Miss World contestants to test their talents in song, dance and other skills. The winner was Lonvette Morizon Hammond (Miss Philippines).

BEER

Beer of the Year Competition

Organised by the Campaign for Real Ale (CAMRA) at the annual Great British Beer Festival, held at Alexandra Palace in September. It is judged by the general public.

Overall Winner
1978 Tie between Fullers ESB and Thwaites Best Mild

Strong Bitter Class
1978 Fullers ESB

Ordinary Bitter Class
1978 Ridleys Bitter

Mild Class
1978 Thwaites Best Mild

The 1978 annual Great British Beer Festival where the 'Beer of the Year' competition is held and judged by the general public (*Courtesy of CAMRA/What's Brewing*)

BIATHLON (See Skiing)

BILLIARDS AND SNOOKER

World Professional Billiards Championship

The first world champion to be recognised was William Cook in 1870. The championship has changed hands as follows:

1870	William Cook	1901	H. W. Stephenson	(*Under Billiards Control Club rules*)	1924 Tom Newman
1870	John Roberts Jnr	1901	Charles Dawson	1909 H. W. Stephenson	1928 Joe Davis
1880	John Bennett	1901	H. W. Stephenson	1912 Melbourne Inman	1933 Walter Lindrum
1885	John Roberts Jnr	1903	Charles Dawson	1920 Willie Smith	1951 Clark McConachy
1889	Charles Dawson	1908	Melbourne Inman	1921 Tom Newman	1968 Rex Williams
				1923 Willie Smith	1971 Leslie Driffield

WPBSA Championship
1971   Rex Williams (retained title in 1973,
        1974 and 1976)

(WPBSA = World Professional Billiards &
Snooker Association)

World Professional Snooker Championship

The championship was held annually from 1927 to 1940 and 1946 to 1952, when the winners were:

1927–40, 1946	Joe Davis (15 contests)	1950	Walter Donaldson
1947	Walter Donaldson	1951	Fred Davis
1948, 1949	Fred Davis	1952	Horace Lindrum

The championship was resumed in 1964 on a challenge basis after the Professional Billiard Players' Association (who had recognised Fred Davis as champion from 1952–1958 and John Pulman as champion from 1958 to 1964) and the Billiards Association and Control Council had reconciled their differences.

The championship reverted to an open tournament in 1969. Champions:

1964–68	John Pulman (6 wins)	1970	John Spencer	1974	Ray Reardon	1977	John Spencer
1969	John Spencer	1972	Alex Higgins	1975	Ray Reardon	1978	Ray Reardon
1970	Ray Reardon	1973	Ray Reardon	1976	Ray Reardon	1979	Terry Griffiths

World Amateur Billiards Championship

First held in 1926 and now contested biennially. Winners:

1926 Joe Earlham (Eng)	1951 Robert Marshall (Aus)	1967 Leslie Driffield (Eng)
1927 Allan Prior (SA)	1952 Leslie Driffield (Eng)	1969 Jack Karnehm (Eng)
1929 Leslie Hayes (Aus)	1954 Tom Cleary (Aus)	1971 Norman Dagley (Eng)
1931 Laurie Steeples (Eng)	1958 Wilson Jones (Ind)	1973 Mohammed Lafir (Sri L)
1933 Sydney Lee (Eng)	1960 Herbery Beetham (Eng)	1975 Norman Dagley (Eng)
1935 Horace Coles (Wal)	1962 Robert Marshall (Aus)	1977 Michael Ferreira (Ind)
1936 Robert Marshall (Aus)	1964 Wilson Jones (Ind)	
1938 Robert Marshall (Aus)		

World Amateur Snooker Championship

First held 1963. Winners:

1963 Gary Owen (Eng)	1968 David Taylor (Eng)	1972 Ray Edmonds (Eng)	1976 Doug Mountjoy (SA)
1966 Gary Owen (Eng)	1970 Jonathan Barron (Eng)	1974 Ray Edmonds (Eng)	1978 Cliff Wilson (Wal)

UK Professional Snooker Championship

First held 1977. Winners:

1977 Patsy Fagan
1978 Doug Mountjoy

Benson & Hedges Masters Snooker Championship

1975 John Spencer	1978 Alex Higgins	
1976 Ray Reardon	1979 Perrie Mans (SA)	
1977 Doug Mountjoy		

Pot Black Snooker Championship

This competition is shown on BBC television, the first event being held in 1969, and the winners since the competition started are:

1969 Ray Reardon	1975 Graham Miles	
1970 John Spencer	1976 John Spencer	
1971 John Spencer	1977 Perrie Mans (SA)	
1972 Eddie Charlton (Aus)	1978 Doug Mountjoy (SA)	
1973 Eddie Charlton (Aus)	(All GB unless otherwise stated)	
1974 Graham Miles		

BOATING

International Bath Tub Racing Championship

This event has been held annually in Canada since 1967. It is run over a course of 37½ miles (60.3km) from Nanaimo to Vancouver, British Columbia. Among the extensive list of race rules it is stated that each tub must conform to the general shape and design of a bathtub, be a minimum length of 3ft 6in (1m) and no tub motor should exceed 6hp. Winners since 1967:

1967	Rusty Harrison (Can) 3hr 15min	1973	Jim (Jamie) Wilmot (Aus) 2hr 25min 3sec
1968	Stan Vollmers (Can) 2hr 1min	1974	Dan Downer (Can) 1hr 53min 3sec
1969	Glen Filipponi (Can) 2hr 9min 21sec	1975	Dan Downer (Can) 1hr 50min
1970	Janice Dorman (Can) 2hr 4min	1976	Phil Holt (Aus) 1hr 35min 4sec
1971	Bill Rathlef (Mex) 2hr 6 min	1977	Phil Holt (Aus) 1hr 32min 15sec
1972	David Lyle (Can) 1hr 49min	1978	Gary Deathbridge (Aus) 1hr 29min 40sec

BOBSLEIGH AND TOBOGGANING

World Champions & Olympic Champions

World Championships were first held for 4-man bobs in 1924 and for 2-man bobs in 1931. In Olympic years the Olympic champions are recognised as world champions. (Olympic champions are identified by an *.)

2-Man World Champions – Bobsleigh
Most titles: Italy 14 (1954, 1956–63, 1966, 1968–69, 1971, 1975) (Eugenio Monti was on 8 of these teams)
Winners since 1972:

1972*	W. Germany (Wolfgang Zimmerer and Peter Utzschneider)
1973	W. Germany (Wolfgang Zimmerer and Peter Utzschneider)
1974	W. Germany (Wolfgang Zimmerer and Peter Utzschneider)
1975	Italy (Giorgio Alvera and Franco Perrugat)
1976*	GDR (Meinhard Nehmer and Bernard Germeshausen)
1977	Switzerland (Hans Hiltebrand and Heinz Meier)
1978	Switzerland (Erich Schärer and Josef Benz)
1979	Switzerland (Erich Schärer and Josef Benz)

4-Man World Champions – Bobsleigh
Most titles: Switzerland 12 (1924, 1936, 1939, 1947, 1954–57, 1971–73, 1975)
Winners since 1972:

1972*	Switzerland (J. Wicki, E. Hubacher, H. Leutenegger, W. Carmichel)
1973	Switzerland (R. Stadler, W. Camchel, K. Schärer, P. Schärer)
1974	W. Germany (W. Zimmerer, A. Wurzer, P. Utzschneider, M. Schumann)
1975	Switzerland (E. Schärer, M. Carmichel, J. Benz, P. Schärer)
1976*	GDR (M. Nehmer, J. Babok, B. Germeshausen, B. Lehmann)
1977	GDR (M. Nehmer, H. Gerhardt, B. Germeshausen, R. Bethge)
1978	GDR (H. Schönau, H. Bernhardt, B. Musiol, H. Seifert)
1979	W. Germany (S. Galsreiter, H. Wagner, H. Bosche, D. Gebhard)

World Champions – Luge Tobogganing – Women
Most titles (first held 1955): 5 Margit Schumann (GDR) 1973–77

Winners since 1972:

1972*	Anna-Maria Muller (GDR)
1973–77	(inc. 1976*) Margit Schumann (GDR)
1978	Vera Sosulya (USSR)
1979	Melitta Sollmann (GDR)

World Champions – Luge Tobogganing – Men
Championships were first held in 1955.
Most titles: 4 Thomas Köhler (GDR) (1962, 1964*, 1966, 1967)
Winners since 1972:

1972*	Wolfgang Scheidel (GDR)
1973	Hans Rinn (GDR)
1974	Josef Fendt (Ger)

The GDR World Champion 4-man bob in 1977 at St Moritz. Two of their team had previously been international athletes – Nehmer at Javelin and Bethge at Hurdles (*Popperfoto*)

1975	Wolfram Fiedler (GDR)
1976*	Detlef Günther (GDR)
1977	Hans Rinn (GDR)
1978	Paul Hildgartner (Ita)
1979	Detlef Günther (GDR)

World Champions – Luge Tobogganing – Men's Two-Seater
Winners since 1972:
1972* Italy (Paul Hildgartner and Walter Plaikner) &
      GDR (Horst Hornlein and Reinhard Bredow)
      shared
1973 GDR (Horst Hornlein and Reinhard Bredow)

1974 GDR (Bernd Hahn and Ulli Hahn)
1975 GDR (Bernd Hahn and Ulli Hahn)
1976* GDR (Hans Rinn and Norbert Hahn)
1977 GDR (Hans Rinn and Norbert Hahn)
1978 USSR (Dainis Bremze and Aigars Krikis)
1979 GDR (Hans Brandner and Balthasar Schwarm)

BODY BUILDING

Mr Universe

Steve Reeves (USA) winner of the 1950 Mr
Universe contest

Bertil Fox (St Kitts) professional winner in 1978
(*Courtesy Arax-Hankey NABBA*)

In 1948 the *Health and Strength* magazine sponsored the first Mr Universe contest in London as a contribution to the Olympic Games held in London.

In 1950 the National Amateur Body Builders' Association was born and so started the unbroken sequence of Mr Universe contests, which are now recognised throughout the world as the greatest annual event of the year. The winners are as follows:

1948 John Grimek (USA)
1949 No contest
1950 Steve Reeves (USA)
1951 Reg Park (GB)
1952 Contest divided into separate classes for Amateurs and Professionals
      Amateur: Mohamed Nasr (Egypt)
      Professional: Juan Ferrero (Spain)
1953 Amateur: Bill Pearl (USA)
      Professional: Arnold Dyson (GB)

1954 Amateur: Enrico Tomas (USA)
      Professional: Jim Park (USA)
1955 Amateur: Mickey Hargitay (USA)
      Professional: Leo Robert (Can)
1956 Amateur: Ray Schaeffer (USA)
      Professional: Jack Dillenger (USA)
1957 Amateur: John Lees (GB)
      Professional: Arthur Robin (Fra)
1958 Amateur: Earl Clark (USA)
      Professional: Reg Park (GB)

1959	Amateur: Len Sell (GB)		1969	Amateur: Boyer Coe (USA)
	Professional: Bruce Randall (USA)			Professional: Arnold Schwarzenegger (Aut)
1960	Amateur: Henry Downs (GB)		1970	Amateur: Frank Zane (USA)
	Professional: Paul Wynter (Antigua)			Professional: Arnold Schwarzenegger (Aut)
1961	Amateur: Ray Routledge (USA)		1971	Amateur: Ken Waller (USA)
	Professional: Bill Pearl (USA)			Professional: Bill Pearl (USA)
1962	Amateur: Joe Abbenda (USA)		1972	Amateur: Elias Petsas (SA)
	Professional: Len Sell (GB)			Professional: Frank Zane (USA)
1963	Amateur: Tom Sansone (USA)		1973	Amateur: Chris Dickerson (USA)
	Professional: Joe Abbenda (USA)			Professional: Boyer Coe (USA)
1964	Amateur: John Hewlett (GB)		1974	Amateur: Roy Duval (GB)
	Professional: Earl Maynard (W. Indies)			Professional: Chris Dickerson (USA)
1965	Amateur: Elmo Santiago (USA)		1975	Amateur: Ian Lawrence (Sco)
	Professional: Reg Park (GB)			Professional: Boyer Coe (USA)
1966	Amateur: Chester Yorton (USA)		1976	Amateur: Sigeru Sugita (Jap)
	Professional: Paul Wynter (Antigua)			Professional: Serge Nubret (Fra)
1967	Amateur: Arnold Schwarzenegger (Aut)		1977	Amateur: Bertil Fox (St. Kitts)
	Professional: Bill Pearl (USA)			Professional: Tony Emmot (GB)
1968	Amateur: Dennis Tinerino (USA)		1978	Amateur: Dave Johns (USA)
	Professional: Arnold Schwarzenegger (Aut)			Professional: Bertil Fox (St. Kitts)

BOWLING (TENPIN)

World Championships

World Championships sponsored by the FIQ, the International Bowling Federation, were first held in 1967. It is now held every four years. Singles winners:

	MEN	**WOMEN**
1967	David Pond (GB)	Helen Weston (USA)
1971	Ed Luther (USA)	Ashie Gonzales (PR)
1975	Marvin Stoudt (USA)	Annedore Haefker (Ger)

BOWLS

World Championships

The first World Championships for Lawn Bowls were held in 1966 in Sydney, Australia, and have subsequently been held in 1972 and 1976. Winners:

Singles

1966 David Bryant (Eng)   1972 Malwyn Evans (Wal)   1976 Doug Watson (SA)

In addition to winning the singles title at the inaugural Bowls World Championships, David Bryant holds a record 15 English Bowls titles, including six singles (*Sport & General*)

Doubles

1966   Geoff Kelley and Bert Palm (Aus)
1972   Cecekio Delgado and Eric Liddell (HK)
1976   Doug Watson and William Moseley (SA)

Triples

1966   John Dobbie, Athol Johnson, Don Collins (Aus)
1972   Richard Folkins, Clive Forrester, William Miller (USA)
1976   Kelvin Lightfoot, Nando Gatti, Kevin Campbell (SA)

Fours

1966   W. O'Neill, G. Jolly, R. Buchan, N. Lash (NZ)
1972   Norman King, Cliff Stroud, Ted Hayward, Peter Line (Eng)
1976   Kelvin Lightfoot, William Moseley, Nando Gatti, Kevin Campbell (SA)

H. K. Leonard Trophy (Team Title All-round)

1966   Australia
1972   Scotland
1976   South Africa

Embassy World Indoor Championship

First held in 1979 and won by David Bryant (Eng).

BOXING

World Champions

Unfortunately it is by no means easy to draw up lists of boxing world champions as there have been different governing bodies that recognise champions. There are now two such governing bodies, the World Boxing Council (WBC) and the World Boxing Association (WBA).

Below is a full list of the Heavyweight World Champions since John L. Sullivan knocked out Paddy Ryan in 1882, and both WBA and WBC Champions at the other weights since 1965.

Heavyweight

1882   John L. Sullivan
1892   James J. Corbett
1897   Bob Fitzsimmons
1899   James J. Jeffries
1905   Marvin Hart
1906   Tommy Burns
1908   Jack Johnson
1915   Jess Willard
1919   Jack Dempsey
1926   Gene Tunney
1930   Max Schmeling
1932   Jack Sharkey
1933   Primo Carnera
1934   Max Baer
1935   James J. Braddock
1937   Joe Louis
1949   Ezzard Charles
1951   Jersey Joe Walcott
1952   Rocky Marciano
1956   Floyd Patterson
1959   Ingemar Johansson
1960   Floyd Patterson
1962   Sonny Liston
1964   Cassius Clay/Muhammad Ali
1965   Ernie Terrell (WBA only) (until 1967)
1968   Joe Frazier (NY State)
1968   Jimmy Ellis (WBA)
1970   Joe Frazier (undisputed)
1973   George Foreman
1974   Muhammad Ali
1978   Leon Spinks   Ken Norton (WBC)
1978   Muhammad Ali (WBA)   Larry Holmes (WBC)

Most successful title defences: 25 Joe Louis between 1937 and 1948, 19 Muhammad Ali between 1965 and 1978 (in addition to winning the title three times)

Light Heavyweight

1965   Jose Torres
1966   Dick Tiger
1968   Bob Foster
1971   Vincente Rondon (WBA) (1972)
1974   John Conteh (WBC)   Victor Galindez (WBA)
1977   Miguel Cuello (WBC)
1978   Mate Parlov (WBC)   Mike Rossman (WBA)
1978   Marvin Johnson (WBC)
1979   Matthew Franklin (WBC)   Victor Galindez (WBA)

Middleweight

1965   Dick Tiger
1966   Emile Griffith
1967   Nino Benvenuti
1967   Emile Griffith
1968   Nino Benvenuti
1970   Carlos Monzon
1974   Carlos Monzon (WBA)   Rodrigo Valdes (WBC)
1976   Carlos Monzon (both)
1977   Rodrigo Valdes
1978   Hugo Corro
1979   Vito Antuofermo

Light Middleweight

1965   Nino Benvenuti
1966   Kim Ki-Soo
1968   Sandro Mazzinghi
1969   Freddie Little
1970   Carmelo Bossi
1971   Koichi Wajima

Joe Louis (*left*) **was world heavyweight champion from 22 June 1937 to 1 March 1949 when he announced his retirement. This reign of 11 years, 8 months, 7 days is the longest for any weight. Here he beats Germany's Max Schmeling** (*Big Fights Inc.*)

1974	Oscar Albarado	
1975	Koichi Wajima	
1975	Jae Do Yuh (WBA)	Miguel De Oliveira (WBC)
1975		Elisha Obed (WBC)
1976	Koichi Wajima (WBA)	Eckhard Dagge (WBC)
1976	Jose Duran (WBA)	
1976	Miguel Castellini (WBA)	
1977	Eddie Gazo (WBA)	Rocky Mattioli (WBC)
1978	Masashi Kudo (WBA)	
1979		Maurice Hope (WBC)

Welterweight

1966	Curtis Cokes	
1969	Jose Napoles	
1970	Billy Backus	
1971	Jose Napoles	
1975	John H. Stracey (WBC)	Angel Espada (WBA)
1976	Carlos Palomino (WBC)	Jose Cuevas (WBA)
1979	Wilfredo Benitez (WBC)	

Light Welterweight (or Super Lightweight)

1965	Carlos Hernandez	
1966	Sandro Lopopolo	
1967	Paul Fuji	
1968	Pedro Adigue (WBC)	Nicholino Loche (WBA)
1970	Bruno Arcari (WBC)	
1972		Alfonso Frazer (WBA)
1972		Antonio Cervantes (WBA)
1974	Perico Fernandez (WBC)	
1975	Saensak Muangsurin (WBC)	
1976	Miguel Velasquez (WBC)	Wilfredo Benitez (WBA)
1976	Saensak Muangsurin (WBC)	
1977		Antonio Cervantes (WBA)
1978	Kim Sang-Hyun (WBC)	

Lightweight

1965	Carlos Ortiz	
1968	Carlos Teo Cruz	
1969	Mando Ramos	
1970	Ismael Laguna	
1970	Ken Buchanan	
1971	Ken Buchanan (WBA & UK)	Pedro Carrasco (WBC)
1972	Roberto Duran (WBA & UK)	Mando Ramos (WBC)
1972		Chango Carmona (WBC)
1972		Rodolfo Gonzalez (WBC)
1974	Roberto Duran (WBA)	Guts Ishimatsu (WBC)
1976		Esteban de Jesus (WBC)
1978	Roberto Duran (both)	
1979	Ernesto Espana (WBA)	Jim Watt (WBC)

Junior Lightweight

1967	Yoshiaki Numata	
1967	Hiroshi Kobayashi	
1969	Hiroshi Kobayashi (WBA)	Rene Barrientos (WBC)
1970		Yoshiaki Numata (WBC)
1971	Alfredo Marcano (WBA)	Ricardo Arredondo (WBC)
1972	Ben Villaflor (WBA)	
1973	Kuniaki Shibata (WBA)	
1973	Ben Villaflor (WBA)	
1974		Kuniaki Shibata (WBC)
1975		Alfredo Escalera (WBC)
1976	Sam Serrano (WBA)	
1978		Alexis Arguello (WBC)

Featherweight

1964	Vincente Saldivar	
1968	Howard Winstone (WBC)	Raul Rojas (WBA)
1968	Jose Legra (WBC)	Shozo Saijyo (WBA)
1969	Johnny Famechon (WBC)	
1970	Vincente Saldivar (WBC)	
1970	Kuniaki Shibata (WBC)	
1971		Antonio Gomez (WBA)
1972	Clemente Sanchez (WBC)	Ernesto Marcel (WBA)
1972	Jose Legra (WBC)	
1973	Eder Jofre (WBC)	
1974	Bobby Chacon (WBC)	Ruben Olivares (WBA)
1974		Alexis Arguello (WBA)
1975	Ruben Olivares (WBC)	
1975	David Kotey (WBC)	
1976	Danny Lopez (WBC)	
1977		Rafael Ortega (WBA)
1977		Cecilio Lastra (WBA)
1978		Eusebio Pedrosa (WBA)

Light Featherweight (Super Bantamweight)

1976	Rigoberto Riasco (WBC)	
1976	Royal Kobayashi (WBC)	
1976	Dong Kyun Yum (WBC)	
1977	Wilfredo Gomez (WBC)	Soo Hwan Hong (WBA)
1978		Ricardo Cardona (WBA)

Bantamweight

1965	Masahiko Harada	
1968	Lionel Rose	
1969	Ruben Olivares	
1970	Jesus Castillo	
1971	Ruben Olivares	
1972	Rafael Herrera	
1972	Enrique Pinder	
1973	Rafael Herrera (WBC)	Romero Anaya (WBA)

1973		Arnold Taylor (WBA)
1974	Rodolfo Martinez (WBC)	Soo Hwan Hong (WBA)
1975		Alfonso Zamora (WBA)
1976	Carlos Zarate (WBC)	
1977		Jorge Lujan (WBA)
1979	Guadalupe Pintor (WBC)	

Flyweight

1965	Salvatore Burruni	
1966	Walter McGowan (WBC)	Horacio Accavallo (WBA)
1966	Chartchai Chionoi (WBC)	
1969	Efren Torres (WBC)	Hiroyuki Ebihara (WBA)
1970	Chartchai Chionoi (WBC)	Bernabe Villacampo (WBA)
1970	Erbito Salavarria (WBC)	Berkrerk Chartvanchai (WBA)
1970		Masao Ohba (WBA)
1971	Betulio Gonzalez (WBC)	
1972	Venice Borkorsor (WBC)	

1973	Betulio Gonzalez (WBC)	Chartchai Chionoi (WBA)
1974	Shoji Oguma (WBC)	Susumu Hanagata (WBA)
1975	Miguel Canto (WBC)	Erbito Salavarria (WBA)
1976		Alfonso Lopez (WBA)
1976		Gustavo Espadas (WBA)
1978		Betulio Gonzalez (WBA)
1979	Park Chan-Hee (WBC)	

Light Flyweight

1975	Franco Udella (WBC)	
1975	Jaime Rios (WBC)	
1975	Luis Espada (WBC)	
1976		Juan Guzman (WBA)
1976		Yoko Gushiken (WBA)
1978	Netranoi Vorasingh (WBC)	
1979	Sung Jun Kim (WBC)	

World Amateur Boxing Championships

First held at Havana in 1974, the world amateur championships are held every four years, the second being held at Belgrade in 1978. Winners:

Heavy:	1974	Teofilio Stevenson (Cub)	1978	Teofilio Stevenson (Cub)
Light-Heavy:	1974	Mate Parlov (Yug)	1978	Sixto Soria (Cub)
Middle:	1974	Rufat Riskiev (USSR)	1978	Jose Gomez (Cub)
Light-Middle:	1974	Rolando Garbey (Cub)	1978	Viktor Savchenko (USSR)
Welter:	1974	Emilio Correa (Cub)	1978	Valeriy Rachkov (USSR)
Light-Welter:	1974	Ayub Kalule (Uga)	1978	Valeriy Lvov (USSR)
Light:	1974	Vasiliy Solomin (USSR)	1978	Andeh Davison (Nig)
Feather:	1974	Howard Davis (USA)	1978	Angel Herrera (Cub)
Bantam:	1974	Wilfredo Gomez (PR)	1978	Adolfo Horta (Cub)
Fly:	1974	Douglas Rodriguez (Cub)	1978	Henryk Srednicki (Pol)
Light-Fly:	1974	Jorge Hernandez (Cub)	1978	Stephen Muchoki (Ken)

Olympic Games

Boxing has been included at each Olympic Games since 1904. Winners of two or more gold medals have been:

3 Laszlo Papp (Hun): Middle 1948, Light-Middle 1952 and 1956

2 Oliver Kirk (USA): Feather and Bantam 1904

2 Harry Mallin (GB): Middle 1920 and 1924

2 Boris Lagutin (USSR): Light-Middle 1964 and 1968

2 Jerzy Kulej (Pol): Light-Welter 1964 and 1968

2 Teofilio Stevenson (Cub): Heavy 1972 and 1976

BRIDES

The Kodak Bride of the Year Competition

The colour photograph of the most radiant bride taken by a professional photographer receives a first prize of £1000. In addition, six monthly regional prizes are awarded, each to the value of £100 cash, or a wedding album of the same value. Winners:

1972 Mrs Gail Mitchelson: won £1000 and a two-week holiday for two in Bermuda

1973 Mrs Sharon Blackgrove: won £1000 and a two-week holiday for two in Bermuda

1974 Mrs Helen Ward: won £1000 and a two-week holiday for two in Barbados

1975 Competition run by *Brides* magazine

1976 No event

1977 No event

1978 Mrs Julia Phillips: won £1000 and a special prize from *Brides and Setting Up Home* magazine

Julia Phillips

BRIDGE

World Championships

World Championships for the Bermuda Bowl were first held in 1951. Winners:

1951	USA	1970	North America	
1952	USA	1971	USA	
1953	USA	1973	Italy	
1954	USA	1974	Italy	
1955	Great Britain	1975	Italy	
1956	France	1976	USA	
1957	Italy	1977	USA	
1958	Italy	1978		
1959	Italy			
1961	Italy			
1962	Italy			
1963	Italy			
1965	Italy			
1966	Italy			
1967	Italy			
1969	Italy			

Women
1960	United Arab Republic
1964	Great Britain
1968	Sweden
1972	Italy
1976	USA

Olympic Pairs Competition (Open)
Men
1962	France
1966	Holland
1970	Austria
1974	USA
1978	Brazil

Team (Four) Olympiad
Men
1960	France
1964	Italy
1968	Italy
1972	Italy
1976	Brazil

CANOEING

Olympic Games
First held in the Olympic Games in 1936.

Most gold medals have been won by Gert Fredriksson (Swe) with six: 1000m Kayak Singles in 1948, 1952, 1956; 10000m Kayak Singles in 1948, 1956; 1000m Kayak Doubles in 1960.

Most gold medals by a woman: three by Lyudmila Pinayeva (née Khvedosyuk) (USSR): 500m Kayak Singles in 1964, 1968; 500m Kayak Doubles in 1972.

Winners at each event in 1976 were:
MEN
Kayak Singles: 500m: Vasile Diba (Rom) 1:46.41; 1000m: Rüdiger Helm (GDR) 3:48.20.
Kayak Pairs: 500m: GDR (Joachim Mattern, Bernd Olbricht) 1:35.87; 1000m: USSR (Sergey Nagorny, Vladimir Romanovsky) 3:29.01.
Kayak Fours: 1000m: USSR (Y. Filatov, V. Morozov, S. Chuhray, A. Degtiaryev) 3:06.69.
Canadian Singles: 500m: Aleksandr Rogov (USSR) 1:59.23; 1000m: Matija Ljubek (Yug) 4:09.51.
Canadian Pairs: 500m: USSR (Sergey Petrenko, Aleksandr Vinogradov) 1:45.81; 1000m: USSR (Sergey Petrenko, Aleksandr Vinogradov) 3:52.76.

WOMEN
Kayak Singles: 500m: Carola Zirzow (GDR) 2:01.05.
Kayak Pairs: 500m: USSR (Galina Kreft, Nina Glopova) 1:51.15.

World Championships

Gert Fredriksson holds the record for the most world titles, as, in addition to his six Olympic Gold Medals, he also won three other world titles: 1000m Kayak Singles in 1950 and 1954; 500m Kayak Singles in 1954.

Double Gold medallists at the 1978 world championships were:
Rudiger Helm (GDR): 1000m K1, 500m K2, 1000m K4 – won most with 3
Rudiger Marg (GDR): 500m K4, 1000m K4
Bernd Olbrecht (GDR): 500m K2, 1000m K4
Bernd Duvigneau (GDR): 500m K4, 1000m K4
Tamas Buday (Hun): 1000m C2, 10000m C2
Istvan Vaskuti (Hun): 500m C2, 10000m C2
Marion Rosiger (GDR): Women's 500m K2, 500m K4
Martina Fischer (GDR): Women's 500m K2, 500m K4
Roswitha Eberl (GDR): Women's 500m K1, 500m K4

CARS

Car of the Year

Sponsored by the *Sunday Telegraph* and five other European publications, the award is given for general design, comfort, handling and general road-worthiness, safety, driver satisfaction, performance, functionalism and value for money.

1974	Mercedes 450	1977	Rover 3500
1975	Citröen CX	1978	Porsche 928
1976	Chrysler Alpine	1979	Chrysler Horizon

In 1979 the vote by an independent jury of 53 motoring writers from 16 European countries gave the winner 251 points, 12 more than a rival front wheel drive model, the Fiat Ritmo. Then came the Audi 80 (181 points), followed by the Opel Senator, and Monza (145), the Peugeot 305 (134), Alfa Romeo Giulietta (112) and Renault 18 (104). The Horizon was designed in Britain at Chrysler UK's Whiley design centre.

CARTOONS

Ally Sloper Award

Founded in 1976, this award is presented at the annual convention of British strip/comic artists, and is given to strip cartoonists only, for work in newspapers and comics. The judges are Denis Gifford and advisers from the Cartoonists Club and the Society of Strip Illustration.

1976–77 **Bronze Award: Humour**
Newspaper Strips: Frank Dickens, Bristow
Comics: Leo Baxendale, Badtime Bedtime Book
Silver Award: Adventure
Newspaper Strips: Steve Dowling, Garth
Comics: Frank Hampson, Dan Dare

Gold Award: Lifetime's Contribution
Terry Wakefield: Laurel and Hardy

1977–78 **Gold Award: Lifetime's Contribution**
Doris White, Link Studios, for Toby, etc.

The Glen Grant Cartoonist of the Year Award

This title, together with £500 and three cases of malt whisky, is given by the Glenlivet Distillers Ltd, in association with the Society of Industrial Artists and Designers. The results for 1978 were:

Overall Winner:
    Michael Heath

Category 1 – Caricature:
    First Prize: Wally Fawkes (Trog)
    Second Prize: Michael ffolkes

Category 2 – Political:
    First Prize: Edward McLachlan
    Second Prize: Edward McLachlan

Category 3 – Humorous:
    First Prize: Michael ffolkes
    Second Prize: Michael ffolkes

Category 4 – Open:
    First Prize: Michael Heath
    Second Prize: Michael Heath

'Apparently they die if they're not put the right way up.'
The 1978 winning cartoon by Michael Heath in the Glen Grant British Cartoonist of the Year Award

The Best Adventure Strip-Writer in the Newspaper category in the 1978 Society of Strip Illustration Awards was Peter O'Donnell with 'Modesty Blaise' (*Evening Standard*)

The Society of Strip Illustration Awards

The first annual awards of the Society were presented on 23 September 1978 by Michael Bentine, chairman of the cartoonists' TV game *Quick on the Draw*.

Category One: Newspapers
Best Adventure Strip-Writer
Peter O'Donnell   'Modesty Blaise'   *Evening Standard*
Best Adventure Strip-Artist
Tony Weare   'Matt Marriott'   *Evening News*
Best Humorous Strip-Writer
Reg Smythe   'Andy Capp'   *Daily Mirror*
Bett Humorous Strip-Artist
Posy Simmonds   'The Silent Three'   *The Guardian*

Category Two: Comics
Best Adventure Strip-Writer
Angus Allen   'The Bionic Woman'   *Look-In*
Best Adventure Strip-Artist
Brian Lewis   'Seven Golden Vampires'   *House of Hammer*
Best Humorous Strip-Writer
Ken Reid   'Faceache'   *Buster*
Best Humorous Strip-Artist
Ken Reid   'Faceache'   *Buster*

Category Three: Best Comic of the Year
Look-In   ITV Publications   Editor: Colin Shelbourn

The Frank Bellamy Award – Most Promising Newcomer
Mike McMahon   'Judge Dredd'   2000 AD

CHEMISTRY

Nobel Prize for Chemistry
(See under separate heading of Nobel Prizes)

1901	Jacobus H. van't Hoff (Hol)		1913	Alfred Werner (Swi) (Ger-born)
1902	Emil Fischer (Ger)		1914	Theodore W. Richards (USA)
1903	Svante A. Arrhenius (Swe)		1915	Richard M. Willstätter (Ger)
1904	Sir William Ramsay (GB)		1916	No award
1905	Johann von Bayer (Ger)		1917	No award
1906	Henri Moissan (Fra)		1918	Fritz Haber (Ger)
1907	Eduard Buchner (Ger)		1919	No award
1908	Ernest Rutherford (GB)		1920	Walther H. Nernst (Ger)
1909	Wilhelm Ostwald (Ger)		1921	Frederick Soddy (GB)
1910	Otto Wallach (Ger)		1922	Francis W. Aston (GB)
1911	Marie Curie (Fra) (Pol-born)		1923	Fritz Pregl (Aut)
1912	Victor Grignard (Fra) and Paul Sabatier (Fra)		1924	No award

1925	Richard A. Zsigmondy (Ger) (Aut-born)

1925 Richard A. Zsigmondy (Ger) (Aut-born)
1926 Theodor Svedberg (Swe)
1927 Heinrich O. Wieland (Ger)
1928 Adolf O. R. Windaus (Ger)
1929 Arthur Harden (GB) and Hans von Eulor-Chelpin (Swe) (Ger-born)
1930 Hans Fischer (Ger)
1931 Friedrich Bergius (Ger) and Carl Bosch (Ger)
1932 Irving Langmuir (USA)
1933 No award
1934 Harold C. Urey (USA)
1935 Frederic Joliot-Curie (Fra) and Irene Joliot-Curie (Fra)
1936 Peter J. W. Debye (Hol)
1937 Walter N. Haworth (GB) and Paul Karrer (Swi) (Russian-born)
1938 Richard Kuhn (Ger) (Aut-born)
1939 Adolf F. J. Butenandt (Ger) and Leopold Ruzicka (Swi)
1940 No award
1941 No award
1942 No award
1943 Georg de Hevesy (Hun)
1944 Otto Hahn (Ger)
1945 Artturi I. Virtanen (Fin)
1946 James B. Sumner (USA), John H. Northrop (USA) and Wendell M. Stanley (USA)
1947 Sir Robert Robinson (GB)
1948 Arne W. K. Tiselius (Swe)
1949 William F. Giauque (USA)
1950 Kurt Alder (Ger) and Otto P. H. Diels (Ger)
1951 Edwin M. McMillan (USA) and Glenn T. Seaborg (USA)
1952 Archer J. P. Martin (GB) and Richard L. M. Synge (GB)

1953 Hermann Staudinger (Ger)
1954 Linus C. Pauling (USA)
1955 Vincent du Vigneaud (USA)
1956 Sir Cyril N. Hinshelwood (GB) and Nikolai N. Semenov (USSR)
1957 Lord Todd (Alexander R. Todd) (GB)
1958 Frederick Sanger (GB)
1959 Jaroslav Heyrovsky (Cze)
1960 Willard F. Libby (USA)
1961 Melvin Calvin (USA)
1962 Sir John C. Kendrew (GB) and Max F. Perutz (GB) (Aut-born)
1963 Giulio Natta (Ita) and Karl Ziegler (Ger)
1964 Dorothy Crowfoot Hodgkin (GB)
1965 Robert B. Woodward (USA)
1966 Robert S. Mulliken (USA)
1967 Manfred Eigen (Ger), Ronald G. W. Norrish (GB) and Sir George Porter (GB)
1968 Lars Onsager (USA) (Nor-born)
1969 Derek H. R. Barton (GB) and Odd Hassel (Nor)
1970 Luis F. Leloir (Arg) (Fr-born)
1971 Gerhard Herzberg (Can) (Ger-born)
1972 Christian B. Anfinsen (USA), Stanford Moore (USA) and William H. Stein (USA)
1973 Ernest Otto Fischer (Ger) and Geoffrey Wilkinson (GB)
1974 Paul J. Flory (USA)
1975 John W. Cornforth (GB) and Vladimir Prelog (Swi) (Yug-born)
1976 William N. Lipscomb Jr (USA)
1977 Ilya Prigogine (Bel) (Russian-born)
1978 Peter Mitchell (GB)

CHESS

World Champions

The first officially recognised match was won by Wilhelm Steinitz in 1886, but included in this list are unofficially recognised champions before that date.

MEN
1851–58 Adolph Anderssen (Ger)
1858–62 Paul Morphy (USA)
1862–66 Adolph Anderssen (Ger)
1866–94 Wilhelm Steinitz (Ger)
1894–1921 Emanuel Lasker (Ger)
1921–27 José Capablanca (Cub)
1927–35 Alexandre Alekhine (Fra)
1935–37 Max Euwe (Hol)
1937–47 Alexandre Alekhine (Fra)
1948–57 Mikhail Botvinnik (USSR)
1957–58 Vassiliy Smyslov (USSR)
1958–61 Mikhail Botvinnik (USSR)
1961–62 Mikhail Tal (USSR)

1962–64 Mikhail Botvinnik (USSR)
1964–69 Tigran Petrosian (USSR)
1969–72 Boris Spassky (USSR)
1972–75 Robert Fischer (USA)
1975– Anatoliy Karpov (USSR)

WOMEN
1927–44 Vera Menchik (GB)
1950–53 Lyudmila Rudenko (USSR)
1953–56 Elizaveta Bykova (USSR)
1956–58 Olga Rubtsova (USSR)
1958–62 Elizaveta Bykova (USSR)
1962– Nona Gaprindashvili (USSR)

World Team Championships (Chess Olympiad)

First held in 1927, and now held every two years. Winners:

MEN

1927	Hungary	1930	Poland	1933	USA	1937	USA	1950	Yugoslavia
1928	Hungary	1931	USA	1935	USA	1939	Germany	1952	USSR

1954	USSR	WOMEN	
1956	USSR	1957	USSR
1958	USSR	1963	USSR
1960	USSR	1966	USSR
1962	USSR	1969	USSR
1964	USSR	1972	USSR
1966	USSR	1974	USSR
1968	USSR	1976	Israel
1970	USSR	1978	USSR
1972	USSR		
1974	USSR		
1976	USA		
1978	Hungary		

Chess concentration by Boris Spassky, World Champion from 1969 until defeated by Bobby Fischer in 1972 (*Syndication International*)

CHILDREN

Champion Children of the Year

The *Daily Mirror*, in association with Dr Barnardo's and C. & A., sponsor this competition, the first year being 1979, to find Britain's 'Superkid'. Readers are asked to nominate a child who does something well, whether sports, dancing, painting, music, drama or literature; and there is a special section for children who have overcome a handicap.

1979 Winners

Sport:	Sandra Arthurton (16), Leeds. Cross-country runner
Mastermind:	Peter Swabey (14), Worthing. Zulu War of 1879
	Roy Collins (9), Shotley Bridge, Co. Durham. Astronomy
Superkid:	Mark Weeks (15), Bournemouth. Karate club organiser
Special interests:	Nick Stevenson (16), Derbyshire and Mark Wilson (14), Derbyshire. Film makers
Triumph over adversity:	Terry Wiles (17), Huntingdon, John Elcock (16), Sheffield, Simon Butterworth (11), Bolton
Painting:	Paul Russell (11), Leytonstone, East London
Dancing:	Gary Edwards (12) and Fiona Bunce (12), Romford, Essex
	Tracey Fitzgerald (9) and Stephen Quarterly (9), Newport, Wales
Music:	Tina Jones (14), Reading

Five-year-old Jemma Bagshaw being kissed by two of the judges, five-year-old Paul Denny (*left*) and six-year-old Tony Watts (*right*), after being crowned 1979 Mini Miss UK (*Keystone*)

Mini Miss UK Competition

The 'Mini Miss United Kingdom' competition is sponsored and organised annually by Harringtons (London) Ltd, the baby wear and children's wear manufacturers.

The first competition was staged in January 1972 and it has been staged annually in January every year since then. It is open to little girls between the ages of three and six years who are invited to enter through entry forms at Harringtons retail stockists throughout the country. The entry form, which calls for details of hobbies, pastimes and a recent photograph, is then forwarded to the Harringtons board of directors who reduce the entry to 10 finalists who then come to London for judging on a different level.

Five judges award five points in each of three categories for Confidence, Personality and Grooming and the winner receives a full selection of Harringtons children's wear, a contract with the Tiny Tots to Teens model agency and numerous other prizes. All 10 finalists receive a prize. Past winners are:

1972	Jeanette Kenny, Coventry	1976	Shona Glover, Surrey
1973	Elizabeth Seal, Hertfordshire	1977	Rowena Cockayne, London
1974	Karen Young, Hertfordshire	1978	Yvette Cowherd, Hertfordshire
1975	Justine Hayles, Middlesex	1979	Jemma Bagshaw, Coventry

CHIVALRY AND COURTESY

Gentleman of the Year

This competition was sponsored in 1978 by Southern Comfort and *Woman's World* magazine, who gave a St Valentine's Day lunch at the Café Royal for the nine finalists, all nominated as ideal gentlemen by the magazine's readers. The winner received a year's supply of the drink Southern Comfort and a weekend for two in Paris.

The winner was the Rev. Donald Rydings, from Great Missenden, Bucks.

CHOIRBOYS

Choirboy of the Year

The Rediffusion Choristers' Award for Choirboy of the Year is promoted by Rediffusion Ltd, in association with the Royal School of Church Music, and it was inaugurated in 1975.

1975 Matthew Billsborough (High Wycombe, All Saints)
1976 Stephen Drummond (Cookridge, Leeds, Holy Trinity)
1977 Andrew March (Tunbridge Wells, Holy Trinity with Christ Church)
1978 Simon Carney (Stockton-on-Tees, St Peter)

Simon Carney from Stockton-on-Tees, St Peter – 1978 Choirboy of the Year

CINEMA

Top Money-Making Women of the Movies

The Motion Picture Almanac publishes an annual poll conducted by exhibitors in the United States to determine the top 10 money-making stars of the year.

WOMEN

1932	Marie Dressler	1956	Marilyn Monroe
1933	Marie Dressler	1957	none
1934	Janet Gaynor	1958	Elizabeth Taylor
1935	Shirley Temple	1959	Doris Day
1936	Shirley Temple	1960	Doris Day
1937	Shirley Temple	1961	Elizabeth Taylor
1938	Shirley Temple	1962	Doris Day
1939	Shirley Temple	1963	Doris Day
1940	Bette Davis	1964	Doris Day
1941	Bette Davis	1965	Doris Day
1942	Betty Grable	1966	Julie Andrews
1943	Betty Grable	1967	Julie Andrews
1944	Betty Grable	1968	Julie Andrews
1945	Greer Garson	1969	Katherine Hepburn
1946	Ingrid Bergman	1970	Barbra Streisand
1947	Betty Grable	1971	Ali MacGraw
1948	Betty Grable	1972	Barbra Streisand
1949	Betty Grable	1973	Barbra Streisand
1950	Betty Grable	1974	Barbra Streisand
1951	Betty Grable	1975	Barbra Streisand
1952	Doris Day	1976	Tatum O'Neal
1953	Marilyn Monroe	1977	Barbra Streisand
1954	Marilyn Monroe	1978	Diane Keaton
1955	Grace Kelly		

Right: **Shirley Temple** (*Popperfoto*)

Top Money-Making Men of the Movies

MEN

1932	Charles Farrell	1956	William Holden
1933	Will Rogers	1957	Rock Hudson
1934	Will Rogers	1958	Glenn Ford
1935	Will Rogers	1959	Rock Hudson
1936	Clark Gable	1960	Rock Hudson
1937	Clark Gable	1961	Rock Hudson
1938	Clark Gable	1962	Rock Hudson
1939	Mickey Rooney	1963	John Wayne
1940	Mickey Rooney	1964	Jack Lemmon
1941	Mickey Rooney	1965	Sean Connery
1942	Abbott and Costello	1966	Sean Connery
1943	Bob Hope	1967	Lee Marvin
1944	Bing Crosby	1968	Sidney Poitier
1945	Bing Crosby	1969	Paul Newman
1946	Bing Crosby	1970	Paul Newman
1947	Bing Crosby	1971	John Wayne
1948	Bing Crosby	1972	Clint Eastwood
1949	Bob Hope	1973	Clint Eastwood
1950	John Wayne	1974	Robert Redford
1951	John Wayne	1975	Robert Redford
1952	Martin and Lewis	1976	Robert Redford
1953	Gary Cooper	1977	Sylvester Stallone
1954	John Wayne	1978	Burt Reynolds
1955	James Stewart		

Right: **Bing Crosby**

Motion Picture Academy Awards (Oscars)

Left: **Marlon Brando was awarded an Oscar for his performance in 'The Godfather' as Best Actor in 1972.** *Centre:* **Ron Moody played the part of Fagin in 'Oliver' which won an award for the Best Picture in 1968** (*Popperfoto*). *Right:* **Milos Forman won an Oscar for Best Director for his film 'One Flew Over the Cuckoo's Nest'. Jack Nicholson starred, as shown in the above scene from the film** (*Popperfoto*)

Given by the Academy of Motion Picture Arts and Sciences, the 'Oscar' statuettes were introduced in 1928 and are the highest accolade of the Hollywood film industry. There are some 25 awards each year, for performances and technical achievements. The main categories of winners are as follows:

BEST ACTOR

1927–28	Emil Jennings, *The Way of All Flesh*
1928–29	Warner Baxter, *In Old Arizona*
1929–30	George Arliss, *Disraeli*
1930–31	Lionel Barrymore, *Free Soul*
1931–32	Fredric March, *Dr Jekyll and Mr Hyde*; Wallace Beery, *The Champ* (tie)
1932–33	Charles Laughton, *Private Life of Henry VIII*
1934	Clark Gable, *It Happened One Night*
1935	Victor McLaglen, *The Informer*
1936	Paul Muni, *Story of Louis Pasteur*
1937	Spencer Tracy, *Captain Courageous*
1938	Spencer Tracy, *Boys Town*
1939	Robert Donat, *Goodbye Mr Chips*
1940	James Stewart, *The Philadelphia Story*
1941	Gary Cooper, *Sergeant York*
1942	James Cagney, *Yankee Doodle Dandy*
1943	Paul Lukas, *Watch on the Rhine*
1944	Bing Crosby, *Going My Way*
1945	Ray Milland, *The Lost Weekend*
1946	Fredric March, *The Best Years of Our Lives*
1947	Ronald Colman, *A Double Life*
1948	Laurence Olivier, *Hamlet*
1949	Broderick Crawford, *All the King's Men*
1950	José Ferrer, *Cyrano de Bergerac*
1951	Humphrey Bogart, *The African Queen*
1952	Gary Cooper, *High Noon*
1953	William Holden, *Stalag 17*
1954	Marlon Brando, *On the Waterfront*
1955	Ernest Borgnine, *Marty*
1956	Yul Brynner, *The King and I*
1957	Alec Guinness, *The Bridge on the River Kwai*
1958	David Niven, *Separate Tables*
1959	Charlton Heston, *Ben Hur*
1960	Burt Lancaster, *Elmer Gantry*
1961	Maximilian Schell, *Judgment at Nuremberg*
1962	Gregory Peck, *To Kill a Mockingbird*
1963	Sidney Poitier, *Lilies of the Field*
1964	Rex Harrison, *My Fair Lady*
1965	Lee Marvin, *Cat Ballou*
1966	Paul Scofield, *A Man for All Seasons*
1967	Rod Steiger, *In the Heat of the Night*
1968	Cliff Robertson, *Charly*
1969	John Wayne, *True Grit*
1970	George C. Scott, *Patton* (refused)
1971	Gene Hackman, *The French Connection*
1972	Marlon Brando, *The Godfather* (refused)
1973	Jack Lemmon, *Save the Tiger*
1974	Art Carney, *Harry and Tonto*
1975	Jack Nicholson, *One Flew Over the Cuckoo's Nest*
1976	Peter Finch, *Network*
1977	Richard Dreyfuss, *The Goodbye Girl*
1978	John Voigt, *Coming Home*

BEST ACTRESS

1927–28	Janet Gaynor, *Seventh Heaven*
1928–29	Mary Pickford, *Coquette*
1929–30	Norma Shearer, *The Divorcee*
1930–31	Marie Dressler, *Min and Bill*
1931–32	Helen Hayes, *Sin of Madelon Claudet*
1932–33	Katharine Hepburn, *Morning Glory*
1934	Claudette Colbert, *It Happened One Night*
1935	Bette Davis, *Dangerous*
1936	Luise Rainer, *The Great Ziegfeld*
1937	Luise Rainer, *The Good Earth*
1938	Bette Davis, *Jezebel*
1939	Vivien Leigh, *Gone With the Wind*
1940	Ginger Rogers, *Kitty Foyle*
1941	Joan Fontaine, *Suspicion*
1942	Greer Garson, *Mrs Miniver*
1943	Jennifer Jones, *The Song of Bernadette*
1944	Ingrid Bergman, *Gaslight*

The Sound of Music was awarded an Oscar in 1965 for the Best Picture

1945	Joan Crawford, *Mildred Pierce*
1946	Olivia de Havilland, *To Each His Own*
1947	Loretta Young, *The Farmer's Daughter*
1948	Jane Wyman, *Johnny Belinda*
1949	Olivia de Havilland, *The Heiress*
1950	Judy Holliday, *Born Yesterday*
1951	Vivien Leigh, *A Streetcar Named Desire*
1952	Shirley Booth, *Come Back, Little Sheba*
1953	Audrey Hepburn, *Roman Holiday*
1954	Grace Kelly, *The Country Girl*
1955	Anna Magnani, *The Rose Tattoo*
1956	Ingrid Bergman, *Anastasia*
1957	Joanne Woodward, *The Three Faces of Eve*
1958	Susan Hayward, *I Want to Live*
1959	Simone Signoret, *Room at the Top*
1960	Elizabeth Taylor, *Butterfield 8*
1961	Sophia Loren, *Two Women*
1962	Anne Bancroft, *The Miracle Worker*
1963	Patricia Neal, *Hud*
1964	Julie Andrews, *Mary Poppins*
1965	Julie Christie, *Darling*
1966	Elizabeth Taylor, *Who's Afraid of Virginia Woolf?*
1967	Katharine Hepburn, *Guess Who's Coming to Dinner*
1968	Katharine Hepburn, *The Lion in Winter*; Barbra Streisand, *Funny Girl* (tie)
1969	Maggie Smith, *The Prime of Miss Jean Brodie*
1970	Glenda Jackson, *Women in Love*
1971	Jane Fonda, *Klute*
1972	Liza Minnelli, *Cabaret*
1973	Glenda Jackson, *A Touch of Class*
1974	Ellen Burstyn, *Alice Doesn't Live Here Anymore*
1975	Louise Fletcher, *One Flew Over the Cuckoo's Nest*
1976	Faye Dunaway, *Network*
1977	Diane Keaton, *Annie Hall*
1978	Jane Fonda, *Coming Home*

BEST PICTURE

1927–28	*Wings*, Paramount
1928–29	*Broadway Melody*, MGM
1929–30	*All Quiet on the Western Front*, Universal
1930–31	*Cimarron*, RKO
1931–32	*Grand Hotel*, MGM
	Special: *Mickey Mouse*, Walt Disney
1932–33	*Cavalcade*, 20th Century-Fox
1934	*It Happened One Night*, Columbia
1935	*Mutiny on the Bounty*, MGM
1936	*The Great Ziegfeld*, MGM
1937	*Life of Emile Zola*, Warner
1938	*You Can't Take It With You*, Columbia
1939	*Gone With the Wind*, Selznick International
1940	*Rebecca*, Selznick International
1941	*How Green Was My Valley*, 20th Century-Fox
1942	*Mrs Miniver*, MGM
1943	*Casablanca*, Warner
1944	*Going My Way*, Paramount
1945	*The Lost Weekend*, Paramount
1946	*The Best Years of Our Lives*, Goldwyn, RKO
1947	*Gentleman's Agreement*, 20th Century-Fox
1948	*Hamlet*, Two Cities Film, Universal International
1949	*All the King's Men*, Columbia
1950	*All About Eve*, 20th Century-Fox
1951	*An American in Paris*, MGM
1952	*Greatest Show on Earth*, Cecil B. De Mille, Paramount
1953	*From Here to Eternity*, Columbia
1954	*On the Waterfront*, Horizon-American Corp. Columbia
1955	*Marty*, Hecht and Lancaster's Steven Productions UA
1956	*Around the World in 80 Days*, Michael Todd Co. UA
1957	*The Bridge on the River Kwai*, Columbia
1958	*Gigi*, Arthur Freed Production, MGM
1959	*Ben-Hur*, MGM
1960	*The Apartment*, Mirisch Co. UA
1961	*West Side Story*, United Artists
1962	*Lawrence of Arabia*, Columbia
1963	*Tom Jones*, Woodfall Prod. UA-Lopert Pictures
1964	*My Fair Lady*, Warner Bros.
1965	*The Sound of Music*, 20th Century-Fox
1966	*A Man for All Seasons*, Columbia
1967	*In the Heat of the Night*, United Artists
1968	*Oliver*, Columbia
1969	*Midnight Cowboy*, United Artists
1970	*Patton*, 20th Century-Fox
1971	*The French Connection*, 20th Century-Fox
1972	*The Godfather*, Paramount
1973	*The Sting*, Universal
1974	*The Godfather, Part II*, Paramount
1975	*One Flew Over the Cuckoo's Nest*, United Artists
1976	*Rocky*, United Artists
1977	*Annie Hall*, United Artists
1978	*The Deer Hunter*, EMI

BEST DIRECTOR

1927–28	Frank Borzage, *Seventh Heaven*, Lewis Milestone, *Two Arabian Knights*
1928–29	Frank Lloyd, *The Divine Lady*
1929–30	Lewis Milestone, *All Quiet on the Western Front*
1930–31	Norman Taurog, *Skippy*
1931–32	Frank Borzage, *Bad Girl*
1932–33	Frank Lloyd, *Cavalcade*
1934	Frank Capra, *It Happened One Night*

1935	John Ford, *The Informer*	1958	Vincente Minnelli, *Gigi*
1936	Frank Capra, *Mr Deeds Goes to Town*	1959	William Wyler, *Ben-Hur*
1937	Leo McCarey, *The Awful Truth*	1960	Billy Wilder, *The Apartment*
1938	Frank Capra, *You Can't Take It With You*	1961	Jerome Robbins, Robert Wise, *West Side Story*
1939	Victor Fleming, *Gone with the Wind*	1962	David Lean, *Lawrence of Arabia*
1940	John Ford, *The Grapes of Wrath*	1963	Tony Richardson, *Tom Jones*
1941	John Ford, *How Green Was My Valley*	1964	George Cukor, *My Fair Lady*
1942	William Wyler, *Mrs Miniver*	1965	Robert Wise, *Sound of Music*
1943	Michael Curtiz, *Casablanca*	1966	Fred Zinnemann, *A Man for All Seasons*
1944	Leo McCarey, *Going My Way*	1967	Mike Nichols, *The Graduate*
1945	Billy Wilder, *The Lost Weekend*	1968	Sir Carol Reed, *Oliver*
1946	William Wyler, *The Best Years of Our Lives*	1969	John Schlesinger, *Midnight Cowboy*
1947	Elia Kazan, *Gentleman's Agreement*	1970	Franklin J. Schaffner, *Patton*
1948	John Huston, *Treasure of Sierra Madre*	1971	William Friedkin, *The French Connection*
1949	Joseph L. Mankiewicz, *A Letter to Three Wives*	1972	Bob Fosse, *Cabaret*
1950	Joseph L. Mankiewicz, *All About Eve*	1973	George Roy Hill, *The Sting*
1951	George Stevens, *A Place in the Sun*	1974	Francis Ford Coppola, *The Godfather, Part II*
1952	John Ford, *The Quiet Man*	1975	Milos Forman, *One Flew Over the Cuckoo's Nest*
1953	Fred Zinnemann, *From Here to Eternity*		
1954	Elia Kazan, *On the Waterfront*	1976	John Avildsen, *Rocky*
1955	Delbert Mann, *Marty*	1977	Woody Allen, *Annie Hall*
1956	George Stevens, *Giant*	1978	Michael Cimino, *The Deer Hunter*
1957	David Lean, *The Bridge on the River Kwai*		

Berlin Film Festival

Gold Medal for feature films: Golden Berlin Bear

1951	*Die Vier im Jeep* (Swi)	1964	*Susuz Yaz* (Tur)
1952	*Hon Dansade en Sommar* (Swe)	1965	*Alphaville* (Fra)
1953	*Le Salaire de la Peur* (Fra)	1966	*Cul-de-Sac* (UK)
1954	*Hobson's Choice* (UK)	1967	*Le Départ*, Jerzy Skolimovski (Bel)
1955	*Die Ratten* (Ger)	1968	*Ole dole doff*, Jan Troell (Swe)
	Marcelino, Pan y Vino (Spa)	1969	*Rani Radovi*, Zelimir Zilnik (Yug)
	Carmen Jones (USA)	1970	No awards
1956	*Invitation to the Dance* (USA)	1971	*Garden of the Finzi Contini*, Vittorio de Sica (Ita)
1957	*Twelve Angry Men* (USA)	1972	*Canterbury Tales*, Pasolini (Ita)
1958	*Smultronstallet* (Swe)	1973	*Tonnerre dans le lointain*, Satyajit Ray (Ind)
1959	*Les Cousins* (Fra)	1974	*The Apprenticeship*, D. Kravitz (Can)
1960	*El Lazarillo de Tormes* (Spa)	1975	*Orokbefogadas* (Hun)
1961	*La Notte* (Ita)	1976	*Buffalo Bill and the Indians or Sitting Bull's History Lesson*, Robert Altman (USA)
1962	*A Kind of Loving* (UK)		
1963	*Bushido Zankoku Monogatari* (Jap)	1977	*Ascension*, Larrisa Skeptiko
	Le Diavolo (Ita)	1978	Spanish contributions (rather than one single film)

British Academy of Film and Television Arts Awards

The major annual awards from the British cinema and TV industries. The academy was known before 1968 as the British Film Academy and after the Society of Film and Television Arts. Until then the awards were known as the British Film Academy Awards.

THE BRITISH FILM ACADEMY AWARDS 1947–67

THE BEST BRITISH FILM OF THE YEAR

1947	*Odd Man Out*	1958	*Room at the Top*
1948	*The Fallen Idol*	1959	*Sapphire*
1949	*The Third Man*	1960	*Saturday Night and Sunday Morning*
1950	*The Blue Lamp*	1961	*A Taste of Honey*
1951	*The Lavender Hill Mob*	1962	*Lawrence of Arabia*
1952	*The Sound Barrier*	1963	*Tom Jones*
1953	*Genevieve*	1964	*Dr Strangelove*
1954	*Hobson's Choice*	1965	*The Ipcress File*
1955	*Richard III*	1966	*The Spy Who Came in from the Cold*
1956	*Reach for the Sky*	1967	*A Man for all Seasons*
1957	*The Bridge on the River Kwai*		

THE BEST FOREIGN ACTRESS
1952 Simone Signoret, *Casque d'Or*
1953 Leslie Caron, *Lili*
1954 Cornell Borchers, *The Divided Heart*
1955 Betsy Blair, *Marty*
1956 Anna Magnani, *The Rose Tattoo*
1957 Simone Signoret, *The Witches of Salem*
1958 Simone Signoret, *Room at the Top*
1959 Shirley MacLaine, *Ask Any Girl*
1960 Shirley MacLaine, *The Apartment*
1961 Sophia Loren, *Two Women*
1962 Anne Bancroft, *The Miracle Worker*
1963 Patricia Neal, *Hud*
1964 Anne Bancroft, *The Pumpkin Eater*
1965 Patricia Neal, *In Harm's Way*
1966 Jeanne Moreau, *Viva Maria*
1967 Anouk Aimee, *Un Homme et Une Femme*

THE BEST FOREIGN ACTOR
1952 Marlon Brando, *Viva Zapata!*
1953 Marlon Brando, *Julius Caesar*
1954 Marlon Brando, *On the Waterfront*
1955 Ernest Borgnine, *Marty*
1956 Francois Perier, *Gervaise*
1957 Henry Fonda, *Twelve Angry Men*
1958 Sidney Poitier, *The Defiant Ones*
1959 Jack Lemmon, *Some Like it Hot*
1960 Jack Lemmon, *The Apartment*
1961 Paul Newman, *The Hustler*
1962 Burt Lancaster, *Birdman of Alcatraz*
1963 Marcello Mastroianni, *Divorce, Italian Style*
1964 Marcello Mastroianni, *Yesterday, Today and Tomorrow*
1965 Lee Marvin, *The Killers* and *Cat Ballou*
1966 Rod Steiger, *The Pawnbroker*
1967 Rod Steiger, *In the Heat of the Night*

THE MOST PROMISING NEWCOMER TO LEADING FILM ROLES

1952 Claire Bloom, *Limelight*
1953 David Kossoff, *The Young Lovers*
1954 Norman Wisdom, *Trouble in Store*
1955 Paul Scofield, *That Lady*
1956 Eli Wallach, *Baby Doll*
1957 Eric Barker, *Brothers in Law*
1958 Paul Massie, *Orders to Kill*
1959 Hayley Mills, *Tiger Bay*
1960 Albert Finney, *Saturday Night and Sunday Morning*
1961 Rita Tushingham, *A Taste of Honey*
1962 Tom Courtenay, *The Loneliness of the Long Distance Runner*
1963 James Fox, *The Servant*
1964 Julie Andrews, *Mary Poppins*
1965 Judi Dench, *Four in the Morning*
1966 Vivien Merchant, *Alfie*
1967 Faye Dunaway, *Bonnie and Clyde*

THE BEST SCREENPLAY OF A BRITISH FILM
1954 *The Young Lovers*, George Tabori and Robin Estridge
1955 *The Ladykillers*, William Rose
1956 *The Man Who Never Was*, Nigel Balchin

1957 *The Bridge on the River Kwai*, Pierre Boulle
1958 *Orders to Kill*, Paul Dehn
1959 *I'm All Right, Jack*, Frank Harvey, John Boulting and Alan Hackney
1960 *The Angry Silence*, Bryan Forbes
1961 *The Day the Earth Caught Fire*, Val Guest and Wolf Mankowitz; *A Taste of Honey*, Shelagh Delaney and Tony Richardson
1962 *Lawrence of Arabia*, Robert Bolt
1963 *Tom Jones*, John Osborne
1964 *The Pumpkin Eater*, Harold Pinter
1965 *Darling*, Frederic Raphael
1966 *Morgan – A Suitable Case for Treatment*, David Mercer
1967 *A Man for All Seasons*, Robert Bolt

THE BEST CINEMATOGRAPHY IN A BRITISH FILM

Colour
1963 *From Russia with Love*, Ted Moore
1964 *Becket*, Geoffrey Unsworth
1965 *The Ipcress File*, Otto Heller
1966 *Arabesque*, Christopher Challis
1967 *A Man for All Seasons*, Ted Moore

Black and White
1963 *The Servant*, Douglas Slocombe
1964 *The Pumpkin Eater*, Oswald Morris
1965 *The Hill*, Oswald Morris
1966 *The Spy Who Came in From the Cold*, Oswald Morris
1967 *The Whisperers*, Gerry Turpin

THE BEST ART DIRECTION IN A BRITISH FILM

Colour
1964 *Becket*, John Bryan
1965 *The Ipcress File*, Ken Adam
1966 *The Blue Max*, Wilfrid Shingleton
1967 *A Man for All Seasons*, John Box

Black and White
1964 *Dr Strangelove*, Ken Adam
1965 *Darling*, Ray Simm
1966 *The Spy Who Came in From the Cold*, Tambi Larsen
1967 No Award

THE BEST SHORT FILM
(Before 1959 Award for the Best Documentary Film)
1947 *The World is Rich*
1948 *The Louisiana Story*
1949 *Daybreak in Udi*
1950 *The Undefeated*
1951 *Beaver Valley*
1952 *Royal Journey*
1953 *The Conquest of Everest*
1954 *The Great Adventure*
1955 *The Vanishing Prairie*
1956 *On the Bowery*
1957 *Journey into Spring*
1958 *Glass*

1959	*Seven Cities of Antarctica*
1960	*High Journey*
1961	*Terminus*
1962	*Incident at Owl Creek*
1963	*Happy Anniversary*
1964	*Kenojuak*
1965	*Rig Move*
1966	*The War Game*
1967	*Indus Waters*

THE BEST SPECIALISED FILM
(Before 1959 Special Award for work lying outside the feature and documentary Fields)

1948	*Atomic Physics*
1949	*La Famille Martin*
1950	*The True Face of Japan*
1951	*Gerald McBoing Boing*
1952	*Animated Genesis*
1953	*The Romance of Transportation*
1954	*Time Out of War*
1955	*The Bespoke Overcoat*
1956	*The Red Balloon*
1957	*A Chairy Tale*
1958	*The Children's Film Foundation*
1959	*This is the BBC*
1960	*Dispute*
1961	Not Awarded
1962	*Four Line Conics*
1963	Not Awarded
1964	*Driving Technique – Passenger Trains*
1965	*I Do – And I Understand*
1966	*Exploring Chemistry*
1967	*Energy and Matter*

THE BEST ANIMATED FILM

1954	*Song of the Prairie*
1955	*Blinkity Blank*
1956	*Gerald McBoing Boing on Planet Moo*
1957	*Pan-Tele-Tron*
1958	*The Little Island*
1959	*The Violinist*
1960	*Universe*
1961	*One Hundred and One Dalmatians*
1962	*The Apple*
1963	*Automania 2000 ; The Critic*
1964	*The Insects*
1965	*Be Careful Boys*
1966	Not Awarded
1967	*Notes on a Triangle*

THE BEST BRITISH ACTRESS

1952	Vivien Leigh, *A Streetcar Named Desire*
1953	Audrey Hepburn, *Roman Holiday*
1954	Yvonne Mitchell, *The Divided Heart*
1955	Katie Johnson, *The Ladykillers*
1956	Virginia McKenna, *A Town Like Alice*
1957	Heather Sears, *The Story of Esther Costello*
1958	Irene Worth, *Orders to Kill*
1959	Audrey Hepburn, *The Nun's Story*
1960	Rachel Roberts, *Saturday Night and Sunday Morning*
1961	Dora Bryan, *A Taste of Honey*
1962	Leslie Caron, *The L-Shaped Room*

1963	Rachel Roberts, *This Sporting Life*
1964	Audrey Hepburn, *Charade*
1965	Julie Christie, *Darling*
1966	Elizabeth Taylor, *Who's Afraid of Virginia Woolf ?*
1967	Edith Evans, *The Whisperers*

THE BEST BRITISH ACTOR

1952	Ralph Richardson, *The Sound Barrier*
1953	John Gielgud, *Julius Caesar*
1954	Kenneth More, *Doctor in the House*
1955	Laurence Olivier, *Richard III*
1956	Peter Finch, *A Town Like Alice*
1957	Alec Guinness, *The Bridge on the River Kwai*
1958	Trevor Howard, *The Key*
1959	Peter Sellers, *I'm All Right, Jack*
1960	Peter Finch, *The Trials of Oscar Wilde*
1961	Peter Finch, *No Love for Johnny*
1962	Peter O'Toole, *Lawrence of Arabia*
1963	Dirk Bogarde, *The Servant*
1964	Richard Attenborough, *Guns at Batasi* and *Seance on a Wet Afternoon*
1965	Dirk Bogarde, *Darling*
1966	Richard Burton, *Who's Afraid of Virginia Woolf ?*
1967	Paul Scofield, *A Man For All Seasons*

THE BEST EDITING OF A BRITISH FILM

1966	*Morgan – A Suitable Case for Treatment*, Tom Priestley
1967	No Award

THE BEST COSTUME DESIGN IN A BRITISH FILM
Colour

1964	*Becket*, Margaret Furse
1965	*Those Magnificent Men in Their Flying Machines*, Osbert Lancaster and Dinah Greet
1966	*The Wrong Box*, Julie Harris
1967	*A Man For All Seasons*, Elizabeth Haffenden and Joan Bridge

Black and White

1964	*The Pumpkin Eater*, Motley
1965	No Award
1966	No Award
1967	*Mademoiselle*, Jocelyn Rickards

THE BAFTA AWARDS FROM 1968

PRODUCTION AND DIRECTION
Best Film (from 1947)

1947	*The Best Years of Our Lives*
1948	*Hamlet*
1949	*Bicycle Thieves*
1950	*All About Eve*
1951	*La Ronde*
1952	*The Sound Barrier*
1953	*Jeux Interdits*
1954	*Le Salaire de la Peur*
1955	*Richard III*
1956	*Gervaise*
1957	*The Bridge on the River Kwai*
1958	*Room at the Top*
1959	*Ben-Hur*

1960	*The Apartment*
1961 {	*Ballad of a Soldier*
	The Hustler
1962	*Lawrence of Arabia*
1963	*Tom Jones*
1964	*Dr Strangelove*
1965	*My Fair Lady*
1966	*Who's Afraid of Virginia Woolf?*
1967	*A Man for all Seasons*
1968	*The Graduate*
1969	*Midnight Cowboy*
1970	*Butch Cassidy and the Sundance Kid*
1971	*Sunday, Bloody Sunday*
1972	*Cabaret*
1973	*Day for Night*
1974	*Lacombe Lucien*
1975	*Alice Doesn't Live Here Anymore*
1976	*One Flew Over the Cuckoo's Nest*
1977	*Annie Hall*
1978	*Julia*

Best Direction

1968	Mike Nichols, *The Graduate*
1969	John Schlesinger, *Midnight Cowboy*
1970	George Roy Hill, *Butch Cassidy and the Sundance Kid*
1971	John Schlesinger, *Sunday, Bloody Sunday*
1972	Bob Fosse, *Cabaret*
1973	Francois Truffaut, *Day for Night*
1974	Roman Polanski, *Chinatown*

'The Graduate', starring Dustin Hoffman as Benjamin, was the 1968 Best Film Award given by BAFTA

1975	Stanley Kubrick, *Barry Lyndon*
1976	Milos Forman, *One Flew over the Cuckoo's Nest*
1977	Woody Allen, *Annie Hall*
1978	Alan Parker, *Midnight Express*

The John Grierson Award

1968	No Award
1969	*Picture to Post*
1970	*Shadow of Progress*
1971	*Alaska – The Great Land*
1972	*Memorial*
1973	*Caring for History*
1974	*Location North Sea*
1975	*Sea Area Forties*

Best Animated Film

1968	*Pas de Deux*
1969	No Award
1970	*Henry Nine 'Til Five*
1971	No Award
1972	No Award
1973	*Tchou Tchou*
1974	*La Faim/Hunger*
1975	*Great*

Best Specialised Film

1968	*The Threat in the Water*
1969	*Let There be Light*
1970	*The Rise and Fall of the Great Lakes*
1971	*The Savage Voyage*
1972	*Cutting Oils and Fluids*
1973	*A Man's World*
1974	*Monet in London*
1975	*The Curiosity that Kills the Cat*
1976	*Hydraulics*
1977	*Path of Paddle*
1978	*Twenty Times More Likely*

The Robert Flaherty Award

For the best-feature-length film, documentary in content

1959	*The Savage Eye*
1960	Not Awarded
1961	*Volcano*
1962	Not Awarded
1963	Not Awarded
1964	*Nobody Waved Goodbye*
1965	*Tokyo Olympiad*
1966	*Goal! The World Cup*
1967	*To Die in Madrid*
1968	*In Need of Special Care*
1969	*Prologue*
1970	*Sad Song of Yellow Skin*
1971	*The Hellstrom Chronicle*
1972	No Award
1973	*Grierson*
1974	*Cree Hunters of Mistassini*
1975	*The Early Americans*
1976	*Los Canadienses*
1977	No Award
1978	*The Silent Witness*

Best Short Factual Film

1976	*The End of the Road*
1977	*The Living City*
1978	*Hokusia – An Animated Sketch book*

Best Short Fictional Film
1976 No Award
1977 *The Bead Game*
1978 No Award

FILM CRAFT AWARDS
Best Screenplay
1968 Calder Willingham, Buck Henry
1969 Waldo Salt
1970 William Goldman
1971 Harold Pinter
1972 Paddy Chayefsky ⎫
     Larry McMurtry ⎬ Tie
     Peter Bogdanovich ⎭
1973 Luis Bunuel, Jean-Claude Carrière
1974 Robert Towne
1975 Robert Getchell
1976 Alan Parker
1977 Woody Allen and Marshall Brickman
1978 Alvin Sargent

Best Cinematography
1968 Geoffrey Unsworth
1969 Gerry Turpin
1970 Conrad Hall
1971 Pasquale de Santis
1972 Geoffrey Unsworth
1973 Anthony Richmond
1974 Douglas Slocombe
1975 John Alcott
1976 Russell Boyd
1977 Geoffrey Unsworth
1978 Douglas Slocombe

Best Production Design/Art Direction
1968 Tony Masters, Harry Lange, Ernie Archer
1969 Don Ashton
1970 Mario Garbuglia
1971 Ferdinando Scarfiotti
1972 Rolf Zehetbaur
1973 Natasha Kroll
1974 John Box
1975 John Box
1976 Geoffrey Kirkland
1977 Danilo Donati
1978 Joe Alives

Best Costume Design
1968 Danilo Donati
1969 Anthony Mendleson
1970 Maria de Matteis, Ugo Pericoli
1971 Piero Tosi
1972 Anthony Mendleson
1973 Phyllis Dalton
1974 Theoni V. Aldredge
1975 Ann Roth
1976 Moidele Bickel
1977 Danilo Donati
1978 Anthony Powell

Best Film Editing
1968 Sam O'Steen
1969 Hugh A. Robertson
1970 John C. Howard, Richard C. Meyer
1971 Richard Marden

1972 Gerry Greenberg
1973 Ralph Kemplen
1974 Walter Murch, Richard Chew
1975 Dede Allen
1976 Richard Chew, Lynzee Klingman, Sheldon Kahn
1977 Ralph Rosenblum, Wendy Greene Bricmont
1978 Gerry Hambling

Best Soundtrack
1968 Winston Ryder
1969 Don Challis, Simon Kaye
1970 Don Hall, David Dockendorf, William Edmundson
1971 Vittorio Trenting, Giuseppe Muratori
1972 David Hildyard, Robert Knudson, Arthur Piantadosi
1973 Les Wiggins, Gordon K. McCallum, Keith Grant
1974 Art Rochester, Nat Boxer, Mike Evje, Walter Murch
1975 William A. Sawyer, Jim Webb, Chris McLaughlin, Richard Portman
1976 Les Wiggins, Clive Winter, Ken Barker
1977 Peter Horrocks, Gerry Humphreys, Simon Kaye, Robin O'Donoghue, Les Wiggins
1978 Team of twelve for *Star Wars*

FILM PERFORMANCE AWARDS
Best Actress
1968 Katherine Hepburn, *Guess Who's Coming to Dinner*, and *Lion in Winter*
1969 Maggie Smith, *The Prime of Miss Jean Brodie*
1970 Katharine Ross, *Butch Cassidy and the Sundance Kid*
1971 Glenda Jackson, *Sunday, Bloody Sunday*
1972 Liza Minnelli, *Cabaret*
1973 Stephane Audran, *The Discreet Charm of the Bourgeoisie*, and *Just before Nightfall*
1974 Joanne Woodward, *Summer Wishes, Winter Dreams*
1975 Ellen Burstyn, *Alice Doesn't Live Here Anymore*
1976 Louise Fletcher, *One Flew Over the Cuckoo's Nest*
1977 Diane Keaton, *Annie Hall*
1978 Jane Fonda, *Julia*

Best Supporting Actress
1968 Billie Whitelaw
1969 Celia Johnson
1970 Susannah York
1971 Margaret Leighton
1972 Cloris Leachman
1973 Valentine Cortese
1974 Ingrid Bergman
1975 Diane Ladd
1976 Jodie Foster
1977 Jenny Agutter
1978 Geraldine Page

Best Actor
1968 Spencer Tracy, *Guess Who's Coming to Dinner*
1969 Dustin Hoffman, *Midnight Cowboy*
1970 Robert Redford, *Butch Cassidy and the Sundance Kid*
1971 Peter Finch, *Sunday, Bloody Sunday*
1972 Gene Hackman, *French Connection*
1973 Walter Matthau, *Pete 'n Tillie*, and *Charley Varrick*

Christopher Reeve as Superman (shown here proving he is 'the man of steel') won the 1978 Most Promising Newcomer to lead in Films' Award given by BAFTA (*Popperfoto*)

1974	Jack Nicholson, *Chinatown*, and *The Last Detail*
1975	Al Pacino, *Dog Day Afternoon*, and *Godfather II*
1976	Jack Nicholson, *One Flew Over the Cuckoo's Nest*
1977	Peter Finch, *Network*
1978	Richard Dreyfuss, *The Goodbye Girl*

Best Supporting Actor

1968	Ian Holm
1969	Laurence Olivier
1970	Colin Welland
1971	Edward Fox
1972	Ben Johnson
1973	Arthur Lowe
1974	John Gielgud
1975	Fred Astaire
1976	Brad Dourif
1977	Edward Fox
1978	John Hurt

The Most Promising Newcomer to Leading Film Roles

1968	Dustin Hoffman, *The Graduate*
1969	Jon Voight, *Midnight Cowboy*
1970	David Bradley, *Kes*
1971	Dominic Guard,
1972	Joel Grey, *Cabaret*
1973	Peter Egan,
1974	Georgina Hale,
1975	Valerie Perrine, *Lennie*
1976	Jodie Foster, *Taxi Driver*
1977	Isabelle Huppert,
1978	Christopher Reeve, *Superman*

UNITED NATIONS AWARD

United Nations Award for the Best Film embodying one or more of the principles of the United Nations Charter.

1949	*The Search*
1950	*Intruder in the Dust*
1951	*Four in a Jeep*
1952	*Cry the Beloved Country*
1953	*World Without End*
1954	*The Divided Heart*
1955	*Children of Hiroshima*
1956	*Race for Life*
1957	*The Happy Road*
1958	*The Defiant Ones*
1959	*On the Beach*
1960	*Hiroshima, Mon Amour*
1961	*Let My People Go*
1962	*Reach for Glory*
1963	*Inheritance*
1964	*Dr Strangelove*
1965	*Tokyo Olympiad*
1966	*The War Game*
1967	*In the Heat of the Night*
1968	*Guess Who's Coming to Dinner?*
1969	*Oh! What a Lovely War*
1970	*M*A*S*H*
1971	*The Battle of Algiers*
1972	*The Garden of the Finzi-Continis*
1973	*State of Siege*
1974	*Lacombe Lucien*
1975	*Conrack*
1976	No Award
1977	No Award
1978	No Award

Cannes Film Festival

Founded in 1946, the Cannes Festival has featured the following major awards: Palme d'Or, Prix special du Jury, Best male and female leads; also awards for the best short film.

Grands Prix (Palmes d'Or until 1954) and Grand Prix International

1946	*La Symphonie pastorale*, J. Delannoy	1951	*Miracle à Milan*, Vittorio de Sica;
1947	*Antoine et Antoinette*, J. Becker		*Mademoiselle Julie*, Alf Sjoberg
1949	*The Third Man*, Carol Reed		

1952	*Deux Sous d'espoir*, Renato Castellani
	Othello, Orson Welles
1953	*Le Salaire de la peur*, H. G. Clouzot
1954	*La Porte de l'Enfer*, T. Kinugasa
1955	*Marty*, Delbert Mann
1956	*Le Monde du silence*, J.-Y Cousteau
1957	*La Loi du Seigneur*, William Wyler
1958	*Quand passent les cigognes*, Mikhail Kalatozov
1959	*Orfeu Negro*, Marcel Camus
1960	*La Dolce Vita*, Federico Fellini
1961	*Une aussi longue absence*, Henri Colpi;
	Viridiana, Luis Bunuel
1962	*La Parole Donnée*, Anselmo Duarte
1963	*Le Guépard*, Luchino Visconti
1964	*Les Parapluies de Cherbourg*, Jacques Demy
1965	*The Knack*, Richard Lester
1966	*Un homme, et une femme*, Claude Lelouch;
	Signore e Signori, Pietro Germi
1967	*Blow up*, Michelangelo Antonioni
1968	No Award
1969	*If*, Lindsay Anderson
1970	*M.A.S.H.*, Robert Altman
1971	*The Go Between*, Joseph Losey
1972	*L'Affaire Mattei*, Francesco Rosi;
	La Classe Ouvrière va au Paradis, Elio Petri
1973	*L'Epouvantail*, Jerry Schatzberg
	La Méprise, Alain Bridges

1974	*The Conversation*, Francis Ford Coppola
1975	*Chronique des années de braise*, Lakhdar Hamina
1976	*Taxi Driver*, Martin Scorsese
1977	*Padre Padrone*, Paolo and Vittorio Taviani
1978	*L'Arbre aux Sabots*, Ermanno Olmi
1979	*Apocalypse Now*, Francis Coppola, and *The Drum*, Volker Schloendorff

Grand Prix Special du Jury

1967	*Accident*, Joseph Losey
	J'ai même rencontré des Tziganes heureux, Alexander Petrovic
1968	No Award
1969	*Adalen 31*, Bo Wilderberg
1970	*Investigation of a Citizen Above Repute*, Elio Petri
1971	*Taking Off*, Milos Forman,
	Johnny Got His Gun, Dalton Trumbo
1972	*Solaris*, Andrei Tarkovski
1973	*La Maman la Putain*, Jean Eustache
1974	*The Thousand and One Nights*, Pier Paolo Passolini
1975	*The Enigma of Kaspar Hauser*, Werner Herzog
1976	*La Marquise d'O*, Eric Rohmer
	Cria Cuervos, Carlos Saura
1977	No Award
1978	*Rêve de Singe*, Marco Ferreri
1979	*The Shout*, Zerzy Skolimowski

New York Film Critics Circle Awards

BEST MOTION PICTURE

1935	*The Informer*, RKO
1936	*Mr Deeds Goes to Town*, Columbia
1937	*The Life of Emile Zola*, Warner Bros.
1938	*The Citadel*, MGM
1939	*Wuthering Heights*, Goldwyn-UA
1940	*The Grapes of Wrath*, 20th Century-Fox
1941	*Citizen Kane*, RKO-Mercury
1942	*In Which We Serve*, UA-Noel Coward
1943	*Watch on the Rhine*, Warner Bros.
1944	*Going My Way*, Paramount
1945	*The Lost Weekend*, Paramount
1946	*The Best Years of Our Lives*, Goldwyn-RKO Radio
1947	*Gentleman's Agreement*, 20th Century-Fox
1948	*Treasure of Sierra Madre*, Warner Bros.
1949	*All the King's Men*, Rossen-Columbia
1950	*All About Eve*, 20th Century-Fox
1951	*A Streetcar Named Desire*, Warner Bros.
1952	*High Noon*, United Artists
1953	*From Here to Eternity*, Columbia
1954	*On the Waterfront*, Columbia
1955	*Marty*, United Artists
1956	*Around the World in 80 Days*, The Michael Todd Co., Inc., UA

1957	*The Bridge on the River Kwai*, Columbia
1958	*The Defiant Ones*, United Artists
1959	*Ben-Hur*, MGM
1960	*The Apartment*, United Artists; *Sons and Lovers*, 20th Century-Fox
1961	*West Side Story*, Mirisch Pictures, Inc.
1962	(No awards given)
1963	*Tom Jones*, Woodfall Productions, Ltd
1964	*My Fair Lady*, Warner Bros.
1965	*Darling*, Embassy Pictures
1966	*A Man for All Seasons*, Columbia
1967	*In the Heat of the Night*, Mirisch Corp.
1968	*The Lion in Winter*, Avco Embassy Pictures
1969	*Z*, Cinema V Distributing
1970	*Five Easy Pieces*, Columbia
1971	*A Clockwork Orange*, Warner Bros.
1972	*Cries and Whispers*, New World
1973	*Day for Night*, Warner Bros.
1974	*Amarcord*, Roger Corman/New World Films
1975	*Nashville*, ABC Entertainment
1976	*All the President's Men*, Warner Bros.
1977	*Annie Hall*

BEST MALE PERFORMANCE

1935	Charles Laughton, *Mutiny on the Bounty* and *Ruggles of Red Gap*
1936	Walter Huston, *Dodsworth*
1937	Paul Muni, *The Life of Emile Zola*
1938	James Cagney, *Angels with Dirty Faces*
1939	James Stewart, *Mr Smith Goes to Washington*

1940	Charles Chaplin, *The Great Dictator* (refused award)
1941	Gary Cooper, *Sergeant York*
1942	James Cagney, *Yankee Doodle Dandy*
1943	Paul Lukas, *Watch on the Rhine*
1944	Barry Fitzgerald, *Going My Way*

1945	Ray Milland, *The Lost Weekend*
1946	Laurence Olivier, *Henry V*
1947	William Powell, *Life with Father*
1948	Sir Laurence Olivier, *Hamlet*
1949	Broderick Crawford, *All the King's Men*
1950	Gregory Peck, *Twelve O'Clock High*
1951	Arthur Kennedy, *Bright Victory*
1952	Ralph Richardson, *Breaking the Sound Barrier*
1953	Burt Lancaster, *From Here to Eternity*
1954	Marlon Brando, *On the Waterfront*
1955	Ernest Borgnine, *Marty*
1956	Kirk Douglas, *Lust for Life*
1957	Alec Guinness, *The Bridge on the River Kwai*
1958	David Niven, *Separate Tables*
1959	James Stewart, *Anatomy of a Murder*
1960	Burt Lancaster, *Elmer Gantry*
1961	Maximilian Schell, *Judgment at Nuremberg*

1962	(No awards given)
1963	Albert Finney, *Tom Jones*
1964	Rex Harrison, *My Fair Lady*
1965	Oskar Werner, *Ship of Fools*
1966	Paul Scofield, *A Man for All Seasons*
1967	Rod Steiger, *In the Heat of the Night*
1968	Alan Arkin, *The Heart Is a Lonely Hunter*
1969	John Voigt. *Midnight Cowboy*
1970	George C. Scott, *Patton*
1971	Gene Hackman, *The French Connection*
1972	Laurence Olivier, *Sleuth*
1973	Marlon Brando, *Last Tango in Paris*
1974	Jack Nicholson, *The Last Detail* and *Chinatown*
1975	Jack Nicholson, *One Flow Over the Cuckoo's Nest*
1976	Robert De Niro. *Taxi Driver*
1977	John Gielgud, *Providence*

BEST FEMALE PERFORMANCE

1935	Greta Garbo, *Anna Karenina*
1936	Luise Rainer, *The Great Ziegfeld*
1937	Greta Garbo, *Camille*
1938	Margaret Sullavan, *Three Comrades*
1939	Vivien Leigh, *Gone with the Wind*
1940	Katharine Hepburn, *The Philadelphia Story*
1941	Joan Fontaine, *Suspicion*
1942	Agnes Moorehead, *The Magnificent Ambersons*
1943	Ida Lupino, *The Hard Way*
1944	Tallulah Bankhead, *Lifeboat*
1945	Ingrid Bergman, *Spellbound, The Bells of St Mary's*
1946	Celia Johnson, *Brief Encounter*
1947	Deborah Kerr, *The Adventuress, Black Narcissus*
1948	Olivia de Havilland, *The Snake Pit*
1949	Olivia de Havilland, *The Heiress*
1950	Bette Davis, *All About Eve*
1951	Vivien Leigh, *A Streetcar Named Desire*
1952	Shirley Booth, *Come Back, Little Sheba*
1953	Audrey Hepburn, *Roman Holiday*
1954	Grace Kelly, *The Country Girl, Rear Window, Dial M for Murder*
1955	Anna Magnani, *The Rose Tattoo*
1956	Ingrid Bergman, *Anastasia*
1957	Deborah Kerr, *Heaven Knows, Mr Allison*
1958	Susan Hayward, *I Want to Live!*
1959	Audrey Hepburn, *The Nun's Story*
1960	Deborah Kerr, *The Sundowners*
1961	Sophia Loren, *Two Women*
1962	(No awards given)
1963	Patricia Neal, *Hud*
1964	Kim Stanley, *Seance on a Wet Afternoon*
1965	Julie Christie, *Darling*
1966	Elizabeth Taylor, *Who's Afraid of Virginia Woolf?*; Lynn Redgrave, *Georgy Girl*
1967	Dame Edith Evans, *The Whisperers*
1968	Joanne Woodward, *Rachel, Rachel*
1969	Jane Fonda, *They Shoot Horses, Don't They?*
1970	Glenda Jackson, *Women in Love*
1971	Jane Fonda, *Klute*
1972	Liv Ullmann, *Cries and Whispers*
1973	Joanne Woodward, *Summer Wishes, Winter Dreams*

Vivien Leigh captivated film audiences with her portrayal of Scarlett O'Hara, the heroine in 'Gone with the Wind'. She won the New York Film Critics Circle Award for the Best Female Performance in 1939 (*Popperfoto*)

1974	Liv Ullmann, *Scenes From a Marriage*
1975	Isabelle Adjani, *The Story of Adele H.*
1976	Liv Ullmann, *Face to Face*
1977	Diane Keaton, *Annie Hall*

BEST DIRECTION

1935	John Ford, *The Informer*	1957	David Lean, *The Bridge on the River Kwai*
1936	Rouben Mamoulian, *The Gay Desperado*	1958	Stanley Kramer, *The Defiant Ones*
1937	Gregory La Cava, *Stage Door*	1959	Fred Zinnermann, *The Nun's Story*
1938	Alfred Hitchcock, *The Lady Vanishes*	1960	Billy Wilder, *The Apartment*; Jack Cardiff, *Sons and Lovers*
1939	John Ford, *Stagecoach*		
1940	John Ford, *How Green Was my Valley*	1961	Robert Rossen, *The Hustler*
1941	John Ford, *The Grapes of Wrath, The Long Voyage Home*	1962	(No awards given)
		1963	Tony Richardson, *Tom Jones*
1942	John Farrow, *Wake Island*	1964	Stanley Kubrick, *Dr Strangelove*
1943	George Stevens, *The More the Merrier*	1965	John Schlesinger, *Darling*
1944	Leo McCarey, *Going My Way*	1966	Fred Zinnemann, *A Man for All Seasons*
1945	Billy Wilder, *The Lost Weekend*	1967	Mike Nichols, *The Graduate*
1946	William Wyler, *The Best Years of Our Lives*	1968	Paul Newman, *Rachel, Rachel*
1947	Elia Kazan, *Gentleman's Agreement, Boomerang*	1969	Costa-Gavras, *Z*
1948	John Huston, *Treasure of Sierra Madre*	1970	Bob Rafelson, *Five Easy Pieces*
1949	Carol Reed, *The Fallen Idol*	1971	Stanley Kubrick, *A Clockwork Orange*
1950	Joseph L. Mankiewicz, *All about Eve*	1972	Ingmar Bergman, *Cries and Whispers*
1951	Elia Kazan, *A Streetcar Named Desire*	1973	François Truffaut, *Day for Night*
1952	Fred Zinnemann, *High Noon*	1974	Federico Fellini, *Amarcord*
1953	Fred Zinnemann, *From Here to Eternity*	1975	Robert Altman, *Nashville*
1954	Elia Kazan, *On the Waterfront*	1976	Alan J. Pakula, *All the President's Men*
1955	David Lean, *Summertime*	1977	Woody Allen, *Annie Hall*
1956	John Huston, *Moby Dick*		

BEST FOREIGN-LANGUAGE FILM 1936–40 and 1946–68 only

1936	*La Kermesse Héroique* (French)	1955	*Diabolique* (French) and *Umberto D.* (Italian)
1937	*Mayerling* (French)	1956	*La Strada* (Italian)
1938	*Grande Illusion* (French)	1957	*Gervaise* (French)
1939	*Harvest* (French)	1958	*Mon Oncle* (French)
1940	*The Baker's Wife* (French)	1959	*The 400 Blows* (French)
1946	*Open City* (Italian)	1960	*Hiroshima, Mon Amour* (French)
1947	*To Live in Peace* (Italian)	1961	*La Dolce Vita* (Italian)
1948	*Paisan* (Italian)	1962	(No awards given)
1949	*The Bicycle Thief* (Italian)	1963	*8½* (Italian)
1950	*Ways of Love* (Franco-Italian)	1964	*The Man from Rio* (French)
1951	*Miracle in Milan* (Italian)	1965	*Juliet of the Spirits* (Italian)
1952	*Forbidden Games* (French)	1966	*The Shop on Main Street* (Czechoslovakian)
1953	*Justice is Done* (French)	1967	*La Guerre est Finie* (French)
1954	*Gate of Hell* (Japanese)	1968	*War and Peace* (Russian)
			Discontinued

SPECIAL AWARD

1938	*Snow White and the Seven Dwarfs*, Disney-RKO		*of Everest* (JARO)
1940	*Fantasia*, Walt Disney	1964	*To Be Alive*, shown by Johnson's Wax Co. at the New York World's Fair
1945	*The True Glory* and *The Fighting Lady*		
1953	*A Queen is Crowned* (JARO) and *The Conquest*	1972	*The Sorrow and the Pity*, French documentary

BEST SCREENPLAY

		1969	Paul Mazursky and Larry Tucker, *Bob & Carol & Ted & Alice*
1958	Nathan E. Douglas and Harold J. Smith, *The Defiant Ones*		
		1970	Eric Rohmer, *Ma Nuit Chez Maud*
1959	Wendell Mayes, *Anatomy of a Murder*	1971	Penelope Gilliat, *Sunday Bloody Sunday*; Larry McMurtry and Peter Bogdanovich, *The Last Picture Show*
1960	Billy Wilder and I. A. L. Diamond, *The Apartment*		
1961	Abby Mann, *Judgment at Nuremberg*	1972	Ingmar Bergman, *Cries and Whispers*
1962	(No awards given)	1973	George Lucas, Gloria Katz, Willard Huyck, *American Graffiti*
1963	Irving Ravetch and Harriet Frank, Jr, *Hud*		
1964	Harold Pinter, *The Servant*	1974	Ingmar Bergman, *Scenes From a Marriage*
1966	Robert Bolt, *A Man for All Seasons*	1975	François Truffaut, Jean Gruault, Suzanne Shiffman, *The Story of Adele H.*
1967	David Newman and Robert Benton, *Bonnie and Clyde*		
		1976	Paddy Chayefsky, *Network*
1968	Lorenzo Semple, Jr, *Pretty Poison*	1977	Woody Allen and Marshall Brickman, *Annie Hall*

BEST SUPPORTING ACTOR		BEST SUPPORTING ACTRESS	
1969	Jack Nicholson, *Easy Rider*	1969	Dyan Cannon, *Bob & Carol & Ted & Alice*
1970	Chief Dan George, *Little Big Man*	1970	Karen Black, *Five Easy Pieces*
1971	Ben Johnson, *The Last Picture Show*	1971	Ellen Burstyn, *The Last Picture Show*
1972	Robert Duvall, *The Godfather*	1972	Jeannie Berlin, *The Heartbreak Kid*
1973	Robert De Niro, *Mean Streets*	1973	Valentina Cortese, *Day for Night*
1974	Charles Boyer, *Stavisky*	1974	Valerie Perrine, *Lenny*
1975	Alan Arkin, *Hearts of the West*	1975	Lily Tomlin, *Nashville*
1976	Jason Robards, *All the President's Men*	1976	Talia Shire, *Rocky*
1977	Maximilian Schell, *Julia*	1977	Sissy Spacek, *Three Women*

Venice Film Festival

The first festival ever to be held, it has been an annual event since 1932, but in 1932–33 and from 1969 there have been no prizes and no jury.

'GRAND PRIX' WINNERS
(including the Mussolini Cup to the Best Foreign Film, 1934–42; Grand Prix International de Venise, 1947–48; and the Lion d'Or de Saint-Marc).

1934	*L'Homme d'Aran*, Robert Flaherty; *Teresa Confalonieri*, G. Brignone
1935	*Anna Karenina*, Clarence Brown; *Casta Diva*, Carmine Gallone
1936	*L'Empereur de Californie*, L. Trenker; *L'Escadron blanc*, A. Genina
1937	*Un carnet de bal*, Julien Duvivier; *Scipion l'Africain*, Carmine Gallone
1938	*Les Olympiades*, Leni Riefenstahl; *Luciano Serra pilote*, G. Alessandrini
1939	*Abuna Messias*, G. Alessandrini
1940	*Le Maître de Poste*, Gustav Ucicky; *L'Alcazar*, Augusto Genina
1941	*Ohm Krueger*, Hans Steinhoff; *La Couronne de fer*, A. Blasetti
1942	*Le Grand Roi*, Veit Harlan; *Bengasi*, Augusto Genina
1943–46	No award
1947	*Sirena*, Karel Stekly
1948	*Hamlet*, Laurence Olivier

1949	*Manon*, H. G. Clouzot
1950	*Justice est faite*, André Cayatte
1951	*Rashomon*, Akira Kurosawa
1952	*Jeux interdits*, René Clément
1953	No Lion d'Or, Lion d'Argent: *Thérèse Raquin*, Marcel Carné
1954	*Roméo et Juliette*, R. Castellani
1955	*Order*, Carl Dreyer
1956	No Award
1957	*Aparajito*, Satyajit Ray
1958	*L'Homme au pousse-pousse*, Hiroshi Inagaki
1959	*Le Général della Rovere*, R. Rossellini; *La Grande Guerre*, M. Monicelli
1960	*Le Passage du Rhin*, André Cayatte
1961	*L'Année dernière à Marienbad*, Alain Resnais
1962	*Journal intime*, Valerio Zurlini; *L'Enfance d'Ivan*, Andrei Tarkovski
1963	*Main basse sur la ville*, F. Rosi
1964	*Le Désert rouge*, M. Antonioni
1965	*Sandra*, Luchino Visconti
1966	*La Bataille d'Alger*, G. Pontecorvo
1967	*Belle de jour*, Luis Bunuel
1968	*Les Artistes sous le chapiteau: perplexes*, Alexander Kluge

CIRCUS

Circus World Championship

Inaugurated in 1976, the competitions are organised by Circus World Championships Ltd, and the 1978 event was staged in London at Gerry Cottle's Circus.

1978 GOLD MEDAL WINNERS

The Flying Oslers, flying trapeze artists, South Africa
Alan Alan, escapologist

Jose Luis Munoz, tightrope walker
The Biochanovi, acrobatic troupe, Bulgaria
Los Rios, acrobats, foot jugglers

COMPOSERS

Ian Whyte Award for British Composers

The major triennial composition prize awarded through the Scottish National Orchestra by a private donor was given for the third time in 1978. The award honours the late Dr Ian Whyte's influence on the musical renaissance of Scotland.

The importance of the competition lies not only in the valuable cash prize of £500 but on the guarantee of many performances of the winning work by the SNO and on BBC Radio. It is often the case that second performances of new works, particularly by young composers, are very difficult to organise, whereas the SNO's scheme ensures that the work of the winning composer is heard by as many people as possible throughout Scotland, and with the help of the BBC, throughout the United Kingdom as a whole. The winners:

1972 Graham Williams
1975 Colin Matthewsin
1978 Lyell Cresswell (33), from New Zealand

The 1978 winning work 'Salm' (inspired by the singing of Gaelic psalms) received its first performance by the SNO under David Atherton on 30 January, 1979 in Aberdeen and later the same week in Dundee, Edinburgh and Glasgow.

Menuhin Prize

This triennial prize for composers is organised jointly by the City of Westminster Arts Council and the Ernest Read Music Association. The winner receives a cash prize of £500 plus a public performance in London of the winning work. Winners to date:

1975 Michael Blake Watkins of Woodford Green, Essex

1978 Adrian Williams of Croxley Green, Rickmansworth, Herts.

CONDUCTORS

The Barbirolli Memorial Trust

Organised by the Royal Academy of Music, this annual contest for young conductors, for an award of approximately £1000, is held in the early part of each year.

1976 Hywel Davies
1978 No award made
1979 Darrell Davison

John Player International Conductors' Award

This award was presented for the first time by Imperial Tobacco in 1974. The award is unique in that it offers a two year engagement for the winning conductor to work on the staff of a professional orchestra – the Bournemouth Symphony Orchestra and the Bournemouth Sinfonietta.

1974 1st Simon Rattle
      2nd Geoffrey Simon
1976 1st Gerard Oskamp
      2nd Wyn Davies
1978 1st Tomasz Bugaj
      2nd Jonathan Del Mar

Rupert Foundation International Young Conductors' Competition

The Foundation holds a competition, called The Rupert Foundation International Competition for Young Conductors, approximately every 18 months.

The competition is held in association with the BBC and the winner receives prize money from the Rupert Foundation and the BBC offers a variety of work with its symphony orchestras during the year of the scholarship. Candidates of either sex and any nationality are eligible to compete, but must have had practical experience of conducting. The winners were as follows:

March 1973   Guido Ajmone-Marsan (USA)
November 1974   Marc Soustrot (Fra)

October 1976   Ivan Fischer (Hun)
April 1978   Gerard Akoka (Fra)

Marc Soustrot (Fra) who won the 1974 Rupert Foundation International Young Conductors' Competition

CONSERVATION

J. Paul Getty $50 000 Wildlife Conservation Prize

The J. Paul Getty Wildlife Conservation Prize is worth $50 000 (about £25 000). The award was made possible by a gift from Mr Getty to the World Wildlife Fund, and is intended to recognise outstanding achievement or service for the benefit of mankind in the conservation of wildlife.

An international jury chaired by HRH The Prince of the Netherlands and including Sir Julian Huxley, Sir Peter Scott, and Maurice Strong (Executive Director of the United Nations Environmental Programme) chose the first winner from 525 nominations from 42 countries.

1974	Felipe Benavides (Peru), conservationist	1977	No Award
1975	Salim A. Ali (Ind), ornithologist	1978	No Award
1976	Ian Grimwood (GB, later Kenya), Chief Game Warden in Kenya	1979	Dr Boonsong Lekagul (Tha), conservationist and educator

Felipe Benavides, winner of the 1974 J. Paul Getty Wildlife Conservation Prize, administered by US National Appeal for the World Wildlife Fund. Sr Benavides is seen here holding two ocelot skins during a visit to the Amazonian town of Leticia, a centre for smuggling the skins of endangered animals out of America. *Inset* **Paul Getty, founder of the J. Paul Getty Wildlife Conservation Prize**

COOKERY

Cook of the Realm

Sponsored jointly by the National Dairy Council and *Woman's Realm*, the contest is featured on BBC Television's Nationwide. The competition involves the preparation of a special meal to suit a particular occasion, for example in 1978 competitors had to devise a fuel saving meal for four which had to be cooked either entirely in the oven or on top of a standard cooker. Food had to be cooked with butter produced in Britain. Prize money amounts to £9500, with £4500 to the winner.

1973	Mary Williamson, Glasgow	1977	Roger Green, Sheffield
1974	Helen Crombie, Edinburgh	1978	Gladys Browne, Weston-super-Mare
1975	Pamela Tickle, Blackpool		
1976	Jill Barge, Exeter		

'Woman's Realm' Junior Cook of the Realm

1976   Sally Horne, Kettering
1977   Claire Baker (14), London
Discontinued

CRAFT

The British Craft Awards

These are sponsored by the *Sunday Telegraph Magazine* and John Player and Sons. First given in 1977, the winners have been:

1977	Rosamund Conway (jewellery)	1978	Michael Lloyd (silver)
	John Hinchcliffe (woven textiles)		Bryan Maynard (musical instrument)
	Judith Gilmore (pottery)		Fred Baier (furniture)
	Sally Lou Smith (book-binding)		Eng Tow (batik/printed textiles)

Goldsmiths', Silversmiths' and Jewellers' Art Council of London Annual Competition of Craftsmanship and Design

The Goldsmiths', Silversmiths' and Jewellers' Art Council of London (nothing to do with the Arts Council of Great Britain) organises an annual competition of craftsmanship and design, which is shown at Goldsmiths' Hall though it is not directly organised by the Company. The 1979 competition was extended to cover the whole of the UK for the first time.

The exhibition in 1978 included eighty prize-winning pieces out of a record total of 292 designs and finished pieces from goldsmiths, silversmiths and jewellers in London and the Home Counties. These included a gold and enamel mask of Tutankhamen, an engraved portrait of Sir Winston Churchill, diamond jewellery, an enamelled egg in Faberge style, massive silver centre-pieces and other examples of modern craftsmanship together worth £100 000.

The most important special prize is the Jacques Cartier Memorial Award for the craftsman of the year.

Full details of the prizewinners can be obtained from the Goldsmiths', Silversmiths' and Jewellers' Art Council direct.

CRICKET

County Championship

17 counties have contested the County Championship since 1921. The method of deciding the

champion has changed several times since the Championship was first recognised as official in 1890. The list of champions can be extended back to 1864.

1864	Surrey		Surrey	1920	Middlesex	1953	Surrey
1865	Nottinghamshire	1889	Lancashire	1921	Middlesex	1954	Surrey
1866	Middlesex		Nottinghamshire	1922	Yorkshire	1955	Surrey
1867	Yorkshire	1890	Surrey	1923	Yorkshire	1956	Surrey
1868	Nottinghamshire	1891	Surrey	1924	Yorkshire	1957	Surrey
1869	Nottinghamshire	1892	Surrey	1925	Yorkshire	1958	Surrey
	Yorkshire	1893	Yorkshire	1926	Lancashire	1959	Yorkshire
1870	Yorkshire	1894	Surrey	1927	Lancashire	1960	Yorkshire
1871	Nottinghamshire	1895	Surrey	1928	Lancashire	1961	Hampshire
1872	Nottinghamshire	1896	Yorkshire	1929	Nottinghamshire	1962	Yorkshire
1873	Gloucestershire	1897	Lancashire	1930	Lancashire	1963	Yorkshire
	Nottinghamshire	1898	Yorkshire	1931	Yorkshire	1964	Worcestershire
1874	Gloucestershire	1899	Surrey	1932	Yorkshire	1965	Worcestershire
1875	Nottinghamshire	1900	Yorkshire	1933	Yorkshire	1966	Yorkshire
1876	Gloucestershire	1901	Yorkshire	1934	Lancashire	1967	Yorkshire
1877	Gloucestershire	1902	Yorkshire	1935	Yorkshire	1968	Yorkshire
1878	Undecided	1903	Middlesex	1936	Derbyshire	1969	Glamorgan
1879	Nottinghamshire	1904	Lancashire	1937	Yorkshire	1970	Kent
	Lancashire	1905	Yorkshire	1938	Yorkshire	1971	Surrey
1880	Nottinghamshire	1906	Kent	1939	Yorkshire	1972	Warwickshire
1881	Lancashire	1907	Nottinghamshire	1946	Yorkshire	1973	Hampshire
1882	Nottinghamshire	1908	Yorkshire	1947	Middlesex	1974	Worcestershire
	Lancashire	1909	Kent	1948	Glamorgan	1975	Leicestershire
1883	Nottinghamshire	1910	Kent	1949	Middlesex	1976	Middlesex
1884	Nottinghamshire	1911	Warwickshire		Yorkshire	1977	Middlesex
1885	Nottinghamshire	1912	Yorkshire	1950	Lancashire		Kent
1886	Nottinghamshire	1913	Kent		Surrey	1978	Kent
1887	Surrey	1914	Surrey	1951	Warwickshire	1979	Essex
1888	Surrey	1919	Yorkshire	1952	Surrey		

One-Day Competitions

GILLETTE CUP

First held 1963, the Gillette Cup is contested on a knock-out basis by the 17 first-class counties and the top 5 minor counties. Matches are played with 60 overs per side.

1963	Sussex
1964	Sussex
1965	Yorkshire
1966	Warwickshire
1967	Kent
1968	Warwickshire
1969	Yorkshire
1970	Lancashire
1971	Lancashire
1972	Lancashire
1973	Gloucestershire
1974	Kent
1975	Lancashire
1976	Northamptonshire
1977	Middlesex
1978	Sussex

JOHN PLAYER LEAGUE

First held in 1969, the John Player League is contested by the 17 first-class counties on an all-play-all basis of 40 over matches.

1969	Lancashire
1970	Lancashire
1971	Worcestershire
1972	Kent
1973	Kent
1974	Leicestershire
1975	Hampshire
1976	Kent
1977	Leicestershire
1978	Hampshire

BENSON & HEDGES CUP

First held in 1972, the Benson & Hedges Cup is contested on a zonal, followed by a knock-out, basis by the 17 first-class counties, a combined team from Oxford and Cambridge Universities and by two minor counties representative teams. Matches played at 55 overs.

1972	Leicestershire
1973	Kent
1974	Surrey
1975	Leicestershire
1976	Kent
1977	Gloucestershire
1978	Kent
1979	Essex

Young Cricketer of the Year

Annual trophy awarded by the Cricket Writers Club.

1950 Roy Tattersall (Lancashire)
1951 Peter May (Surrey)
1952 Freddie Trueman (Yorkshire)
1953 Colin Cowdrey (Kent)
1954 Peter Loader (Surrey)
1955 Ken Barrington (Surrey)
1956 Brian Taylor (Essex)
1957 Michael Stewart (Surrey)
1958 Colin Ingleby-Mackenzie (Hampshire)
1959 Geoff Pullar (Lancashire)
1960 David Allen (Gloucestershire)
1961 Peter Parfitt (Middlesex)
1962 Phil Sharpe (Yorkshire)
1963 Geoff Boycott (Yorkshire)
1964 Michael Brearley (Middlesex)
1965 Alan Knott (Kent)
1966 Derek Underwood (Kent)
1967 Tony Greig (Sussex)
1968 Bob Cottam (Hampshire)
1969 Alan Ward (Derbyshire)
1970 Chris Old (Yorkshire)
1971 John Whitehouse (Warwickshire)
1972 Dudley Owen-Thomas (Surrey)
1973 Michael Hendrick (Derbyshire)
1974 Philippe Edmonds (Middlesex)
1975 Andrew Kennedy (Lancashire)
1976 Geoff Miller (Derbyshire)
1977 Ian Botham (Somerset)
1978 David Gower (Leicestershire)

Three great England cricketers bound for Australia in 1978. One achievement they have in common is that of being elected Young Cricketer of the Year. David Gower (*back left*) in 1978, Ian Botham (*back right*) in 1977 and Geoff Boycott (*front*) in 1963 (*Keystone*)

Sheffield Shield

The Australian state championship for the Sheffield Shield is contested annually. First held in the 1892–93 season following the gift of the trophy by Lord Sheffield to the Australian Cricket Council. Winners (year shown is that of the second half of each season):

Victoria 1893, 1895, 1898–99, 1901, 1908, 1915, 1922, 1924–25, 1928, 1930–31, 1934–35, 1937, 1947, 1951, 1963, 1970, 1974, 1979

South Australia 1894, 1910, 1913, 1927, 1936, 1939, 1953, 1964, 1969, 1971, 1976

New South Wales 1896–97, 1900, 1902–07, 1909, 1911–12, 1914, 1920–21, 1923, 1926, 1929, 1932–33, 1938, 1940, 1949–50, 1952, 1954–62, 1965–66

Western Australia 1948, 1968, 1972–73, 1975, 1977–78

Currie Cup

The Cup was presented by Sir Donald Currie and first contested in 1889–90. Competing teams are from the South African provinces and Rhodesia. In some seasons the event has not been held due to the presence of an overseas touring team. Winners (= tied for championship):

Transvaal 1890, 1895, 1903–05, 1907, 1922(=), 1924, 1926–27, 1930, 1935, 1938(=), 1951, 1959, 1966(=), 1969, 1970(=), 1971–73, 1979

Griqualand West 1891

Western Province 1893–94, 1897–98, 1909, 1921, 1922(=), 1932, 1953, 1956, 1970(=), 1975, 1978

Natal 1911, 1913, 1922(=), 1934, 1937, 1947–48, 1952, 1955, 1960–61, 1963–64, 1966(=), 1967–68, 1974, 1976–77

Shell Shield

The Shell Shield, first held in 1966, is contested by the West Indian nations. Winners:

Barbados 1966–67, 1972, 1974, 1976(=), 1977, 1978, 1979

Jamaica 1969

Trinidad & Tobago 1970–71, 1976(=)

Guyana 1973, 1975

Plunket Shield

From the 1906–7 season until 1974–75 the New Zealand provinces contested the Plunket Shield, a trophy presented by Lord Plunket. From 1906 to 1921 the trophy was contested on a challenge basis. Since then winners were:

Auckland   1922, 1927, 1929, 1934, 1937–40, 1947, 1959, 1964, 1969

Canterbury   1923, 1931, 1935, 1946, 1949, 1952, 1956, 1960, 1965

Wellington   1924, 1926, 1928, 1930, 1932, 1936, 1950, 1955, 1957, 1961–62, 1966, 1973, 1974

Otago   1925, 1933, 1948, 1951, 1953, 1958, 1970, 1972, 1975

Central Districts   1954, 1967–68, 1971

Northern Districts   1963

Shell Cup and Trophy

From the 1975–76 season, cricket in New Zealand, the Shell Series, has replaced the Plunket Shield. The provincial competition is now in two parts, the Shell Cup and the Shell Trophy. Winners:

Shell Cup: 1976 Canterbury
1977 Northern Districts
1978 Canterbury
1979 Otago

Shell Trophy: 1976 Canterbury
1977 Otago
1978 Auckland
1979 Otago

Ranji Trophy

The Ranji Trophy, established in memory of K. S. Ranjitsinhji, is contested by the Indian states and provinces. First held in 1934–35 season.

Most wins have been achieved by Bombay: 1935–36, 1942, 1945, 1949, 1952, 1954, 1956–57, 1959–73, 1975–77.

Other winners in recent years: 1958 Baroda; 1974 Karnataka; 1978 Karnataka; 1979 Delhi

Test Cricket

The first Test Match was played between England and Australia in 1876 at Melbourne. Winners of Test series:

ENGLAND v AUSTRALIA

Season	Won by Eng.	Won by Aus.	Drawn
1876–77	1	1	0
1878–79	0	1	0
1880	1	0	0
1881–82	0	2	2
1882	0	1	0
1882–83	2	2	0
1884	1	0	2
1884–85	3	2	0
1886	3	0	0
1886–87	2	0	0
1887–88	1	0	0
1888	2	1	0
1890	2	0	0
1891–92	1	2	0
1893	1	0	2
1894–95	3	2	0
1896	2	1	0
1897–98	1	4	0
1899	0	1	4
1901–02	1	4	0
1902	1	2	2
1903–04	3	2	0
1905	2	0	3
1907–08	1	4	0
1909	1	2	2
1911–12	4	1	0
1912	1	0	2
1920–21	0	5	0
1921	0	3	2
1924–25	1	4	0
1926	1	0	4
1928–29	4	1	0
1930	1	2	2
1932–33	4	1	0
1934	1	2	2
1936–37	2	3	0
1938	1	1	2
1946–47	0	3	2
1948	0	4	1
1950–51	1	4	0
1953	1	0	4
1954–55	3	1	1
1956	2	1	2
1958–59	0	4	1
1961	1	2	2
1962–63	1	1	3
1964	0	1	4
1965–66	1	1	3
1968	1	1	3
1970–71	2	0	4
1972	2	2	1
1974–75	1	4	1
1975	0	1	3
1976–77	0	1	0
1977	3	0	2
1978–79	5	1	0
Total	79	89	68

Summary of other Test series showing number of wins to each country and the number of draws:

England 46	South Africa 18	Drawn 38		Australia 7	Pakistan 3	Drawn 4
England 21	West Indies 22	Drawn 28		South Africa 9	New Zealand 2	Drawn 6
England 27	New Zealand 1	Drawn 25		West Indies 5	New Zealand 2	Drawn 7
England 25	India 7	Drawn 21		West Indies 17	India 5	Drawn 21
England 11	Pakistan 1	Drawn 21		West Indies 6	Pakistan 4	Drawn 5
Australia 29	South Africa 11	Drawn 13		New Zealand 3	India 10	Drawn 9
Australia 25	West Indies 10	Drawn 10	Tied 1	New Zealand 1	Pakistan 8	Drawn 12
Australia 5	New Zealand 1	Drawn 3		India 2	Pakistan 3	Drawn 13
Australia 19	India 5	Drawn 6		(As at 1 July 1979)		

World Cup

A knock-out one-day competition, contested by the leading cricketing nations. First held 1975. Winners:

1975   West Indies
1979   West Indies

Women's Cricket
WORLD CUP

First held in 1973. Winners:
1973   England
1978   Australia

CROQUET

MacRobertson International Shield

Contested periodically by Great Britain, New Zealand and Australia.

1925	Great Britain	1937	Great Britain	1969	Great Britain
1928	Australia	1950	New Zealand	1974	Great Britain
1930	Australia	1956	Great Britain	1979	New Zealand
1935	Australia	1963	Great Britain		

The Open Croquet Championship

First held in 1867. Most wins:

10   John W. Solomon   (1953, 1956, 1959, 1961, 1963–68)

7   Humphrey Hicks   (1932, 1939, 1947–50, 1952)
5   Cyril Corbally   (1902–03, 1906, 1908, 1913)

Most wins by a woman:

4   Dorothy Steel   (1925, 1933, 1935–36)

CROSS-COUNTRY RUNNING

International/World Cross-Country Championship

The International Cross-Country Championship was instituted at Hamilton Park Racecourse, Glasgow, Scotland in 1903. The four British countries competed first, with France competing in 1907 for the first time. Gradually the event became more international in character, and this process was completed when the IAAF included it in its jurisdiction from 1973.

Individual winners and team winners:

MEN

	Individual	Team			
	Individual	*Team*	1907	A. Underwood (Eng)	England
1903	Alfred Shrubb (Eng)	England	1908	Archie Robertson (Eng)	England
1904	Alfred Shrubb (Eng)	England	1909	Edward Wood (Eng)	England
1905	Albert Aldridge (Eng)	England	1910	Edward Wood (Eng)	England
1906	Charles Straw (Eng)	England	1911	Jean Bouin (Fra)	England

Individual		Team
1912	Jean Bouin (Fra)	England
1913	Jean Bouin (Fra)	England
1914	Arthur Nicholls (Eng)	England
1920	James Wilson (Sco)	England
1921	W. Freeman (Eng)	England
1922	Joseph Guillemot (Fra)	France
1923	Charles Blewitt (Eng)	France
1924	William Cotterell (Eng)	England
1925	Jack Webster (Eng)	England
1926	Ernest Harper (Eng)	France
1927	L. Payne (Eng)	France
1928	H. Eckersley (Eng)	France
1929	William Cotterell (Eng)	France
1930	Thomas Evenson (Eng)	England
1931	Tim Smythe (Ire)	England
1932	Thomas Evenson (Eng)	England
1933	Jack Holden (Eng)	England
1934	Jack Holden (Eng)	England
1935	Jack Holden (Eng)	England
1936	William Eaton (Eng)	England
1937	James Flockhart (Sco)	England
1938	John Emery (Eng)	England
1939	Jack Holden (Eng)	France
1946	Raphael Pujazon (Fra)	France
1947	Raphael Pujazon (Fra)	France
1948	John Doms (Bel)	Belgium
1949	Alain Mimoun (Fra)	France
1950	Lucien Theys (Bel)	France
1951	Geoffrey Saunders (Eng)	England
1952	Alain Mimoun (Fra)	France
1953	Franjo Mihalic (Yug)	England
1954	Alain Mimoun (Fra)	England
1955	Frank Sando (Eng)	England
1956	Alain Mimoun (Fra)	France
1957	Frank Sando (Eng)	Belgium
1958	Stanley Eldon (Eng)	England
1959	Fred Norris (Eng)	England
1960	Abdesselem Rhadi (Fra)	England
1961	Basil Heatley (Eng)	Belgium
1962	Gaston Roelants (Bel)	England
1963	Roy Fowler (Eng)	Belgium
1964	Francesco Arizmendi (Spa)	England
1965	Jean Fayolle (Fra)	England
1966	Ben Assou El Ghazi (Mor)	England
1967	Gaston Roelants (Bel)	England
1968	Mohamed Gammoudi (Tun)	England
1969	Gaston Roelants (Bel)	England
1970	Michael Tagg (Eng)	England

The first three in the International Cross-Country Championship of 1972 at Cambridge. On the left Mariano Haro, who four times in succession came second in the event, in the centre Gaston Roelants, winner on a record four occasions, and on the right Ian Stewart, third in 1972, who won in 1975 (*Keystone*)

1971	David Bedford (Eng)	England
1972	Gaston Roelants (Bel)	England
1973	Pekka Paivarinta (Fin)	Belgium
1974	Eric De Beck (Bel)	Belgium
1975	Ian Stewart (Sco)	New Zealand
1976	Carlos Lopes (Por)	England
1977	Leon Schots (Bel)	Belgium
1978	John Treacy (Ire)	France
1979	John Treacy (Ire)	England

WOMEN (race first held 1967)

Year	Individual	Team
1967	Doris Brown (USA)	England
1968	Doris Brown (USA)	USA
1969	Doris Brown (USA)	USA
1970	Doris Brown (USA)	England
1971	Doris Brown (USA)	England
1972	Joyce Smith (Eng)	England
1973	Paola Cacchi (Ita)	England
1974	Paola Cacchi (Ita)	England
1975	Julie Brown (USA)	USA
1976	Carmen Valero (Spa)	USSR
1977	Carmen Valero (Spa)	USSR
1978	Grete Waitz (Nor)	Romania
1979	Grete Waitz (Nor)	USA

CROSSWORDS

Logogriphist of the Year

The first ever Logogriphist of the Year competition (sponsored by *The Guardian* and Cutty Sark) was held 4–6 November 1977. It was a 'word weekend' of crosswords, anagrams and other word games. The word 'logogriphist' was coined by *The Guardian* with the approval of Dr J. E. Sykes of the *Oxford English Dictionary*, and describes one who is addicted to word puzzles.   **Winner:**   1977   David Meadows, Alvaston, Derby

'The Times'/Cutty Sark Championship

Sponsored by the London whisky company since 1970, the competition attracts over 3000 entries. After an initial qualifying round, competitors are obliged to complete four puzzles under gruelling examination conditions.

1970	Roy Dean (record holder for the fastest solver of a *Times* crossword)
1971	James Atkins
1972	Dr John Sykes
1973	Dr John Sykes
1974	Dr John Sykes

1975	Dr John Sykes
1976	James Atkins
1977	Dr John Sykes
1978	Eric Rodick
1979	Roy Dean

(Dr Sykes did not compete in 1976 and 1978)

CURLING

World Championships

Contested for the Scotch Cup from 1959 and for the Air Canada Silver Broom from 1968.

1959	Canada	1966	Canada	1973	Sweden
1960	Canada	1967	Scotland	1974	USA
1961	Canada	1968	Canada	1975	Switzerland
1962	Canada	1969	Canada	1976	USA
1963	Canada	1970	Canada	1977	Sweden
1964	Canada	1971	Canada	1978	USA
1965	USA	1972	Canada	1979	Norway

CUSTARD PIES

The World Custard Pie Throwing Championship

The target (face) must be 8ft 3¾in (2.53m) from the thrower who must throw a pie, with his left hand, which is no more than 10¾in (27.3cm) in diameter.

Winners since inception in 1968
1968	Custard Kings
1969	Coxheath Men
1970	Coxheath Men
1971	The Birds
1972	The Birds
1973	The Bashers
1974	The Clowns
1975	The Hadlow Haystackers
1976	The Magnificent Seven
1977	The Kent Messenger Girls
1978	Anglian Angels
1979	Anglian Angels

Scene from the 1978 World Custard Pie Championship. The 'Anglian Angels' won the event in 1978 and 1979

CYCLING

World Championships

The first cycling world championships were held for amateurs in 1893, and the first for professionals in 1895.

Track champions at each event since 1965 (with the most wins at each event) have been:

MEN
Professional

| | *Sprint* | *Pursuit* | *Motor Paced* (100km) |
| 1965 | G. Beghetto (Ita) | L. Faggin (Ita) | G. Timoner (Spa) |

1966	G. Beghetto (Ita)	L. Faggin (Ita)	R. de Loof (Bel)
1967	P. Sercu (Bel)	T. Groen (Hol)	L. Proost (Bel)
1968	G. Beghetto (Ita)	H. Porter (GB)	L. Proost (Bel)
1969	P. Sercu (Bel)	F. Bracke (Hol)	J. Oudkerk (Hol)
1970	G. Johnson (Aus)	H. Porter (GB)	E. Rudolph (Ger)
1971	L. Loeveseijn (Hol)	D. Baert (Bel)	T. Verschueren (Bel)
1972	R. van Lancker (Bel)	H. Porter (GB)	T. Verschueren (Bel)
1973	R. van Lancker (Bel)	H. Porter (GB)	C. Stam (Hol)
1974	P. Pedersen (Den)	R. Schuiten (Hol)	C. Stam (Hol)
1975	J. Nicholson (Aus)	R. Schuiten (Hol)	D. Kemper (Ger)
1976	J. Nicholson (Aus)	F. Moser (Ita)	W. Peffgen (Ger)
1977	K. Nakano (Jap)	G. Braun (Ger)	C. Stam (Hol)
1978	K. Nakano (Jap)	G. Braun (Ger)	W. Peffgen (Ger)

Most: 7 Jeff Scherens (Bel)
(1932–37, 1947)
7 Antonio Maspes (Ita)
(1955–56, 1959–62, 1964)

4 Hugh Porter (GB)
(*as above*)

6 Guillermo Timoner (Spa)
(1955, 1959–60, 1962, 1964–65)

Amateur (* = Olympic champions)

	Sprint	*Pursuit*	*Motor Paced*
1965	O. Phakadze (USSR)	T. Groen (Hol)	M. Mas (Spa)
1966	D. Morelon (Fra)	T. Groen (Hol)	P. de Wit (Hol)
1967	D. Morelon (Fra)	G. Bongers (Hol)	P. de Wit (Hol)
1968	L. Borghetti (Ita)	M. Frey (Den)	G. Grassi (Ita)
1969	D. Morelon (Fra)	X. Kurmann (Swi)	A. Boom (Hol)
1970	D. Morelon (Fra)	X. Kurmann (Swi)	C. Stam (Hol)
1971	D. Morelon (Fra)	M. Rodriguez (Col)	H. Gnas (Ger)
1972	*D. Morelon (Fra)	*K. Knudsen (Nor)	H. Gnas (Ger)
1973	D. Morelon (Fra)	K. Knudsen (Nor)	H. Gnas (Ger)
1974	A. Tkac (Cze)	H. Lutz (Ger)	J. Breuer (Ger)
1975	D. Morelon (Fra)	T. Huschke (GDR)	G. Minneboo (Hol)
1976	*A. Tkac (Cze)	*G. Braun (Ger)	G. Minneboo (Hol)
1977	H.-J. Geschke (GDR)	N. Durpisch (GDR)	G. Minneboo (Hol)
1978	A. Tkac (Cze)	D. Macha (GDR)	G. Minneboo (Hol)

Most: 8 Daniel Morelon (Fra)
(*as above*)

3 Guido Messina (Ita)
(1947–48, 1953)
3 Tiemen Groen (Hol)
(1964–66)

7 Leon Meredith (GB)
(1904–05, 1907–09, 1911, 1913)

Amateur (* = Olympic champions)
1000 Metres Time Trial

1966	P. Trentin (Fra)
1967	N. Fredborg (Den)
1968	N. Fredborg (Den)
1969	G. Sartori (Ita)
1970	N. Fredborg (Den)
1971	E. Rapp (USSR)
1972	*N. Fredborg (Den)
1973	J. Kierzkowski (Pol)
1974	E. Rapp (USSR)
1975	K.-J. Grünke (GDR)
1976	*K.-J. Grünke (GDR)
1977	L. Thoms (GDR)
1978	L. Thoms (GDR)

The great Belgian road cyclist Eddy Merckx won the Tour de France five times and the World Professional road race title three times (*UPI*)

The 1979 Dada Silver Award for the most Outstanding Photography Campaign sponsored by the *Illustrated London News*. Client: Clark Son & Morland Ltd, Agency: Cherry Hedger & Seymour Ltd (see pp 13–15)

The 1979 Nationwide Glamorous Grannies line-up. The winner was Patricia Stables (No. 16) from Brigg, South Humberside (*BBC copyright*)

Bjorn Borg, seen here winning the 1979 Wimbledon Men's Singles Championship, is the only man to have consecutively won the championship four times since the abolition of the Challenge Round in 1922 (*All Sport*)

Amateur (* = Olympics)

	Team Pursuit	Tandem Sprint	Road Race
1965	USSR	Not held	J. Botherell (Fra)
1966	Italy	Fra (D. Morelon, P. Trentin)	E. Dolman (Hol)
1967	USSR	Ita (D. Verzini, B. Gonzato)	G. Webb (GB)
1968	Italy	Ita (Gorini, G. Turrini)	V. Marcelli (Ita)
1969	USSR	GDR (H.-J. Geschke, W. Otto)	L. Mortensen (Den)
1970	W. Germany	WG (J. Barth, R. Müller)	J. Schmidt (Den)
1971	Italy	GDR (H.-J. Geschke, W. Otto)	R. Ovion (Fra)
1972	*W. Germany	USSR (V. Sements, I. Tselovalnikov)	*H. Kuiper (Hol)
1973	W. Germany	Cze (V. Vackar, M. Vymarzal)	R. Szurkowski (Pol)
1974	W. Germany	Cze (V. Vackar, M. Vymarzal)	J. Kowalski (Pol)
1975	W. Germany	not held	A. Gevers (Hol)
1976	*W. Germany	Pol (B. Kokot, J. Kotlinski)	*B. Johansson (Swe)
1977	GDR	Cze (V. Vackar, M. Vymarzal)	C. Corti (Ita)
1978	GDR	Cze (V. Vackar, M. Vymarzal)	G. Glaus (Swi)

Professional Road Race

1965	T. Simpson (GB)	1971	E. Merckx (Bel)	1976	F. Maertens (Bel)
1966	R. Altig (Ger)	1972	M. Basso (Ita)	1977	F. Moser (Ita)
1967	E. Merckx (Bel)	1973	F. Gimondi (Ita)	1978	G. Kneteman (Hol)
1968	V. Adorni (Ita)	1974	E. Merckx (Bel)		
1969	H. Ottenbroos (Hol)	1975	H. Kuiper (Hol)		
1970	J.-P. Monsere (Bel)				

Most wins: 3 Alfredo Binda (Ita) (1927, 1930, 1932); 3 Henri van Steenbergen (Bel) (1949, 1956–57); 3 Eddy Merckx (Bel) (*as above*)

WOMEN

	Sprint	Pursuit	Road Race
1965	V. Savina (USSR)	Y. Reynders (Bel)	E. Eicholz (GDR)
1966	I. Kirichenko (USSR)	B. Burton (GB)	Y. Reynders (Bel)
1967	V. Savina (USSR)	T. Garkushkina (USSR)	B. Burton (GB)
1968	I. Baguiniantz (USSR)	R. Obodovskaya (USSR)	K. Hage (Hol)
1969	G. Tsareva (USSR)	R. Obodovskaya (USSR)	A. McElmiry (USA)
1970	G. Tsareva (USSR)	T. Garkushkina (USSR)	A. Konkina (USSR)
1971	G. Tsareva (USSR)	T. Garkushkina (USSR)	A. Konkina (USSR)
1972	G. Yermolayeva (USSR)	T. Garkushkina (USSR)	G. Gambillon (Fra)
1973	S. Young (USA)	T. Garkushkina (USSR)	N. van den Broeck (Bel)
1974	T. Piltsikova (USSR)	T. Garkushkina (USSR)	G. Gambillon (Fra)
1975	S. Novarra (USA)	K. van Oosten (Hage) (Hol)	T. Fopma (Hol)
1976	S. Young (USA)	K. van Oosten (Hage) (Hol)	K. van Oosten (Hage) (Hol)
1977	G. Tsareva (USSR)	V. Kuznyetsova (USSR)	J. Bost (Fra)
1978	G. Tsareva (USSR)	K. van Oosten (Hage) (Hol)	B. Habetz (Ger)

Most: 6 Galina Yermolayeva (USSR) (1958–61, 1963, 1972)   6 Tamara Garkushkina (USSR) (*as above*)   4 Yvonne Reynders (Bel) (1959, 1961, 1963, 1966)

Tour de France

Perhaps the greatest French sporting event, the Tour de France is a stage race all round France, and in some cases into the surrounding countries. Individual winners since the race's inception in 1903:

1903	Maurice Garin (Fra)	1919	Firmin Lambot (Bel)	1931	Antonin Magne (Fra)
1904	Henri Cornet (Fra)	1920	Philippe Thys (Bel)	1932	André Leducq (Fra)
1905	Louis Trousselier (Fra)	1921	Léon Scieur (Bel)	1933	Georges Speicher (Fra)
1906	René Pottier (Fra)	1922	Firmin Lambot (Bel)	1934	Antonin Magne (Fra)
1907	Lucien Petit-Breton (Fra)	1923	Henri Pelissier (Fra)	1935	Romain Maes (Bel)
1908	Lucien Petit-Breton (Fra)	1924	Ottavio Bottecchia (Ita)	1936	Sylvere Maes (Bel)
1909	François Faber (Lux)	1925	Ottavio Bottecchia (Ita)	1937	Roger Lapebie (Fra)
1910	Octave Lapize (Fra)	1926	Lucien Buysse (Bel)	1938	Gino Bartali (Ita)
1911	Gustave Garrigou (Fra)	1927	Nicholas Frantz (Lux)	1939	Sylvere Maes (Bel)
1912	Odile Defraye (Bel)	1928	Nicholas Frantz (Lux)	1947	Jean Robic (Fra)
1913	Philippe Thys (Bel)	1929	Maurice Dewaele (Bel)	1948	Gino Bartali (Ita)
1914	Philippe Thys (Bel)	1930	André Leducq (Fra)	1949	Fausto Coppi (Ita)

1950	Ferdinand Kubler (Swi)	1960	Gastone Nencini (Ita)	1970	Eddy Merckx (Bel)
1951	Hugo Koblet (Swi)	1961	Jacques Anquetil (Fra)	1971	Eddy Merckx (Bel)
1952	Fausto Coppi (Ita)	1962	Jacques Anquetil (Fra)	1972	Eddy Merckx (Bel)
1953	Louison Bobet (Fra)	1963	Jacques Anquetil (Fra)	1973	Luis Ocana (Spa)
1954	Louison Bobet (Fra)	1964	Jacques Anquetil (Fra)	1974	Eddy Merckx (Bel)
1955	Louison Bobet (Fra)	1965	Felice Gimondi (Ita)	1975	Bernard Thevenet (Fra)
1956	Roger Walkowiak (Fra)	1966	Lucien Aimar (Fra)	1976	Lucien van Impe (Bel)
1957	Jacques Anquetil (Fra)	1967	Roger Pingeon (Fra)	1977	Bernard Thevenet (Fra)
1958	Charly Gaul (Lux)	1968	Jan Janssen (Hol)	1978	Bernard Hinault (Fra)
1959	Federico Bahamontes (Spa)	1969	Eddy Merckx (Bel)	1979	Bernard Hinault (Fra)

Tour of Britain

The Tour of Britain, first held in 1951, is a stage race for amateurs.

	Individual	*Team*		*Individual*	*Team*
1951	Ian Steel (GB)	Viking	1966	Josef Gawliczek (Pol)	USSR
1952	Kenneth Russell (GB)	BSA	1967	Les West (GB)	USSR
1953	Gordon Thomas (GB)	Wearwell	1968	Gosta Pettersson (Swe)	USSR
1954	Eugene Tamburlini (Fra)	France	1969	Fedor Den Hertog (Hol)	Poland
1955	Anthony Hewson (GB)	Viking	1970	Jiri Mainus (Cze)	Poland
1956–57	Not held		1971	Fedor Den Hertog (Hol)	Holland
1958	Richard Durlacher (Aut)	Belgium	1972	Hennie Kuiper (Hol)	Holland
1959	Bill Bradley (GB)	Belgium	1973	Piet van Katwijk (Hol)	Sweden
1960	Bill Bradley (GB)	England	1974	Roy Schuiten (Hol)	Holland
1961	Billy Holmes (GB)	Northern	1975	Bernt Johansson (Swe)	Czechoslovakia
1962	Eugen Pokorny (Pol)	England	1976	Bill Nickson (GB)	Great Britain
1963	Peter Chisman (GB)	Poland	1977	Said Gusseinov (USSR)	USSR
1964	Arthur Metcalfe (GB)	England	1978	Jan Brzezny (Pol)	USSR
1965	Les West (GB)	Poland	1979	Yuriy Kachinine (USSR)	USSR

CYCLO-CROSS

The first cross-country world championships were held in 1950 and since 1967 have been divided into amateur and professional categories.

OPEN (1950–1966)

1950	Jean Robic (Fra)
1951–53	Roger Rondeaux (Fra) (3)
1954–58	André Dufraisse (Fra)
1959	Renato Longo (Ita)
1960–61	Rolf Wolfshohl (Ger) (2)
1962	Renato Longo (Ita)
1963	Rolf Wolfshohl (Ger)
1964–65	Renato Longo (Ita) (2)
1966	Eric de Vlaeminck (Bel)

AMATEUR

1967	Michel Pelchat (Fra)
1968	Roger de Vlaeminck (Bel)
1969	René Declercq (Bel)
1970–71	Robert Vermeier (Bel)
1972	Norbert de Deckere (Bel)
1973	Klaus-Peter Thaler (Ger)
1974–75	Robert Vermeier (Bel) (2)
1976	Klaus-Peter Thaler (Ger)
1977	Robert Vermeier (Bel)
1978	Roland Liboton (Bel)
1979	Vito di Tano (Ita)

PROFESSIONAL

1967	Renato Longo (Ita)
1968–73	Eric de Vlaeminck (Bel)
1974	Albert Van Damme (Bel)
1975	Roger de Vlaeminck (Bel)
1976–79	Albert Zweifel (Swi)

DANCING

Carl Alan Awards

Originated in 1954 by Eric D. Morley, over 300 Carl Alans have been presented to date. The awards cover amateur and professional ballroom dancers, formation team coaches, dance teachers, band leaders, groups, and singers.

There are approximately twelve awards made each year, and winners include the Beatles and Abba, bandleaders like Victor Silvester and Joe Loss, jazz musicians like Kenny Ball and Acker Bilk and of course a host of dancers. (*See* Mecca p. 99.)

BBC Inter-Regional 'Come Dancing' Championship

This is the final award in the popular television ballroom dancing series which is organised each year by the BBC.

1956	South of England
1957	South of England
1958	Wales
1959	Midlands
1960	South London
1961	West Midlands
1962	North West
1963	North London
1964	South London
1965	Home Counties North
1966	Home Counties North
1967	North West
1968	Home Counties South
1969	Home Counties North
1970	North
1971	Wales
1972	North
1973	South Wales
1974	England
1975	Midlands and West
1976	Midlands and West
1977	Midlands and West
1978	Midlands and West

Stuart and Lesley Cole dancing the Paso Doble for Midlands and West in the final of the 1977 Come Dancing competition (*BBC copyright photograph*)

FORMATION TEAM TROPHY WINNERS

1958	Sybil Marks and Phil Williams, Cardiff
1959	Thorpe-Hancock School of Dance, Mansfield
1960	Frank and Peggy Spencer, Penge
1961	Laura Dixon School of Dance, Birmingham
1962	Frank and Peggy Spencer, Penge
1963	Russell-Vale Team (N. London), and James Stevenson Team (E. Midlands)
1964	Frank and Peggy Spencer, Penge
1965	Ada Unsworth
1966	Tony Smith
1967	John Stead, and Frank and Peggy Spencer
1968	Frank and Peggy Spencer
1969	Stanley Jackson
1970	Jack and Joyce Briggs
1971	Sybil Marks
1972	Sybil Marks, and Jack and Joyce Briggs
1973	Jack and Joyce Briggs
1974	Stanley Jackson, and Sybil Marks
1975	Janet and Stanley Jackson
1976	John and Joan Knight
1977	Jack and Joyce Briggs
1978	Ted Burroughs

Mecca

The following are the major championships and their winners organised by Mecca.

CARL-ALAN AWARD AMATEUR DANCING CHAMPIONSHIP

1969	Richard Gleave and Janet Wade
1970	Stan Shippy and Iris Kane
1971	Michael Barr and Vicky Green
1972	Alan and Hazel Fletcher
1973	Frank Venables and Lynda Horwood
1974	Peter Maxwell and Lyn Harman
1975	Glen and Lynette Boyce
1976	Keith and Judy Clifton
1977	Greg Smith and Marion Alleyne
1978	Stephen and Lindsey Hillier, and David Sycamore and Denise Weaver

CARL-ALAN AWARD PROFESSIONAL DANCING CHAMPIONSHIP

1969	Anthony Hurley and Fay Saxton
1970	Michael Needham and Monica Dunsford
1971	Anthony Hurley and Fay Saxton, and John and Betty Westley
1972	Richard Gleave and Janet Wade
1973	Richard and Janet Gleave
1974	Michael Stylianos and Lorna Lee
1975	Richard and Janet Gleave, and Robin and Rita Short
1976	Peter Maxwell and Lyn Harman
1977	Alan and Hazel Fletcher
1978	Michael and Vicky Barr

WORLD AMATEUR MODERN DANCING CHAMPIONSHIP

1969   Richard Gleave and Janet Wade
1970   Richard Gleave and Janet Wade
1971   Byron Charlton and Maureen Alexander
1972   Michael Barr and Vicky Green
1973   Michael Barr and Vicky Green
1974   Frank Venables and Lynda Horwood
1975   Glen and Lynette Boyce
1976   Bob and Barbara Grover
1977   Greg Smith and Marion Alleyne
1978   Stephen and Lindsay Hillier

WORLD AMATEUR LATIN DANCING CHAMPIONSHIP

1969   Raymond Root and Francis Spires
1970   P. Neubeck and H. Kaufmann
1971   P. Neubeck and H. Kaufmann
1972   Alan and Hazel Fletcher
1973   Alan and Hazel Fletcher
1974   Peter Maxwell and Lyn Harman
1975   Ian and Ruth Walker
1976   Espen and Kirsten Salberg
1977   Jeffrey Dobinson and Debbie-Lee London
1978   David Sycamore and Denise Weaver
1979   David Sycamore and Denise Weaver

WORLD PROFESSIONAL MODERN DANCING CHAMPIONSHIP

1969   Peter Eggleton and Brenda Winslade
1970   Peter Eggleton and Brenda Winslade
1971   Anthony Hurley and Fay Saxton
1972   Anthony Hurley and Fay Saxton
1973   Richard and Janet Gleave
1974   Richard and Janet Gleave
1975   Richard and Janet Gleave
1976   Richard and Janet Gleave
1977   Richard and Janet Gleave
1978   Richard and Janet Gleave

WORLD PROFESSIONAL LATIN DANCING CHAMPIONSHIP

1969   Rudolf and Mechthild Trautz
1970   Rudolf and Mechthild Trautz
1971   Rudolf and Mechthild Trautz
1972   Wolfgang and Evelyn Opitz
1973   Hans Peter and Ingeborg Fischer
1974   Hans Peter and Ingeborg Fischer
1975   Hans Peter and Ingeborg Fischer
1976   Peter Maxwell and Lynn Harman
1977   Alan and Hazel Fletcher
1978   Alan and Hazel Fletcher

DARTS

World Cup

First held in December 1977 at the Wembley Conference Centre, London.

1977   Team Winners: Wales
        Individual Winner: Leighton Rees (Wal)

World Masters Individual

First held in the West Centre Hotel, London, December 1974.

1974   Cliff Inglis (Eng)   1977   Eric Bristow (Eng)
1975   Alan Evans (Wal)   1978   Ronnie Davis (Eng)
1976   John Lowe (Eng)

British Open Championship

First held in January 1975.

1975   Alan Evans (Wal)   1978   Eric Bristow (Eng)
1976   Jack North (Eng)   1979   Tony Brown (Eng)
1977   John Lowe (Eng)

Embassy World Professional Championship

First held in February 1978 in Stoke-on-Trent.

1978   Leighton Rees (Wal)   1979   John Lowe (Eng)

British Gold Cup

First held in November 1978 in Stoke-on-Trent.

1978   Gold Cup Singles Champion: John Lowe (Eng)
        Gold Cup Pairs Champions: Tim Stedman & Bill Duddy (Eng)

Nations Cup

Team Championships first held in March 1977 at West Centre Hotel, London.

1977 Scotland
1978 Sweden
1979 England

Home International Series

First held in 1973 in Bristol (England, Ireland, Scotland & Wales).

1973 England
1974 England
1975 Wales
1976 Scotland & England
1977 Wales
1978 England

Europe Cup

First held in September 1978 in Copenhagen, Denmark.

1978 Team Winners: England
      Individual Champion: John Lowe (Eng)

John Lowe with a triple bullseye and a double armful of Danish fans, after winning the British Open Darts Championship in 1977 (*Syndication International*)

DISC JOCKEYS

Sounds Alive with Tea

Amid the plethora of dance competitions that sprang up in 1978 with the current interest in disco dancing, the Tea Council sponsored a very different competition of great interest to that other integral part of the disco scene – the DJ.

'Sounds Alive With Tea' is what they called their contest to find Britain's best young amateur DJ. It was open to both sexes (although sadly no ladies won through to the final) and the only other qualification was that entrants had to be between 18 and 25.

A prize of £1000 worth of DJ disco equipment and an appearance on Kid Jensen's BBC Radio show was offered and there were 500 entrants. At the Grand Final, held at the Empire Ballroom, Leicester Square, London, the ten finalists had to impress a panel of judges. The aim for the young contestants was stated to be 'to get the crowd dancing, keep them dancing, project a good personality – but not get in the way of the music'.

The winner was Graham Thornton, age 21, a call-boy for Yorkshire TV from Leeds.

DISCO DANCING

British Disco Dancing Championship

Organised for the first time in 1978, and featured on London Weekend Television's Bruce Forsyth's Big Night.

1978 Grant Santino

United Kingdom Disco Doubles Competition

This was organised in 1979 at Regine's Nightclub in Kensington, London, and it was featured

on BBC Television's Nationwide.
The winners were Everet Jervis and Rita Maria Boxhill.

Above: **Grant Santino winner of the 1978 British Disco Dancing Championship. The competition was featured on London Weekend Television's Bruce Forsyth's Big Night** (*London Weekend Television*)

Right: **Phil Ton and Karen Sparks, dancing partners in Nationwide's competition Disco Doubles** (*BBC copyright photograph*)

The World Disco Dancing Championships

Organised by EMI Dancing Ltd, the first competition was held in London in December 1978. There were thirty six competitors, including only five women dancers, and the prizes were valued at over £15 000. The winner for 1978–79 was Takaaki Dan (Japan).

DIVING (*See* Swimming)

DOGS

Cruft's Dog Show

Although the first dog show was held at Newcastle-upon-Tyne in 1859, Cruft's was not started until 1886, but this famous national dog show now enjoys both tremendous popular interest and an international reputation. Before 1928 there was no award of Best-in-Show.

BEST IN SHOW WINNERS

1928   Greyhound. Primely Sceptre. H. Whitley
1929   Scottish Terrier. Heather Necessity. E. Chapman
1930   Spaniel (Cocker). Luckystar of Ware. H. S. Lloyd
1931   Spaniel (Cocker). Luckystar of Ware. H. S. Lloyd
1932   Retriever (Labrador). Bramshaw Bob. Lorna Countess Howe
1933   Retriever (Labrador). Bramshaw Bob. Lorna Countess Howe
1934   Greyhound. Southball Moonstone. B. Hartland Worden
1935   Pointer. Pennine Prima Donna. A. Eggleston

1936   Chow Chow. Ch Choonam Hung Kwong. Mrs V. A. M. Mannooch
1937   Retriever (Labrador). Ch. Cheveralla Ben of Banchory. Lorna Countess Howe
1938   Spaniel (Cocker). Exquisite Model of Ware. H. S. Lloyd
1939   Spaniel (Cocker). Exquisite Model of Ware. H. S. Lloyd
1948   Spaniel (Cocker). Tracey Witch of Ware. H. S. Lloyd
1950   Spaniel (Cocker). Tracey Witch of Ware. H. S. Lloyd

1951 Welsh Terrier. Twynstar Dyma-Fi. Fl. Capt. and Mrs I. M. Thomas
1952 Bulldog. Ch. Noways Chuckles. J. T. Barnard
1953 Great Dane. Ch. Elch Elder of Ouborough. W. G. Siggers
1954 (Cancelled)
1955 Poodle (Standard). Ch. Tzigane Aggri of Nashend. Mrs A. Proctor
1956 Greyhound. Treetops Golden Falcon. Mrs W. de Casembroot and Miss H. Greenish
1957 Keeshond. Ch. Volkrijk of Vorden. Mrs I. M. Tucker
1958 Pointer. Ch. Chiming Bells. Mrs W. Parkinson
1959 Welsh Terrier. Ch. Sandstorm Saracen. Mesdames Leach and Thomas
1960 Irish Wolfhound. Sulhamstead Merman. Mrs Nagle and Miss Clark
1961 Airedale Terrier. Ch. Riverina Tweedsbairn. Miss P. McCaughey and Mrs D. Schuth
1962 Fox Terrier (Wire). Ch. Crackwyn Cockspur. H. L. Gill
1963 Lakeland Terrier. Rogerholm Recruit. W. Rogers
1964 English Setter. Sh. Ch. Silbury Soames of Madavale. Mrs A. Williams
1965 Alsatian (GSD). Ch. Fenton of Kentwood. Miss S. H. Godden
1966 Poodle (Toy). Oakington Puckshill Amber Sunblush. Mrs C. E. Perry
1967 Lakeland Terrier. Ch. Stingray of Derryabah. Mr and Mrs W. Postlewaite
1968 Dalmatian. Ch. Fanhill Faune. Mrs E. J. Woodyatt
1969 Alsatian (GSD). Ch. Hendrawen's Nibelung of Charavigne. Mr and Mrs E. J. White
1970 Pyrenean Mountain Dog. Bergerie Knur. Mr and Mrs F. S. Prince
1971 Alsatian (GSD). Ch. Ramacon Swashbuckler. Prince Ahmed Husain

The Best in Show – Crufts 1979 (*Hartley Campbell*)

1972 Bull Terrier. Ch. Abraxas Audacity. Miss V. Drummond-Dick
1973 Cavalier King Charles Spaniel. Alansmere Aquarius. Messrs Hall and Evans
1974 St Bernard. Ch. Burtonswood Bossy Boots. Miss M. Hindes
1975 Fox Terrier (Wire). Ch. Brookewire Brandy of Layven. Messrs Benelli and Dondina
1976 West Highland White Terrier. Ch. Dianthus Buttons. Mrs K. Newstead
1977 English Setter. Bournehouse Dancing Master. Mr G. F. Williams
1978 Fox Terrier (Wire). Ch. Harrowhill Huntsman. Miss E. Howles
1979 Kerry Blue Terrier. Ch. Callaghan of Leander. Mrs W. Streatfield

236

DRAMA

Pulitzer Prizes

The pre-eminent award for play writers in the United States (*see* Pulitzer Prizes).

1918 Jesse Lynch Williams, *Why Marry?*
1920 Eugene O'Neill, *Beyond the Horizon*
1921 Zona Gale, *Miss Lulu Bett*
1922 Eugene O'Neill, *Anna Christie*
1923 Owen Davis, *Icebound*
1924 Hatcher Hughes, *Hell-Bent for Heaven*
1925 Sidney Howard, *They Knew What They Wanted*
1926 George Kelly, *Craig's Wife*
1927 Paul Green, *In Abraham's Bosom*
1928 Eugene O'Neill, *Strange Interlude*
1929 Elmer Rice, *Street Scene*
1930 Marc Connelly, *The Green Pastures*
1931 Susan Glaspell, *Alison's House*
1932 George S. Kaufman, Morris Ryskind and Ira Gershwin, *Of Thee I Sing*
1933 Maxwell Anderson, *Both Your Houses*
1934 Sidney Kingsley, *Men in White*
1935 Zoe Akins, *The Old Maid*
1936 Robert E. Sherwood, *Idiot's Delight*

1937 George S. Kaufman and Moss Hart, *You Can't Take It With You*
1938 Thornton Wilder, *Our Town*
1939 Robert E. Sherwood, *Abe Lincoln in Illinois*
1940 William Saroyan, *The Time of Your Life*
1941 Robert E. Sherwood, *There Shall Be No Night*
1943 Thornton Wilder, *The Skin of Our Teeth*
1945 Mary Chase, *Harvey*
1946 Russel Crouse and Howard Lindsay, *State of the Union*
1948 Tennessee Williams, *A Streetcar Named Desire*
1949 Arthur Miller, *Death of a Salesman*
1950 Richard Rodgers, Oscar Hammerstein (2nd) and Joshua Logan, *South Pacific*
1952 Joseph Kramm, *The Shrike*
1953 William Inge, *Picnic*
1954 John Patrick, *Teahouse of the August Moon*
1955 Tennessee Williams, *Cat on a Hot Tin Roof*
1956 Frances Goodrich and Albert Hackett, *The Diary of Anne Frank*

1957 Eugene O'Neill, *Long Day's Journey Into Night*
1958 Ketti Frings, *Look Homeward, Angel*
1959 Archibald MacLeish, *J.B.*
1960 George Abbott, Jerome Weidman, Sheldon Harnick and Jerry Bock, *Fiorello*
1961 Tad Mosel, *All the Way Home*
1962 Frank Loesser and Abe Burrows, *How To Succeed In Business Without Really Trying*
1965 Frank D. Gilroy, *The Subject Was Roses*
1967 Edward Albee, *A Delicate Balance*
1969 Howard Sackler, *The Great White Hope*

1970 Charles Gordone, *No Place to Be Somebody*
1971 Paul Zindel, *The Effect of Gamma Rays on Man-in-the Moon Marigolds*
1973 Jason Miller, *That Championship Season*
1975 Edward Albee, *Seascape*
1976 Michael Bennett, James Kirkwood, Nicholas Dante, Marvin Hamlisch, Edward Kleban, *A Chorus Line*
1977 Michael Cristofer, *The Shadow Box*
1978 Donald L. Coburn, *The Gin Game*

DRESSAGE (*See* Equestrian Events)

DRIVING

Driver of the Year

Run by the BBC, the competition aims to find the best amateur driver in Britain. Both men and women are encouraged to enter this motor-sport-orientated competition, which tests driving skills in a variety of situations and vehicles.

Competitors who pass the preliminaries are invited to take part in regional heats which, together with the national grand final, are shown on BBC Television. The competition is organised with the help of the RAC Motor Sports Division and the major British Motor manufacturers.

1977   Christopher Townrow
1978–79 Sam Brennan

RAC L Driver of the Year Competition

	Winner	Age		Winner	Age
1964	Stephen Jackson	18	1971	Anthony Powell	17
1965	David Evenett	18	1972	Keith Taylor	18
1966	Peter Jeffery	18	1973	Malcolm Smith	19
1967	Gordon Aitchison	41	1974	Stephen Mann	20
1968	Gay Harker	17½	1975	Christopher Hill	18
1969	Barry Garner	21	1976	David Wright	17
1970	Paul Nuttall	18	The competition has not been held since 1976.		

DUELLING

This ancient way of settling disputes has, for many years, been illegal. In 1613 Charles I issued a proclamation against duelling and this was reinforced by a decree of Star Chamber of 1614. The present prohibition of duelling is contained in the 1881 Army Act. Despite this prohibition some notable contests have taken place.

May 1652   Lord Chandos killed Colonel Compton.
Jan 1668   The Duke of Buckingham, with Holmes and and Jenkins, fought the Earl of Shrewsbury, with Sir J. Talbot and Bernard Howard; Jenkins was killed, the Earl mortally wounded, and the rest wounded more or less severely.

The duel in November 1712 between the Duke of Hamilton and Lord Mohun resulted in both their deaths
(*Mary Evans Picture Library*)

Nov 1712	Lord Mohun and the Duke of Hamilton, in Hyde Park; both killed.	Jun 1808	Captain Boyd killed by Major Campbell (who was hanged in Oct).
Jan 1765	Lord Byron killed Mr Chaworth.	Sep 1809	Lord Castlereagh wounded George Canning.
Nov 1779	C. J. Fox wounded by Mr Adair.		
Mar 1780	Mr Fullerton wounded Lord Shelburne.	Jan 1815	Daniel O'Connell killed Mr D'Esterre.
Jun 1782	Rev. Mr Allen killed Lloyd Dulaney.	Aug 1827	Rev. Mr Hodgson wounded Mr Grady.
May 1789	The Duke of York (second son of George III) and Colonel Lennox (later Duke of Richmond); neither injured.	Nov 1835	Mr Roebuck, MP, and Mr Black, editor of the *Morning Chronicle.*
May 1798	Wm. Pitt the Younger and George Tierney	Sep 1840	The Earl of Cardigan wounded Captain Tuckett (the Earl was tried in the House of Lords, but acquitted).

ECONOMICS
Nobel Economics Prize

1969	Ragnar Frisch (Nor)	1974	Gunnar Myrdal (Swe)
	Jan Tinbergen (Hol)		Friedrich A. von Hayek (Aut)
1970	Paul A. Samuelson (USA)	1975	Leonid V. Kantorovich (USSR)
1971	Simon Kuznets (USA)		Tjalling C. Koopmans (USA) (Dutch-born)
1972	Kenneth J. Arrow (USA)	1976	Milton Friedman (USA)
	Sir John R. Hicks (GB)	1977	Bertil Ohlin (Swe)
1973	Vassily Leontief (USA) (Russian-born)		James Edward Meade (GB)
		1978	Herbert Simon (USA)

EISTEDDFOD
Royal National Eisteddfod of Wales

The principal annual event in the cultural life of Wales. Competitions range across a wide field of literature, music and the arts, the medium of communication being Welsh.

WINNERS OF THE BARDIC CHAIR AND CROWN FOR POETRY FROM 1900 (founded 1861)

	Chair	Crown
1900	Pedrog (Rev. John Owen Williams)	Job (Rev. John Thomas Job)
1901	Dyfed (Rev. Evan Rees)	Gwili (Rev. John Gwili Jenkins)
1902	T. Gwynn Jones	Robert Silyn Roberts
1903	Job (Rev. John Thomas Job)	Rhuddawr (Rev. John Evans Davies)
1904	J. Machreth Rees	Machno (Rev. Richard Machno Humphreys)
1905		Mafonwy (Thomas Mafonwy Davies)
1906	Rev. John James Williams	Rev. Hugh Emyr Davies
1907	Thomas Davies	Rev. John Dyfnallt Owen
1908	Rev. John James Williams	Emyr (Rev. Hugh Emyr Davies)
1909	T. Gwynn Jones	W. J. Gruffydd
1910	R. Williams Parry	Crwys (Rev. William Crwys Williams)
1911	Gwilym Ceiriog (W. Roberts)	Crwys (Rev. William Crwys Williams)
1912	T. H. Parry-Williams	T. H. Parry-Williams
1913	Sarnicol (Thomas Jacob Thomas)	Wil Ifan (Rev. William Evans)
1915	T. H. Parry-Williams	T. H. Parry-Williams
1916	J. Ellis Williams	
1917	Hedd Wyn	Wil Ifan (Rev. William Evans)
1918	Job (Rev. John Thomas Job)	Rev. D. Emrys Lewis
1919	Cledlyn Davies	Crwys (Rev. William Crwys Williams)
1920		Rev. James Evans
1921	Meuryn (Robert John Rowlands)	Cynan (Rev. Albert Evans Jones)
1922	J. Lloyd-Jones	Rev. Robert Beynon
1923	Cledlyn Davies	Cynan (Rev. Albert Evans Jones)
1924	Cynan (Rev. Albert Evans Jones)	Edward Prosser Rhys
1925	Dewi Morgan	Wil Ifan (Rev. William Evans)
1926	Gwenallt (David James Jones)	Dewi Emrys (Rev. David Emrys James)
1927		Caradog Prichard
1928		Caradog Prichard

1929	Dewi Emrys (Rev. David Emrys James)	Caradog Prichard
1930	Dewi Emrys (Rev. David Emrys James)	Gwilym Myrddin (William Jones)
1931	Gwenallt (David James Jones)	Cynan (Rev. Albert Evans Jones)
1932	Rev. D. J. Davies	Rev. Thomas Eurig Davies
1933	Trefin (Rev. Edgar Phillips)	Rev. Simon B. Jones
1934	Rev. William Morris	Rev. Thomas Eurig Davies
1935	Gwyndaf (Rev. E. Gwyndaf Evans)	Gwilym R. Jones
1936	Rev. Simon B. Jones	David Jones
1937	T. Rowland Hughes	J. M. Edwards
1938	Gwilym R. Jones	Edgar H. Thomas
1939		
1940	T. Rowland Hughes	
1941	Rolant o Fôn (Roland Jones)	J. M. Edwards
1942		Rev. Herman Jones
1943	Dewi Emrys (Rev. David Emrys James)	Rev. Dafydd Owen
1944	D. Lloyd Jenkins	J. M. Edwards
1945	Tom Parri-Jones	
1946	Geraint Bowen	Rev. Rhydwen Williams
1947	John Eilian	Rev. Griffith John Roberts
1948	Dewi Emrys (Rev. David Emrys Jones)	Rev. Euros Bowen
1949	Rolant o Fôn (Roland Jones)	John Eilian
1950	Rev. Gwilym R. Tilsley	Rev. Euros Bowen
1951	Brinley Richards	T. Glyn Davies
1952	John Evans	
1953	Rev. Erni Llwyd Williams	Dilys Cadwaladr
1954	John Evans	Rev. Erni Llwyd Williams
1955	Rev. Gwilym Ceri Jones	Rev. W. J. Gruffydd
1956	Mathonwy Hughes	
1957	Rev. Gwilym R. Tilsley	Dyfnallt Morgan
1958	T. Llew Jones	Llewelyn Jones
1959	T. Llew Jones	Tom Huws
1960		Rev. W. J. Gruffydd
1961	Rev. Emrys Edwards	Rev. L. Haydn Lewis
1962	Caradog Prichard	Rev. D. Emlyn Lewis
1963		Tom Parri-Jones
1964	Rev. R. Bryn Williams	Rev. Rhydwen Williams
1965	W. D. Williams	Tom Parri-Jones
1966	Dio Jones	Dafydd Jones
1967	Emrys Roberts	Eluned Phillips
1968	Rev. R. Bryn Williams	Rev. Lewis Haydn Lewis
1969	James Nicholas	Rev. Dafydd Rowlands
1970	Tomi Evans	Bryan Martin Davies
1971	Emrys Roberts	Bryan Martin Davies
1972	Rev. Dafydd Owen	Rev. Dafydd Rowlands
1973	Alan Llwyd	Alan Llwyd
1974	Moses Glyn Jones	W. R. P. George
1975	Gerallt Lloyd Owen	Elwyn Roberts
1976	Alan Llwyd	Alan Llwyd
1977	Donald Evans	Donald Evans
1978		Siôn Eirian

ELECTIONS

WINNERS OF GENERAL ELECTIONS IN GREAT BRITAIN 1900–1979

		Liberal	Labour	Others	Turnout (per cent)
28 Sep–24 Oct 1900	CONSERVATIVE 402	184	2	82	74·6

					Turnout (per cent)
12 Jan–7 Feb 1906	LIBERAL 400	Conservative 157	Labour 30	Others 83	82.6
14 Jan–9 Feb 1910	LIBERAL 275	Conservative 273	Labour 40	Others 82	86.6
2–19 Dec 1910	LIBERAL 272	Conservative 272	Labour 42	Others 84	81.1
14 Dec 1918	CONSERVATIVE 383	Liberal 161	Labour 73	Others 90	58.9
15 Nov 1922	CONSERVATIVE 345	Labour 142	Liberal 116	Others 12	71.3
6 Dec 1923	CONSERVATIVE* 258	Labour 191	Liberal 159	Others 7	70.8
29 Oct 1924	CONSERVATIVE 419	Labour 151	Liberal 40	Others 5	76.6
30 May 1929	LABOUR 288	Conservative 260	Liberal 59	Others 8	76.1
27 Oct 1931	CONSERVATIVE 521	Labour 52	Liberal 37	Others 5	76.3
14 Nov 1935	CONSERVATIVE 432	Labour 154	Liberal 20	Others 9	71.2
5 July 1945	LABOUR 393	Conservative 213	Liberal 12	Others 22	72.7
23 Feb 1950	LABOUR 315	Conservative 298	Liberal 9	Others 3	84.0
25 Oct 1951	CONSERVATIVE 321	Labour 295	Liberal 6	Others 3	82.5
25 May 1955	CONSERVATIVE 344	Labour 277	Liberal 6	Others 3	76.7
8 Oct 1959	CONSERVATIVE 365	Labour 258	Liberal 6	Others 1	78.8
15 Oct 1964	LABOUR 317	Conservative 303	Liberal 9	Others 1	77.1
31 Mar 1966	LABOUR 363	Conservative 253	Liberal 12	Others 2	75.9
18 June 1970	CONSERVATIVE 330	Labour 288	Liberal 6	Others 6	72.0
28 February 1974	LABOUR 301	Conservative 297	Liberal 14	Others 23	78.8
10 Oct 1974	LABOUR 319	Conservative 277	Liberal 13	Others 26	72.8
3 May 1979	CONSERVATIVE 339	Labour 268	Liberal 11	Others 17	76.0

*Although the Conservatives won the most seats, Labour went on to form a minority government

Margaret Thatcher in buoyant mood, in the Conservative Headquarters, as she heads for victory for the Conservatives on 3 May 1979. She is Britain's first woman prime minister (*Popperfoto*)

FAMOUS BY-ELECTION WINNERS SINCE 1958

	Party	Constituency	Date	Remarks
Mark Bonham Carter	Liberal	Torrington	27 Mar 1958	First Liberal victory at a by-election since 1929.
Eric Lubbock	Liberal	Orpington	14 Mar 1962	The most sensational Liberal victory of the 1960s. The party swept to victory in a safe Tory seat.
Sir Alec Douglas-Home	Conservative	Kinross & W. Perthshire	7 Nov 1963	The by-election in which the former 14th Earl of Home returned to the Commons as Sir Alec Douglas-Home.
Ronald Buxton	Conservative	Leyton	21 Jan 1965	Defeated Labour's Foreign Secretary Patrick Gordon Walker in a normally safe East London Labour stronghold.
David Steel	Liberal	Roxburgh, Selkirk and Peebles	24 Mar 1965	David Steel won a safe Conservative seat to become the 'baby of the House' and eventual Liberal Party leader.
Gwynfor Evans	Plaid Cymru	Carmarthen	14 July 1966	The first – and so far the only – Welsh Nationalist to win a seat in a by-election.
Winifred Ewing	Scottish National Party	Hamilton	2 Nov 1967	The first SNP by-election victory since the party won Motherwell in a wartime by-election in April 1945. Hamilton heralded the revival of the SNP.
Don Williams	Conservative	Dudley	28 Mar 1968	The by-election which saw the largest swing ever recorded to the Conservatives during the 1966–70 Wilson Government.
Cyril Smith	Liberal	Rochdale	26 Oct 1972	First of the famous series of Liberal by-election victories of 1972–1973.
Graham Tope	Liberal	Sutton & Cheam	7 Dec 1972	A sensational Liberal victory in one of the safest Tory areas – the London suburbs.
Dick Taverne	Democratic Labour	Lincoln	1 Mar 1973	Dick Taverne won a personal triumph as a Democratic Labour Candidate having previously been the town's Labour MP.
Margo MacDonald	Scottish National Party	Glasgow Govan	Oct 1973	The first SNP by-election victory since Hamilton in 1967.
R. G. Hodgson	Conservative	Walsall North	4 Nov 1976	The safe Labour stronghold formerly held by John Stonehouse fell on a swing of 22.6 per cent to the Conservatives – the largest swing of the 1974–79 Parliament to a Conservative.
Austin Mitchell	Labour	Grimsby	28 Apr 1977	Labour's best result of the 1974–79 Parliament – held the same day that Ashfield fell to the Tories on a 20.8 per cent swing.
David Alton	Liberal	Liverpool Edge Hill	29 Mar 1979	A sweeping Liberal victory by 8133 votes in a hitherto safe Labour seat. The 32 per cent swing to the Liberals was the highest in post-war politics.

European Parliament

The first direct elections to the 410-member European Parliament took place in June 1979. In Great Britain the result was as follows:

Party	Votes	Votes (per cent)	Seats
Conservative	6 504 481	50.6	60
Labour	4 253 210	33.0	17
Liberal	1 690 600	13.1	—
Others	421 553	3.3	1 (SNP)

In Northern Ireland, where proportional representation was used, the three MPs elected were: Rev. Ian Paisley (Democratic Unionist): John Hume (SDLP) and John Taylor (Official Unionist).

AMERICAN PRESIDENTIAL ELECTIONS 1789–1976

	Presidential Candidates	*Party*	*Electoral Vote*
1789	George Washington	No party	69
	John Adams	No party	34
	Scattering	No party	35
	Votes not cast	—	8
1792	George Washington	Federalist	132
	John Adams	Federalist	77
	George Clinton	Anti-Federalist	50
	Thomas Jefferson	Anti-Federalist	4
	Aaron Burr	Anti-Federalist	1
	Votes not cast	—	6
1796	John Adams	Federalist	71
	Thomas Jefferson	Dem-Rep	68
	Thomas Pinckney	Federalist	59
	Aaron Burr	Dem-Rep	30
	Scattering	—	48
1800	Thomas Jefferson	Dem-Rep	73
	Aaron Burr	Dem-Rep	73
	John Adams	Federalist	65
	Charles C. Pinckney	Federalist	64
	John Jay	Federalist	1
1804	Thomas Jefferson	Dem-Rep	162
	Charles C. Pinckney	Federalist	14
1808	James Madison	Dem-Rep	122
	Charles C. Pinckney	Federalist	47
	George Clinton	Dem-Rep	6
	Votes not cast	—	1
1812	James Madison	Dem-Rep	128
	De Witt Clinton	Federalist	89
	Votes not cast	—	1
1816	James Monroe	Dem-Rep	183
	Rufus King	Federalist	34
	Votes not cast	—	4
1820	James Monroe	Dem-Rep	231
	John Quincy Adams	Ind (no party)	1
	Votes not cast	—	3
1824	John Quincy Adams	No party	84
	Andrew Jackson	No party	99
	William H. Crawford	No party	41
	Henry Clay	No party	37
1828	Andrew Jackson	Democratic	178
	John Quincy Adams	Natl Rep	83
1832	Andrew Jackson	Democratic	219
	Henry Clay	Natl Rep	49
	John Floyd	Ind (no party)	11
	William Wirt	Antimasonic	7
	Votes not cast	—	2
1836	Martin Van Buren	Democratic	170
	William H. Harrison	Whig	73
	Hugh L. White	Whig	26
	Daniel Webster	Whig	14
	W. P. Mangum	Ind (no party)	11
1840	William H. Harrison	Whig	234
	Martin Van Buren	Democratic	60
1844	James K. Polk	Democratic	170
	Henry Clay	Whig	105
1848	Zachary Taylor	Whig	163
	Lewis Cass	Democratic	127
1852	Franklin Pierce	Democratic	254
	Winfield Scott	Whig	42
1856	James Buchanan	Democratic	174
	John C. Fremont	Republican	114
	Willard Filmore	American	8

George Washington, the first American President (*Popperfoto*)

Abraham Lincoln who rose from being in turn farm labourer, boat-hand, log-chopper and storekeeper to be President (*Popperfoto*)

Woodrow Wilson, 28th President of the United States (*Popperfoto*)

Year	Candidate	Party	Electoral	Popular Vote
1860	Abraham Lincoln	Republican	180	
	John C. Breckinridge	Democratic	72	
	John Bell	Const Union	39	
	Stephen A. Douglas	Democratic	12	
1864	Abraham Lincoln	Union	212	
	George B. McClellan	Democratic	21	
1868	Ulysses S. Grant	Republican	214	
	Horatio Seymour	Democratic	80	
	Votes not counted	—	23	
1872	Ulysses S. Grant	Republican	286	
	Horace Greeley	Dem Liberal Rep	—	
	Thomas A. Hendricks	Democratic	42	
	B. Gratz Brown	Dem Liberal Rep	18	
	Charles J. Jenkins	Democratic	2	
	David Davis	Democratic	1	
	Votes not counted	—	17	
1876	Rutherford B. Hayes	Republican	185	
	Samuel J. Tilden	Democratic	184	
	Peter Cooper	Greenback	0	
1880	James A. Garfield	Republican	214	
	Winfield S. Hancock	Democratic	155	
	James B. Weaver	Greenback	0	
1884	Grover Cleveland	Democratic	219	
	James G. Blaine	Republican	182	
	Benjamin F. Butler	Greenback	0	
	John P. St. John	Prohibition	0	
1888	Benjamin Harrison	Republican	233	
	Grover Cleveland	Democratic	168	
	Clinton B. Fisk	Prohibition	0	
	Aaron J. Streeter	Union Labor	0	
1892	Grover Cleveland	Democratic	277	
	Benjamin Harrison	Republican	145	
	James B. Weaver	People's	22	
	John Bidwell	Prohibition	0	
1896	William McKinley	Republican	271	
	William J. Bryan	Dem People's	176	
	John M. Palmer	Natl Dem	0	
	Joshua Levering	Prohibition	0	
1900	William McKinley	Republican	292	7 219 530
	William J. Bryan	Dem People's	155	6 358 071
	Eugene V. Debs	Social Democratic	0	94 768
1904	Theodore Roosevelt	Republican	336	7 628 834
	Alton B. Parker	Democratic	140	5 084 491
	Eugene V. Debs	Socialist	0	402 400
1908	William H. Taft	Republican	321	7 679 006
	William J. Bryan	Democratic	162	6 409 106
	Eugene V. Debs	Socialist	0	420 820
1912	Woodrow Wilson	Democratic	435	6 286 214
	Theodore Roosevelt	Progressive	88	4 126 020
	William H. Taft	Republican	8	3 483 922
	Eugene V. Debs	Socialist	0	897 011
1916	Woodrow Wilson	Democratic	277	9 129 606
	Charles E. Hughes	Republican	254	8 538 221
	A. L. Benson	Socialist	0	585 113
1920	Warren G. Harding	Republican	404	16 152 200
	James M. Cox	Democratic	127	9 147 353
	Eugene V. Debs	Socialist	0	917 799
1924	Calvin Coolidge	Republican	382	15 725 016
	John W. Davis	Democratic	136	8 385 586
	Robert M. LaFollette	Progressive, Socialist	13	4 822 856
1928	Herbert Hoover	Republican	444	21 392 190
	Alfred E. Smith	Democratic	87	15 016 443
	Norman Thomas	Socialist	0	267 420
1932	Franklin D. Roosevelt	Democratic	472	22 821 857
	Herbert Hoover	Republican	59	15 761 841
	Norman Thomas	Socialist	0	884 781

Franklin Roosevelt (*Popperfoto*)

Jimmy Carter holding his first press conference in August 1977 (*Popperfoto*)

1936	Franklin D. Roosevelt	Democratic	523	27 751 597
	Alfred M. Landon	Republican	8	16 679 583
	Norman Thomas	Socialist	0	187 720
1940	Franklin D. Roosevelt	Democratic	449	27 244 160
	Wendell L. Willkie	Republican	82	22 305 198
	Norman Thomas	Socialist	0	99 557
1944	Franklin D. Roosevelt	Democratic	432	25 602 504
	Thomas E. Dewey	Republican	99	22 006 285
	Norman Thomas	Socialist	0	80 518
1948	Harry S. Truman	Democratic	303	24 179 345
	Thomas S. Dewey	Republican	189	21 991 291
	J. Strom Thurmond	States' Rights Dem	39	1 176 125
	Henry A. Wallace	Progressive	0	1 157 326
	Norman Thomas	Socialist	0	139 572
1952	Dwight D. Eisenhower	Republican	442	33 936 234
	Adlai E. Stevenson	Democratic	89	27 314 992
1956	Dwight D. Eisenhower	Republican	457	35 590 472
	Adlai E. Stevenson	Democratic	73	26 022 752
1960	John F. Kennedy	Democratic	303	34 226 731
	Richard M. Nixon	Republican	219	34 108 157
1964	Lyndon B. Johnson	Democratic	486	43 129 484
	Barry M. Goldwater	Republican	52	27 178 188
1968	Richard M. Nixon	Republican	301	31 785 480
	Hubert H. Humphrey	Democratic	191	31 275 166
	George C. Wallace	American Ind	46	9 906 473
1972	Richard M. Nixon	Republican	520	47 169 911
	George McGovern	Democratic	17	29 170 383
	John G. Schmitz	American	0	1 099 482
1976	Jimmy Carter	Democratic	297	40 828 657
	Gerald R. Ford	Republican	240	39 145 520
	Eugene J. McCarthy	Independent	0	756 605

ENTERTAINMENT

Variety Club of Great Britain Show Business Awards

Britain's entertainment industry honours its leading members with these annual awards. The presentations were first made in 1952.

1952 Musical comedy star: Jean Carson
1953 Showman of the year: Jack Hylton
Actress: Dorothy Tutin
1954 Showman of the year: Sir Arthur Elvin
Star: Jack Hawkins
Most promising actress: Diane Cilento
Actor who made most progress: Donald Sinden
1955 Show Business personality: Diana Dors
Most promising international star: Kenneth More
Theatrical manager: Peter Saunders
Actor who made most progress: Ian Carmichael
1956 Show Business personality: Tommy Trinder
Best actor: Paul Scofield
Best actress: Mary Ure
Most promising newcomer: Elizabeth Seal
1957 Show business personality: Frankie Vaughan
Best actor: Sir Laurence Olivier
Best film actor: Alec Guiness
Best actress: Yvonne Mitchell
Most promising newcomer: Heather Sears
Best playwright: John Osborne
For her international triumphs in *My Fair Lady*:
Julie Andrews
1958 Show Business personality: Max Bygraves
Best actor: Michael Redgrave

Best film actor: Richard Attenborough
Best film actress: Sylvia Sims
Most promising newcomer: Bernard Bresslaw
1959 Show Business personality: Harry Secombe
Best film actress: Audrey Hepburn
Best film actor: Laurence Harvey
Best actress: Elizabeth Seal
Best actor: Peter O'Toole
Most promising newcomer: Anthony Newley
BBC TV personality: Richard Dimbleby
ITV personality: Bruce Forsyth
For unique contribution to the English theatre:
Sir Bernard Miles
1960 Show Business personality: Lionel Bart
Best film actor: Peter Sellers
Best film actress: Hayley Mills
Best actor: Nigel Patrick
Best actress: Billie Whitelaw
Most promising newcomer: Albert Finney
BBC TV personality: David Jacobs
Joint ITV personalities: Alfie Bass and Bill Fraser
BBC Sound Radio personality: Freddie
Grisewood
Cinderella award: Shirley Ann Field

1961   Show Business personality: Cliff Richard
Most promising newcomer: Helen Shapiro
BBC Sound Radio personality: Franklin Engelman
Best film actress: Deborah Kerr
ITV personality: Arthur Haynes
BBC TV personality: Cliff Michelmore
Most promising newcomer: Rita Tushingham
Best actor: Albert Finney
Best actress: Vanessa Redgrave
For services to the theatre: Hugh 'Binkie' Beaumont

1962   Show Business personality: Billy Cotton
Joint most promising newcomers: Tom Courtenay and Sarah Miles
Best actor: Paul Scofield
Best film actress: Leslie Caron
Best film actor: Peter O'Toole
Best actress: Sheila Hancock
BBC TV personality: Harry Worth
ITV personality: Violet Carson
BBC Sound Radio personality: Eamonn Andrews

1963   Joint Show Business personalities: The Beatles
Joint most promising newcomers: Julie Christie and James Fox
Joint BBC TV personalities: Wilfred Brambell and Harry H. Corbett
Joint ITV personalities: Honor Blackman and Patrick Macnee
Best actor: Sir Michael Redgrave
Best actress: Maggie Smith
Best film actress: Margaret Rutherford
Best film actor: Dirk Bogarde
BBC Sound Radio personality: Jean Metcalfe
Special award: Sean Connery

1964   Joint Show Business personalities: Morecambe and Wise
Best actor: Sir Laurence Olivier
Best actress: Dame Peggy Ashcroft
Best film actor: Richard Attenborough
Joint best film actresses: Rita Tushingham and Millicent Martin
BBC TV personality: Eric Sykes
ITV personality: Bernard Braden
BBC Sound Radio personality: Jack De Manio
Most promising newcomer: Jimmy Tarbuck

1965   Show Business personality: Ken Dodd
Best film actor: Sean Connery
Best film actress: Julie Christie
Best actor: Robert Stephens
Best actress: Dorothy Tutin
BBC TV personality: Benny Hill
ITV personality: Patrick McGoohan
Special award: Michael Miles
Special award: Hughie Green
BBC Sound Radio personality: Peter Haigh
Most promising artiste: Michael Crawford

1966   Show Business personality: Frankie Howerd
Best film actor: Michael Caine
Best film actress: Virginia McKenna
Best actor: David Warner
Best actress: Vanessa Redgrave
BBC TV personality: Val Doonican
ITV personality: David Frost
BBC Sound Radio personality: Nicholas Parsons

Most promising artiste: Barbara Ferris
Special award: Anna Neagle

1967   Show Business personality: Englebert Humperdinck
Best film actor: Paul Scofield
Best film actress: Edith Evans
Best actor: Donald Pleasance
Best actress: Irene Worth
BBC TV personality: Warren Mitchell
ITV personality: Dave Allen
BBC Sound Radio personality: Kenneth Horne
Most promising star: Carol White
Special award: Stanley Baker
Special award: Dame Gladys Cooper

1968   Show Business personality: Tom Jones
Best film actor: Ron Moody
Best film actress: Maggie Smith
Best actor: Sir John Gielgud
Best actress: Jill Bennett
Joint BBC TV personalities: Marty Feldman and Rolf Harris
Joint ITV personalities: Ronnie Corbett and Tommy Cooper
BBC Sound Radio personality: Jimmy Young
Most promising star: Alan Bennett
Special award: Dame Sybil Thorndike

1969   Show Business personality: Danny La Rue
Best film actor: Nicol Williamson
Best film actress: Glenda Jackson
Best actor: Leonard Rossiter
Best actress: Margaret Leighton
BBC TV personality: Wendy Craig
ITV personality: Ronnie Barker
BBC Radio personality: Eric Robinson
Most promising artiste: Polly James
Special award: Bernard Delfont

1970   Show Business personality: Derek Nimmo
Best film actor: Albert Finney
Best film actress: Sarah Miles
Best actor: Alec McCowen
Best actress: Eileen Atkins
Joint BBC TV personalities: Arthur Lowe, John Le Mesurier, Clive Dunn, John Laurie, Arnold Ridley, James Beck and Ian Lavender
Joint ITV personalities: Reg Varney, Doris Hare, Michael Robbins, Bob Grant, Stephen Lewis and Anna Karen
BBC Radio personality: Sam Costa
Most promising artiste: Jenny Agutter
Special award: Fred Emney

1971   Show Business personality: Frankie Howerd
Best film actor: Peter Finch
Best film actress: Nanette Newman
Best actor: Alan Badel
Best Actress: Moira Lister
BBC TV personality: Stratford Johns
ITV personality: Benny Hill
Show Business writer: David Storey
Most promising artiste: Murray Head
BBC Radio personality: Tony Blackburn
Special award: Keith Michell
Special award: Cicely Courtneidge and Jack Hulbert

1972   Show Business personality: Jimmy Savile

David Essex and Elaine Paige, stars in Evita, receive the Variety Club of Great Britain Joint Show Business Personalities Award from Lord Delfont

Tom Conti whose performance in 'Whose Life is it Anyway?' won him the Variety Club of Great Britain Best Stage Actor Award in 1978

Best film actor: Simon Ward
Best film actress: Dorothy Tutin
Best actor: Tom Courtenay
Best actress: Maggie Smith
BBC TV personality: Dick Emery
Joint ITV personalities: Jack Smethurst, Rudolph Walker, Nina Baden-Semper and Kate Williams
Show Business writer: Carl Foreman
BBC Radio personality: Pete Murray
Most promising artiste: Jon Finch
Special award: Jack Warner
1973 Show Business personality: Max Bygraves
Best film actor: Malcolm McDowell
Best film actress: Glenda Jackson
Best actor: Alastair Sim
Best actress: Wendy Hiller
BBC TV personality: Mike Yarwood
ITV personality: Wendy Craig
Show Business writer: William Douglas Home
BBC Radio personality: Terry Wogan
Most promising artiste: David Essex
Special award: Lord Willis
Special award: Evelyn Laye
1974 Show Business personality: Michael Crawford
Best actor: Tom Courtenay
Best actress: Claire Bloom
Best film actor: Albert Finney
Best film actress: Susannah York
BBC TV personality: Ronnie Barker
ITV personality: Jean Marsh
BBC Radio personality: Ed Stewart
Most promising artiste: Felicity Kendal
Playwright: Alan Ayckbourne
Special award: John Woolf
1975 Show Business personality: Bruce Forsyth
Best film actor: Robert Shaw
Best film actress: Glenda Jackson
Best actor: Alan Bates
Best actress: Helen Mirren
Joint BBC TV personalities: John Cleese and Esther Rantzen
ITV personality: Gordon Jackson
Show Business writer: Simon Gray

BBC Radio personality: David Jacobs
Most promising artiste: Lisa Harrow
Special award: Max Wall
1976 Show Business personality: Penelope Keith
Best film actor: Sir Laurence Olivier
Best film actress: Gemma Craven
Best actor: Donald Sinden
Best actress: Joan Plowright
Joint BBC TV personalities: John Inman and Derek Jacobi
Joint ITV personalities: Dennis Waterman, John Thaw, Yootha Joyce and Brian Murphy
BBC Radio personality: Roy Hudd
Most promising artiste: Andrew Sachs
Special award: Richard Goolden
1977 Joint Show Business personalities: John Dankworth and Cleo Laine
Best Actor: Sir Alec Guinness
Best actress: Glynis Johns
Best film actor: Norman Beaton
Best film actress: Billie Whitelaw
Joint BBC TV personalities: Terry Scott and June Whitfield
Joint ITV personalities: Jim Henson and Frank Oz
Joint BBC Radio personalities: Frank Muir and Denis Norden
Independent Radio personality: Kenny Everett
Most promising artiste: Susan Littler
Special award: Stanley Holloway
1978 Joint Show Business personalities: David Essex and Elaine Paige, *Evita*
Best stage actor: Tom Conti, *Whose Life is it Anyway?*
Best stage actress: Felicity Kendal, *Clouds*
Best film actor: Peter Ustinov, *Death on the Nile*
Best film actress: Glenda Jackson, *House Calls* and *Stevie*
Joint BBC TV personalities: Christopher Timothy, Robert Hardy, Carol Drinkwater and Peter Davidson, *All Creatures Great and Small*
ITV personality: Francesca Annis, *Lillie*
BBC Radio personality: Charlie Chester, *Sunday Soapbox*

ENVIRONMENT

Britain in Bloom

Sponsored by the British Tourist Authority, the Britain in Bloom competition is a nationwide campaign aimed at encouraging people to make our cities, towns and villages as attractive as possible by the imaginative and decorative use of trees, shrubs and flowers.

Many cities, towns and villages entering the competition establish local Britain in Bloom action committees which enlist the support of private and public organisations, businesses, societies and private citizens in the area. They compete with their counterparts on a regional basis through the regional and national tourist boards of England, Scotland, Wales and the Isle of Man. Finalists – who are entered for the nationwide competition – are chosen by each region. In early autumn a panel of eminent horticulturists visits the cities, towns and villages which have been chosen as finalists. The judging panel travels the length and breadth of the country by air and road to decide which outstanding places shall win the national trophies. In recent years British cities, towns and villages have competed with European communities to win international honours in the Entente Florale competition.

National trophies are awarded annually to the winning city, the winning town and the winning village in the Britain in Bloom competition. A 'Keep Britain Tidy' trophy goes to the Britain in Bloom finalist most active in litter prevention and another trophy is awarded to the city, town or village where the commercial sector of the community has made the greatest contribution. Winners since 1964:

1964   Bath
1965   Aberdeen
1966   Exeter and Middlesbrough (jointly)
1967   City of London
1968   Bath
1969   Aberdeen
1970   City: Aberdeen
          Town: Falmouth
          Village: Abington

The City of Bath – Britain in Bloom and Entente Florale Winner in 1978

1971   City: Aberdeen
          Town: Falmouth
          Village: Abington
          Gordon Ford Trophy: Bath
1972   City: Bath
               Hartlepool
          Town: Ayr
          Village: Chagford
          Gordon Ford Trophy: Bath
1973   City: Aberdeen
          Town: Bridlington
               Falmouth
          Village: Ryton
          Keep Britain Tidy Award: Bridlington
          Gordon Ford Trophy: Bath
1974   City: Aberdeen
               City of London
          Town: Shrewsbury
          Village: Clovelly
          Keep Britain Tidy Award: Clovelly
          Gordon Ford Trophy: Bath
1975   City: Bath
          Town: Sidmouth
          Village: Clovelly
          Keep Britain Tidy Award: London Borough of Camden
          Gordon Ford Trophy: City of London
1976   City: Bath
          Town: Harrogate
          Village: Bampton
          Keep Britain Tidy Award: Wolviston
          Gordon Ford Trophy: Bath
          Parks Department Trophy: Department of Leisure and Recreation in Aberdeen
1977   City: Aberdeen
          Town: Harrogate
          Village: Wolviston

1977 *Cont.*
Keep Britain Tidy Award: Exeter
Gordon Ford Trophy: Bath
Moran Memorial Award: Mr P. C. Conn

1978   City: Bath
Large Town: Douglas
Small Town: Sidmouth
Village: Aberdovey
    Carrington
Keep Britain Tidy Award: Holywell, North-
umberland
Gordon Ford Trophy: Swansea

EQUESTRIAN EVENTS

Show Jumping

WORLD CHAMPIONS
Men
First held 1953. Team Championship first held 1978.
1953   Francisco Goyoago (Spa) on *Quorum*
1954   Hans Günter Winkler (Ger) on *Halla*
1955   Hans Günter Winkler (Ger) on *Halla*
1956   Raimondo d'Inzeo (Ita) on *Merano*
1960   Raimondo d'Inzeo (Ita) on *Gowran Girl*
1966   Pierre d'Oriola (Fra) on *Pomone*
1970   David Broome (GB) on *Beethoven*
1974   Hartwig Steenken (Ger) on *Simona*
1978   Gerd Wiltfang (Ger) on *Roman*

Women
First held 1965.
1965   Marion Coakes (GB) on *Stroller*
1970   Janou Lefebvre (Fra) on *Rocket*
1974   Janou Tissot (née Lefebvre) (Fra) on *Rocket*

Team
1978   Great Britain

OLYMPIC CHAMPIONS
First held 1900. Individual and Team winners since 1948 have been:

	Individual	*Team*
1948	Humberto Cortes (Mex) on *Arete*	Mexico
1952	Pierre d'Oriola (Fra) on *Ali Baba*	Great Britain
1956	Hans Günter Winkler (Ger) on *Halla*	Germany
1960	Raimondo d'Inzeo (Ita) on *Merano*	Germany
1964	Pierre d'Oriola (Fra) on *Lutteur*	Germany
1968	William Steinkraus (USA) on *Snowbound*	Canada
1972	Graziano Mancinelli (Ita) on *Ambassador*	W. Germany
1976	Alwin Schockemöhle (Ger) on *Warwick Rex*	France

Pierre d'Oriola on *Pomone* (*E. D. Lacey*)

PRESIDENT'S CUP
The award for the world Team championship, based on each country's best six Nations Cup results in a season.

1965	Great Britain	1969	W. Germany	1973	Great Britain	1977	Great Britain
1966	USA	1970	Great Britain	1974	Great Britain	1978	Great Britain
1967	Great Britain	1971	W. Germany	1975	W. Germany		
1968	USA	1972	Great Britain	1976	W. Germany		

Three-Day Event

WORLD CHAMPIONS
First held 1966.

	Individual	*Team*
1966	Carlos Moratorio (Arg) on *Chalan*	Ireland
1970	Mary Gordon-Watson (GB) on *Cornishman V*	Great Britain
1974	Bruce Davidson (USA) on *Irish Cap*	USA
1978	Bruce Davidson (USA) on *Might Tango*	Canada

OLYMPIC CHAMPIONS
First held 1912. Winners since 1948 have been:

		Team
1948	Bernard Chevallier (Fra) on *Aiglonne*	USA
1952	Hans von Blixen-Finecke (Swe) on *Jubal*	Sweden
1956	Petrus Kastenman (Swe) on *Iluster*	Great Britain
1960	Lawrence Morgan (Aus) on *Salad Days*	Australia

OLYMPIC CHAMPIONS *continued*

1964	Mauro Checcoli (Ita) on *Syrbean*	Italy
1968	Jean-Jacques Guyon (Fra) on *Pitou*	Great Britain
1972	Richard Meade (GB) on *Laurieston*	Great Britain
1976	Edmund Coffin (USA) on *Ballycor*	USA

DRESSAGE

WORLD CHAMPIONS

First held 1966

1966	Josef Neckermann (Ger) on *Mariano*	W. Germany
1970	Elena Petouchkova (USSR) on *Pepel*	USSR
1974	Reiner Klimke (Ger) on *Dux*	W. Germany
1978	Christine Stückelberger (Swi) on *Granat*	W. Germany

OLYMPIC CHAMPIONS

First held 1912. Team and Individual winners since 1948 have been:

1948	Hans Moser (Swi) on *Hummer*	France
1952	Henri St Cyr (Swe) on *Master Rufus*	Sweden
1956	Henri St Cyr (Swe) on *Juli*	Sweden
1960	Sergey Filatov (USSR) on *Absent*	Not held
1964	Henri Chammartin (Swi) on *Woermann*	W. Germany
1968	Ivan Kizimov (USSR) on *Ichor*	W. Germany
1972	Liselott Linsenhoff (Ger) on *Piaff*	USSR
1976	Christine Stückelberger (Swi) on *Granat*	W. Germany

EYES

Miss Beautiful Eyes

The original concept of Miss Beautiful Eyes, organised since 1968 by the British Safety Council, was to hold a competition in order to find a girl with beautiful eyes to feature on a British Safety Council eye safety poster.

During the last few years the campaign has changed in that the winner of the title fulfils a year of duties, visiting factories and workplaces all over the country communicating a safety message.

1968	Fay Bird	1975	Penny Hilditch
1969	Moira-Ann Harley	1976	Helene Granville
1970	Linda Cunningham	1977	Judith Platt,
1971	Penelope Dussek		Moya Ann Church
1972	Teresa Flanagan	1978	Suzanne Stead
1973	Maralyn Roberson	1979	Pauline Hegarty
1974	Jacqui Horgan		

Right: **Pauline Hegarty – Miss Beautiful Eyes 1979**

FASHION

Clothing Manufacturers' Federation: The Ten Well-Dressed Men

Members are primarily concerned with the men's and boys' outerwear sector of the clothing industry, a small number of members are also engaged in the women's outerwear sector, such as Aquascutum. Current membership stands at 270 firms, who provide something like 80 per cent of the outerwear (male) sold in this country.

Between the years 1959 and 1964 the Federation ran an event called the Ten Well-Dressed Men, which was always interpreted by the press as the Ten Best-Dressed Men. Each nominee

or winner received a suitably inscribed silver shield mounted on mahogany.
The nominees for the period concerned were:

1959	Sir Malcolm Sargent	1962	Leo Abse, MP
	Sir David Eccles		Paul Getty
	J. Birkmyre Rowan		Lord Gladwyn
	Charles Glenny		Sir William Holford
	Leslie Gamage		Innes Ireland
	Douglas Fairbanks		David Jacobs
	Malcolm Northcote		Michael Mander
	A. C. Grover		Cliff Richard
	Hardy Amies		John Taylor
	Rex Harrison	1963	Sebastian de Ferranti

1959
Sir Malcolm Sargent
Sir David Eccles
J. Birkmyre Rowan
Charles Glenny
Leslie Gamage
Douglas Fairbanks
Malcolm Northcote
A. C. Grover
Hardy Amies
Rex Harrison
1960
Peter Dimmock
Peter Trench
Gerald Nabarro, MP
Donald Campbell
Peter May
Sir William McFadzean
The Earl of Sefton
Lonnie Donegan
Lord Netherthorpe
Sir Miles Thomas
1961
The Duke of Bedford
Basil Boothroyd
Douglas Fairbanks
Ian Forbes-Leith
Col. Colin Gray
Edward Marsh
Nigel Patrick
Sir William Piggott-Brown
Sir Stanley Rous
Nubar Gulbenkian

1962
Leo Abse, MP
Paul Getty
Lord Gladwyn
Sir William Holford
Innes Ireland
David Jacobs
Michael Mander
Cliff Richard
John Taylor
1963
Sebastian de Ferranti
Adam Faith
Lionel Fraser
John Freeman
Sidney Greene
Jack Hawkins
Edward Heath MP
Sir Patrick Hennessy
Ivan Sanderson
Harry Wheatcroft

1964
Richard Baker
Anthony Chambers
Sir Christopher Chancellor
Christopher Chataway
Luigi Donzelli
Brian Epstein
Bruce Forsyth
Patrick McNee
Norman Parkinson
Sir David Webster
1965
Sir Thomas Bland
John Edrich
William Edwards
Sir Harold Evans
Peter Evans
Hugh Gatehorne Hardy
Det. Supt. Francis Lea
Patrick McGoohan
Herman Noone
The Hon. Tim Tollemache

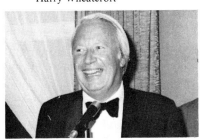

Edward Heath, MP, one
of the ten well-dressed
men in 1963

Tie Manufacturers' Association: Top Tie Men

Although the Association had previously named certain people as Top Tie Men, it was not until 1973 that the event was placed on a formal footing with a presentation of awards. Throughout the year by monitoring newspaper and magazines photographs and television the Association compiles its list. Here are the six years' names: all 10 winners are equal, though their names are listed alphabetically.

1973
Leo Abse, MP
Richard Baker
The Duke of Bedford
John Bentley
Gordon Honeycombe
Kenneth Kendall
Rodney Marsh
Eric Morley
Sir Gerald Nabarro, MP
Derek Nimmo
1974
Malcolm Allison
Kingsley Amis
Michael Barratt
Patrick Cargill
Frank Chapple
Henry Cooper
Norman Lamont, MP
Roy Mason, MP
Leonard Parkin
Peter Woods

1975
The Marquess of Bath
Raymond Baxter
Ronnie Corbett
Dickie Davies
Jimmy Hill
Robert Maxwell
Nicholas Parsons
Paul Raymond
Don Revie
Nicholas Winterton, MP
1976
Reginald Bosanquet
Tony Britton
Eric Deakins, MP
Noel Edmonds
Stuart Hall
Victor Hill
Peter Parker
Geoffrey Pattie, MP
Sir Harold Wilson, MP
John Young

1977
Richard Baker
Nicholas Fairbairn, MP
Bruce Forsyth
Gerald Harper
Gordon Honeycombe
David Jacobs
Kenneth Kendall
Terry Neill
Leonard Parkin
Jimmy Perry
1978
Trevor Bannister
Lionel Blair
Ted Croker
Sir Charles Forte
Denis Healey, MP
Derek Hobson
Reginald Maudling, MP
Michael Smithwick
David Steel, MP
Alan Weeks

FENCING

Olympic Games and World Championships

Fencing has been included in each of the modern Olympic Games, and Olympic Championships are recognised as World Championships in Olympic years. World Championships are held annually, and have had official status since 1936, but followed European Championships which were first held in 1921. Women's events were first held in 1929.

Winners since 1965 (Olympic Champions identified by *):

INDIVIDUAL

Men's Foil

1965	Jean-Claude Magnan (Fra)
1966	Gherman Sveshnikov (USSR)
1967	Viktor Putyatin (USSR)
1968	*Ion Drimba (Rom)
1969	Friedrich Wessel (Ger)
1970	Friedrich Wessel (Ger)
1971	Vassily Stankovich (USSR)
1972	*Witold Woyda (Pol)
1973	Christian Nöel (Fra)
1974	Alexandr Romankov (USSR)
1975	Christian Nöel (Fra)
1976	*Fabio dal Zotto (Ita)
1977	Alexandr Romankov (USSR)
1978	Didier Flament (Fra)

Most: 6   Christian d'Oriola (Fra):
1947, *1948, 1949, *1952, 1953, 1954

Men's Sabre

1965	Jerzy Pawlowski (Pol)
1966	Jerzy Pawlowski (Pol)
1967	Mark Rakita (USSR)
1968	*Jerzy Pawlowski (Pol)
1969	Viktor Sidiak (USSR)
1970	Tibor Pezsa (Hun)
1971	Michele Maffei (Ita)
1972	*Viktor Sidiak (USSR)
1973	Mario Aldo Montano (Ita)
1974	Mario Aldo Montano (Ita)
1975	Vladimir Nazlimov (USSR)
1976	*Viktor Krovopouskov (USSR)
1977	Pal Gerevich (Hun)
1978	Viktor Krovopouskov (USSR)

Most: 4   Rudolf Karpati (Hun): 1954, *1956, 1959, *1960
4   Aladar Gerevich (Hun): 1935, *1948, 1951, 1955
4   Jerzy Pawlowski (Pol): 1957, 1965, 1966, *1968

Men's Épée

Zoltan Nemere (Hun)
Aleksey Nikanchikov (USSR)
Aleksey Nikanchikov (USSR)
*Gyözö Kulcsar (Hun)
Bogdan Andrzejewski (Pol)
Aleksey Nikanchikov (USSR)
Grigory Kriss (USSR)
*Csaba Fenyvesi (Hun)
Rolf Edling (Swe)
Rolf Edling (Swe)
Alexander Pusch (Ger)
*Alexander Pusch (Ger)
Johan Harmenberg (Swe)
Alexander Pusch (Ger)

3   Georges Buchard (Fra): 1927, 1931, 1933
3   Aleksey Nikanchikov: *as above*
3   Alexander Pusch: *as above*

Women's Foil

Galina Gorokhova (USSR)
Tatyana Samusenko (USSR)
Alexandra Zabelina (USSR)
*Elena Novikova (USSR)
Elena Novikova (USSR)
Galina Gorokhova (USSR)
Marie-Chantal Demaille (Fra)
*Antonella Ragno-Lonzi (Ita)
Valentina Nikonova (USSR)
Ildiko Bobis (Hun)
Ecaterina Stahl (Rom)
*Ildiko Schwarczenberger (Hun)
Valentina Sidorova (USSR)
Valentina Sidorova (USSR)

5   Ilona Elek (Hun): 1934, 1935, *1936, *1948, 1951

TEAM

	Men's Foil	**Men's Épée**	**Men's Sabre**	**Women's Foil**
1965	USSR	France	USSR	USSR
1966	USSR	France	Hungary	USSR
1967	Romania	USSR	USSR	Hungary
1968	*France	*Hungary	*USSR	*USSR
1969	USSR	USSR	USSR	Romania
1970	USSR	Hungary	USSR	USSR
1971	France	Hungary	USSR	USSR
1972	*Poland	*Hungary	*Italy	*USSR

1973	USSR	W. Germany	Hungary	Hungary
1974	USSR	Sweden	USSR	USSR
1975	France	Sweden	USSR	USSR
1976	*W. Germany	*Sweden	*USSR	*USSR
1977	W. Germany	Sweden	USSR	USSR
1978	Poland	Hungary	Hungary	USSR

Most: 16   USSR   16   Italy   24   Hungary   12   USSR

FISHING (*See* Angling)

FLORISTRY

The Huxley Cup

This competition for members of the Women's Institute is staged annually by the Royal Agricultural Society of England and judged in the Floral Arrangement Section of the Flower Show at the Royal Show. The competition aims to find a flower arranger who can create an artistic arrangement at low cost using the most basic materials. The theme changes each year, that for 1978 being the 'Village Green' and 1979 'The Secret Garden'. Each of the 65 County Federations in the WI movement are permitted to place one entry with the exception of last year's winners who are not eligible.

The most recent winners were:

1974	'Gardener's Reward'	Kesteven	1976	'Summer Simplicity'	Gwent
1975	WI Diamond Jubilee – '60 years Then and Now'	Warwickshire	1977	'The Crown Jewels'	Avon
			1978	'The Village Green'	Gloucester

National Association of Flower Arrangement Societies of Great Britain: Annual Festival of Flower Arrangement

This Association has held an annual Festival of Flower Arrangement since 1962, at which the national competitions are held. The national festival and competitions are organised by one of the twenty areas into which the National Association is divided, and is therefore held in a different part of the country each year.

The Julia Clements Challenge Trophy for the Best Exhibit in the national competitions has been awarded to the following members of NAFAS:

1962	Mrs D. Starling, London and Overseas Area
1963	Mrs P. Mann, Wessex Area
1964	Mrs K. M. Nicol, North Midlands Area
1965	Mrs J. Taylor, Mercia and North Wales Area
1966	Mrs K. Young, London and Overseas Area
1967	Mrs J. Taylor, Mercia and North Wales Area
1968	Mrs J. M. Abbott, London and Overseas Area
1969	Miss E. Tomkinson, Mercia and North Wales Area
1970	Mrs A. Horsley, South Midlands Area
1971	Mrs R. Hewitt, County of Surrey Area
1972	Mrs C. Jephcott, South West England Area
1973	Mr D. Bridges, North East England Area
1974	Mrs A. Wiltshire, Wessex Area
1975	Mrs S. Lewis, Three Counties and South Wales Area
1976	Mrs D. Da Rosa, Surrey
1977	Mrs N. Hegarty, London and Overseas Area
1978	Mrs M. MacFarlane, Scotland

The Best Exhibit in the class entitled 'The Magic Carpet'. This was won by Mrs M. MacFarlane from Scotland. This annual Festival of Flower Arrangement is arranged by the National Association of Flower Arrangement Societies of Great Britain

FOOD

Gourmet of the Year

This contest, first held in 1976, is organised by the London *Evening Standard* and sponsored by Mouton Cadet. In 1978 competitors had to identify three mystery recipes, and in the second round 25 winners answered questions about their lunch menu at Mayfair's Greenhouse Restaurant. The champion was later chosen at the Miller Howe Hotel in the Lake District from three finalists who had to identify the ingredients of the following meal: (a) Tomato, apple and celery soup, also containing butter, onion, sherry, chicken stock, cream, sugar, salt and freshly-ground black pepper; (b) Duck liver pies, flavoured with onion, fennel, garlic, marjoram and thyme, with a puff pastry topping and served with purée sprouts cooked in a rich egg custard and sprinkled with finely chopped French beans tossed in walnut oil, cheese and breadcrumbs; and (c) Brown bread and rum cream ice.

1976   Bill Vellutini of London was the *Evening Standard*'s very first Gourmet of the Year – a teacher of English at Godolphin and Latymer School. The two runners up were housewives Gail Wright and Susan Keville.

1977   Judith Hitching is the wife of writer and film producer Francis Hitching and the mother of 3 daughters, and lives in Twickenham. The two runners up were Peter Aprile of Surrey and Mrs Brenda Holroyd of London.

1978   The winner was Sue Morgan of Islington, and the runners up were Judith Wilkinson of Frognal and Fiona Fraser-Thomson from Richmond.

FOOTBALL   (*See* American Football, Association Football, Gaelic Football, Rugby League, Rugby Union)

GAELIC FOOTBALL

All-Ireland Championship

First contested in 1887. Winners since 1965:

1965	Galway	1970	Kerry	1975	Kerry
1966	Galway	1971	Offaly	1976	Dublin
1967	Meath	1972	Offaly	1977	Dublin
1968	Down	1973	Cork	1978	Kerry
1969	Kerry	1974	Dublin	**Most wins:** 24 Kerry	

GAMES

Game of the Year Award

The *Games & Puzzles* Game Award of the Year, first given in 1975, is the proprietary indoor game voted best by readers of the magazine. It is awarded to the manufacturer. Traditional games (eg chess), card games with usual pack(s) and similar are not eligible. Recent winners are set out below:

1975	Scrabble	1977	Diplomacy
1976	Diplomacy	1978	Kingmaker

It's a Knockout

The British competition is organised by BBC television. Teams from various towns take part in a number of events, designed to test skills, ingenuity and speed but above all to provide entertainment for the viewer.

Prior to 1972 no team was designated British champion team. From 1972 to 1975 the *Radio Times* trophy was awarded to the team which gained the highest number of points in the domestic competition. The winners were as follows:

1972	Luton	1974	Southport
1973	Ely	1975	Onchen (Isle of Man)

From 1976 the *Radio Times* trophy was awarded for 'It's A Championship Knockout' which is a competition between the seven teams of 'It's a Knockout' (ie the seven heat winners of the domestic competition). The winners of this competition were as follows:

1976	Blackpool	1977	Macclesfield	1978	Sandwell

Jeux Sans Frontières

This is the European Competition of 'It's a Knockout'. Since Britain began competing the results have been as follows:

1967	Bardenberg	West Germany		1973	Ely	Great Britain
1968	Osterholz Scharmbeck	West Germany		1974	Muotathal	Switzerland
1969	Shrewsbury	Great Britain	tie	1975	Nancy	France
	Wolfsburg	West Germany		1976	Ettlinden	West Germany
1970	Como	Italy		1977	Schliersee	West Germany
1971	Blackpool	Great Britain		1978	Abano Therme	Italy
1972	La Chaux de Fonds	France				

Master Mind

Master Mind – the code-breaking game, not the TV quiz – achieved seven million sales in the UK alone.

World Championship
(Started in 1977)
1977* John Serjeant (UK)
1978   John Serjeant (UK)

British Championship
1975   Stephen Winters
1976   Maxine Hobbs
1977   (No contest)
1978   John Serjeant

* The 1977 World Championship was run in conjunction with the British Championship: John Serjeant was thus winner of both.

Three-times champion John Serjeant, a 16-year-old student from Nottingham, and 18-year-old Canadian Cindy Forth during the final of the World Invicta Master Mind Championships in November 1978

GLIDING

World Championships

The first World Gliding (or Soaring) Championships were held in 1937. They are held biennially, and there are now three categories – Open, Standard and 15 metres. Winners at each category:

OPEN

1937	Heini Dittmar (Ger)	1972	Goran Ax (Swe)
1948	Per Persson (Swe)	1974	George Moffat (USA)
1950	Billy Nilsson (Swe)	1976	George Lee (GB)
1952	Phillip Wills (GB)	1978	George Lee (GB)
1954	Gerard Pierre (Fra)		
1956	Paul MacCready (USA)	**2-Seater**	
1958	Ernst Haase (Ger)	1952	Luis Juez and J. Ara (Spa)
1960	Rudolf Hossinger (Arg)	1954	Z. Rain and P. Komac (Yug)
1963	Edward Makula (Pol)	1956	Nick Goodhard and Frank Foster (GB)
1965	Jan Wroblewski (Pol)		
1968	Harro Wodl (Aut)		
1970	George Moffat (USA)		

Standard

1958	Adam Witek (Pol)
1960	Heinz Huth (Ger)
1963	Heinz Huth (Ger)
1965	François Henry (Fra)
1968	A. J. Smith (USA)
1970	Helmut Reichmann (Ger)
1972	Jan Wroblewski (Pol)
1974	Helmut Reichmann (Ger)
1976	Ingo Renner (Aus)
1978	Baer Selen (Hol)

15 metres

1978	Helmut Reichmann (Ger)

GOLF

British Open Championship

The first Championship was held at Prestwick in 1860. In 1892 the competition was extended from 36 to 72 holes. Winners (GB except where shown):

Year	Winner	Score	Year	Winner	Score	Year	Winner	Score
1860	Willie Park, Sr	174	1898	Harry Vardon	307	1946	Sam Snead (USA)	290
1861	Tom Morris, Sr	163	1899	Harry Vardon	310	1947	Fred Daly	293
1862	Tom Morris, Sr	163	1900	John H. Taylor	309	1948	Henry Cotton	284
1863	Willie Park, Sr	168	1901	James Braid	309	1949	Bobby Locke (SA)	283
1864	Tom Morris, Sr	167	1902	Alexander Herd	307	1950	Bobby Locke (SA)	279
1865	Andrew Strath	162	1903	Harry Vardon	300	1951	Max Faulkner	285
1866	Willie Park, Sr	169	1904	Jack White	296	1952	Bobby Locke (SA)	287
1867	Tom Morris, Sr	170	1905	James Braid	318	1953	Ben Hogan (USA)	282
1868	Tom Morris, Jr	170	1906	James Braid	300	1954	Peter Thomson (Aus)	283
1869	Tom Morris, Jr	154	1907	Arnaud Massy	312	1955	Peter Thomson (Aus)	281
1870	Tom Morris, Jr	149	1908	James Braid	291	1956	Peter Thomson (Aus)	286
1872	Tom Morris, Jr	166	1909	John H. Taylor	295	1957	Bobby Locke (SA)	279
1873	Tom Kidd	179	1910	James Braid	299	1958	Peter Thomson (Aus)	278
1874	Mungo Park	159	1911	Harry Vardon	303	1959	Gary Player (SA)	284
1875	Willie Park, Sr	166	1912	Edward (Ted) Ray	295	1960	Kel Nagle (Aus)	278
1876	Robert Martin	176	1913	John H. Taylor	304	1961	Arnold Palmer (USA)	284
1877	Jamie Anderson	160	1914	Harry Vardon	306	1962	Arnold Palmer (USA)	276
1878	Jamie Anderson	157	1920	George Duncan	303	1963	Bob Charles (NZ)	277
1879	Jamie Anderson	170	1921	Jock Hutchison (USA)	296	1964	Tony Lema (USA)	279
1880	Robert Ferguson	162	1922	Walter Hagen (USA)	300	1965	Peter Thomson (Aus)	285
1881	Robert Ferguson	170	1923	Arthur G. Havers	295	1966	Jack Nicklaus (USA)	282
1882	Robert Ferguson	171	1924	Walter Hagen (USA)	301	1967	Roberto de Vincenzo	
1883	Willie Fernie	159	1925	James M. Barnes (USA)	300		(Arg)	278
1884	Jack Simpson	160	1926	Robert T. Jones, Jr (USA)	291	1968	Gary Player (SA)	299
1885	Bob Martin	171	1927	Robert T. Jones, Jr (USA)	285	1969	Tony Jacklin	280
1886	David Brown	157	1928	Walter Hagen (USA)	292	1970	Jack Nicklaus (USA)	283
1887	Willie Park, Jr	161	1929	Walter Hagen (USA)	292	1971	Lee Trevino (USA)	278
1888	Jack Burns	171	1930	Robert T. Jones, Jr (USA)	291	1972	Lee Trevino (USA)	278
1889	Willie Park, Jr	155	1931	Tommy D. Armour (USA)	296	1973	Tom Weiskopf (USA)	276
1890	John Ball	164	1932	Gene Sarazen (USA)	283	1974	Gary Player (SA)	282
1891	Hugh Kirkaldy	169	1933	Denny Shute (USA)	292	1975	Tom Watson (USA)	279
1892	Harold H. Hilton	305	1934	Henry Cotton	283	1976	Johnny Miller (USA)	279
1893	William Auchterlonie	322	1935	Alfred Perry	283	1977	Tom Watson (USA)	268
1894	John H. Taylor	326	1936	Alfred Padgham	287	1978	Jack Nicklaus (USA)	281
1895	John H. Taylor	322	1937	Henry Cotton	290	1979	Severiano Ballesteros	
1896	Harry Vardon	316	1938	R. A. Whitcombe	295		(Spa)	283
1897	Harold H. Hilton	314	1939	Richard Burton	290			

US Masters Championship

Played each year at the Augusta National Golf Course, Augusta, Georgia. Instituted in 1934. Stroke play over 72 holes. Winners (USA except where shown):

Year	Winner	Score	Year	Winner	Score	Year	Winner	Score
1934	Horton Smith	284	1948	Claude Harmon	279	1959	Art Wall	284
1935	Gene Sarazen	282	1949	Sam Snead	282	1960	Arnold Palmer	282
1936	Horton Smith	285	1950	Jimmy Demaret	283	1961	Gary Player (SA)	280
1937	Byron Nelson	283	1951	Ben Hogan	280	1962	Arnold Palmer	280
1938	Henry Picard	285	1952	Sam Snead	286	1963	Jack Nicklaus	286
1939	Ralph Guldahl	279	1953	Ben Hogan	274	1964	Arnold Palmer	276
1940	Jimmy Demaret	280	1954	Sam Snead	289	1965	Jack Nicklaus	271
1941	Craig Wood	280	1955	Cary Middlecoff	279	1966	Jack Nicklaus	288
1942	Byron Nelson	280	1956	Jack Burke	289	1967	Gay Brewer	280
1946	Herman Keiser	282	1957	Doug Ford	283	1968	Bob Goalby	277
1947	Jimmy Demaret	281	1958	Arnold Palmer	284	1969	George Archer	281

		Score			Score			Score
1970	Billy Casper	279	1974	Gary Player (SA)	278	1978	Gary Player (SA)	277
1971	Charles Coody	279	1975	Jack Nicklaus	276	1979	Fuzzy Zoeller	280
1972	Jack Nicklaus	286	1976	Ray Floyd	271			
1973	Tommy Aaron	283	1977	Tom Watson	276			

US Open Championship

First held in 1894. Stroke play over 72 holes. Winners (USA except where shown):

		Score			Score			Score
1895	Horace Rawling	173	1924	Cyril Walker	297	1955	Jack Fleck	287
1896	James Foulis	152	1925	Willie Macfarlane	291	1956	Cary Middlecoff	281
1897	Joe Lloyd	162	1926	Robert T. Jones, Jr	293	1957	Dick Mayer	282
1898	Fred Herd	328	1927	Tommy Armour	301	1958	Tommy Bolt	283
1899	Willie Smith	315	1928	Johnny Farrell	294	1959	Billy Casper	282
1900	Harry Vardon (GB)	313	1929	Robert T. Jones, Jr	294	1960	Arnold Palmer	280
1901	Willie Anderson	331	1930	Robert T. Jones, Jr	287	1961	Gene Littler	281
1902	Laurie Auchterlonie	307	1931	Billy Burke	292	1962	Jack Nicklaus	283
1903	Willie Anderson	307	1932	Gene Sarazen	286	1963	Julius Boros	293
1904	Willie Anderson	303	1933	John Goodman	287	1964	Ken Venturi	278
1905	Willie Anderson	314	1934	Olin Dutra	293	1965	Gary Player (SA)	282
1906	Alex Smith	295	1935	Sam Parks, Jr	299	1966	Billy Casper	278
1907	Alex Ross	302	1936	Tony Manero	282	1967	Jack Nicklaus	275
1908	Fred McLeod	322	1937	Ralph Guldahl	281	1968	Lee Trevino	275
1909	George Sargent	290	1938	Ralph Guldahl	284	1969	Orville Moody	281
1910	Alex Smith	298	1939	Byron Nelson	284	1970	Tony Jacklin (GB)	281
1911	John McDermott	307	1940	Lawson Little	287	1971	Lee Trevino	280
1912	John McDermott	294	1941	Craig Wood	284	1972	Jack Nicklaus	290
1913	Francis Ouimet	304	1946	Lloyd Mangrum	284	1973	Johnny Miller	279
1914	Walter Hagen	290	1947	Lew Worsnam	282	1974	Hale Irwin	287
1915	Jerome D. Travers	297	1948	Ben Hogan	276	1975	Lou Graham	287
1916	Charles Evans, Jr	286	1949	Cary Middlecoff	286	1976	Jerry Pate	277
1919	Walter Hagen	301	1950	Ben Hogan	287	1977	Hubert Green	278
1920	Edward Ray (GB)	295	1951	Ben Hogan	287	1978	Andy North	285
1921	Jim Barnes	289	1952	Julius Boros	281	1979	Hale Irwin	284
1922	Gene Sarazen	288	1953	Ben Hogan	283			
1923	Robert T. Jones, Jr	296	1954	Ed Furgol	284			

US Professional Golfers' Association Championship

First played in 1916. From then until 1957 it was a knock-out match play tournament, but since 1958 has been decided over 36 holes of stroke play.

								Score
1916	James M. Barnes		1939	Henry Picard		1961	Jerry Barber	277
1919	James M. Barnes		1940	Byron Nelson		1962	Gary Player (SA)	278
1920	Jock Hutchinson		1941	Vic Ghezzi		1963	Jack Nicklaus	279
1921	Walter Hagen		1942	Sam Snead		1964	Bob Nichols	271
1922	Gene Sarazen		1944	Bob Hamilton		1965	Dave Marr	280
1923	Gene Sarazen		1945	Byron Nelson		1966	Al Geiberger	280
1924	Walter Hagen		1946	Ben Hogan		1967	Don January	281
1925	Walter Hagen		1947	Jim Ferrier		1968	Julius Boros	281
1926	Walter Hagen		1948	Ben Hogan		1969	Ray Floyd	276
1927	Walter Hagen		1949	Sam Snead		1970	Dave Stockton	279
1928	Leo Diegel		1950	Chandler Harper		1971	Jack Nicklaus	281
1929	Leo Diegel		1951	Sam Snead		1972	Gary Player (SA)	281
1930	Tommy Armour		1952	Jim Turnesa		1973	Jack Nicklaus	277
1931	Tom Creavy		1953	Walter Burkemo		1974	Lee Trevino	276
1932	Olin Dutra		1954	Chick Harbert		1975	Jack Nicklaus	276
1933	Gene Sarazen		1955	Doug Ford		1976	Dave Stockton	281
1934	Paul Runyan		1956	Jack Burke		1977	Lanny Wadkinsz	282
1935	Johnny Revolta		1957	Lionel Hebert	Score	1978	John Mahaffey	276
1936	Denny Shute		1958	Dow Finsterwald	276	1979	David Graham (Aus)	272
1937	Denny Shute		1959	Bob Rosburg	277			
1938	Paul Runyan		1960	Jay Hebert	281			

World Match Play Tournament

Sponsored by Piccadilly from 1964 to 1976, and by Colgate from 1977.

1964	Arnold Palmer (USA)	1969	Bob Charles (NZ)	1974	Hale Irwin (USA)
1965	Gary Player (SA)	1970	Jack Nicklaus (USA)	1975	Hale Irwin (USA)
1966	Gary Player (SA)	1971	Gary Player (SA)	1976	David Graham (Aus)
1967	Arnold Palmer (USA)	1972	Tom Weiskopf (USA)	1977	Graham Marsh (Aus)
1968	Gary Player (SA)	1973	Gary Player (SA)	1978	Isao Aoki (Jap)

British Amateur Championship

First played in 1885, the Amateur Championship is a knock-out match play event. Winners since 1965:

1965	Michael Bonallack (GB)	1970	Michael Bonallack (GB)	1975	Marvin Giles (USA)
1966	Bobby Cole (SA)	1971	Steve Melnyk (USA)	1976	Dick Siderowf (USA)
1967	Bob Dickson (USA)	1972	Trevor Homer (GB)	1977	Peter McAvoy (GB)
1968	Michael Bonallack (GB)	1973	Dick Siderowf (USA)	1978	Peter McAvoy (GB)
1969	Michael Bonallack (GB)	1974	Trevor Homer (GB)	1979	Jay Sigel (USA)

Most wins: 8   John Ball (GB): 1888, 1890, 1892, 1894, 1899, 1907, 1910, 1912

US Amateur Championship

First played in 1893, a match play tournament over 36 holes per round. Winners since 1965:

1965	Bob Murphy	1970	Lanny Wadkins	1975	Fred Ridley
1966	Gary Cowan	1971	Gary Cowan	1976	Bill Sander
1967	Bob Dickson	1972	Marvin Giles	1977	John Fought
1968	Bruce Fleisher	1973	Craig Stadler	1978	John Cook
1969	Steve Melnyk	1974	Jerry Pate		

(all the above from the USA)

Most wins: 5   Robert T. Jones: 1924, 1925, 1927, 1928, 1930

Colgate European Women's Open Championship

First held in 1974. 72 holes stroke play. Winners:

1974	Judy Rankin (USA) 218 (54 holes)	1977	Judy Rankin (USA) 281
1975	Donna Caponi/Young (USA) 283	1978	Nancy Lopez (USA) 289
1976	Chako Higuchi (Jap) 284	1979	Nancy Lopez (USA) 282

US Women's Open Championship

First held in 1946 as match play, but since 1947 has been at 72 holes stroke play. Winners since 1965 (all USA except where stated):

1965	Carol Mann 290	1970	Donna Caponi 287	1975	Sandra Palmer 295
1966	Sandra Spuzich 277	1971	Jo Anne Carner 288	1976	Jo Anne Carner 292
1967	Catherine Lacoste (Fra) 294	1972	Sue Maxwell Berning 299	1977	Hollis Stacy 292
1968	Sue Maxwell Berning 289	1973	Sue Maxwell Berning 290	1978	Hollis Stacy 289
1969	Donna Caponi 294	1974	Sandra Haynie 295		

Most wins: 4   Betsy Rawls: 1951, 1953, 1957, 1960
4   Mickey Wright: 1958, 1959, 1961, 1964

British Ladies Amateur Championship

First held in 1893, a knock-out match play event. Winners since 1965:

1965	Brigitte Varangot (Fra)	1968	Brigitte Varangot (Fra)	1971	Michelle Walker (GB)
1966	Elizabeth Chadwick (GB)	1969	Catherine Lacoste (Fra)	1972	Michelle Walker (GB)
1967	Elizabeth Chadwick (GB)	1970	Dinah Oxley (GB)	1973	Ann Irvin (GB)

1974	Carol Semple (USA)
1975	Nancy Syms (USA)
1976	Catherine Panton (GB)
1977	Angela Uzielli (GB)
1978	Edwina Kennedy (Aus)

Most wins: 4 Cecilia Leitch: 1914, 1920, 1921, 1926
4 Joyce Wethered: 1922, 1924, 1925, 1929

World Cup

Contested by 2-man national teams of professionals. Instituted in 1953 as the Canada Cup.

1953	Argentina	1960	USA	1967	USA	1973	USA
1954	Australia	1961	USA	1968	Canada	1974	South Africa
1955	USA	1962	USA	1969	USA	1975	USA
1956	USA	1963	USA	1970	Australia	1976	Spain
1957	Japan	1964	USA	1971	USA	1977	Spain
1958	Ireland	1965	South Africa	1972	Taiwan	1978	USA
1959	Australia	1966	USA				

Ryder Cup

Contested every two years by professional teams from the United States and Great Britain. First held in 1927. The USA have won on 18 occasions, most recently in 1971, 1973, 1975 and 1977. Great Britain/British Isles won in 1929, 1933 and 1957 and the 1969 match was halved.

Walker Cup

Contested every two years by amateur teams from the United States and Great Britain. First held in 1922. The USA have won on 24 occasions, most recently in 1973, 1975, 1977 and 1979. Great Britain won in 1947 and 1971 and the 1965 match was halved.

Curtis Cup

Contested every two years by teams of lady golfers from the United States and Great Britain. First held in 1932. The USA have won on 16 occasions, most recently in 1970, 1972, 1974, 1976 and 1978. Great Britain won in 1952 and 1956 and the 1936 and 1958 matches were halved.

Eisenhower Trophy

Contested by 4-man amateur national teams. First held in 1958.

1958	Australia	1970	USA
1960	USA	1972	USA
1962	USA	1974	USA
1964	GB and Ireland	1976	GB and Ireland
1966	Australia	1978	USA
1968	USA		

World Women's Amateur Team Championship

Contested every two years for the Espirito Santo Trophy.

| 1964 | France | 1968 | USA | 1972 | USA | 1976 | USA |
| 1966 | USA | 1970 | USA | 1974 | USA | 1978 | Australia |

British Ladies Open Championship

First held 1976; this tournament succeeded the British Ladies' Amateur Stroke Play Championship which had been inaugurated in 1969.

| 1976 | Jennifer Lee Smith (GB) 299 | 1977 | Vivien Saunders (GB) 306 | 1978 | Janet Melville (GB) 310 |
| | | 1979 | Alison Sheard (SA) 301 | | |

GRANDMOTHERS

Glamorous Grannies Award

There are many competitions at local level throughout Britain to find the most glamorous granny, and since 1978 BBC Television's Nationwide organises a national award scheme. As well as the silver challenge trophy, the winner received £1000 and a holiday for two in Sierra Leone.

1978   Pamela Burnell
1979   Patricia Stables (45) of Brigg, South Humberside

GREYHOUND RACING

Greyhound Derby

Britain's premier race, the Greyhound Derby, is held at the White City Stadium over a distance of 500 metres. It was first held in 1927. Winners have been:

1927	Entry Badge	1939	Highland Rum	1955	Rushton Mack	1967	Tric-Trac
1928	Boher Ash	1940	G. R. Archduke	1956	Dunmore King	1968	Camira Flash
1929	Mick The Miller	1945	Ballyhennessy Seal	1957	Ford Spartan	1969	Sand Star
1930	Mick The Miller	1946	Mondays News	1958	Pigalle Wonder	1970	John Silver
1931	Seldom Lad	1947	Trevs Perfection	1959	Mile Bush Pride	1971	Dolores Rocket
1932	Wild Woolley	1948	Priceless Border	1960	Duleek Dandy	1972	Patricia's Hope
1933	Future Cutlet	1949	Narrogar Ann	1961	Palms Printer	1973	Patricia's Hope
1934	Davesland	1950	Ballmac Ball	1962	The Grand Canal	1974	Jimsun
1935	Greta Ranee	1951	Ballylanigan Tanist	1963	Lucky Boy Boy	1975	Tartan Khan
1936	Fine Jubilee	1952	Endless Gossip	1964	Hack Up Chieftain	1976	Mutts Silver
1937	Wattle Bark	1953	Daws Dancer	1965	Chittering Clapton	1977	Balliniska Band
1938	Lone Keel	1954	Pauls Fun	1966	Faithful Hope	1978	Lacca Champion
						1979	Sarah's Bunny

The most famous greyhound of all time, Mick the Miller, was the first dog to win the Greyhound Derby twice – in 1929 and 1930. Here in his retirement at the age of eight in 1934 he meets some of the Crazy Gang and showgirls from the Palladium (*Syndication International*)

Greyhound Grand National

First held in 1927 and run over 500 metres hurdles at the White City Stadium.

1927	Bonzo	1930	Stylish Cutlet	1933	Scapegoat	1936	Kilganny Bridge
1928	Cormorant	1931	Rule the Roost	1934	Lemonition	1937	Flying Wedge
1929	Levator	1932	Long Hop	1935	Quarter Day	1938	Juvenile Classic

1939	Valiant Bob	1953	Denver Berwick	1962	Corsican Reward	1971	Sherry's Prince
1940	Juvenile Classic	1954	Prince Lawrence	1963	Indoor Sport	1972	Sherry's Prince
1946	Barry from Limerick	1955	Barrowside	1964	Two Aces	1973	Killone Flash
1947	Baytown Pigeon	1956	Blue Sand	1965	I'm Crazy	1974	Shanney's Darkie
1948	Joves Reason	1957	Tanyard Tulip	1966	Halfpenny King	1975	Pier Hero
1949	Blossom of Annagura	1958	Fodda Champion	1967	The Grange Santa	1976	Weston Pete
1950	Blossom of Annagura	1959	Prince Poppit	1968	Ballintore Tiger	1977	Salerno
1951	XPDNC	1960	Bruff Chariot	1969	Tony's Friend	1978	Top O' The Tide
1952	Whistling Laddie	1961	Ballinatona Special	1970	Sherry's Prince	1979	Top O' The Tide

The Laurels

First held in 1930 and run over 500 metres at Wimbledon.

1930	Kilbrean Boy	1950	Ballymac Ball	1966	Super Fame
1931	Future Cutlet	1951	Ballylanigan Tanist	1967	Carry on Oregon
1932	Beef Cutlet	1952	Endless Gossip	1968	Ambiguous
1933	Wild Woolley	1953	Polonius	1969	Ardine Flame
1934	Brilliant Bob	1954	Coolkill Chieftain	1970	Sole Aim
1935	Kitshine	1955	Duet Leader	1971	Black Andrew
1936	Top O' The Carlow Road	1956	Duet Leader	1972	Cricket Bunny
1937	Ballyhennessy Sandhills	1957	Ford Spartan	1973	Black Banjo
1938	Ballyhennessy Sandhills	1958	Granthamian	1974	Over Protected
1939	Musical Duke	1959	Mighty Hassan	1975	Pineapple Grand
1940	April Burglar	1960	Dunstown Paddy	1976	Xmas Holiday
1945	Burhill Moon	1961	Clonalvy Pride	1977	Greenfield Fox
1946	Shannon Shore	1962	Tuturama	1978	Jet Control
1947	Rimmells Black	1963	Dalcassion Son		
1948	Good Worker	1964	Conna Count		
1949	Ballymac Ball	1965	Conna Count		

GYMNASTICS

Olympic Games

First held in the Olympics in 1896; since the 1948 Games the events have been: Men: Floor exercises, Side Horse, Rings, Horse Vault, Parallel Bars, Horizontal Bar. Women: Horse Vault, Asymmetrical Bars, Balance Beam, Floor Exercises. Competitors compete for medals in both these events and the Combined Exercises for which points in individual events are totalled. Winners of the Combined Exercises (Team and Individual) since 1948:

MEN

	Team	Individual	Most Individual Gold Medals	
1948	Finland	Veikko Huhtanen (Fin)	2	Veikko Huhtanen and Paavo Aaltonen (Fin)
1952	USSR	Viktor Chukarin (USSR)	3	Viktor Chukarin
1956	USSR	Viktor Chukarin (USSR)	2	Viktor Chukarin and Valentin Muratov (USSR)
1960	Japan	Boris Shakhlin (USSR)	4	Boris Shakhlin
1964	Japan	Yukio Endo (Jap)	2	Yukio Endo
1968	Japan	Sawao Kato (Jap)	2	Kato, Akinori Nakayama (Jap), and Mikhail Voronin (USSR)
1972	Japan	Sawao Kato (Jap)	2	Sawao Kato
1976	Japan	Nikolai Andrianov (USSR)	4	Nikolai Andrianov

Overall most individual Gold Medals have been won by Boris Shakhlin (USSR) with 6: one in 1956, four in 1960 and one in 1964.

WOMEN

	Team	Individual	Most Individual Gold Medals	
1948	Czechoslovakia	(Only a team competition)		
1952	USSR	Maria Gorokhovskaya (USSR)	1	by several girls
1956	USSR	Larissa Latynina (USSR)	3	Latynina and Agnes Keleti (Hun)
1960	USSR	Larissa Latynina (USSR)	2	Larissa Latynina
1964	USSR	Vera Caslavska (Cze)	3	Vera Caslavska
1968	USSR	Vera Caslavska (Cze)	4	Vera Caslavska

	Team	Individual	Most Individual Gold Medals
1972	USSR	Lyudmila Tourischeva (USSR)	2 Olga Korbut (USSR) and Karin Janz (GDR)
1976	USSR	Nadia Comaneci (Rom)	3 Nadia Comaneci (Rom)

Overall most individual Gold Medals have been won by Vera Caslavska (Cze) with 7.

World Championships

Combined Exercises World Champions since 1950:

MEN

	Team	Individual	Most Individual Gold Medals
1950	Switzerland	Walter Lehmann (Swi)	2 Lehmann and Josef Stalder (Swi)
1954	USSR	Valentin Muratov (USSR) and Viktor Chukharin (USSR)	3 Valentin Muratov (USSR)
1958	USSR	Boris Shakhlin (USSR)	4 Boris Shakhlin (USSR)
1962	Japan	Yuriy Titov (USSR)	2 Titov and Miroslav Cerar (Yug)
1966	Japan	Mikhail Voronin (USSR)	2 Mikhail Voronin (USSR)
1970	Japan	Eizo Kenmotsu (Jap)	3 Akinori Nakayama (Jap)
1974	Japan	Shigeru Kasamatsu (Jap)	3 Shigeru Kasamatsu (Jap)
1978	Japan	Nikolai Andrianov (USSR)	2 Nikolai Andrianov (USSR)

WOMEN

	Team	Individual	Most Individual Gold Medals
1950	Sweden	Helena Rakoczy (Pol)	4 Helena Rakoczy (Pol)
1954	USSR	Galina Roudiko (USSR)	2 Tamara Minina (USSR)
1958	USSR	Larissa Latynina (USSR)	4 Larissa Latynina (USSR)
1962	USSR	Larissa Latynina (USSR)	2 Larissa Latynina (USSR)
1966	Czechoslovakia	Vera Caslavska (Cze)	3 Natalia Kuchinskaya (USSR)
1970	USSR	Lyudmila Tourischeva (USSR)	2 Tourischeva and Erika Zuchold (GDR)
1974	USSR	Lyudmila Tourischeva (USSR)	3 Tourischeva
1978	USSR	Elena Mukhina (USSR)	2 Nelli Kim (USSR)

HAIRDRESSING

Guild Young Hairstylists Championship

The Incorporated Guild of Hairdressers, Wigmakers and Perfumers dates back to the late 1800s and for many years they ran an annual event known as the 'National Junior Hairstyling Competition'. This was changed in 1972 to the 'Guild Young Hairstylists Championship of Great Britain'.

Competitors are required to produce a free style for any occasion. Hair style may be produced on any length of hair, but female models only are permitted. One hair-piece is allowed and use of hair ornaments is optional. The time allowed is 45 minutes. The jury looks for originality of the dressing, the suitability of the hair style to the model, and the 'total look' of the model. The winners to date are as follows:

1972	Miss Sandra Bicknell of Leamington Spa	1976	Miss Vivienne Limbrey of Porthcawl
1973	Mr Neil Tapscott of High Bickington, N. Devon	1977	Mr Bruce Patrick of York
1974	Miss Lynda Hoddinott of Selsey, Sussex	1978	Miss Della Reeves of Brockenhurst, Hants
1975	Mr Kevin Murphy of Bedworth, Warwicks	1979	George Romeo Brown of Liverpool

Student of the Year Award

The Hairdressing Council, which was established by the provisions of the Hairdressers (Registration) Act 1964, is required to approve, or otherwise, courses and examinations in hairdressing. However, in the UK a person is not compelled by law to follow an approved course of training or pass an approved examination in order to practice as a hairdresser. As a consequence, the Hairdressing Council devised the 'Student of the Year' Award to encourage all those young people entering hairdressing as a career to follow an approved course of training.

The 'Student of the Year' Award is an educational award and not a hairdressing competition.

Mary Stavin, Miss World 1977 (see p 59) (*Mike Hallson/ JEM Int*)

John Hinchcliffe, a winner of the 1977 British Craft Awards (see p 89) (*Daily Telegraph*)

Above: **Winner of the 1975** *Garden News* **tallest sunflower competition—21 ft 6 in (6.5 m) (see p 231)**

Right: **Fred Pearce, foreman, with a display of giant begonias at Totteridge Station, voted 1978 Best Underground Station Garden (see p 205)**

Tom Baker in a scene from Dr Who, winner of several awards, in the 'Terror of the Zygons' shown in 1975 (*BBC copyright*)

A scene from Fawlty Towers during 'The Gourmet Evening' episode. The series received a BAFTA award in 1975 for the Best Light Entertainment Production (*BBC copyright*)

The Goodies programme was awarded a Silver Rose of Montreux in 1974 (*BBC copyright*)

The winners since it began in 1968 are:

1968   Minnie Harrop, Olive Ioannou,
       Marilyn Derby
1969   Margaret Stevens
1970   Wendy Heyball
1971   Joanna Long
1972   Sally Ann Maunder
1973   Wendy Payne
1974   Caroline Ridgewell
1975   Dayle Taylor
1976   Carole Nickson
1977   Sian Lewis
1978   Julie Bates

Julie Bates, 1978 Student of the Year, at the Jingles School of Advanced Hairdressing

HANDBALL

First held in the Olympic Games in 1936, the sport for men was re-introduced in 1972, and is now held indoors.

OLYMPIC CHAMPIONS	WORLD CHAMPIONS		Women
	Men		*Outdoor*
1936 Germany	*Outdoors*	*Indoor*	1949 Hungary
1972 Yugoslavia	1938 Germany	1954 Sweden	1956 Romania
1976 USSR	1948 Sweden	1958 Sweden	1960 Romania
	1952 W. Germany	1961 Romania	
	1955 W. Germany	1964 Romania	*Indoor*
	1959 Germany	1967 Czechoslovakia	1957 Czechoslovakia
	1963 GDR	1970 Romania	1962 Romania
	1966 W. Germany	1974 Romania	1965 Hungary
		1978 W. Germany	1971 GDR
			1973 Yugoslavia

HEROISM

Greatest Heroes in History

The winner of a competition in 1970 to select the 25 greatest heroes in history, organised by the British Parliamentary Group for World Government and the World Confederation of Organisations of the Teaching Profession, was Daniel Jaussaud, aged 20, a student teacher at the Ecole Normale, Digne, France. The prize was a trip round the world. His selection of heroes, in alphabetical order, was:

Avicenna (the Islamic philosopher)
Simon Bolivar   Jesus Christ
Buddha   Martin Luther King
Charlemagne   Lincoln
Marie Curie   Marx
Henri Dunant   Michelangelo
Einstein   St. Thomas More
Erasmus   Pasteur
St. Francis of Assisi Plato
Galen   Rousseau
Gandhi   Schweitzer
Gutenberg   Tolstoy
Hippocrates   Leonardo da Vinci

One of the 'Greatest Heroes in History'. Marie Curie, voted one of the greatest heroes in this competition which was held in 1970 (*Popperfoto*)

HOCKEY

Olympic Games

Winners of the men's Hockey title at the Olympic Games – first included in 1908:

1908	England	1932	India	1952	India	1964	India
1920	Great Britain	1936	India	1956	India	1968	Pakistan
1928	India	1948	India	1960	Pakistan	1972	West Germany
						1976	New Zealand

World Cup

MEN

The first men's World Cup was held in 1971. Winners:

1971   Pakistan
1973   Holland
1975   India
1978   Pakistan

WOMEN

The FIH, the International Federation governing Hockey for both men and women, organised the first official world championship for women – the World Cup – in 1974.

1974   Holland
1976   West Germany
1978   Holland

World Championship

The IFWHA, the International Federation of Women's Hockey Associations organised a World Championship in 1975, and a second in August 1979.

1975   England

European Cup

MEN

First held in 1970. Winners:

1970   West Germany   1974   Spain   1978   West Germany

County Championships

MEN (First held 1957–58 season):

1958	Lincolnshire	1969	Lancashire
1959	Middlesex	1970	Wiltshire
1960	Hertfordshire	1971	Staffordshire
1961	Middlesex	1972	Wiltshire
1962	Durham	1973	Surrey
1963	Surrey	1974	Hertfordshire
1964	Kent	1975	Kent
1965	Kent	1976	Hertfordshire
1966	Cheshire	1977	Middlesex
1967	Wiltshire	1978	Lancashire
1968	Wiltshire	1979	Kent

WOMEN (First held 1958–59 season)

1969	Hertfordshire & Lancashire
1970	Lancashire
1971	Hertfordshire & Lancashire
1972	Essex
1973	Lancashire
1974	Lancashire
1975	Surrey & Leicestershire
1976	Lancashire
1977	Lancashire
1978	Hertfordshire
1979	Lancashire

HORSE RACING

The Classics

The five English Classics are all for 3-year-old horses. They are the 2000 Guineas, the 1000 Guineas, the Derby, the Oaks, and the St. Leger. The 1000 Guineas and the Oaks are restricted to fillies.

Two horses have won four classics: *Formosa* (1868) and *Sceptre* (1902), each won all bar the Derby.

Fifteen horses have won the 2000 Guineas, Derby and St. Leger – the only horse since 1935 being *Nijinsky* in 1970.

Six horses have won the 1000 Guineas, Oaks and St. Leger – since 1942 the only one to do so being *Meld* in 1955.

1000 GUINEAS

Run at Newmarket over 1 mile. First run in 1814.
Winning horses and jockeys since 1946 have been:

		Jockey
1946	Hypericum	D. Smith
1947	Imprudence	W. Johnstone
1948	Queenpot	G. Richards
1949	Musidora	E. Britt
1950	Camaree	W. Johnstone
1951	Belle of All	G. Richards
1952	Zabara	K. Gethin
1953	Happy Laughter	E. Mercer
1954	Festoon	A. Breasley
1955	Meld	H. Carr
1956	Honeylight	E. Britt
1957	Rose Royale	C. Smirke
1958	Bella Paola	S. Boullenger
1959	Petite Etoile	D. Smith
1960	Never Too Late	R. Poincelet
1961	Sweet Solera	W. Rickaby
1962	Abermaid	W. Williamson
1963	Hula Dancer	R. Poincelet
1964	Pourparler	G. Bougoure
1965	Night Off	W. Williamson
1966	Glad Rags	P. Cook
1967	Fleet	G. Moore
1968	Caergwrle	A. Barclay
1969	Full Dress II	R. Hutchinson
1970	Humble Duty	L. Piggott
1971	Altesse Royale	Y. Saint-Martin
1972	Waterloo	E. Hide
1973	Mysterious	G. Lewis
1974	Highclere	J. Mercer
1975	Nocturnal Spree	J. Roe
1976	Flying Water	Y. Saint-Martin
1977	Mrs McArdy	E. Hide
1978	Enstone Spark	E. Johnson
1979	One In a Million	J. Mercer

2000 GUINEAS

Run at Newmarket over 1 mile. First run in 1809.
Winning horses and jockeys since 1946 have been:

1946	Happy Knight	T. Weston
1947	Tudor Minstrel	G. Richards
1948	My Babu	C. Smirke
1949	Nimbus	E. C. Elliott
1950	Palestine	C. Smirke
1951	Ki Ming	A. Breasley
1952	Thunderhead II	R. Poincelet
1953	Nearula	E. Britt
1954	Darius	E. Mercer
1955	Our Babu	D. Smith
1956	Gilles de Retz	F. Barlow
1957	Crepello	L. Piggott
1958	Pall Mall	D. Smith
1959	Taboun	G. Moore
1960	Martial	R. Hutchinson
1961	Rockavon	N. Stirk
1962	Privy Councillor	W. Rickaby
1963	Only For Life	J. Lindley
1964	Baldric II	W. Pyers
1965	Niksar	D. Keith

1966	Kashmir II	J. Lindley
1967	Royal Palace	G. Moore
1968	Sir Ivor	L. Piggott
1969	Right Tack	G. Lewis
1970	Nijinsky	L. Piggott
1971	Brigadier Gerard	J. Mercer
1972	High Top	W. Carson
1973	Mon Fils	F. Durr
1974	Nonoalco	Y. Saint-Martin
1975	Bolkonski	G. Dettori
1976	Wollow	G. Dettori
1977	Nebbiolo	G. Curran
1978	Roland Gardens	F. Durr
1979	Tap On Wood	S. Cauthen

THE DERBY

Run at Epsom over 1½ miles. First run in 1780. Winning horses and jockeys since 1946 have been:

1946	Airborne	T. Lowrey
1947	Pearl Diver	G. Bridgland
1948	My Love	W. Johnstone
1949	Nimbus	E. C. Elliott
1950	Galcador	W. Johnstone
1951	Arctic Prince	C. Spares
1952	Tulyar	C. Smirke
1953	Pinza	G. Richards
1954	Never Say Die	L. Piggott
1955	Phil Drake	F. Palmer
1956	Lavandin	W. Johnstone
1957	Crepello	L. Piggott
1958	Hard Ridden	C. Smirke
1959	Parthia	H. Carr
1960	St Paddy	L. Piggott
1961	Psidium	R. Poincelet
1962	Larkspur	N. Sellwood
1963	Relko	Y. Saint-Martin
1964	Santa Claus	A. Breasley
1965	Sea Bird II	T. P. Glennon
1966	Charlottown	A. Breasley
1967	Royal Palace	G. Moore
1968	Sir Ivor	L. Piggott
1969	Blakeney	E. Johnson
1970	Nijinsky	L. Piggott
1971	Mill Reef	G. Lewis
1972	Roberto	L. Piggott
1973	Morston	E. Hide
1974	Snow Knight	B. Taylor
1975	Grundy	P. Eddery
1976	Empery	L. Piggott
1977	The Minstrel	L. Piggott
1978	Shirley Heights	G. Starkey
1979	Troy	W. Carson

THE OAKS

Run at Epsom over 1½ miles. First run in 1779. Winning horses and jockeys since 1946:

1946	Steady Aim	H. Wragg
1947	Imprudence	W. Johnstone
1948	Masaka	W. Nevett
1949	Musidora	E. Britt
1950	Asmena	W. Johnstone
1951	Neasham Belle	S. Clayton

1952	*Frieze*	E. Britt
1953	*Ambiguity*	J. Mercer
1954	*Sun Cap*	W. Johnstone
1955	*Meld*	H. Carr
1956	*Sicarelle*	F. Palmer
1957	*Carrozza*	L. Piggott
1958	*Bella Paola*	M. Garcia
1959	*Petite Etoile*	L. Piggott
1960	*Never Too Late*	R. Poincelet
1961	*Sweet Solera*	W. Rickaby
1962	*Monade*	Y. Saint-Martin
1963	*Noblesse*	G. Bougoure
1964	*Homeward Bound*	G. Starkey
1965	*Long Look*	J. Purtell
1966	*Valoris*	L. Piggott
1967	*Pia*	E. Hide
1968	*La Lagune*	G. Thiboeuf
1969	*Sleeping Partner*	J. Gorton
1970	*Lupe*	A. Barclay
1971	*Altesse Royale*	G. Lewis
1972	*Ginevra*	A. Murray
1973	*Mysterious*	G. Lewis
1974	*Polygamy*	P. Eddery
1975	*Juliette Marny*	L. Piggott
1976	*Pawneese*	Y. Saint-Martin
1977	*Dunfermline*	W. Carson
1978	*Fair Salinia*	G. Starkey
1979	*Scintillate*	P. Eddery

ST. LEGER

Run at Doncaster over 1 mile 6 furlongs 132 yards. First run in 1776. Winning horses and jockeys since 1946:

1946	*Airborne*	T. Lowrey
1947	*Sayajirao*	E. Britt
1948	*Black Tarquin*	E. Britt
1949	*Ridge Wood*	M. Beary
1950	*Scratch II*	W. Johnstone
1951	*Talma II*	W. Johnstone
1952	*Tulyar*	C. Smirke
1953	*Premonition*	E. Smith
1954	*Never Say Die*	C. Smirke
1955	*Meld*	H. Carr
1956	*Cambremer*	F. Palmer
1957	*Ballymoss*	T. P. Burns
1958	*Alcide*	H. Carr
1959	*Cantelo*	E. Hide
1960	*St. Paddy*	L. Piggott
1961	*Aurelius*	L. Piggott
1962	*Hethersett*	H. Carr
1963	*Ragusa*	G. Bougoure
1964	*Indiana*	J. Lindley
1965	*Provoke*	J. Mercer
1966	*Sodium*	F. Durr
1967	*Ribocco*	L. Piggott
1968	*Ribero*	L. Piggott
1969	*Intermezzo*	R. Hutchinson
1970	*Nijinsky*	L. Piggott
1971	*Athens Wood*	L. Piggott
1972	*Boucher*	L. Piggott
1973	*Peleid*	F. Durr
1974	*Bustino*	J. Mercer
1975	*Bruni*	A. Murray
1976	*Crow*	Y. Saint-Martin
1977	*Dunfermline*	W. Carson
1978	*Julio Mariner*	E. Hide

Prix de L'Arc de Triomphe

Europe's most prestigious race was first run in 1920. It is run at Longchamp, Paris, over $1\frac{1}{2}$ miles and is open to all ages. Winning horses and jockeys since 1946 have been:

1946	*Caracalla*	E. C. Elliott
1947	*Le Paillon*	F. Rochetti
1948	*Migoli*	C. Smirke
1949	*Coronation*	R. Poincelet
1950	*Tantième*	J. Doyasbère
1951	*Tantième*	J. Doyasbère
1952	*Nuccio*	R. Poincelet
1953	*La Sorellina*	M. Larraun
1954	*Sica Boy*	W. Johnstone
1955	*Ribot*	E. Camici
1956	*Ribot*	E. Camici
1957	*Oroso*	S. Boullenger
1958	*Ballymoss*	A. Breasley
1959	*Saint Crespin*	G. Moore
1960	*Puissant Chef*	M. Garcia
1961	*Molvedo*	E. Camici
1962	*Soltikoff*	M. Depalmas
1963	*Exbury*	J. Deforge
1964	*Prince Royal II*	R. Poincelet
1965	*Sea Bird II*	T. Glennon
1966	*Bon Mot III*	F. Head
1967	*Topyo*	W. Pyers
1968	*Vaguely Noble*	W. Williamson
1969	*Levmoss*	W. Williamson
1970	*Sassafras*	Y. Saint-Martin
1971	*Mill Reef*	G. Lewis
1972	*San San*	F. Head
1973	*Rheingold*	L. Piggott
1974	*Allez France*	Y. Saint-Martin
1975	*Star Appeal*	G. Starkey
1976	*Ivanjica*	F. Head
1977	*Alleged*	L. Piggott
1978	*Alleged*	L. Piggott

Washington D.C. International

Run at Laurel Park, Washington, over $1\frac{1}{2}$ miles and held annually since 1952. Winning horses and jockeys have been (open by invitation to horses from all over the world, 3-year-olds and over):

1952	*Wilwyn* (GB)	E. Mercer
1953	*Worden II* (Fra)	C. Smirke
1954	*Fisherman* (USA)	E. Arcaro
1955	*El Chama* (Ven)	R. Bustamante
1956	*Master Boing* (Fra)	G. Chancelier
1957	*Mahan* (USA)	S. Boulmetis
1958	*Sailor's Guide* (Aus)	H. Grant
1959	*Bald Eagle* (USA)	M. Ycaza
1960	*Bald Eagle* (USA)	M. Ycaza
1961	*T.V. Lark* (USA)	J. Longden
1962	*Match III* (Fra)	Y. Saint-Martin
1963	*Mongo* (USA)	W. Chambers
1964	*Kelso* (USA)	I. Valenzuela
1965	*Diatome* (Fra)	J. Deforge

1966	*Behistoun* (Fra)	J. Deforge
1967	*Fort Marcy* (USA)	M. Ycaza
1968	*Sir Ivor* (Ire)	L. Piggott
1969	*Karabas* (Eng)	L. Piggott
1970	*Fort Marcy* (USA)	J. Velasquez
1971	*Run the Gauntlet* (USA)	R. Woodhouse
1972	*Droll Role* (USA)	B. Baeza
1973	*Dahlia* (Fra)	W. Pyers
1974	*Admetus* (Fra)	M. Philipperon
1975	*Nobiliary* (Fra)	S. Hawley
1976	*Youth* (Fra)	S. Hawley
1977	*Johnny D* (USA)	S. Cauthen
1978	*MacDiarmida* (USA)	J. Cruguet

National Hunt Racing

GRAND NATIONAL

Held at Aintree, Liverpool – a steeplechase over 4 miles 856 yards. (In 1916, 1917 and 1918 the race was held at Gatwick in Surrey.) Winning horses and jockeys since 1946 have been:

1946	*Lovely Cottage*	R. Petre
1947	*Caughoo*	E. Dempsey
1948	*Sheila's Cottage*	A. Thompson
1949	*Russian Hero*	L. McMorrow
1950	*Freebooter*	J. Power
1951	*Nickel Coin*	J. Bullock
1952	*Teal*	A. Thompson
1953	*Early Mist*	B. Marshall
1954	*Royal Tan*	B. Marshall
1955	*Quare Times*	P. Taaffe
1956	*E.S.B.*	D. Dick
1957	*Sundew*	F. Winter
1958	*Mr. What*	A. Freeman
1959	*Oxo*	M. Scudamore
1960	*Merryman II*	G. Scott
1961	*Nicolaus Silver*	H. Beasley
1962	*Kilmore*	F. Winter
1963	*Ayala*	P. Buckley
1964	*Team Spirit*	W. Robinson
1965	*Jay Trump*	C. Smith
1966	*Anglo*	T. Norman
1967	*Foinavon*	J. Buckingham
1968	*Red Alligator*	B. Fletcher
1969	*Highland Wedding*	E. Harty
1970	*Gay Trip*	P. Taaffe
1971	*Specify*	J. Cook

In five attempts, 1973–77, *Red Rum*, here with his trainer, Donald McCain, won the Grand National a record three times and was runner-up twice (*Syndication International*)

1972	*Well To Do*	G. Thorner
1973	*Red Rum*	B. Fletcher
1974	*Red Rum*	B. Fletcher
1975	*L'Escargot*	T. Carberry
1976	*Rag Trade*	J. Burke
1977	*Red Rum*	T. Stack
1978	*Lucius*	R. Davies
1979	*Rubstic*	M. Barnes

CHELTENHAM GOLD CUP

Held at Cheltenham – a steeplechase run over $3\frac{1}{4}$ miles. Distance: 1924–28, about $3\frac{1}{4}$ miles; 1929–35, 3 miles and about 3 furlongs; 1936–39, 3 miles and about 2 furlongs; 1940–45, 3 miles; 1946–57, 3 miles and about 2 furlongs; 1958, $3\frac{1}{4}$ miles and 130 yards; from 1965, 3 miles 2 furlongs and 76 yards. (All horses now carry 12st.) Winning horses and jockeys since 1946:

1946	*Prince Regent*	T. Hyde
1947	*Fortina*	Mr R. Black
1948	*Cottage Rake*	A. Brabazon
1949	*Cottage Rake*	A. Brabazon
1950	*Cottage Rake*	A. Brabazon
1951	*Silver Fame*	M. Molony
1952	*Mont Tremblant*	D. Dick
1953	*Knock Hard*	T. Molony

1954	*Four Ten*	T. Cusack
1955	*Gay Donald*	A. Grantham
1956	*Limber Hill*	J. Power
1957	*Linwell*	M. Scudamore
1958	*Kerstin*	S. Hayhurst
1959	*Roddy Owen*	H. Beasley
1960	*Pas Seul*	W. Rees
1961	*Saffron Tartan*	F. Winter
1962	*Mandarin*	F. Winter
1963	*Mill House*	W. Robinson
1964	*Arkle*	P. Taaffe
1965	*Arkle*	P. Taaffe
1966	*Arkle*	P. Taaffe
1967	*Woodland Venture*	T. W. Biddlecombe
1968	*Fort Leney*	P. Taaffe
1969	*What a Myth*	P. Kelleway

1970	*L'Escargot*	T. Carberry
1971	*L'Escargot*	T. Carberry
1972	*Glencaraig Lady*	F. Berry
1973	*The Dikler*	R. Barry
1974	*Captain Christy*	H. Beasley

1975	*Ten Up*	T. Carberry
1976	*Royal Frolic*	J. Burke
1977	*Davy Lad*	D. T. Hughes
1978	*Midnight Court*	J. Francome
1979	*Alverton*	J. J. O'Neill

CHAMPION HURDLE

Held at Cheltenham – a steeplechase over 2 miles 200 yards. Distance: 1927–28, 2 miles: 1929–57, 2 miles and a few yards; 1958–60, 2 miles; 1961–64, 2 miles 100 yards; from 1965, 2 miles 200 yards. Winning horses and jockeys since 1946:

1946	*Distel*	R. O'Ryan
1947	*National Spirit*	D. Morgan
1948	*National Spirit*	R. Smyth
1949	*Hatton's Grace*	A. Brabazon
1950	*Hatton's Grace*	A. Brabazon
1951	*Hatton's Grace*	T. Molony
1952	*Sir Ken*	T. Molony
1953	*Sir Ken*	T. Molony
1954	*Sir Ken*	T. Molony
1955	*Clair Soleil*	F. Winter
1956	*Doorknocker*	H. Sprague
1957	*Merry Deal*	G. Underwood
1958	*Bandalore*	G. Slack
1959	*Fare Time*	F. Winter

1960	*Another Flash*	H. Beasley
1961	*Eborneezer*	F. Winter
1962	*Anzio*	W. Robinson
1963	*Winning Flair*	Mr A. Lillingston
1964	*Magic Court*	P. McCarron
1965	*Kirriemuir*	W. Robinson
1966	*Salmon Spray*	J. Haine
1967	*Saucy Kit*	R. Edwards
1968	*Persian War*	J. Uttley
1969	*Persian War*	J. Uttley
1970	*Persian War*	J. Uttley
1971	*Bula*	P. Kelleway
1972	*Bula*	P. Kelleway
1973	*Comedy of Errors*	W. Smith
1974	*Lanzarote*	R. Pitman
1975	*Comedy of Errors*	K. White
1976	*Night Nurse*	P. Broderick
1977	*Night Nurse*	P. Broderick
1978	*Monksfield*	T. Kinane
1979	*Monksfield*	D. Hughes

British Flat Racing – Champion Jockeys

The rider of the most winners on the flat each year.

Most years as champion:

27 Gordon Richards: 1925, 1927–29, 1931–40, 1942–53; **most wins in a year:** 269 in 1947, 261 in 1949, 259 in 1933, 231 in 1952, 227 in 1951, 224 in 1948, 214 in 1937, 212 in 1934 and 1946, 210 in 1935, 206 in 1938, 201 in 1950.

14 George Fordham: 1855–63, 1865, 1867–69, 1871 (shared); **most wins in a year:** 166 in 1862.

13 Fred Archer: 1874–86; **most wins in a year:** 246 in 1885, 241 in 1884, 232 in 1883, 229 in 1878, 220 in 1881, 218 in 1887, 210 in 1882, 207 in 1876.

13 Elnathan Flatman: 1840–52; **most wins in a year:** 104 in 1848.

10 Steve Donoghue: 1914–22, 1923 (shared); **most wins in a year:** 143 in 1920.

Champions since 1946:

1946	Gordon Richards 212
1947	Gordon Richards 269
1948	Gordon Richards 224
1949	Gordon Richards 261
1950	Gordon Richards 201
1951	Gordon Richards 227
1952	Gordon Richards 231
1953	Gordon Richards 191
1954	Doug Smith 129
1955	Doug Smith 168
1956	Doug Smith 155
1957	Scobie Breasley 173

1958	Doug Smith 165
1959	Doug Smith 157
1960	Lester Piggott 170
1961	Scobie Breasley 171
1962	Scobie Breasley 179
1963	Scobie Breasley 176
1964	Lester Piggott 140
1965	Lester Piggott 166
1966	Lester Piggott 191
1967	Lester Piggott 117
1968	Lester Piggott 139
1969	Lester Piggott 163

1970	Lester Piggott 162
1971	Lester Piggott 162
1972	Willie Carson 132
1973	Willie Carson 163
1974	Pat Eddery 148
1975	Pat Eddery 164
1976	Pat Eddery 162
1977	Pat Eddery 176
1978	Willie Carson 182

National Hunt Racing – Champion Jockeys

From 1900 to 1925 champions were listed for the calendar year, but since 1925/26 they have been accepted for the season from one year to another. The years shown below denote the second half of the season.

Most years as champion:

7 Gerry Wilson: 1933–38, 1941; **most wins in a year:** 73 in 1935

6 F. Mason: 1901–02, 1904–07; **most wins in a year:** 73 in 1905

5   Frederick Rees: 1920–21, 1923–24, 1927; **most wins in a year:** 108 in 1924

5   Billy Stott; 1928–32; **most wins in a year:** 88 in 1928
5   Tim Molony: 1949–52, 1955

Champions since 1946:

1946	Fred Rimell 54	
1947	Jack Dowdeswell 58	
1948	Brian Marshall 66	
1949	Tim Molony 60	
1950	Tim Molony 95	
1951	Tim Molony 83	
1952	Tim Molony 99	
1953	Fred Winter 121	
1954	Dick Francis 76	
1955	Tim Molony 67	
1956	Fred Winter 74	
1957	Fred Winter 80	

1958	Fred Winter 82
1959	Tim Brookshaw 83
1960	Stan Mellor 68
1961	Stan Mellor 118
1962	Stan Mellor 80
1963	Josh Gifford 70
1964	Josh Gifford 94
1965	Terry Biddlecombe 114
1966	Terry Biddlecombe 102
1967	Josh Gifford 122
1968	Josh Gifford 82

1969	{ Bob Davies / Terry Biddlecombe } 77
1970	Bob Davies 91
1971	Graham Thorner 74
1972	Bob Davies 89
1973	Ron Barry 125
1974	Ron Barry 94
1975	Tommy Stack 82
1976	Johnny Francome 96
1977	Tommy Stack 97
1978	Jon Jo O'Neill 149
1979	Johnny Francome 95

American Triple Crown

The American Triple Crown is made up of three races for three-year-olds.

KENTUCKY DERBY
$1\frac{1}{4}$ miles at Churchill Downs, Louisville, Kentucky; first held in 1875.

BELMONT STAKES
$1\frac{1}{2}$ miles at Belmont Park, New York; first held in 1867.

PREAKNESS STAKES
$1\frac{3}{16}$ miles at Pimlico, Baltimore, Maryland; first held in 1873.

Horses to have won all three races have been:

1919	*Sir Barton*
1930	*Gallant Fox*
1935	*Omaha*
1937	*War Admiral*
1941	*Whirlaway*
1943	*Count Fleet*
1946	*Assault*
1948	*Citation*
1973	*Secretariat*
1977	*Seattle Slew*
1978	*Affirmed*

HOSPITALITY

Ideal Hostess

This was organised by *Ideal Home* magazine, in conjunction with EKCO Heating and Appliances. First prize in 1973 was a five-day French cookery course in Dieppe, with £25 spending money and other prizes. There were over 50 runner-up prizes. The first prize in 1972 was £1000.

1972   Shelagh Heaver, Chichester
1973   Sarah Losse, London
1974   Susan Swan, Chorley
(The contest was discontinued)

HOTELS

Egon Ronay Hotel of the Year

The Gold Plate Awards are not necessarily given to the best establishment, but to the hotel or restaurant whose consistent excellence or enterprise is outstanding.

1969   Lygon Arms, Broadway (Hereford and Worcester)
1970   Inn on the Park, London W1
1971   Inverlochy Castle, Fort William (Highlands)

1972   Berkeley Hotel, London SW1
1973   Gleneagles Hotel, Auchterarder (Tayside)
1974   Sharrow Bay Country House Hotel, Ullswater (Cumbria)

1975   Ashford Castle, Cong, Co. Mayo, Eire
1976   Chewton Glen Hotel, New Milton (Hampshire)
1977   Gravetye Manor, East Grinstead (West Sussex)
1978   The Ritz, London W1

LONDON'S HOTELS
The following were billed as 'de luxe' by Egon Ronay in
1978, with the percentage score awarded to each.
Berkeley Hotel (93%)
Connaught Hotel (92%)
Dorchester Hotel (91%)
Claridge's Hotel (90%)
Inn on the Park (88%)
Carlton Tower Hotel (87%)
Grosvenor House Hotel (87%)
Ritz Hotel (87%)
Howard Hotel (86%)
Inter-Continental Hotel (85%)

**The Palm Court at the Ritz, London – Egon Ronay
Hotel of The Year in 1978**

HURLING

All-Ireland Championship
First contested in 1887. Winners since 1965:

1965	Tipperary	1971	Tipperary	1977	Cork
1966	Kilkenny	1972	Kilkenny	1978	Cork
1967	Kilkenny	1973	Limerick	**Most wins:** 24	Cork
1968	Wexford	1974	Kilkenny		
1969	Tipperary	1975	Kilkenny		
1970	Cork	1976	Cork		

ICE HOCKEY

Stanley Cup
The Stanley Cup, the premier trophy in North American Ice Hockey, is contested by the
professional teams in the National Hockey League. It was first competed for in 1893. Winners
since 1965:

1964–65	Montreal Canadiens	1969–70	Boston Bruins	1974–75	Philadelphia Flyers
1965–66	Montreal Canadiens	1970–71	Montreal Canadiens	1975–76	Montreal Canadiens
1966–67	Toronto Maple Leafs	1971–72	Boston Bruins	1976–77	Montreal Canadiens
1967–68	Montreal Canadiens	1972–73	Montreal Canadiens	1977–78	Montreal Canadiens
1968–69	Montreal Canadiens	1973–74	Philadelphia Flyers	1978–79	Montreal Canadiens

Most wins: 21   Montreal Canadiens – 1916, 1924, 1930–31, 1944, 1946, 1953, 1956–60, 1965–66, 1968–69, 1971, 1973,
1976–78

World Championship
First held in conjunction with the Olympics, and amateur only until 1976, but now held
annually. Winners since 1965:

1965	USSR	1970	USSR	1975	USSR
1966	USSR	1971	USSR	1976	Czechoslovakia
1967	USSR	1972	Czechoslovakia	1977	Czechoslovakia
1968	USSR	1973	USSR	1978	USSR
1969	USSR	1974	USSR	1979	USSR

Most wins: Canada 19, USSR 15

Olympic Champions
First held 1920.

1920	Canada	1932	Canada	1952	Canada	1964	USSR	1976	USSR
1924	Canada	1936	Great Britain	1956	USSR	1968	USSR		
1928	Canada	1948	Canada	1960	USA	1972	USSR		

ICE SKATING

World Champions

World figure skating championships were first held in 1896 for men, and in 1906 for women. Pair skating titles have been decided since 1908 and Ice Dancing since 1952. The championships were not held in 1961.

MEN'S FIGURE SKATING
Winners since 1947:

1947	Hans Gerschwiler (Swi)
1948	Richard Button (USA)
1949	Richard Button (USA)
1950	Richard Button (USA)
1951	Richard Button (USA)
1952	Richard Button (USA)
1953	Hayes Jenkins (USA)
1954	Hayes Jenkins (USA)
1955	Hayes Jenkins (USA)
1956	Hayes Jenkins (USA)
1957	David Jenkins (USA)
1958	David Jenkins (USA)
1959	David Jenkins (USA)
1960	Alain Giletti (Fra)
1962	Donald Jackson (Can)
1963	Donald McPherson (Can)
1964	Manfred Schnelldorfer (Ger)
1965	Alain Calmat (Fra)
1966	Emmerich Danzer (Aut)
1967	Emmerich Danzer (Aut)
1968	Emmerich Danzer (Aut)
1969	Tim Wood (USA)
1970	Tim Wood (USA)
1971	Ondrej Nepela (Cze)
1972	Ondrej Nepela (Cze)
1973	Ondrej Nepela (Cze)
1974	Jan Hoffmann (GDR)
1975	Sergei Volkov (USSR)
1976	John Curry (GB)
1977	Vladimir Kovalev (USSR)
1978	Charles Tickner (USA)
1979	Vladimir Kovalev (USSR)

Most titles: 10   Ulrich Salchow (Swe): 1901–05, 1907–11; 7   Karl Schäfer (Aut): 1930–36

WOMEN'S FIGURE SKATING
Winners since 1947:

1947	Barbara Ann Scott (Can)
1948	Barbara Ann Scott (Can)
1949	Aja Vrzanova (Cze)
1950	Aja Vrzanova (Cze)
1951	Jeanette Altwegg (GB)
1952	Jeanette Altwegg (GB)
1953	Tenley Albright (USA)
1954	Gundi Busch (Ger)
1955	Tenley Albright (USA)
1956	Carol Heiss (USA)
1957	Carol Heiss (USA)
1958	Carol Heiss (USA)
1959	Carol Heiss (USA)
1960	Carol Heiss (USA)
1962	Sjoukje Dijkstra (Hol)
1963	Sjoukje Dijkstra (Hol)
1964	Sjoukje Dijkstra (Hol)
1965	Petra Burka (Can)
1966	Peggy Fleming (USA)
1967	Peggy Fleming (USA)
1968	Peggy Fleming (USA)
1969	Gabriele Seyfert (GDR)
1970	Gabriele Seyfert (GDR)
1971	Beatrix Schuba (Aut)
1972	Beatrix Schuba (Aut)
1973	Karen Magnussen (Can)
1974	Christine Errath (GDR)
1975	Dianne de Leeuw (Hol)
1976	Dorothy Hamill (USA)
1977	Linda Fratianne (USA)
1978	Annette Pötzsch (GDR)
1979	Linda Fratianne (USA)

Most titles: 10   Sonja Henie (Nor) 1927–36

PAIR'S SKATING

1947, 1948	Pierre Baugniet and Micheline Lannoy (Bel)
1949	Ede Király and Andrea Kékessy (Hun)
1950	Peter Kennedy and Karol Kennedy (USA)
1951, 1952	Paul Falk and Ria Baran/Falk (Ger)
1953	John Nicks and Jennifer Nicks (GB)
1954, 1955	Norris Bowden and Frances Dafoe (Can)
1956	Kurt Oppelt and Sissy Schwarz (Aut)
1957–1960	Robert Paul and Barbara Wagner (Can)
1962	Otto Jelinek and Maria Jelinek (Can)
1963–1964	Hans-Jürgen Bäumler and Marika Kilius (Ger)
1965–1968	Oleg Protopopov and Lyudmila Protopopov (USSR)
1969–1972	Alexei Ulanov and Irina Rodnina (USSR)
1973–1978	Aleksandr Zaitsev and Irina Rodnina (USSR)
1979	Randy Gardner and Tai Babilonia (USA)

ICE DANCE SKATING

1952–1955	Lawrence Demmy and Jean Westwood (GB)
1956	Paul Thomas and Pamela Weight (GB)
1957–1958	Courtney Jones and June Markham (GB)
1959–1960	Courtney Jones and Doreen Denny (GB)
1962–1965	Pavel Roman and Eva Romanova (Cze)
1966–1969	Bernard Ford and Diane Towler (GB)
1970–1974	Aleksandr Gorshkov and Lyudmila Pakhomova (USSR)
1975	Andrei Minenkov and Irina Moiseyeva (USSR)
1976	Aleksandr Gorshkov and Lyudmila Pakhomova (USSR)
1977	Andrei Minenkov and Irina Moiseyeva (USSR)
1978–1979	Gennadiy Karponosov and Natalia Linichuk (USSR)

Olympic Champions

Figure Skating was first included in the Olympic Games in 1908, and has been included at each celebration since 1920. Winners since 1948:

MEN'S FIGURE SKATING
1948   Richard Button (USA)
1952   Richard Button (USA)
1956   Hayes Jenkins (USA)
1960   David Jenkins (USA)
1964   Manfred Schnelldorfer (Ger)
1968   Wolfgang Schwarz (Aut)
1972   Ondrej Nepela (Cze)
1976   John Curry (GB)

WOMEN'S FIGURE SKATING
1948   Barbara Ann Scott (Can)
1952   Jeanette Altwegg (GB)
1956   Tenley Albright (USA)
1960   Carol Heiss (USA)
1964   Sjoukje Dijkstra (Hol)
1968   Peggy Fleming (USA)
1972   Beatrix Schuba (Aut)
1976   Dorothy Hamill (USA)

PAIR'S SKATING
1948   Pierre Baugniet and Micheline Lannoy (Bel)
1952   Paul Falk and Ria Falk (Ger)
1956   Kurt Oppelt and Sissy Schwarz (Aut)
1960   Robert Paul and Barbara Wagner (Can)
1964   Oleg Protopopov and Lyudmila Protopopov (USSR)
1968   Oleg Protopopov and Lyudmila Belousova (Protopopov) (USSR)
1972   Alexei Ulanov and Irina Rodnina (USSR)
1976   Aleksandr Zaitsev and Irina Rodnina (USSR)

ICE DANCE
First held 1976
1976   Aleksander Gorshkov and Lyudmila Pakhomova (USSR)

SPEED SKATING

World Champions

World championships were first held in 1893. For men they are contested at 500, 1500, 5000 and 10 000 metres and for women at 500, 1000, 3000 and 5000 metres. Overall world champions are determined over the four distances. Overall world champions since 1947 have been:

MEN
1947   Lauri Parkkinen (Fin)
1948   Odd Lundberg (Nor)
1949   Kornel Pajor (Hun)
1950   Hjalmar Andersen (Nor)
1951   Hjalmar Andersen (Nor)
1952   Hjalmar Andersen (Nor)
1953   Oleg Goncharenko (USSR)
1954   Boris Schilkov (USSR)
1955   Sigvard Ericsson (Swe)
1956   Oleg Goncharenko (USSR)
1957   Knut Johannesen (Nor)
1958   Oleg Goncharenko (USSR)
1959   Juhani Järvinen (Fin)
1960   Boris Stenin (USSR)
1961   Hendrik van der Grift (Hol)
1962   Viktor Kosichkin (USSR)
1963   Jonny Nilsson (Swe)
1964   Knut Johannesen (Nor)
1965   Per Moe (Nor)
1966   Kees Verkerk (Hol)
1967   Kees Verkerk (Hol)
1968   Anton Maier (Nor)
1969   Dag Fornaess (Nor)
1970   Ard Schenk (Hol)
1971   Ard Schenk (Hol)
1972   Ard Schenk (Hol)
1973   Goran Claesson (Swe)
1974   Sten Stensen (Nor)
1975   Harm Kuipers (Hol)
1976   Piet Kleine (Hol)

1977   Eric Heiden (USA)
1978   Eric Heiden (USA)
1979   Eric Heiden (USA)

WOMEN
1947   Verne Lesche (Fin)
1948   Maria Isakova (USSR)
1949   Maria Isakova (USSR)
1950   Maria Isakova (USSR)
1951   Eva Huttunen (Fin)
1952   Lydia Selichova (USSR)
1953   Khalida Schegoleyeva (USSR)
1954   Lydia Selichova (USSR)
1955   Rimma Zhukova (USSR)
1956   Sofia Kondakova (USSR)
1957   Inga Artamonova (USSR)
1958   Inga Artamonova (USSR)
1959   Tamara Rylova (USSR)
1960   Valentina Stenina (USSR)
1961   Valentina Stenina (USSR)
1962   Inga Voronina (née Artamonova) (USSR)
1963   Lydia Skoblikova (USSR)
1964   Lydia Skoblikova (USSR)
1965   Inga Voronina (USSR)
1966   Valentina Stenina (USSR)
1967   Stein Kaiser (Hol)
1968   Stein Kaiser (Hol)
1969   Lasma Kauniste (USSR)
1970   Atje Keulen-Deelstra (Hol)
1971   Nina Statkevich (USSR)

1972	Atje Keulen-Deelstra (Hol)	1976	Sylvia Burka (Can)
1973	Atje Keulen-Deelstra (Hol)	1977	Vera Bryndzey (USSR)
1974	Atje Keulen-Deelstra (Hol)	1978	Tatiana Averina (USSR)
1975	Karin Kessow (GDR)	1979	Elizabeth Heiden (USA)

Olympic Champions

Speed Skating has been included on the Olympic programme since 1924 for men, and since 1960 for women. Winners since 1948:

MEN
500 metres
1948	Finn Helgesen (Nor)	43.1
1952	Kenneth Henry (USA)	43.2
1956	Yevgeniy Grischin (USSR)	40.2
1960	Yevgeniy Grischin (USSR)	40.2
1964	Richard McDermott (USA)	40.1
1968	Erhard Keller (Ger)	40.3
1972	Erhard Keller (Ger)	39.44
1976	Yevgeniy Kulikov (USSR)	39.17

1000 metres
1976	Peter Muller (USA)	1:19.32

1500 metres
1948	Sverre Farstad (Nor)	2:17.6
1952	Hjalmar Andersen (Nor)	2:20.4
1956	Yevgeniy Grischin (USSR) and Yuriy Mikhailov (USSR)	2:08.6
1960	Roald Aas (Nor) and Yevgeniy Grischin (USSR)	2:10.4
1964	Ants Antson (USSR)	2:10.3
1968	Cornelis Verkerk (Hol)	2:03.4
1972	Ard Schenk (Hol)	2:02.96
1976	Jan Egil Storholt (Nor)	1:59.38

5000 metres
1948	Reidar Liaklev (Nor)	8:29.4
1952	Hjalmar Andersen (Nor)	8:10.6
1956	Boris Schilkov (USSR)	7:48.7
1960	Viktor Kositschkin (USSR)	7:51.3
1964	Knut Johannesen (Nor)	7:38.4
1968	Anton Maier (Nor)	7:22.4
1972	Ard Schenk (Hol)	7:23.61
1976	Sten Stensen (Nor)	7:24.48

10 000 metres
1948	Åke Seyffarth (Swe)	17:26.3
1952	Hjalmar Andersen (Nor)	16:45.8
1956	Sigvard Ericsson (Swe)	16:35.9
1960	Knut Johannesen (Nor)	15:46.6
1964	Jonny Nilsson (Swe)	15:50.1
1968	Johnny Hoeglin (Swe)	15:23.6
1972	Ard Schenk (Hol)	15:01.35
1976	Piet Kleine (Hol)	14:50.59

WOMEN
500 metres
1960	Helga Haase (Ger)	45.9
1964	Lydia Skoblikova (USSR)	45.0
1968	Lyudmila Titova (USSR)	46.1
1972	Anne Henning (USA)	43.33
1976	Sheila Young (USA)	42.76

1000 metres
1960	Klala Guseva (USSR)	1:34.1
1964	Lydia Skoblikova (USSR)	1:33.2
1968	Corolina Geijssen (Hol)	1:32.6
1972	Monika Pflug (Ger)	1:31.40
1976	Tatyana Averina (USSR)	1:28.43

1500 metres
1960	Lydia Skoblikova (USSR)	2:25.2
1964	Lydia Skoblikova (USSR)	2:22.6
1968	Kaija Mustonen (Fin)	2:22.4
1972	Dianne Holum (USA)	2:20.85
1976	Galina Stepanskaya (USSR)	2:16.58

3000 metres
1960	Lydia Skoblikova (USSR)	5:14.3
1964	Lydia Skoblikova (USSR)	5:14.9
1968	Johanna Schut (Hol)	4:56.2
1972	Stein Baas-Kaiser (Hol)	4:52.14
1976	Tatyana Averina (USSR)	4:45.19

JAI ALAI (Pelota)

World Amateur Jai Alai Championships

Under the auspices of the Federación Internacional de Pelota Vasca, which is based in Spain. First held in 1952. Recent winners:

1966	Mexico	1974	France
1968	Spain	1975	United States
1970	France	1976	France
1971	Spain	1978	Spain

JOURNALISM

British Press Awards

These began in 1962 as the Hannen Swaffer National Press Awards, sponsored by Odhams Press in memory of Hannen Swaffer. The title was changed to the IPC Press Awards in 1967 when the International Publishing Corporation took over Odhams, and a further change was made in 1975 when the present name was adopted. The *Daily Mirror* gave up its control over the awards, which are now sponsored by several major newspaper groups. In 1976 photographic classes were introduced for the first time.

JOURNALIST OF THE YEAR

1962   Walter Terry, *Daily Mail*
1963   D. H. Hopkinson, *Sheffield Telegraph*
1964   Denis Hamilton, *The Sunday Times*
1965   Michael Randall, *Daily Mail*
1966   Sir Gordon Newton, *Financial Times*
1967   John Pilger, *Daily Mirror*
1968   Victor Zorza, *The Guardian*
1969   Anthony Grey, *Reuter's*
1970   Alastair Hetherington, *The Guardian*
1971   Simon Winchester, *The Guardian*
1972   Harold Evans, *The Sunday Times*
1973   Adam Raphael, *The Guardian*
1974   Harry Longmuir, *Daily Mail*
1975   Jon Swain, *The Sunday Times*
1976   No award
1977   *Lancashire Evening Post* (editor, assistant editor and chief reporter)
1978   Martin Bailey, Bernard Rivers and Peter Kelluer, *The Sunday Times*

YOUNG JOURNALIST OF THE YEAR

1967   June Sparey, Reading *Evening Post*
1968   Kevin Rafferty, *The Sun*
1969   Raymond Fitzwalker, Bradford *Telegraph and Argus*
1970   Janice Cave, Southend *Evening Echo*
1971   Yvonne Roberts, Northampton *Chronicle and Echo*
1972   Andrew Kruyer, Southend *Evening Echo*
1973   Roger Beam, Lancs *Evening Post*
1974   Gordon Ogilvie, Aberdeen *Evening Express*
1975   Melanie Phillips, Hemel Hempstead *Evening Post Echo*
1976   Richard Woolveridge, *South London Press*
1977   Tina Brown, *Telegraph Sunday Magazine* and Jad Adams, South East London and Kentish *Mercury*
1978   Andrew Cooper, Walsall *Observer*

REPORTER OF THE YEAR

1963   Henry Brandon, *The Sunday Times*
1964   Michael Gabbert, *The People*
1965   Anthony Carthew, *Sun* and *Daily Mail*
1966   Ken Gardner, *The People*
1967   David Farr, *The People*
1968   Harold Jackson, *The Guardian*
1969   Mary Holland, *The Observer*
1970   Monty Meth, *Daily Mail*
1971   John Clare, *The Times*
1972   Peter Harvey, *The Guardian*

1973   John Burns, Belfast *Telegraph*
1974   John Pilger, *Daily Mail*
1975   John Edwards, *Daily Mail*
1976   Geraldine Norman, *The Times*
1977   Richard Stott, *Daily Mirror*
1978   *Daily Mirror:* Team of Roger Beam, Barry Wigmore, Frank Palmer, Kent Gavin

INTERNATIONAL REPORTER OF THE YEAR

1966   Louis Heren, *The Times*
1967   Christopher Dobson, *Daily Mail*
1968   Walter Partington, *Daily Express*
1969   Murray Sayle, *The Sunday Times*
1970   John Pilger, *Daily Mirror*
1971   Peter Hazelhurst, *The Times*, and Gavin Young, *The Observer*
1972   John Fairhall, *The Guardian*
1973   Peter Niesewand, *The Guardian*
1924   Colin Smith, *The Observer*
1975   Martin Wollacott, *The Guardian*
1976   Peter Niesewand, *The Guardian*
1977   Robin Smyth, *The Observer*
1978   Peter Lewis, *Daily Mail*

PROVINCIAL JOURNALIST OF THE YEAR

1964   Anthony Hancox, *Sunday Mercury*
1965   Frank Laws, *Yorks Evening Post*
1966   Peter Williams, Burnley *Evening Star*
1967   Ernest Moore, Lancs *Evening Post*
1968   Len Doherty, Sheffield *Star*
1969   Eric Forster, Newcastle *Evening Chronicle*
1970   Alfred McCreary, Belfast *Telegraph*
1971   Barry Lloyd Jones, *The Birmingham Post*
1972   Chris Fuller, *The Birmingham Post*
1973   Frank Branston, Bedfordshire *Times*
1974   John Marquis, Watford *Echo*
1975   Carol Robertson, Sunderland *Echo*
1976   Geoffrey Parkhouse, *Glasgow Herald*, and Alan Whitsett, *Belfast News Letter*
1977   Carol Robertson and John Bailey, Sunderland *Echo*
1978   Team at Oldham *Evening Chronicle*

CRITIC OF THE YEAR

1963   Alan Brien, *Sunday Telegraph*
1964   Philip Purser, *Sunday Telegraph*
1965   Michael Foot, *Evening Standard*
1966   Milton Shulman, *Evening Standard*
1967   Alan Brien, *Sunday Telegraph*
1968   Peter Black, *Daily Mail*
1969   Alexander Walker, London *Evening Standard*
1970   George Melly, *The Observer*

1971   Derek Malcolm, *The Guardian*
1972   T. C. Worsley, *Financial Times*
1973   Alexander Walker, *Evening Standard*
1974   Michael Billington, *The Guardian*
1975   Paul Allen, *Sheffield Morning Telegraph*
1976   Chris Dunkley, *Financial Times*
1977   Clive James, *The Observer*
1978   Fay Maschler, *Evening Standard*

DESCRIPTIVE WRITER OF THE YEAR
1962   William Neil Connor, *Daily Mirror*
1963   Vincent Mulchrone, *Daily Mail*
1964   Anne Sharpley, *Evening Standard*
1965   James Cameron, *Evening Standard*
1966   John Pilger, *Daily Mirror*
1967   Donald Zec, *Daily Mirror*
1968   Angus McGill, *Evening Standard*
1969   Michael Frayn, *The Observer*
1970   Vincent Mulchrone, *Daily Mail*, and Keith
       Waterhouse, *Daily Mirror*
1971   Geoffrey Goodman, *Daily Mirror*
Discontinued

SPORTS WRITER OF THE YEAR
1963   J. L. Manning, *Daily Mail*
1964   George Whiting, *Evening Standard*
1965   Peter Wilson, *Daily Mirror*
1966   Hugh McIlvanney, *The Observer*
1967   Sam Leitch, *Sunday Mirror*
1968   Christopher Brasher, *The Observer*
1969   Hugh McIlvanney, *The Observer*
1970   Frank Butler, *News of the World*
1971   Ian Wooldridge, *Daily Mail*
1972   John Morgan, *Daily Express*
1973   Peter Batt, *The Sun*
1974   Ian Wooldridge, *Daily Mail*
1975   David Gray, *The Guardian*
1976   Chris Brasher, *The Observer*
1977   Hugh McIlvanney, *The Observer*
1978   Hugh McIlvanney, *The Observer*

WOMAN'S PAGE JOURNALIST OF THE YEAR
1967   Christine Galpin, Freelance/*News of the World*
1968   Marjorie Proops, *Daily Mirror*
1969   Felicity Green, *Daily Mirror*
1970   Elizabeth Prosser, *The Sun*
1971   Shirley Kaye, Halifax *Evening Post*, and Jill
       Tweedie, *The Guardian*
1972   Sue Hercombe, Newcastle *Evening Chronicle*
Discontinued

CAMPAIGNING JOURNALIST OF THE YEAR
1965   R. Stuart Campbell, *The People*
1966   Harold Evans, *Northern Echo*
1967   Colin McGlashan, *The Observer*
1968   Michael Leapman, *The Sun*, and Peter Harland,
       Bradford *Telegraph and Argus*
1969   Ken Gardner, *The People*
1970   Colin Brannigan, Sheffield *Star*
1971   Barry Askew, Lancs *Evening Post*
1972   Caren Meyer, *Evening News*
1973   Christopher Booker and Benny Gray, freelance
1974   No award
1975   Mary Beith, *Sunday People*, and Angus King,
       Yorkshire Post

1976   Douglas Thain, Alan Hurndall and Graham
       Hind, *Sheffield Star*
1977   John Pilger, *Daily Mirror*
1978   Team at Liverpool *Echo*

SPECIAL AWARD
1966   David Rhys Davies, *Merthyr Express*
1967   Peter Preston, *The Guardian*, Susanne Proudfoot,
       The Times
1968   Henry Longhurst, *The Sunday Times*
1969   Sir Neville Cardus, *The Guardian*
1970   Ken Gardner, *The People*
1971   William Rees-Mogg, *The Times*, and Anthony
       Mascarenhas, *The Sunday Times*
1972   Laurie Manifold, *Sunday People*, and David
       Williams, Southend *Evening Echo*
1973   David English, *Daily Mail*
1974   Brian Roberts, *Sunday Telegraph*
1975   No award
1976   Stephen Fay with Hugo Young, *The Sunday Times*
1977   Charles Raw, *The Sunday Times*
1978   Stephen Fay, Hugo Young, *The Sunday Times*

WOMAN JOURNALIST OF THE YEAR
1962   Clare Hollingworth, *The Guardian*
1963   Anne Sharpley, *Evening Standard*
1964   Joan Seddon, Lancashire *Evening Telegraph*
1965   Wendy Cooper, Birmingham *Post*
1966   Barbara Buchanan, Bristol *Evening Post*
Discontinued

SPECIALIST WRITER OF THE YEAR
1972   John Graham, *Financial Times*
1973   John Davis, *The Observer*
1974   Richard Milner, *The Sunday Times*
1975   Andrew Alexander, *Daily Mail*
1976   Andrew Alexander, *Daily Mail*
1977   Oliver Gillie, *The Sunday Times*
1978   John McCririck, *Sporting Life*

COLUMNIST OF THE YEAR
1973   Keith Waterhouse, *Daily Mirror*, and Bernard
       Levin, *The Times*
1974   Bernard Levin, *The Times*
1975   Ian Wooldridge, *Daily Mail*
1976   Ian Wooldridge, *Daily Mail*
1977   Anthony Holden, *The Sunday Times*
1978   Keith Waterhouse, *Daily Mirror*

CHAIRMAN'S AWARDS
1974   Sydney Jacobson, IPC
1977   David Holden, *The Sunday Times*

PRESS PHOTOGRAPHER OF THE YEAR
1976   David Cairns, *Daily Express*

PHOTOGRAPHER OF THE YEAR
1977   John Downing, *Daily Express*
1978   Mike Lloyd, freelance

NEWS PHOTOGRAPHER OF THE YEAR
1977   J. A. Jedrej, Cambridge *Evening News*
1978   Reg Lancaster, *Daily Express*

DAVID HOLDEN AWARD
1978   Ian Wright and Altaf Gauhar, *The Guardian*

British Press Photographer of the Year

This has been an annual award since 1969, sponsored by the Midland Bank Limited from 1974.

1969 Kent Gavin, *Daily Mirror*	1974 Jim McLagan, *The Argus* (Cape Town)
1970 Michael Brennan, *The Sun*	1975 Ronald G. Bell, The Press Association
1971 David Cairns, *Daily Express*	1976 Monty Fresco, *Daily Mail*
1972 William Lovelace, *Daily Express*	1977 Frank Barrett, Keystone Press Agency
1973 David Cairns, *Daily Express*	1978 Monty Fresco, *Daily Mail*

Monte Fresco of the *Daily Mail* was the British Press Photographer of 1978. Mr Fresco won the accolade for the best portfolio of 10 prints

Pulitzer Prizes
See Pulitzer Prizes. The following is a selection of the award winners.

LOCAL INVESTIGATIVE REPORTING
Founded 1953. The winners from 1970 are:
1970 Harold E. Martin, *Montgomery* (Ala.) *Advertiser*
1971 William Hugh Jones, *Chicago Tribune*
1972 Ann De Santis, S. A. Kurkjian, T. Leland, and G. M. O'Neill, *Boston Globe*
1973 *Sun* Newspapers, Omaha, Nebr.
1974 William Sherman, *New York Daily News*
1975 *Indianapolis Star*
1976 Staff of *Chicago Tribune* for exposing conditions in two hospitals that led to their closing and for discovering abuses in federal housing programmes
1977 Acel Moore and Wendell Rawls Jr, *Philadelphia Inquirer*, for investigation of state mental hospital
1978 Anthony R. Dolan, *Stamford* (Conn.) *Advocate*

LOCAL GENERAL REPORTING
Founded in 1953. The winners from 1970 are:
1970 Thomas Fitzpatrick, *Chicago Sun-Times*
1971 *Akron* (Ohio) *Beacon Journal*
1972 R. I. Cooper and J. W. Machacek, *Rochester* (NY) *Times-Union*
1973 *Chicago Tribune*
1974 Arthur M. Petacque and Hugh F. Hough, *Chicago Sun-Times*
1975 *Xenia* (Ohio) *Daily Gazette*
1976 Gene Miller, *Miami Herald*, who dug up evidence that freed two men convicted of murder. He previously won a Pulitzer Prize in 1967 for uncovering evidence that freed a man and woman convicted of separate murders.
1977 Margo Huston, *Milwaukee Journal*
1978 Richard Whitt, *Louisville* (Ky.) *Courier-Journal*

NATIONAL REPORTING
The winners from foundation:
1942 Louis Stark, *New York Times*
1943 No award
1944 Dewey L. Fleming, *Sun*, Baltimore
1945 James B. Reston, *New York Times*
1946 Edward A. Harris, *St. Louis Post-Dispatch*
1947 Edward T. Folliard, *Washington Post*
1948 Bert Andrews, *New York Herald Tribune*, and Nat. S. Finney, *Minneapolis Tribune*
1949 Charles P. Trussell, *New York Times*
1950 Edwin O. Guthman, *Seattle Times*
1951 No award
1952 Anthony Leviero, *New York Times*
1953 Don Whitehead, Associated Press
1954 Richard Wilson, Cowles Newspapers
1955 Anthony Lewis, *Washington Daily News*
1956 Charles Bartlett, *Chattanooga* (Tenn.) *Times*
1957 James Reston, *New York Times*
1958 Relman Morin, Associated Press
1959 Howard Van Smith, *Miami News*
1960 Vance Trimble, Scripps-Howard
1961 Edward R. Cony, *Wall Street Journal*
1962 Nathan G. Caldwell and Gene S. Graham, *Nashville Tennessean*
1963 Anthony Lewis, *New York Times*
1964 Merriman Smith, United Press International

1965 Louis Kohlmeier, *Wall Street Journal*
1966 Haynes Johnson, *Washington Evening Star*
1967 Monroe W. Karmin and Stanley W. Penn, *Wall Street Journal*
1968 Howard James, *Christian Science Monitor*, and Nathan Kotz, *Register*, Des Moines, Iowa
1969 Robert Cahn, *Christian Science Monitor*
1970 William J. Eaton, *Chicago Daily News*
1971 Lucinda Franks and Thomas Powers, United Press International
1972 Jack Anderson, syndicated columnist
1973 Robert Boyd and Clark Hoyt, Knight Newspapers
1974 James R. Polk, *Washington Star-News*, and Jack White, *Providence* (RI) *Journal-Bulletin*
1975 Donald L. Barlett and James B. Steel, *Philadelphia Inquirer*
1976 James Risser, *Register*, Des Moines, Iowa, who as Washington correspondent broke story on corruption in American grain export trade
1977 Walter Mears, Associated Press chief political writer
1978 Gaylord Shaw, *Los Angeles* (Calif.) *Times*

INTERNATIONAL REPORTING
The winners from foundation:
1942 Laurence E. Allen, Associated Press
1943 Ira Wolfert, North American Newspaper Alliance
1944 Daniel DeLuce, Associated Press
1945 Mark S. Watson, *Sun*, Baltimore
1946 Homer W. Bigart, *New York Herald Tribune*
1947 Eddy Gilmore, Associated Press
1948 Paul W. Ward, *Sun*, Baltimore
1949 Price Day, *Sun*, Baltimore
1950 Edmund Stevens, *Christian Science Monitor*
1951 Keyes Beech and Fred Sparks, *Chicago Daily News*, Homer Bigart and Marguerite Higgins, *New York Herald Tribune*, Relman Morin and Don Whitehead, Associated Press
1952 John M. Hightower, Associated Press
1953 Austin Wehrwein, *Milwaukee Journal*
1954 Jim. G. Lucas, Scripps-Howard Newspapers
1955 Harrison Salisbury, *New York Times*
1956 William Randolph Hearst Jr, Kingsbury Smith, and Frank Conniff, International News Service
1957 Russell Jones, United Press
1958 *New York Times*
1959 Joseph Martin and Philip Santora, *New York Daily News*
1960 A. M. Rosenthal, *New York Times*
1961 Lynn Heinzerling, Associated Press
1962 Walter Lippmann, *New York Herald Tribune* Syndicate
1963 Hal Hendrix, *Miami News*
1964 Malcolm W. Browne, Associated Press, David Halberstam, *New York Times*
1965 J. A. Livingston, *Philadelphia Bulletin*
1966 Peter Arnett, Associated Press
1967 R. J. Hughes, *Christian Science Monitor*
1968 Alfred Friendly, *Washington Post*
1969 William Tuohy, *Los Angeles Times*
1970 Seymour M. Hersh, Dispatch News Service

1971   Jimmie Lee Hoagland, *Washington Post*
1972   Peter R. Kann, *Wall Street Journal*
1973   Max Frankel, *New York Times*
1974   Hedrick Smith, *New York Times*
1975   William Mullen and Ovie Carter, *Chicago Tribune*
1976   Sydney H. Schanberg, *New York Times*, who stayed behind when the Cambodian government was defeated by the communists on 17 April 1975, finally leaving with a convoy on 8 May to send story on the fall of Phnom Penh.
1977   No award
1978   Henry Kamm, *New York Times*

EDITORIAL WRITING
Founded in 1917. The winners from 1970 are:
1970   Philip Geyelin, *Washington Post*
1971   Horance G. Davis Jr, *Gainesville (Fla.) Sun*
1972   J. Strohmeyer, *Bethlehem (Pa.) Globe-Times*
1973   Roger B. Linscott, *Berkshire Eagle*, Pittsfield, Mass.
1974   F. Gilman Spencer, *Trenton (N.J.) Trentonian*
1975   John Daniell Maurice, *Charleston (W.Va) Daily Mail*
1976   Philip P. Kerby, *Los Angeles Times*
1977   Warren L. Lerude, Foster Church, Norman F. Cardoza, *Reno Evening Gazette* and *Nevada State Journal*
1978   Meg Greenfield, *The Washington (D.C.) Post*

CARTOON
Founded in 1922. Winners since 1970 are:
1970   Thomas Darcy, *Newsday*, Garden City, NY
1971   Paul Conrad, *Los Angeles Times*
1972   J. K. MacNelly, *Richmond (Va.) News Leader*
1973   No award
1974   Paul Szep, *Boston Globe*
1975   Garry Trudeau, creator of 'Doonesbury' comic strip
1976   Tony Auth, political cartoonist, *Philadelphia Inquirer*
1977   Paul Szep, *Boston Globe*
1978   J. K. MacNelly, *Richmond (Va.) News Leader*

NEWS PHOTOGRAPHY
Founded in 1942. The winners since 1970 are:
1970   Steve Starr, Associated Press
1971   John Paul Filo, amateur photographer
1972   H. Faas, M. Laurent, Associated Press
1973   Huynh Cong Ut, Associated Press
1974   Anthony K. Roberts, freelance
1975   Gerald H. Gay, *Seattle Times*
1976   Stanley Forman, *Boston Herald-American*
1977   Stanley Forman, *Boston Herald-American* and Neal Ulevich, Associated Press
1978   J. Ross Baughman, Associated Press; John W. Blair, freelance; and UPI Indianapolis

FEATURE PHOTOGRAPHY
1968   Toshio Sakai, United Press International
1969   Moneta Sleet Jr, *Ebony* magazine
1970   Dallas Kinney, *Palm Beach (Fla.) Post*
1971   Jack Dykinga, *Chicago Sun-Times*
1972   Dave Kennerly, United Press International
1973   B. Lanker, *Topeka (Kans.) Capital-Journal*

1974   Slava Veder, Associated Press
1975   Matthew Lewis, *Washington Post*
1976   Photographic staff of *Louisville Courier-Journal and Times*
1977   Robin Hood, *News-Free Press*. Chattanooga, Tenn.
1978   J. Ross Baughman, Associated Press

MERITORIOUS PUBLIC SERVICE
1917   No award
1918   *New York Times*
1919   *Milwaukee Journal*
1920   No award
1921   *Boston Post*
1922   *World*, New York
1923   *Memphis Commercial Appeal*
1924   *World*, New York
1925   No award
1926   *Enquirer Sun*, Columbus, Ga.
1927   *Canton (Ohio) Daily News*
1928   *Indianapolis Times*
1929   *Evening World*, New York
1930   No award
1931   *Atlanta Constitution*
1932   *Indianapolis News*
1933   *New York World-Telegram*
1934   *Medford (Oreg.) Mail Tribune*
1935   *Sacramento (Calif.) Bee*
1936   *Cedar Rapids (Iowa) Gazette*
1937   *St. Louis Post-Dispatch*
1938   *Bismarck (N.D.) Tribune*
1939   *Miami Daily News*
1940   *Waterbury (Conn.) Republican and American*
1941   *St. Louis Post-Dispatch*
1942   *Los Angeles Times*
1943   *World-Herald*, Omaha, Nebr.
1944   *New York Times*
1945   *Detroit Free Press*
1946   *Scranton (Pa.) Times*
1947   *Baltimore Sun*
1948   *St. Louis Post-Dispatch*
1949   *Nebraska State Journal*
1950   *Chicago Daily News*
         St. Louis Post-Dispatch
1951   *Miami Herald*
         Brooklyn Eagle
1952   *St. Louis Post-Dispatch*
1953   *News Reporter*, Whiteville, N.C.
         Tabor City (N.C.) Tribune
1954   *Newsday*, Garden City N.Y.
1955   *Columbus (Ga.) Ledger and Sunday Ledger-Enquirer*
1956   *Watsonville (Calif.) Register-Pajaronian*
1957   *Chicago Daily News*
1958   *Arkansas Gazette*, Little Rock
1959   *Utica (N.Y.) Observer-Dispatch*
         Utica (N.Y.) Daily Press
1960   *Los Angeles Times*
1961   *Amarillo (Tex.) Globe-Times*
1962   *Panama City (Fla.) News-Herald*
1963   *Chicago Daily News*
1964   *St. Petersburg (Fla.) Times*
1965   *Hutchinson (Kans.) News*
1966   *Boston Globe*
1967   *Louisville Courier-Journal and Milwaukee Journal*

1968	*Riverside* (Calif.) *Press*
1969	*Los Angeles Times*
1970	*Newsday*, Garden City, N.Y.
1971	*Winston-Salem* (N.C.) *Journal and Sentinel*
1972	*New York Times*
1973	*Washington Post*
1974	*Newsday*, Garden City, N.Y.
1975	*Boston Globe*
1976	*Anchorage* (Alaska) *Daily News*
1977	*Lufkin* (Tex) *News*, for inquiry on death of local marine in training camp
1978	*Philadelphia* (Pa.) *Inquirer*

CRITICISM

The winners since 1970 were:

1970	Ada Louise Huxtable, *New York Times*
1971	Harold C. Schonberg, *New York Times*
1972	Frank L. Peters Jr., *St. Louis Post-Dispatch*
1973	Ronald Powers, *Chicago Sun-Times*
1974	Emily Genauer, *Newsday* syndicate
1975	Roger Ebert, *Chicago Sun-Times*
1976	Alan M. Kriegsman, dance critic, *Washington Post*
1977	William McPherson, book critic, *Washington Post*
1978	Walter Kerr, *New York Times*

COMMENTARY

The winners since 1970:

1970	Marquis Childs, *St. Louis Post-Dispatch*
1971	William A. Caldwell, *Record*, Hackensack, N.J.
1972	Mike Royko, *Chicago Daily News*
1973	David S. Broder, *Washington Post*
1974	Edwin A. Roberts Jr., *National Observer*
1975	Mary McGrory, *Washington Star*
1976	Walter W. (Red) Smith, sports columnist, *New York Times*
1977	George F. Will, syndicated columnist, *Washington Post* Writers Group
1978	Walter Safire, *New York Times*

SPECIAL PULITZER PRIZE CITATIONS

1938	*Edmonton Journal*, for defending freedom of the press in Alberta, Canada.
1941	*New York Times*, for the public educational value of its foreign news reporting, exemplified by its scope, excellence of writing and presentation, and supplementary background information and interpretation.
1944	Mrs William Allen White, indicating appreciation of Mrs White's interest and services during the

previous seven years as a member of the Advisory Board of the Graduate School of Journalism, Columbia University. Byron Price, Director of the Office of Censorship, for the creation and administration of the newspaper and radio codes.

1945	The cartographers of the American press, whose maps of the war fronts helped notably to clarify and increase public information on the progress of the armies and navies engaged in World War II.
1947	(Pulitzer Centennial year) Columbia University and the Graduate School of Journalism, for their efforts to maintain and advance the high standards governing the Pulitzer Prize awards.
1948	Dr Frank Diehl Fackenthal, indicating appreciation of his interest and service during the preceding years.
1951	Cyrus L. Sulzberger, *New York Times*, for his exclusive interview with Archbishop Aloysius Stepinac of Yugoslavia.
1952	*Kansas City Star*, for the news coverage of the great regional flood of 1951 in Kansas and northwestern Missouri. Max Case, *New York Journal-American*, for his exposures of corruption in basketball.
1953	*New York Times*, for the section of its Sunday edition headed Review of the Week, which for 17 years brought enlightened commentary to its readers.
1958	Walter Lippmann, nationally syndicated columnist of *New York Herald Tribune*, for the wisdom, perception, and high sense of responsibility with which he commented on national and international affairs.
1964	Gannett Newspapers, Rochester, NY, for their programme 'The Road to Integration', a distinguished example of the use of a newspaper group's resources to complement the work of its individual newspapers.
1973	James T. Flexner, for 'George Washington', a four-volume biography.
1976	Scott Joplin (1868–1917), special bicentennial year award for his contributions to American music with such compositions as 'Maple Leaf Rag'.
1976	John Hohenberg, for 22 years of service as administrator of the Pulitzer Prizes.
1977	Alex Haley, for 'Roots', an 'important contribution to the literature of slavery'.
1978	E. B. White, *The New Yorker*

JUDO

World Championships

Judo World Championships were first held in 1956 and are now held biennially, but were cancelled in 1977. Winners at each weight category:

OPEN

1956	Shokichi Natsui (Jap)	1965	Isao Inokuma (Jap)	1971	Masatoshi Shinomaki (Jap)
1958	Koji Sone (Jap)	1967	Matsuo Matsunaga (Jap)	1973	Kazuhiro Nimomiya (Jap)
1961	Anton Geesink (Hol)	1969	Masatoshi Shinomaki (Jap)	1975	Haruki Uemura (Jap)

HEAVYWEIGHT (over 93 kg)
1965   Anton Geesink (Hol)
1967   Wim Ruska (Hol)
1969   Shuja Suma (Jap)
1971   Wim Ruska (Hol)
1973   Chonofuhe Tagaki (Jap)
1975   Sumio Endo (Jap)

LIGHT HEAVYWEIGHT (over 80 kg)
1967   Nobuyaki Sato (Jap)
1969   Fumio Sasahara (Jap)
1971   Fumio Sasahara (Jap)
1973   Nobuyaki Sato (Jap)
1975   Jean-Luc Rouge (Fra)

MIDDLEWEIGHT (over 70 kg)
1965   Isao Okano (Jap)
1967   Eiji Maruki (Jap)
1969   Isomu Sonoda (Jap)
1971   Shozo Fujii (Jap)
1973   Shozo Fujii (Jap)
1975   Shozo Fujii (Jap)

LIGHT MIDDLEWEIGHT (Welterweight) (over 63 kg)
1967   Hiroshi Minatoya (Jap)
1969   Hiroshi Minatoya (Jap)
1971   Hizashi Tsuzawa (Jap)
1973   Kazutoyo Nomura (Jap)
1975   Vladimir Nevzova (USSR)

LIGHTWEIGHT (under 63 kg)
1965   H. Matsuda (Jap)
1967   Takosumi Shigeoka (Jap)
1969   Yoshio Sonoda (Jap)
1971   Takao Kawaguchi (Jap)
1973   Yoshiharu Minamo (Jap)
1975   Yoshiharu Minamo (Jap)

Olympic Champions

Judo was first held in the Olympic Games at Tokyo in 1964, but was not included in 1968.

Winners:

OPEN
1964   Anton Geesink (Hol)

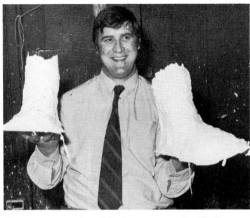

To the consternation of the host country, the 6ft 6in Dutchman, Anton Geesink, won the 1964 Olympic Open Judo Championship in Tokyo, Japan (*Keystone*)

HEAVY
1964   Isao Inokuma (Jap)
1972   Wim Ruska (Hol)
1976   Sergei Novikov (USSR)

LIGHT HEAVY
1972   Shota Chochoshvily (USSR)
1976   Kazuhiro Ninomiya (Jap)

MIDDLE
1964   Isao Okano (Jap)
1972   Shinobu Sekine (Jap)
1976   Isamu Sonoda (Jap)

LIGHT MIDDLE
1972   Kazutoyo Nomura (Jap)
1976   Vladimir Nevzorov (USSR)

LIGHT
1964   Takehide Nakatani (Jap)
1972   Takao Kawaguchi (Jap)
1976   Hector Rodriguez (Cub)

1972   Wim Ruska (Hol)
1976   Haruko Uemura (Jap)

KARATE

World Championships (Karate-do)

TEAM
First held in 1970. Winners:
1970   Japan
1972   France
1975   Great Britain
1977   Holland

INDIVIDUAL
1977   Otti Roethof (Hol)

Japan Karate Association (JKA) World Championships (Shotoku style)

JUI-KUMITE (free-style fighting)

Individual		Team
1975	Masahiko Tanaka (Jap)	Japan
1977	Masahiko Tanaka (Jap)	Japan

KATA (training dances)

Team	Men	Women
1977	Japan	Japan

KENDO

World Kendo Championships

First held in 1970 in Japan; and subsequently in the USA in 1973 and in Britain in 1976.

Individual winners:		Team prize:	
1970	Kobayashi (Jap)	1970	Japan
1973	Sakuragi (Jap)	1973	Japan
1976	Eiji Yoko (Jap)	1976	Japan

LACROSSE

World Championships

The first men's world championships for field lacrosse were held in 1967 in Toronto. Winners:

1967 USA	1974 USA	1978 Canada

The first women's world championships were held in 1969. Winners:

1969 Great Britain	1974 USA

LAWN TENNIS

Davis Cup

The world's premier international team competition is contested on a best of 5 match basis by men's teams. The Cup was first contested as a challenge match between USA and Great Britain in 1900.

Most wins; USA   25 (1900, 1902, 1913, 1920–26, 1937–38, 1946–49, 1954, 1958, 1963, 1968–72, 1978)
Australia/Australasia   24 (1907–09, 1911, 1914, 1919, 1939, 1950–53, 1955–57, 1959–62, 1964–67, 1973, 1977)
Great Britain/British Isles   9 (1903–06, 1912, 1933–36)
France   6 (1927–32)

Winners since 1974
1974	South Africa
1975	Sweden
1976	Italy
1977	Australia
1978	USA

Wightman Cup

Contested annually by women's teams from the USA and Great Britain on a best of seven matches basis. First held in 1923, the United States have won 41 times to 1977, Great Britain have won 10 times – 1924, 1925, 1928, 1930, 1958, 1960, 1968, 1974, 1975, 1978.

Federation Cup

Contested by women's teams annually on a knock-out basis. First played in 1963.

1963	USA	1969	USA	1975	Czechoslovakia
1964	Australia	1970	Australia	1976	USA
1965	Australia	1971	Australia	1977	USA
1966	USA	1972	South Africa	1978	USA
1967	USA	1973	Australia	1979	USA
1968	Australia	1974	Australia		

Wimbledon Championships

The most celebrated of the world's major championships, the Wimbledon Championships were first played in 1877. Winners:

MEN'S SINGLES

1877 Spencer W. Gore (GB)	1878 Frank Hadow (GB)	1879 Rev. John Hartley (GB)

1880   Rev. John Hartley (GB)
1881   William Renshaw (GB)
1882   William Renshaw (GB)
1883   William Renshaw (GB)
1884   William Renshaw (GB)
1885   William Renshaw (GB)
1886   William Renshaw (GB)
1887   Herbert Lawford (GB)
1888   Ernest Renshaw (GB)
1889   William Renshaw (GB)
1890   Willoughby Hamilton (GB)
1891   Wilfred Baddeley (GB)
1892   Wilfred Baddeley (GB)
1893   Joshua Pim (GB)
1894   Joshua Pim (GB)
1895   Wilfred Baddeley (GB)
1896   Harold Mahony (GB)
1897   Reginald Doherty (GB)
1898   Reginald Doherty (GB)
1899   Reginald Doherty (GB)
1900   Reginald Doherty (GB)
1901   Arthur Gore (GB)
1902   Laurence Doherty (GB)
1903   Laurence Doherty (GB)
1904   Laurence Doherty (GB)
1905   Laurence Doherty (GB)
1906   Laurence Doherty (GB)
1907   Norman Brookes (Aus)
1908   Arthur W. Gore (GB)
1909   Arthur W. Gore (GB)
1910   Tony Wilding (NZ)
1911   Tony Wilding (NZ)
1912   Tony Wilding (NZ)
1913   Tony Wilding (NZ)
1914   Norman Brookes (Aus)
1919   Gerald Patterson (Aus)
1920   Bill Tilden (USA)
1921   Bill Tilden (USA)
1922   Gerald Patterson (Aus)
1923   William Johnston (USA)
1924   Jean Borotra (Fra)
1925   René Lacoste (Fra)
1926   Jean Borotra (Fra)
1927   Henri Cochet (Fra)
1928   René Lacoste (Fra)
1929   Henri Cochet (Fra)
1930   Bill Tilden (USA)
1931   Sidney Wood (USA)
1932   Ellsworth Vines (USA)
1933   Jack Crawford (Aus)
1934   Fred Perry (GB)
1935   Fred Perry (GB)
1936   Fred Perry (GB)
1937   Donald Budge (USA)
1938   Donald Budge (USA)
1939   Bobby Riggs (USA)

Rod Laver won four successive Wimbledon singles titles (1961, 1962, 1968 and 1969). The five-year gap in the middle represents the period after he turned professional and before the game went open in 1968 (*E. D. Lacey*)

1946   Yvon Petra (Fra)
1947   Jack Kramer (USA)
1948   Bob Falkenburg (USA)
1949   Ted Schroeder (USA)
1950   Budge Patty (USA)
1951   Dick Savitt (USA)
1952   Frank Sedgman (Aus)
1953   Vic Seixas (USA)
1954   Jaroslav Drobny (Cze)
1955   Tony Trabert (USA)
1956   Lew Hoad (Aus)
1957   Lew Hoad (Aus)
1958   Ashley Cooper (Aus)
1959   Alex Olmedo (USA)
1960   Neale Fraser (Aus)
1961   Rod Laver (Aus)
1962   Rod Laver (Aus)
1963   Chuck McKinley (USA)

1964   Roy Emerson (Aus)
1965   Roy Emerson (Aus)
1966   Manuel Santana (Spa)
1967   John Newcombe (Aus)
1968   Rod Laver (Aus)
1969   Rod Laver (Aus)
1970   John Newcombe (Aus)
1971   John Newcombe (Aus)
1972   Stan Smith (USA)
1973   Jan Kodes (Cze)
1974   Jimmy Connors (USA)
1975   Arthur Ashe (USA)
1976   Bjorn Borg (Swe)
1977   Bjorn Borg (Swe)
1978   Bjorn Borg (Swe)
1979   Bjorn Borg (Swe)

(Note: Hamilton, Pim and Mahony were Irish.)

WOMEN'S SINGLES
First played in 1884. Winners:
1884   Maud Watson (GB)
1885   Maud Watson (GB)
1886   Blanche Bingley (GB)

1887   Lottie Dod (GB)
1888   Lottie Dod (GB)
1889   Blanche Hillyard (née Bingley) (GB)
1890   Helene Rice (GB-Ire)

1891   Lottie Dod (GB)
1892   Lottie Dod (GB)
1893   Lottie Dod (GB)
1894   Blanche Hillyard (GB)

1895   Charlotte Cooper (GB)
1896   Charlotte Cooper (GB)
1897   **Blanche Hillyard (GB)**
1898   Charlotte Cooper (GB)
1899   Blanche Hillyard (GB)
1900   Blanche Hillyard (GB)
1901   Charlotte Sterry (née Cooper) (GB)
1902   Muriel Robb (GB)
1903   Dorothea Douglass (GB)
1904   Dorothea Douglass (GB)
1905   May Sutton (USA)
1906   Dorothea Douglass (GB)
1907   May Sutton (USA)
1908   Charlotte Sterry (GB)
1909   Dora Boothby (GB)
1910   Dorothea Lambert Chambers
       (née Douglass) **(GB)**
1911   Dorothea Lambert Chambers (GB)
1912   Ethel Larcombe (GB)
1913   Dorothea Lambert Chambers (GB)
1914   Dorothea Lambert Chambers (GB)
1919   Suzanne Lenglen (Fra)
1920   Suzanne Lenglen (Fra)
1921   Suzanne Lenglen (Fra)
1922   Suzanne Lenglen (Fra)
1923   Suzanne Lenglen (Fra)
1924   Kathleen McKane (GB)
1925   Suzanne Lenglen (Fra)
1926   Kathleen Godfree (née McKane)
       (GB)
1927   Helen Wills (USA)
1928   Helen Wills (USA)
1929   Helen Wills (USA)
1930   Helen Wills Moody (USA)
1931   Cilly Aussem (Ger)
1932   Helen Wills Moody (USA)
1933   Helen Wills Moody (USA)
1934   Dorothy Round (GB)
1935   Helen Wills Moody (USA)
1936   Helen Jacobs (USA)
1937   Dorothy Round (GB)
1938   Helen Wills Moody (USA)
1939   Alice Marble (USA)
1946   Pauline Betz (USA)
1947   Margaret Osborne (USA)

Suzanne Lenglen was unbeaten in 32 singles matches at Wimbledon, winning the title every year from 1919 to 1925, except for 1924 when she retired through illness

1948   Louise Brough (USA)
1949   Louise Brough (USA)
1950   Louise Brough (USA)
1951   Doris Hart (USA)
1952   Maureen Connolly (USA)
1953   Maureen Connolly (USA)
1954   Maureen Connolly (USA)
1955   Louise Brough (USA)
1956   Shirley Fry (USA)
1957   Althea Gibson (USA)

1958   Althea Gibson (USA)
1959   Maria Bueno (Bra)
1960   Maria Bueno (Bra)
1961   Angela Mortimer (GB)
1962   Karen Susman (USA)
1963   Margaret Smith (Aus)
1964   Maria Bueno (Bra)
1965   Margaret Smith (Aus)
1966   Billie Jean King (USA)
1967   Billie Jean King (USA)
1968   Billie Jean King (USA)

1969   Ann Jones (GB)
1970   Margaret Court (née Smith) (Aus)
1971   Evonne Goolagong (Aus)
1972   Billie Jean King (USA)
1973   Billie Jean King (USA)
1974   Christine Evert (USA)
1975   Billie Jean King (USA)
1976   Christine Evert (USA)
1977   Virginia Wade (GB)
1978   Martina Navratilova (Cze)
1979   Martina Navratilova (Cze)

MEN'S DOUBLES
First held 1884.
Most wins: 8   Laurence Doherty and Reginald Doherty
(GB): 1897–1901, 1903–05

Winners since 1965:
1965   John Newcombe and Tony Roche (Aus)
1966   Ken Fletcher and John Newcombe (Aus)

1967   Bob Hewitt and Frew McMillan (SA)
1968   John Newcombe and Tony Roche (Aus)
1969   John Newcombe and Tony Roche (Aus)
1970   John Newcombe and Tony Roche (Aus)
1971   Roy Emerson and Rod Laver (Aus)
1972   Bob Hewitt and Frew McMillan (SA)
1973   Jimmy Connors (USA) and Ilie Nastase (Rom)
1974   John Newcombe and Tony Roche (Aus)

1975	Vitas Gerulaitis and Sandy Mayer (USA)	1978	Bob Hewitt and Frew McMillan (SA)
1976	Brian Gottfried (USA) and Raul Ramirez (Mex)	1979	Peter Fleming and John McEnroe (USA)
1977	Ross Case and Geoff Masters (Aus)		

WOMEN'S DOUBLES

First held 1899, but not a championship event until 1913.

Most wins: 12 Elizabeth Ryan (USA): 1 with Agatha Morton 1914, 6 with Suzanne Lenglen 1919–23, 1925; 1 with Mary Browne 1926, 2 with Helen Wills Moody 1927, 1930; 2 with Simone Mathieu 1933–34

Winners since 1965:

1965	Maria Bueno (Bra) and Billie Jean Moffitt (USA)
1966	Maria Bueno (Bra) and Nancy Richey (USA)
1967	Rosemary Casals and Billie Jean King (née Moffitt) (USA)
1968	Rosemary Casals and Billie Jean King (USA)
1969	Margaret Court and Judy Tegart (Aus)
1970	Rosemary Casals and Billie Jean King (USA)
1971	Rosemary Casals and Billie Jean King (USA)
1972	Billie Jean King (USA) and Betty Stove (Hol)
1973	Rosemary Casals and Billie Jean King (USA)
1974	Evonne Goolagong (Aus) and Peggy Michel (USA)
1975	Ann Kiyomura (USA) and Kazuko Sawamatsu (Jap)
1976	Christine Evert (USA) and Martina Navratilova (Cze)
1977	Helen Cawley (Aus) and Joanne Russell (USA)
1978	Kerry Reid and Wendy Turnbull (Aus)
1979	Billie Jean King (USA) and Martina Navratilova (Cze)

MIXED DOUBLES

First held 1900, but not a championship event until 1913.

Most wins: 7 Elizabeth Ryan (USA): 1919, 1921, 1923, 1927–28, 1930, 1932 with 5 different partners

Winners since 1965:

1965	Ken Fletcher and Margaret Smith (Aus)
1966	Ken Fletcher and Margaret Smith (Aus)
1967	Owen Davidson (Aus) and Billie Jean King (USA)
1968	Ken Fletcher and Margaret Court (née Smith) (Aus)
1969	Fred Stolle (Aus) and Ann Jones (GB)
1970	Ilie Nastase (Rom) and Rosemary Casals (USA)
1971	Owen Davidson (Aus) and Billie Jean King (USA)
1972	Ilie Nastase (Rom) and Rosemary Casals (USA)
1973	Owen Davidson (Aus) and Billie Jean King (USA)
1974	Owen Davidson (Aus) and Billie Jean King (USA)
1975	Marty Reissen (USA) and Margaret Court (Aus)
1976	Tony Roche (Aus) and Françoise Durr (Fra)
1977	Bob Hewitt and Greer Stevens (SA)
1978	Frew McMillan (SA) and Betty Stove (Hol)
1979	Bob Hewitt and Greer Stevens (USA)

United States Championships

The USLTA Championships were first held in 1881 and continued until 1969. The Tournament was superseded in 1970 by the US Open Championships which had first been held in 1968. Now held at Flushing Meadow, New York.

Most wins in the USLTA Championships:
Men's Singles: 7 Richard D. Sears 1881–87: 7 William T. Tilden 1920–25, 1929
Women's Singles: 7 Helen Wills Moody 1923–25, 1927–29, 1931

US Open Winners:

MEN'S SINGLES

1968	Arthur Ashe (USA)
1969	Rod Laver (Aus)
1970	Ken Rosewall (Aus)
1971	Stan Smith (USA)
1972	Ilie Nastase (Rom)
1973	John Newcombe (Aus)
1974	Jimmy Connors (USA)
1975	Manuel Orantes (Spa)
1976	Jimmy Connors (USA)
1977	Guillermo Vilas (Arg)
1978	Jimmy Connors (USA)

WOMEN'S SINGLES

1968	Virginia Wade (GB)
1969	Margaret Court (Aus)
1970	Margaret Court (Aus)
1971	Billie Jean King (USA)
1972	Billie Jean King (USA)
1973	Margaret Court (Aus)
1974	Billie Jean King (USA)
1975	Christine Evert (USA)
1976	Christine Evert (USA)
1977	Christine Evert (USA)
1978	Christine Evert (USA)

French Championships

First held in 1891. Held on hard courts at the Stade Roland Garros, near Paris. Singles winners since 1968:

MEN'S SINGLES

1968	Ken Rosewall (Aus)	1970	Jan Kodes (Cze)	1972	Andres Gimeno (Spa)
1969	Rod Laver (Aus)	1971	Jan Kodes (Cze)	1973	Ilie Nastase (Rom)

1974 Bjorn Borg (Swe)	**WOMEN'S SINGLES**	1973 Margaret Court (Aus)
1975 Bjorn Borg (Swe)	1968 Nancy Richey (USA)	1974 Christine Evert (USA)
1976 Adriano Panatta (Ita)	1969 Margaret Court (Aus)	1975 Christine Evert (USA)
1977 Guillermo Vilas (Arg)	1970 Margaret Court (Aus)	1976 Susan Barker (GB)
1978 Bjorn Borg (Swe)	1971 Evonne Goolagong (Aus)	1977 Mima Jausovec (Yug)
1979 Bjorn Borg (Swe)	1972 Billie Jean King (USA)	1978 Virginia Ruzici (Rom)
		1979 Christine Evert-Lloyd (USA)

Australian Championships

First held in 1905. Singles' winners since 1968 (year shown is second half of winter season):

MEN'S SINGLES	1976 Mark Edmondson (Aus)	1971 Margaret Court (Aus)
1968 William Bowrey (Aus)	1977 Roscoe Tanner (USA)	1972 Virginia Wade (GB)
1969 Rod Laver (Aus)	1978 Vitas Gerulaitis (USA)	1973 Margaret Court (Aus)
1970 Arthur Ashe (USA)	1979 Guillermo Vilas (Arg)	1974 Evonne Goolagong (Aus)
1971 Ken Rosewall (Aus)		1975 Evonne Goolagong (Aus)
1972 Ken Rosewall (Aus)	**WOMEN'S SINGLES**	1976 Evonne Cawley (née Goola-
1973 John Newcombe (Aus)	1968 Billie Jean King (USA)	gong) (Aus)
1974 Jimmy Connors (USA)	1969 Margaret Court (Aus)	1977 Kerry Reid (Aus)
1975 John Newcombe (Aus)	1970 Margaret Court (Aus)	1978 Evonne Cawley (Aus)
		1979 Christine O'Neill (Aus)

Grand Slam

Winners of the Grand Slam are those players who have won the Singles' events at the world's four major tournaments in the same year. Tournaments are Wimbledon, USA, French and Australian Championships. Grand slams have been achieved by:

Men: Donald Budge (USA) 1938; Rod Laver (Aus) 1962, 1969

Women: Maureen Connolly (USA) 1953; Margaret Court (Aus) 1970

WCT Champions

World Championship Tennis (WCT) has held a series of championships since 1971.

1971 Ken Rosewall (Aus)	1974 John Newcombe (Aus)	1977 Jimmy Connors (USA)
1972 Ken Rosewall (Aus)	1975 Arthur Ashe (USA)	1978 Vitas Gerulaitis (USA)
1973 Stan Smith (USA)	1976 Bjorn Borg (Swe)	1979 John McEnroe (USA)

Grand Prix

Winners on points gained in major tournaments since 1970:

1970 Cliff Richey (USA)	1973 Ilie Nastase (Rom)	1976 Raul Ramirez (Mex)
1971 Stan Smith (USA)	1974 Guillermo Vilas (Arg)	1977 Guillermo Vilas (Arg)
1972 Ilie Nastase (Rom)	1975 Guillermo Vilas (Arg)	1978 Jimmy Connors (USA)

Grand Prix Masters Tournament

Contested annually since 1970 by the top points scorers in the Grand Prix.

1970 Stan Smith (USA)
1971 Ilie Nastase (Rom)
1972 Ilie Nastase (Rom)
1973 Ilie Nastase (Rom)
1974 Guillermo Vilas (Arg)
1975 Ilie Nastase (Rom)
1976 Manuel Orantes (Spa)
1977 Jimmy Connors (USA)
1978 John McEnroe (USA) (held in 1979)

LITERATURE

The Booker Prize

Inaugurated in 1968, this most prestigious annual prize for fiction of £5000 is sponsored by Booker McConnell Ltd, and administered by the National Book League. The prize is awarded to the best novel, in the opinion of the judges, published each year. The prize is open to novels written in English by citizens of the British Commonwealth, the Republic of Ireland and the Republic of South Africa, and published for the first time in the UK by a British publisher.

1969　*Something to Answer For*, P. H. Newby, Faber & Faber

1970　*The Elected Member*, Bernice Rubens, Eyre and Methuen

1971　*In a Free State*, V. S. Naipaul, Andre Deutsch

1972　*G*, John Berger, Weidenfeld & Nicolson

1973　*The Siege of Krishnapur*, J. G. Farrell, Weidenfeld & Nicolson

1974　*The Conservationist*, Nadine Gordimer, Jonathan Cape;
Holiday, Stanley Middleton, Hutchinson

1975　*Heat and Dust*, Ruth Prawer Jhabvada, John Murray

1976　*Saville*, David Storey, Jonathan Cape

1977　*Staying On*, Paul Scott, William Heinemann

1978　*The Sea, The Sea*, Iris Murdoch, Chatto & Windus

Michael Caine, vice chairman and chief executive of Booker McConnell, presenting a leatherbound copy of her prize winning novel, 'The Sea, The Sea' to Iris Murdoch at the Booker Prize Dinner 1978

The Hawthornden Prize

The Hawthornden Prize, the oldest of the famous British literary prizes, was founded in 1919 by Miss Alice Warrender. It consists of £100 awarded annually to an English writer under 41 years of age for the best work of imaginative literature. It is especially designed to encourage young authors, and the word 'imaginative' is given a broad interpretation. Biographies are not necessarily excluded. Books do not have to be submitted for the prize. It is awarded without competition, and a panel of judges decides upon the winner.

1919	*The Queen of China*	Edward Shanks
1920	*Poems New and Old*	John Freeman
1921	*The Death of Society*	Romer Wilson
1922	*The Shepherd*	Edmund Blunden
1923	*Lady into Fox*	David Garnett
1924	*The Spanish Farm*	Ralph Hale Mottram
1925	*Juno and the Paycock*	Sean O'Casey
1926	*The Land*	Victoria Sackville-West
1927	*Tarka the Otter*	Henry Williamson
1928	*Memoirs of a Fox-Hunting Man*	Siegfried Sassoon
1929	*The Stricken Deer*	Lord David Cecil
1930	*The End of the World*	Geoffrey Dennis
1931	*Without My Cloak*	Kate O'Brien
1932	*The Fountain*	Charles Morgan
1933	*Collected Poems*	Victoria Sackville-West
1934	*Lost Horizon*	James Hilton
1935	*I Claudius*	Robert Graves
1936	*Edmund Campion*	Evelyn Waugh
1937	*A Trophy of Arms*	Ruth Pitter
1938	*In Parenthesis*	David Michael Jones
1939	*Penthesperon*	Christopher Hassall
1940	*London Fabric*	James Pope-Hennessy

1941	*The Labyrinthine Ways* (English title: *The Power and the Glory*)	Graham Greene
1942	*England is my Village*	John Llewellyn Rhys
1943	*The Cruel Solstice* and *The Iron Laurel*	Sidney Keyes
1944	*Letters to Malaya*	Martyn Skinner
1945–57	No award	
1958	*A Beginning*	Dom Moraes
1959	No award	
1960	*The Loneliness of the Long Distance Runner*	Alan Sillitoe
1961	*Lupercal*	Ted Hughes
1962	*The Sun Doctor*	Robert Shaw
1963	*The Price of Glory: Verdun 1916*	Alistair Horne
1964	*Mr Stone and the Knights Companions*	V. S. Naipaul
1965	*The Old Boys*	William Trevor
1966	No award	
1967	*The Russian Interpreter*	Michael Frayn
1968	*Early Renaissance*	Michael Levey
1969	*King Log*	Geoffrey Hill
1970	*Monk Dawson*	Piers Paul Read
1971	No award	
1972	No award	
1973	No award	
1974	*Awakenings*	Oliver Sacks
1975	*Changing Places*	David Lodge
1976	*Falstaff*	Robert Nye
1977	*In Patagonia*	Bruce Chatwin
1978	*Walter*	David Cook

International Book Award

Established in 1973 by the International Book Committee, the award recognises outstanding services rendered by a person or institution to the cause of books in such fields as authorship, publishing, production, book design, translation, library services, bookselling, encouragement of the reading habit, and promotion of international co-operation. This follows the UNESCO aim of furthering the use of books in the service of mutual understanding. The award is an honorary distinction consisting of a diploma bestowed annually at various international book fairs.

1973 Herman Liebaers, Chairman, International Book Year Support Committee; President, IFLA; Royal Librarian of Belgium

1974 Shoichi Noma, President, Japanese Publishers Association; President, Kodansha Ltd

1975 USSR National Committee for International Book Year, for its initiative in having 1972 proclaimed International Book Year

1976 Ronald Barker, Secretary of the Publishers Association (awarded posthumously)

1977 Julian Behrstock (USA), UNESCO staff

1978 Virginia Betancourt, Director of the Autonomous Institute of the National Library of Venezuela

Nobel Prize for Literature

The Nobel Prize in literature is one of the awards stipulated in the will of the late Alfred Nobel, the Swedish scientist who invented dynamite. The awarding authority is the Swedish Academy (for Literature). (*See* Nobel Prizes.)

1901	Sully Prudhomme (René Prudhomme) (Fra)
1902	C. M. T. Mommsen (Ger)
1903	Bjornstjerne Bjornson (Nor)
1904	Frederic Mistral (Fra)
	Jose Echegaray (Spa)
1905	Henryk Sienkiewicz (Pol)
1906	Giosue Carducci (Ita)
1907	Rudyard Kipling (GB)
1908	Rudolf C. Eucken (Ger)
1909	Selma Lagerlof (Swe)
1910	Paul J. L. Heyse (Ger)
1911	Count Maurice Maeterlinck (Bel)
1912	Gerhart Hauptmann (Ger)
1913	Rabindranath Tagore (Ind)
1914	No award
1915	Romain Rolland (Fra)

Rudyard Kipling is the youngest Literature Nobel Prize Winner. He won the prize in 1907 at the age of 41 (*Mansell*)

1916	Carl G. von Heidenstam (Swe)
1917	Karl A. Gjellerup (Den)
	Henrik Pontoppidan (Den)
1918	No award
1919	Carl F. G. Spitteler (Swi)
1920	Knut Hamsun (Nor)
1921	Anatole France (Fra)
1922	Jacinto Benavente (Spa)
1923	William Butler Yeats (Ire)
1924	Wladyslaw S. Reymont (Pol)
1925	George Bernard Shaw (GB) (Irish-born)
1926	Grazia Deledda (Ita)
1927	Henri Bergson (Fra)
1928	Sigrid Undset (Nor) (Danish-born)
1929	Thomas Mann (Ger)
1930	Sinclair Lewis (USA)
1931	Erik A. Karlfeldt (Swe)
1932	John Galsworthy (GB)
1933	Ivan A. Bunin (Fra) (Russian-born)

1934	Luigi Pirandello (Ita)
1935	No award
1936	Eugene O'Neill (USA)
1937	Roger Martin du Gard (Fra)
1938	Pearl S. Buck (USA)
1939	Frans E. Sillanpaa (Fin)
1940	No award
1941	No award
1942	No award
1943	No award
1944	Johannes V. Jensen (Den)
1945	Gabriela Mistral (Chi)
1946	Hermann Hesse (Swi) (German-born)
1947	André Gide (Fra)
1948	T. S. Eliot (GB) (USA-born)
1949	William Faulkner (USA)
1950	Bertrand Russell (GB)
1951	Par F. Lagerkvist (Swe)
1952	François Mauriac (Fra)
1953	Sir Winston Churchill (GB)
1954	Ernest Hemingway (USA)
1955	Halldor K. Laxness (Ice)
1956	Juan Ramon Jimenez (PR) (Spanish-born)
1957	Albert Camus (Fra)
1958	Boris L. Pasternak (USSR) Prize declined
1959	Salvatore Quasimodo (Ita)
1960	Saint-John Perse (Fra)
1961	Ivo Andric (Yug)
1962	John Steinbeck (USA)
1963	George Seferis (Gre)
1964	Jean-Paul Sartre (Fra) Prize declined
1965	Mikhail Sholokhov (USSR)
1966	Shmuel Yosef Agnon (Isr) (Austrian-born)
	Nelly Sachs (Swe) (German-born)
1967	Miguel Angel Asturias (Gua)
1968	Yasunari Kawabata (Jap)
1969	Samuel Beckett (Ire)
1970	Aleksandr I. Solzhenitsyn (USSR)
1971	Pablo Neruda (Chi)
1972	Heinrich Boll (Ger)
1973	Patrick White (Aus)
1974	Eyvind Johnson (Swe)
	Harry Edmund Martinson (Swe)
1975	Eugenio Montale (Ita)
1976	Saul Bellow (USA)
1977	Vicente Aleixandre (Spa)
1978	Isaac Bashevis Singer (USA)

Pulitzer Prizes
(*See* Pulitzer Prizes.)

FICTION

1917	No award	
1918	*His Family*	Ernest Poole
1919	*The Magnificent Ambersons*	Booth Tarkington
1920	No award	
1921	*The Age of Innocence*	Edith Wharton
1922	*Alice Adams*	Booth Tarkington
1923	*One of Ours*	Willa Cather
1924	*The Able McLaughlins*	Margaret Wilson
1925	*So Big*	Edna Ferber
1926	*Arrowsmith*	Sinclair Lewis
1927	*Early Autumn*	Louis Bromfield
1928	*The Bridge of San Luis Rey*	Thornton Wilder

1929	*Scarlet Sister Mary*	Julia Peterkin
1930	*Laughing Boy*	Oliver LaFarge
1931	*Years of Grace*	Margaret Ayer Barnes
1932	*The Good Earth*	Pearl S. Buck
1933	*The Store*	T. S. Stribling
1934	*Lamb in His Bosom*	Caroline Miller
1935	*Now in November*	Josephine Winslow Johnson
1936	*Honey in the Horn*	Harold L. Davis
1937	*Gone with the Wind*	Margaret Mitchell
1938	*The Late George Apley*	John Phillips Marquand
1939	*The Yearling*	Marjorie Kinnan Rawlings
1940	*The Grapes of Wrath*	John Steinbeck

1941	No award	
1942	*In This Our Life*	Ellen Glasgow
1943	*Dragon's Teeth*	Upton Sinclair
1944	*Journey in the Dark*	Martin Flavin
1945	*A Bell for Adano*	John Hersey
1946	No award	
1947	*All the King's Men*	Robert Penn Warren
1948	*Tales of the South Pacific*	James Michener
1949	*Guard of Honor*	James Gould Cozzens
1950	*The Way West*	A. B. Guthrie Jr
1951	*The Town*	Conrad Richter
1952	*The Caine Mutiny*	Herman Wouk
1953	*The Old Man and the Sea*	Ernest Hemingway
1954	No award	
1955	*A Fable*	William Faulkner
1956	*Andersonville*	MacKinlay Kantor
1957	No award	
1958	*A Death in the Family*	James Agee
1959	*The Travels of Jaime McPheeters*	Robert Lewis Taylor
1960	*Advise and Consent*	Allen Drury

1961	*To Kill a Mockingbird*	Harper Lee
1962	*The Edge of Sadness*	Edwin O'Connor
1963	*The Reivers*	William Faulkner
1964	No award	
1965	*The Keepers of the House*	Shirley Ann Grau
1966	*The Collected Stories of Katherine Anne Porter*	Katherine Anne Porter
1967	*The Fixer*	Bernard Malamud
1968	*The Confessions of Nat Turner*	William Styron
1969	*House Made of Dawn*	N. Scott Momaday
1970	*Collected Stories*	Jean Stafford
1971	No award	
1972	*Angle of Repose*	Wallace Stegner
1973	*The Optimist's Daughter*	Eudora Welty
1974	No award	
1975	*The Killer Angels*	Michael Shaara
1976	*Humboldt's Gift*	Saul Bellow
1977	No award	
1978	*Elbow Room*	James Allan McPherson

HISTORY

1917	*With Americans of Past and Present Days*	J. J. Jusserand
1918	*A History of the Civil War, 1861–65*	James Ford Rhodes
1919	No award	
1920	*The War with Mexico*	Justin H. Smith
1921	*The Victory at Sea*	William Sowden Sims and Burton J. Hendrick
1922	*The Founding of New England*	James Truslow Adams
1923	*The Supreme Court in United States History*	Charles Warren
1924	*The American Revolution – A Constitutional Interpretation*	Charles McIlwain
1925	*A History of the American Frontier*	Frederic L. Paxson
1926	*The History of the United States*	Edward Channing
1927	*Pinckney's Treaty*	Samuel Flagg Bemis
1928	*Main Currents in American Thought* (2 vols.)	Vernon Louis Parrington
1929	*The Organization and Administration of the Union Army, 1861–1865*	Fred Albert Shannon
1930	*The War of Independence*	Claude H. Van Tyne
1931	*The Coming of the War, 1914*	Bernadotte E. Schmitt
1932	*My Experiences in the World War*	John J. Pershing
1933	*The Significance of Sections in American History*	Frederick J. Turner
1934	*The People's Choice*	Herbert Agar
1935	*The Colonial Period of American History*	Charles McLean Andrews
1936	*The Constitutional History of the United States*	Andrew C. McLaughlin
1937	*The Flowering of New England*	Van Wyck Brooks
1938	*The Road to Reunion, 1865–1900*	Paul Herman Buck
1939	*A History of American Magazines*	Frank Luther Mott
1940	*Abraham Lincoln: The War Years*	Carl Sandburg
1941	*The Atlantic Migration, 1607–1860*	Marcus Lee Hansen
1942	*Reveille in Washington*	Margaret Leech
1943	*Paul Revere and the World He Lived In*	Esther Forbes
1944	*The Growth of American Thought*	Merle Curti
1945	*Unfinished Business*	Stephen Bonsal
1946	*The Age of Jackson*	Arthur M. Schlesinger Jr
1947	*Scientists Against Time*	James Phinney Baxter III
1948	*Across the Wide Missouri*	Bernard De Voto
1949	*The Disruption of American Democracy*	Roy Franklin Nichols
1950	*Art and Life in America*	Oliver W. Larkin
1951	*The Old Northwest: Pioneer Period, 1815–1840*	R. Carlyle Buley
1952	*The Uprooted*	Oscar Handlin
1953	*The Era of Good Feelings*	George Dangerfield
1954	*A Stillness at Appomattox*	Bruce Catton
1955	*Great River: The Rio Grande in North American History*	Paul Horgan

1956	*Age of Reform*	Richard Hofstadter
1957	*Russia Leaves the War; Soviet-American Relations, 1917–1920*	George F. Kennan
1958	*Banks and Politics in America – From the Revolution to the Civil War*	Bray Hammond
1959	*The Republican Era: 1869–1901*	Leonard D. White, assisted by Jean Schneider
1960	*In the Days of McKinley*	Margaret Leech
1961	*Between War and Peace: The Potsdam Conference*	Herbert Feis
1962	*The Triumphant Empire: Thunder-Clouds Gather in the West*	Lawrence H. Gipson
1963	*Washington: Village and Capital, 1800–1878*	Constance McLaughlin Green
1964	*Puritan Village: The Formation of a New England Town*	Sumner Chilton Powell
1965	*The Greenback Era*	Irwin Unger
1966	*Life of the Mind in America: From the Revolution to the Civil War*	Perry Miller
1967	*Exploration and Empire: The Explorer and Scientist in the Winning of the American West*	William H. Goetzmann
1968	*The Ideological Origins of the American Revolution*	Bernard Bailyn
1969	*Origins of the Fifth Amendment*	Leonard Levy
1970	*Present at the Creation: My Years in the State Department*	Dean G. Acheson
1971	*Roosevelt: The Soldier of Freedom, 1940–1945*	James MacGregor Burns
1972	*Neither Black Nor White*	C. N. Degler
1973	*People of Paradox: An Inquiry Concerning the Origin of American Civilization*	Michael Kammen
1974	*The Americans: The Democratic Experience*	Daniel J. Boorstin
1975	*Jefferson and His Time*	Dumas Malone
1976	*Lamy of Santa Fe*	Paul Horgan
1977	*The Impending Crisis*	David M. Potter
1978	*The Invisible Hand: The Managerial Revolution in American Business*	Alfred D. Chandler

BIOGRAPHY/AUTOBIOGRAPHY

1917	*Julia Ward Howe*	Laura E. Richards, Maude H. Elliot, and Florence H. Hall
1918	*Benjamin Franklin, Self-Revealed*	William Cabell Bruce
1919	*The Education of Henry Adams*	Henry Adams
1920	*The Life of John Marshall* (4 vols)	Albert J. Beveridge
1921	*The Americanization of Edward Bok*	Edward Bok
1922	*A Daughter of the Middle Border*	Hamlin Garland
1923	*The Life and Letters of Walter H. Page*	Burton J. Hendrick
1924	*From Immigrant to Inventor*	Michael Idvorsky Pupin
1925	*Barrett Wendell and His Letters*	M. A. DeWolfe Howe
1926	*The Life of Sir William Osler* (2 vols)	Harvey Cushing
1927	*Whitman*	Emory Holloway
1928	*The American Orchestra and Theodore Thomas*	Charles Edward Russell
1929	*The Training of an American: The Earlier Life and Letters of Walter H. Page*	Burton J. Hendrick
1930	*The Raven*	Marquis James
1931	*Charles W. Eliot*	Henry James
1932	*Theodore Roosevelt*	Henry F. Pringle
1933	*Grover Cleveland*	Allan Nevins
1934	*John Hay*	Tyler Dennett
1935	*R. E. Lee*	Douglas Southall Freeman
1936	*The Thought and Character of William James*	Ralph Barton Perry
1937	*Hamilton Fish*	Allan Nevins
1938	*Pedlar's Progress*	Odell Shepard
	Andrew Jackson	Marquis James
1939	*Benjamin Franklin*	Carl Van Doren
1940	*Woodrow Wilson, Life and Letters, Volumes VII and VIII*	Ray Stannard Baker
1941	*Jonathan Edwards*	Ola E. Winslow

1942	*Crusader in Crinoline*	Forrest Wilson
1943	*Admiral of the Ocean Sea*	Samuel Eliot Morison
1944	*The American Leonardo: The Life of Samuel F. B. Morse*	Carleton Mabee
1945	*George Bancroft: Brahmin Rebel*	Russell Blaine Nye
1946	*Son of the Wilderness*	Linnie M. Wolfe
1947	*The Autobiography of William Allen White*	William Allen White
1948	*Forgotten First Citizen: John Bigelow*	Margaret Clapp
1949	*Roosevelt and Hopkins*	Robert E. Sherwood
1950	*John Quincy Adams and the Foundations of American Foreign Policy*	Samuel Bemis
1951	*John C. Calhoun: American Portrait*	Margaret Louise Coit
1952	*Charles Evans Hughes*	Merlo J. Pusey
1953	*Edmund Pendleton 1721–1803*	David J. Mays
1954	*The Spirit of St. Louis*	Charles A. Lindbergh
1955	*The Taft Story*	William S. White
1956	*Benjamin Henry Latrobe*	T. F. Hamlin
1957	*Profiles in Courage*	John F. Kennedy
1958	*George Washington, Volumes I-VI,*	Douglas Southall Freeman
	Volume VII	Mary Ashworth and John Carroll
1959	*Woodrow Wilson, American Prophet*	Arthur Walworth
1960	*John Paul Jones*	Samuel Eliot Morison
1961	*Charles Sumner and the Coming of the Civil War*	David Donald
1962	No award	
1963	*Henry James*	Leon Edel
1964	*John Keats*	Walter Jackson Bate
1965	*Henry Adams*	Ernest Samuels
1966	*A Thousand Days*	Arthur Schlesinger Jr
1967	*Mr Clemens and Mark Twain*	Justin Kaplan
1968	*Memoirs (1925–1950)*	George F. Kennan
1969	*The Man from New York: George Quinn and His Friends*	Benjamin Reid
1970	*Huey Long*	T. Harry Williams
1971	*Robert Frost: The Years of Triumph, 1915–1938*	Lawrance R. Thompson
1972	*Eleanor and Franklin*	J. P. Lash
1973	*Luce and His Empire*	W. A. Swanberg
1974	*O'Neill, Son and Artist*	Louis Sheaffer
1975	*The Power Broker: Robert Moses and the Fall of New York*	Robert A. Caro
1976	*Edith Wharton: A Biography*	Richard Warrington Baldwin Lewis
1977	*A Prince of our Disorder (T. E. Lawrence)*	John E. Mack
1978	*Samuel Johnson*	Walter Jackson Bate

GENERAL NONFICTION
This prize was first awarded in 1962.

1962	*The Making of the President 1960*	Theodore H. White
1963	*The Guns of August*	Barbara Tuchman
1964	*Anti-intellectualism in American Life*	Richard Hofstadter
1965	*O Strange New World*	Howard Mumford Jones
1966	*Wandering Through Winter*	Edwin Way Teale
1967	*The Problem of Slavery in Western Culture*	David Brion Davis
1968	*Rousseau and Revolution*	Will and Ariel Durant
1969	*So Human an Animal: How We are Shaped by Surroundings and Events*	Rene Dubos
	The Armies of the Night	Norman Mailer
1970	*Gandhi's Truth*	Erik H. Erikson
1971	*The Rising Sun*	John Toland
1972	*Stilwell and the American Experience in China, 1911–1945*	Barbara W. Tuchman
1973	*Fire in the Lake*	Frances Fitzgerald
	Children of Crisis	Robert Coles
1974	*The Denial of Death*	Ernest Becker
1975	*Pilgrim at Tinker Creek*	Annie Dillard
1976	*Why Survive? Being Old in America*	Robert N. Butler

| 1977 | *Beautiful Swimmers: Watermen, Crabs and the Chesapeake Bay* | William W. Warner |
| 1978 | *The Dragons of Eden* | Carl Sagan |

The Royal Society of Literature Benson Medal

Established in 1916, the award is given from time to time by the Council of the Royal Society of Literature for meritorious work in poetry, fiction, history, biography, and belles-lettres.

1917	Gabrielle d'Annunzio	1929	Helen Waddell	1940	John Galsworthy
	Benito Peréz Galdós		F. A. Simpson		Christopher Hassall
	Maurice Parrès	1932	Stella Benson	1941	Christopher La Farge
1923	Lytton Strachey	1934	Dame Edith Sitwell	1952	Frederick S. Boas
1926	Percy Lubbock	1938	E. M. Forster	1966	J. R. R. Tolkien
	Robert Lynd		G. M. Young		Dame Rebecca West
	Harold Nicolson	1939	F. L. Lucas	1968	E. V. Rieu
1928	Gordon Bottomley		Andrew Young	1969	C. Woodham-Smith
	George Santayana			1975	Philip Larkin

The Royal Society of Literature Heinemann Award

Established in 1944 through the will of the late William Heinemann. The award, organised by the Royal Society of Literature, is 'primarily to reward those classes of literature which are less remunerative, namely, poetry, criticism, biography, history, etc.' and 'to encourage the production of works of real merit'.

1945	*Five Rivers*	Norman Nicholson	Dutton
1946	*In Search of Two Characters*	D. Colston-Baynes	Scribner
	Prospect of Flowers	Andrew Young	Cape
1947	*History of Western Philosophy*	Bertrand Russell	Simon & Schuster
	The Garden	V. Sackville-West	Doubleday
1948	*Down to Earth*	J. Stuart Collis	Irwin Clarke
	Letters to Malaya	Martyn Skinner	Putnam
1949	*Selected Poems*	John Betjeman	John Murray
	Travelling Home	Frances Cornford	Cresset Press
1950	*Broken Images*	John Guest	Longmans
	John Ruskin	Peter Quennell	Collins
1951	*Travellers Tree*	Patrick Leigh-Fermor	Harper
	Glassblowers and Gormanghast	Mervyn Peake	Eyre & Spottiswoo.le
1952	*The Cruel Sea*	Nicholas Monsarrat	Knopf
	Mountains with a Difference	G. Winthrop Young	British Book Centre
1953	*Collected Poems*	Edwin Muir	Grove
	Arnold Bennett	Reginald Pound	Harcourt
1954	*The Ermine*	Ruth Pitter	Cresset Press
	The Go-Between	L. P. Hartley	Knopf
1955	*John Keats: The Living Years*	Robert Gittings	Harvard Univ. Press
	Song at the Years Turning	R. S. Thomas	Hart-Davis
1956	*Wise Man from the West*	Vincent Cronin	Dutton
	Thomas Gray	R. W. Ketton-Cremer	Cambridge Univ. Press
1957	*The Bourbons of Naples*	Harold Acton	Humanities
	Roman Mornings	James Lees-Milne	British Book Centre
1958	*Sword of Pleasure*	Peter Green	World
	A Reed Shaken by the Wind	Gavin Maxwell	Longmans
1959	*The Last Tudor King*	Hester Chapman	Macmillan
	The Chequer'd Shade	John Press	Oxford Univ. Press
1960	*The Cocks of Hades*	C. A. Trypanis	Faber & Faber
	The Devil's Advocate	Morris West	Morrow
1961	*Venice*	James Morris	Pantheon
	The Masks of Love	Vernon Scannell	Putnam
1962	*Curtmantle*	Christopher Fry	Oxford Univ. Press
	The Destruction of Lord Raglan	Christopher Hibbert	Little
1963	*Mrs. Browning*	Alethea Hayter	Barnes & Noble

1964	*Rosebery*	Robert Rhodes James	Weidenfeld
	Cooper's Creek	Alan Moorehead	Harper
1965	*Journey from Obscurity, II, Youth*	Harold Owen	Oxford Univ. Press
	The Marsh Arabs	Wilfred Thesiger	Dutton
1966	*Jonathan Swift*	Nigel Dennis	Macmillan
	The Castaway	Derek Walcott	Cape
1967	*Wide Sargasso Sea*	Jean Rhys	Deutsch
	Surroundings	Norman MacCaig	Wesleyan Univ. Press
	Tolstoy and the Novel	John Bayley	Viking
1968	*Charlotte Brontë*	W. Gérin	Oxford Univ. Press
	The Maze Maker	Michael Ayrton	Holt
1969	*George Eliot*	Gordon S. Haight	Oxford Univ. Press
	Writing in the Dust	Jasmine Rose Innes	Deutsch
	A Cab at the Door	V. S. Pritchett	Chatto & Windus
1970	*Akenfield: Portrait of an English Village*	Ronald Blythe	A. Lane
	Sir William Hamilton	Brian Fothergill	Faber
	Pharaoh's Chicken	Nicholas Wollaston	Lippincott
1971	*Britain and Her Army*	Corelli Barnett	A. Lane
	Medieval Humanism	R. W. Southern	Blackwell
1972	*Granite Islands: Portrait of Corsica*	Dorothy Carrington	Longman
	Mercian Hymns	Geoffrey Hill	Deutsch
	The Big Chapel	Thomas Kilroy	Faber
1973	*That Greece Might Still Be Free*	William St. Clair	Oxford Univ. Press
	The Chant of Jimmy Blacksmith	Thomas Keneally	Angus & Roberson
1974	*Alexander the Great*	Robin Lane Fox	Dial
	From the Wilderness	Alasdair Maclean	Harper
	Mooncranker's Gift	Barry Unsworth	Houghton
1975	*Samuel Johnson*	John Wain	Macmillan
	William Wilberforce	Robin Furneaux	Hamilton
1976	*Melbourne*	Philip Ziegler	Collins
	Shadow of the Winter Palace	Edward Crankshaw	Macmillan
1977	*Parnell*	F. S. L. Lyons	Collins
	The First Fabians	N. & J. Mackenzie	Weidenfeld and Nicolson
	Milton and the English Revolution	C. Hill	Faber and Faber
1978	*Live Bait*	Frank Tuohy	Macmillan
	The Older Hardy	Robert Gittings	Heinemann Educational

The W.H. Smith & Son Annual Literary Award

The prize of £1000, awarded annually since 1959, goes to a Commonwealth author (including a citizen of the UK) whose book, written in English and published in the UK, within 12 months ending on December 31st preceding the date of the award, in the opinion of the judges makes the most outstanding contribution to literature. Previous winners include:

1959	Patrick White, *Voss*	1970	John Fowles, *The French Lieutenant's Woman*
1960	Laurie Lee, *Cider with Rosie*	1971	Nan Fairbrother, *New Lives, New Landscapes*
1961	Nadine Gordimer, *Friday's Footprint*	1972	Kathleen Raine, *The Lost Country*
1962	J. R. Ackerley, *We think the World of You*	1973	Brian Moore, *Catholics*
1963	Gabriel Fielding, *The Birthday King*	1974	Anthony Powell, *Temporary Kings*
1964	E. H. Gombrich, *Meditations on a Hobby Horse*	1975	Jon Stallworthy, *Wilfred Owen: A Biography*
1965	Leonard Woolf, *Beginning Again*	1976	Seamus Heaney, *North*
1966	R. C. Hutchinson, *A Child Possessed*	1977	Ronald Lewin, *Slim: The Standardbearer*
1967	Jean Rhys, *Wide Sargasso Sea*	1978	Patrick Leigh Fermor, *A Time of Gifts*
1968	V. S. Naipaul, *The Mimic Men*	1979	Mark Girouard, *Life in the English Country House*
1969	Robert Gittings, *John Keats*		

The Whitbread Literary Awards

Instituted in 1971, the awards of £1500 each in three categories, Novel, Biography/Auto-biography and Children's Book, are selected from books by writers who have lived in Great Britain and Ireland for five or more years.

1971	Fiction:	*The Destiny Waltz*, Gerda Charles
	Biography:	*Henrik Ibsen*, Michael Meyer
	Poetry:	*Mercian Hymns*, Geoffrey Hill
1972	Fiction:	*The Bird of Night*, Susan Hill
	Biography:	*Trollope*, James Pope-Hennessy
	Children's Book	*The Diddakoi*, Rumer Godden
1973	Fiction:	*The Chip Chip Gatherers*, Shiva Naipaul
	Biography:	*CB – A Life of Sir Henry Campbell-Bannerman*, John Wilson
	Children's Book:	*The Butterfly Ball and the Grasshopper's Feast*, Alan Aldridge and William Plomer
1974	Fiction:	*The Sacred and Profane Love Machine*, Iris Murdoch
	Biography:	*Poor Dear Brendan*, Andrew Boyle
	Joint Children's Books:	*How Tom Beat Captain Najork and His Hired Sportsmen*, Russel Hoban and Quentin Blake
		The Emperor's Winding Sheet, Jill Paton Walsh
	First Book:	*The Life and Death of Mary Wollstonecraft*, Claire Tomalin
1975	Fiction:	*Docherty*, William McIlvanney
	Biography:	*In Our Infancy (An Autobiography 1882–1912)*, Helen Corke
	First Book:	*The Improbable Puritan (A Life of Bulstrode Whitelock 1605–1675)*, Ruth Spalding
1976	Fiction:	*The Children of Dynmouth*, William Trevor
	Biography:	*Elizabeth Gaskell*, Winifred Gerin
	Children's Book:	*A Stitch in Time*, Penelope Lively
1977	Fiction:	*Injury Time*, Beryl Bainbridge
	Biography:	*Mary Curzon*, Nigel Nicolson
	Children's Book:	*No End of Yesterday*, Shelagh Macdonald
1978	Fiction:	*Picture Palace*, Paul Theroux
	Biography:	*Lloyd George: The People's Champion, 1902–1911*, John Grigg
	Children's Book:	*The Battle of Bubble and Squeak*, Philippa Pearce

LIVESTOCK

The Royal Smithfield Show Livestock Champions

The Royal Smithfield Club has held its annual show at Earls Court, London, since 1949, but the club dates from 1798 when the original Smithfield Cattle and Sheep Society was founded. The first Smithfield Show was organised in Wootton's Dolphin Yard, Smithfield, London, in 1799. The club then had 113 members; there were two competitions for cattle and five for sheep, and the prize money amounted to £52 10s. By 1978 the Club could boast 2200 members, there were competitions in 148 classes, and the prizes offered were valued at over £20 000.

The greatest number of wins, within each category, by one owner are given below. For full detail of results contact the Royal Smithfield Club direct.

CHAMPION CATTLE

Supreme Champion Beast of the Show	Scottish Malt Distillers Ltd, Pencaitland, E. Lothian	Shorthorn × Aberdeen Angus Steer (1949)
		Aberdeen Angus × Shorthorn Steer (1952)
		Aberdeen Angus Steer (1953)
		Aberdeen Angus × Shorthorn Steer (1954)
Best Beast in the Show bred by Exhibitor	David B. Sinclair, Inchture, Perthshire	Aberdeen Angus Heifer (1968)
		Aberdeen Angus Cross Steer (1971)
		Charolais × Aberdeen Angus Steer (1972)
Supreme Champion Beast of the Show Sold for Show Record Price Fetched £7800 at Auction. Bought by J. H. Dewhurst Ltd	James Donald, Glenalmond, Perthshire	Charolais × Aberdeen Angus Steer – Named Super Star (1974)

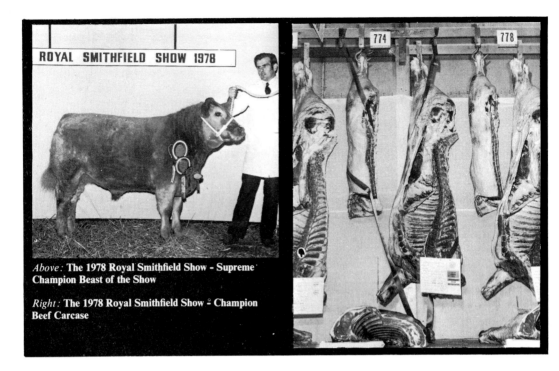

ROYAL SMITHFIELD SHOW 1978

Above: **The 1978 Royal Smithfield Show - Supreme Champion Beast of the Show**

Right: **The 1978 Royal Smithfield Show - Champion Beef Carcase**

CHAMPION SHEEP

Champion Pen of Lambs in the Show	Late Sir Wm. Rootes, Nr. Hungerford, Berks	Hampshire Down (1950, 1954, 1955, 1956, 1957)
Best Pen of Lambs in the Show bred by Exhibitor	Late Sir Wm. Rootes, Nr. Hungerford, Berks	Hampshire Down (1950, 1954, 1955, 1956, 1957)

CHAMPION PIGS

Champion Pen of Two Pigs in the Show	C. N. Flack & Co. Ltd, Culford, Bury St. Edmunds, Suffolk	Large White (1955, 1956, 1977) Landrace (1973)
	Croxton Park Ltd, Thetford, Norfolk	Welsh (1963, 1971, 1974, 1978)
Champion Single Pig in the Show	C. N. Flack & Co. Ltd, Culford, Bury St. Edmunds, Suffolk	Large White (1955, 1965, 1973) Landrace (1970)

CHAMPION CARCASE

Champion Beef Carcase	Hatch Gate Farms Ltd, Wargrave, Berks	Aberdeen Angus Steer (1960, 1965, 1968) Aberdeen Angus Heifer (1961)
Champion Beef Carcase Sold for Show Record Price Fetched £5319 at Auction. (591 lbs at £9) World Record	J. H. Cridlan, Henley-on-Thames, Oxon	Aberdeen Angus Steer (1971)
Champion Lamb Carcase	J. M. Lenthall, Burton Bradstock, Dorset	Dorset Horn (1957, 1959) Polled Dorset Horn (1960) Suffolk × Dorset Horn (1963)
	A. W. Lang, Curry Rivel, Langport, Somerset	Dorset Down (1965, 1969, 1970, 1976)
Champion Pork Carcase	D. W. P. Gough & Co. Ltd, Lackford, Bury St. Edmunds, Suffolk	Landrace (1965, 1970, 1977)

| Champion Bacon Carcase | Alan Tew, Bledlow Ridge, High Wycombe, Bucks | Welsh (1976, 1977, 1978) |
| Champion Veal Carcase | Mrs B. Wrixon, Toller Porcorum, Dorchester, Dorset | British Friesian (1970, 1971) British Friesian × Aberdeen Angus (1977) |

LUGE (*See* Bobsleigh and Tobogganing)

MAGIC

The Magic Circle Awards

The first award is a direct competition open to boys (aged 12 to 18), who have to present a short magic act which is judged on standard of technique, ability, personality and presentation. The competition is held every two years and is open to entrants from all over the world. The eliminating rounds are held wherever necessary with the final in London at the Magic Circle headquarters.

YOUNG MAGICIAN OF THE YEAR

1961	Johnny Hart	1971	Christopher Payne
1963	Airaksinen	1973	Colin Boardman
1965	Keith Cooper	1975	*Joint:* David Owen, Martin Welford
1967	Colin Rose	1977	*Joint:* Stephen Hill, David Metcalf
1969	David Lait	1979	Phillip Theodore

The other award made by the Magic Circle is the Maskelyne. This is given to the magician who has made an outstanding contribution either by performance, invention, writing or, in fact, in any way that will help to develop the art of magic. The award takes the shape of a bronze head of John Nevil Maskelyne who was a great magician 100 years ago and who did much to help the Magic Circle when it was founded in 1905.

THE MASKELYNE

1970	Robert Harbin	1974	Peter Warlock
1971	David Nixon	1975	No award
1972	Ali Bongo	1976	No award
1973	John Nevil Maskelyne (posthumously)	1977	No award
		1978	'Goodliffe'

MEDICINE

The British Medical Association

The British Medical Association organises a number of awards and honours, including the triennial Brackenbury Prize for a particular subject in public health, medical-politics, medical-sociology, or medical education; the biennial Katherine Bishop Harman Prize for successful medical practice in the fields of pregnancy and childbearing risks to health and life; the annual Nathanial Bishop Harman Prize for exceptionally good hospital practices; the annual Sir Charles Hastings and Charles Oliver Hawthorne Clinical Prize for systematic observation, research and recording in general practice; the biennial Insole Research Award for research into causes and cure of venereal disease; the Middlemore Prize for a contribution to ophthalmic medicine or surgery; the Milburn Award for outstanding contributions in forensic medicine; the biennial Occupational Health Prize for contributions to occupational health; and the biennial Doris Odlum Prize for a contribution to mental health medicine. Further details on winners are available direct from the Association.

Nobel Prize for Medicine (*See* Nobel Prizes)

1901	Emil A. von Behring (Ger)	1951	Max Theiler (USA) (S. African-born)
1902	Sir Ronald Ross (GB)	1952	Selman A. Waksman (USA)
1903	Niels R. Finsen (Den)	1953	Hans A. Krebs (GB) (German-born)
1904	Ivan P. Pavlov (Rus)		Fritz A. Lipmann (USA) (German-born)
1905	Robert Koch (Ger)	1954	John F. Enders (USA)
1906	Camillo Golgi (Ita)		Frederick C. Robbins (USA)
	Santiago Ramon y Cajal (Spa)		Thomas H. Weller (USA)
1907	Charles L. A. Laveran (Fra)	1955	Alex H. T. Theorell (Swe)
1908	Paul Ehrlich (Ger)	1956	André F. Cournand (USA) (French-born)
	Elie Metchnikoff (Fra) (Russian-born)		Werner Forssmann (Ger)
1909	Emil T. Kocher (Swi)		Dickinson W. Richards Jr (USA)
1910	Albrecht Kossel (Ger)	1957	Daniel Bovet (Ita) (Swiss-born)
1911	Allvar Gullstrand (Swe)	1958	George W. Beadle (USA)
1912	Alexis Carrel (USA)		Edward L. Tatum (USA)
1913	Charles R. Richet (Fra)		Joshua Lederberg (USA)
1914	Robert Bárány (Hun)	1959	Arthur Kornberg (USA)
1915–18	No award		Severo Ochoa (USA) (Spanish-born)
1919	Jules Bordet (Bel)	1960	Sir F. Macfarlane Burnet (Aus)
1920	Schack A. S. Krogh (Den)		Peter B. Medawar (GB) (Brazilian-born)
1921	No award	1961	Georg von Békèsy (USA) (Hungarian-born)
1922	Archibald V. Hill (GB)	1962	Francis H. C. Crick (GB)
	Otto F. Meyerhof (Ger)		James D. Watson (USA)
1923	Frederick G. Banting (Can)		Maurice H. F. Wilkins (GB)
	John J. R. Macleod (Can)	1963	Sir John C. Eccles (Aus)
1924	Willem Einthoven (Hol)		Alan L. Hodgkin (GB)
1925	No award		Andrew F. Huxley (GB)
1926	Johannes A. G. Fibiger (Den)	1964	Konrad E. Bloch (USA)
1927	Julius Wagner-Jauregg (Aut)		Feodor Lynen (Ger)
1928	Charles J. H. Nicolle (Fra)	1965	François Jacob (Fra)
1929	Christiaan Eijkman (Hol)		André Lwoff (Fra)
	Sir Frederick G. Hopkins (GB)		Jacques Monod (Fra)
1930	Karl Landsteiner (USA) (Austrian-born)	1966	Charles B. Huggins (USA)
1931	Otto H. Warburg (Ger)		Francis Peyton Rous (USA)
1932	Edgar D. Adrian (GB)	1967	Ragnar Granit (Swe) (Finnish-born)
	Sir Charles S. Sherrington (GB)		Haldan Keffer Hartline (USA)
1933	Thomas H. Morgan (USA)		George Wald (USA)
1934	George R. Minot (USA)	1968	Robert W. Holley (USA)
	William P. Murphy (USA)		Har Gobind Khorana (USA) (Indian-born)
	George H. Whipple (USA)		Marshall W. Nirenberg (USA)
1935	Hans Spemann (Ger)	1969	Max Delbrück (USA) (German-born)
1936	Sir Henry H. Dale (GB)		Alfred D. Hershey (USA)
	Otto Loewi (USA) (Austrian-born)		Salvador D. Luria (USA) (Italian-born)
1937	Albert Szent-Györgyi von Nagyrapolt (USA)	1970	Julius Axelrod (USA)
	(Hungarian-born)		Ulf von Euler (Swe)
1938	Corneille J. F. Heymans (Bel)		Bernard Katz (GB)
1939	Gerhard Domagk (Ger)	1971	Earl W. Sutherland Jr (USA)
1940	No award	1972	Gerald M. Edelman (USA)
1941	No award		Rodney Porter (GB)
1942	No award	1973	Karl von Frisch (Aut)
1943	Henrik C. P. Dam (Den)		Konrad Lorenz (Aut)
	Edward A. Doisy (USA)		Nikolaas Tinbergen (GB) (Dutch-born)
1944	Joseph Erlanger (USA)	1974	Albert Claude (USA) (Lux-born)
	Herbert S. Gasser (USA)		Christian René de Duve (Bel)
1945	Sir Alexander Fleming (GB)		George Emil Palade (USA) (Romanian-born)
	Ernst B. Chain (GB) (German-born)	1975	David Baltimore (USA)
	Sir Howard W. Florey (GB) (Australian-born)		Howard Martin Temin (USA)
1946	Hermann J. Muller (USA)		Renato Dulbecco (USA) (Italian-born)
1947	Carl F. Cori (USA) (Czech-born)	1976	Baruch S. Blumberg (USA)
	Gerty T. Cori (USA) (Czech-born)		D. Carleton Gajdusek (USA)
	Bernardo A. Houssay (Arg)	1977	Rosalyn S. Yalow (USA)
1948	Paul H. Müller (Swi)		Roger C. L. Guillemin (USA) (French-born)
1949	Walter R. Hess (Swi)		Andrew V. Schally (USA)
	Antonio Moniz (Por)	1978	Werner Arber (Swi)
1950	Philip S. Hench (USA)		Daniel Nathans (USA)
	Edward C. Kendall (USA)		Hamilton Smith (USA)
	Tadeus Reichstein (Swi) (Polish-born)		

MILK

There are now various competitions in Britain for the Milkman of the Year or Personality Milkman.

One of the winners in 1979 was Bob Ayotte from Woolwich, London, who delivered more than 600 000 pints during a three-month spell – and won a fortnight's holiday in Florida plus £500 spending money.

The National Dairy Council's Personality Milkman for 1979, chosen from thousands of nominations by customers throughout England and Wales, was William Jones of Blackwood, Gwent. He received a £500 prize. The customer who nominated Mr Jones, Mrs Mary Charles of Blackwood, also received £500. Her summing up: 'He is always very pleasant in all winds and weathers and very helpful.'

MODERN PENTATHLON

Modern Pentathlon comprises the sports of Cross-Country Riding, Fencing, Shooting, Swimming and Cross-Country Running. It was first included in the Olympic Games of 1912 and World Championships were first held in 1949.

OLYMPIC CHAMPIONS
Since 1948:

	Individual	Team
1948	William Grut (Swe)	
1952	Lars Hall (Swe)	Hungary
1956	Lars Hall (Swe)	USSR
1960	Ferenc Németh (Hun)	Hungary
1964	Ferenc (Török (Hun)	USSR
1968	Bjorn Ferm (Swe)	Hungary
1972	Andras Balczo (Hun)	USSR
1976	Janusz Pyciak-Peciak (Pol)	G. Britain

MEN'S WORLD CHAMPIONS

	Individual	Team
1949	Tage Bjurefelt (Swe)	Sweden
1950	Lars Hall (Swe)	Sweden
1951	Lars Hall (Swe)	Sweden
1953	Dabor Benedek (Hun)	Sweden
1954	Björn Thofelt (Swe)	Hungary
1955	Konstantin Salnikov (USSR)	Hungary
1957	Igor Novikov (USSR)	USSR

	Individual	Team
1958	Igor Novikov (USSR)	USSR
1959	Igor Novikov (USSR)	USSR
1961	Igor Novikov (USSR)	USSR
1962	S. Dobnikov (USSR)	USSR
1963	Andras Balczo (Hun)	Hungary
1965	Andras Balczo (Hun)	Hungary
1966	Andras Balczo (Hun)	Hungary
1967	Andras Balczo (Hun)	Hungary
1969	Andras Balczo (Hun)	USSR
1970	Paul Kelemen (Hun)	Hungary
1971	Boris Onischenko (USSR)	USSR
1973	Pavel Lednev (USSR)	USSR
1974	Pavel Lednev (USSR)	USSR
1975	Pavel Lednev (USSR)	Hungary
1977	Janusz Pyciak-Peciak (Pol)	Poland
1978	Pavel Lednev (USSR)	Poland

WOMEN'S WORLD CHAMPIONS
First contested 1977.

1977	Virginia Swift (USA)
1978	Wendy Norman (GB)

MOTO CROSS

European Championships were first held at 500 cc in 1952 and World Championships were first held at this category in 1957, at which time a 250 cc category was introduced as a European Championship. The latter was upgraded to World Championships status in 1962. Winners since 1957:

250 cc

European Championships

1957	Fritz Betzelbacher (Ger)
1958	Jaromir Cizek (Cz)
1959	Rolf Tibblin (Swe)
1960	Dave Bickers (GB)
1961	Dave Bickers (GB)

World Championships

1962	Torsten Hallman (Swe)
1963	Torsten Hallman (Swe)
1964	Joël Robert (Bel)
1965	Victor Arbekov (USSR)
1966	Torsten Hallman (Swe)
1967	Torsten Hallman (Swe)

1968	Joël Robert (Bel)
1969	Joël Robert (Bel)
1970	Joël Robert (Bel)
1971	Joël Robert (Bel)
1972	Joël Robert (Bel)
1973	Hakan Andersson (Swe)

1974   Gennadiy Moisseyev (USSR)
1975   Harry Everts (Bel)
1976   Heikki Mikkola (Fin)
1977   Gennadiy Moisseyev (USSR)
1978   Gennadiy Moisseyev (USSR)

500 cc
World Championships
1957   Bill Nilsson (Swe)
1958   René Baeten (Bel)
1959   Sten Lundin (Swe)
1960   Bill Nilsson (Swe)
1961   Sten Lundin (Swe)
1962   Rolf Tibblin (Swe)
1963   Rolf Tibblin (Swe)
1964   Jeff Smith (GB)
1965   Jeff Smith (GB)
1966   Paul Friedrichs (GDR)
1967   Paul Friedrichs (GDR)
1968   Paul Friedrichs (GDR)
1969   Bengt Aberg (Swe)
1970   Bengt Aberg (Swe)
1971   Roger de Coster (Bel)
1972   Roger de Coster (Bel)
1973   Roger de Coster (Bel)
1974   Heikki Mikkola (Fin)
1975   Roger de Coster (Bel)
1976   Roger de Coster (Bel)
1977   Heikki Mikkola (Fin)
1978   Heikki Mikkola (Fin)
1979   Graham Noyce (GB)

125 cc
World Championships
1975   Gaston Rahier (Bel)
1976   Gaston Rahier (Bel)
1977   Gaston Rahier (Bel)
1978   Akira Watanabe (Jap)
1979   Harry Everts (Bel)

MOTO-CROSS DES NATIONS
The international Team championship for 500 cc has been contested annually since 1947. Winning nations:
Great Britain: 1947, 1949–50, 1952–54, 1956–57, 1959–60, 1963–67
Belgium: 1948, 1951, 1969, 1972–73, 1976–77
Sweden: 1955, 1958, 1961–62, 1971, 1974
USSR: 1968, 1978
Czechoslovakia: 1975

TROPHEE DES NATIONS
The international Team championship for 250 cc has been contested annually since 1961. Winning nations:
Great Britain: 1961–62, 1965
Sweden: 1963–64, 1966–68
Belgium: 1969–78

TRIALS
World Champions (first recognised 1975)
1975   Martin Lampkin (GB)
1976   Yrjo Vesterinen (Fin)
1977   Yrjo Vesterinen (Fin)
1978   Yrjo Vesterinen (Fin)

'MOTOR CYCLE NEWS' 'MAN OF THE YEAR' COMPETITION
This prestigious annual poll is for the man voted by readers of *Motor Cycle News* as their most popular motorcycle racer. Inaugurated in 1958. Winners:

1958 John Surtees	1966 Giacomo Agostini (Ita)	1973 Barry Sheene
1959 John Surtees	1967 Mike Hailwood	1974 Phil Read
1960 Dave Bickers	1968 Helmut Fath (Ger)	1975 Barry Sheene
1961 Mike Hailwood	1969 Rod Gould	1976 Barry Sheene
1962 Derek Minter	1970 John Cooper	1977 Barry Sheene
1963 Mike Hailwood	1971 John Cooper	1978 Mike Hailwood
1964 Jeff Smith	1972 Ray Pickrell	(Except where otherwise stated all are British)
1965 Bill Ivy		

MOTORCYCLING

World Championship

The most important World Championship category is undoubtedly the 500 cc. For this and the other categories riders gain points based on their performances in a series of Grand Prix events. The World Championships were first held under the auspices of the FIM in 1949. Individual winners:

500 cc

1949 Leslie Graham (GB)	1955 Geoff Duke (GB)	1961 Gary Hocking (Rho)
1950 Umberto Masetti (Ita)	1956 John Surtees (GB)	1962 Mike Hailwood (GB)
1951 Geoff Duke (GB)	1957 Libero Liberati (Ita)	1963 Mike Hailwood (GB)
1952 Umberto Masetti (Ita)	1958 John Surtees (GB)	1964 Mike Hailwood (GB)
1953 Geoff Duke (GB)	1959 John Surtees (GB)	1965 Mike Hailwood (GB)
1954 Geoff Duke (GB)	1960 John Surtees (GB)	1966 Giacomo Agostini (Ita)

1967　Giacomo Agostini (Ita)
1968　Giacomo Agostini (Ita)
1969　Giacomo Agostini (Ita)
1970　Giacomo Agostini (Ita)
1971　Giacomo Agostini (Ita)
1972　Giacomo Agostini (Ita)
1973　Phil Read (GB)
1974　Phil Read (GB)
1975　Giacomo Agostini (Ita)
1976　Barry Sheene (GB)
1977　Barry Sheene (GB)
1978　Kenny Roberts (USA)
1979　Kenny Roberts (USA)

250 cc
1949　Bruno Ruffo (Ita)
1950　Dario Ambrosini (Ita)
1951　Bruno Ruffo (Ita)
1952　Enrico Lorenzetti (Ita)
1953　Werner Haas (Ger)
1954　Werner Haas (Ger)
1955　Herman Müller (Ger)
1956　Carlo Ubbiali (Ita)
1957　Cecil Sandford (GB)
1958　Tarquinio Provini (Ita)
1959　Carlo Ubbiali (Ita)
1960　Carlo Ubbiali (Ita)
1961　Mike Hailwood (GB)
1962　Jim Redman (Rho)
1963　Jim Redman (Rho)
1964　Phil Read (GB)
1965　Phil Read (GB)
1966　Mike Hailwood (GB)
1967　Mike Hailwood (GB)
1968　Phil Read (GB)
1969　Kel Carruthers (Aus)
1970　Rod Gould (GB)
1971　Phil Read (GB)
1972　Jarno Saarinen (Fin)
1973　Dieter Braun (Ger)
1974　Walter Villa (Ita)
1975　Walter Villa (Ita)
1976　Walter Villa (Ita)
1977　Mario Lega (Ita)
1978　Kork Ballington (SA)
1979　Kork Ballington (SA)

350 cc
1949　Freddie Frith (GB)
1950　Bob Foster (GB)
1951　Geoff Duke (GB)
1952　Geoff Duke (GB)
1953　Fergus Anderson (GB)
1954　Fergus Anderson (GB)
1955　Bill Lomas (GB)
1956　Bill Lomas (GB)
1957　Keith Campbell (Aus)
1958　John Surtees (GB)
1959　John Surtees (GB)
1960　John Surtees (GB)
1961　Gary Hocking (Rho)
1962　Jim Redman (Rho)
1963　Jim Redman (Rho)
1964　Jim Redman (Rho)
1965　Jim Redman (Rho)
1966　Mike Hailwood (GB)
1967　Mike Hailwood (GB)

Giacomo Agostini (Ita) won a record 15 motorcycling World Championships. In 12 seasons from 1968 to 1976 he won 122 races in the World Championships series (*Popperfoto*)

1968　Giacomo Agostini (Ita)
1969　Giacomo Agostini (Ita)
1970　Giacomo Agostini (Ita)
1971　Giacomo Agostini (Ita)
1972　Giacomo Agostini (Ita)
1973　Giacomo Agostini (Ita)
1974　Giacomo Agostini (Ita)
1975　Johnnie Cecotto (Ven)
1976　Walter Villa (Ita)
1977　Takazumi Katayama (Jap)
1978　Kork Ballington (SA)
1979　Kork Ballington (SA)

50 cc
1962　Ernst Degner (Ger)
1963　Hugh Anderson (NZ)
1964　Hugh Anderson (NZ)
1965　Ralph Bryans (Ire)
1966　Hans-Georg Anscheidt (Ger)
1967　Hans-Georg Anscheidt (Ger)
1968　Hans-Georg Anscheidt (Ger)
1969　Angel Nieto (Spa)
1970　Angel Nieto (Spa)
1971　Jan de Vries (Hol)
1972　Angel Nieto (Spa)
1973　Jan de Vries (Hol)
1974　Henk van Kessel (Hol)
1975　Angel Nieto (Spa)
1976　Angel Nieto (Spa)
1977　Angel Nieto (Spa)
1978　Rocardo Tormo (Spa)

FORMULA 750
1977　Steve Baker (USA)
1978　Johnnie Cecotto (Ven)

125 cc
1949　Nello Pagani (Ita)
1950　Bruno Ruffo (Ita)

1951　Carlo Ubbiali (Ita)
1952　Cecil Sandford (GB)
1953　Werner Haas (Ger)
1954　Rupert Hollaus (Aut)
1955　Carlo Ubbiali (Ita)
1956　Carlo Ubbiali (Ita)
1957　Tarquinio Provini (Ita)
1958　Carlo Ubbiali (Ita)
1959　Carlo Ubbiali (Ita)
1960　Carlo Ubbiali (Ita)
1961　Tom Phillis (Aus)
1962　Luigi Taveri (Swi)
1963　Hugh Anderson (NZ)
1964　Luigi Taveri (Swi)
1965　Hugh Anderson (NZ)
1966　Luigi Taveri (Swi)
1967　Bill Ivy (GB)
1968　Phil Read (GB)
1969　Dave Simmonds (GB)
1970　Dieter Braun (Ger)
1971　Angel Nieto (Spa)
1972　Angel Nieto (Spa)
1973　Kent Andersson (Swe)
1974　Kent Andersson (Swe)
1975　Paolo Pileri (Ita)
1976　Pier-Paolo Bianchi (Ita)
1977　Pier-Paolo Bianchi (Ita)
1978　Eugenio Lazzarini (Ita)
1979　Angel Nieto (Spa)

SIDE-CARS
1949　Eric Oliver (GB)
1950　Eric Oliver (GB)
1951　Eric Oliver (GB)
1952　Cyril Smith (GB)
1953　Eric Oliver (GB)
1954　Wilhelm Noll (Ger)
1955　Wilhelm Faust (Ger)

1956	Wilhelm Noll (Ger)	1964	Max Deubel (Ger)	1972	Klaus Enders (Ger)
1957	Fritz Hillebrand (Ger)	1965	Fritz Scheidegger (Swi)	1973	Klaus Enders (Ger)
1958	Walter Schneider (Ger)	1966	Fritz Scheidegger (Swi)	1974	Klaus Enders (Ger)
1959	Walter Schneider (Ger)	1967	Klaus Enders (Ger)	1975	Rolf Steinhausen (Ger)
1960	Helmut Fath (Ger)	1968	Helmut Fath (Ger)	1976	Rolf Steinhausen (Ger)
1961	Max Deubel (Ger)	1969	Klaus Enders (Ger)	1977	George O'Dell (GB)
1962	Max Deubel (Ger)	1970	Klaus Enders (Ger)	1978	Rolf Biland (Swi)
1963	Max Deubel (Ger)	1971	Horst Owesle (Ger)	1979	Rolf Biland (Swi)

MOTORING

Automobile Association National Motoring Awards

These awards are given annually to mark notable inventions and developments which help the motoring public. The awards made are as follows:

1965

Gold Medal   The Rover Company Ltd
(for the Rover 2000 car)

Silver Medals   The Dunlop Rubber Company Ltd
(for tyre safety research)
Harry Ferguson Research Ltd
(for 4-wheel drive and anti-locking brake system)
The Ford Motor Company Ltd
(for aero-flow ventilation)

1966

Silver Medals   Cox of Watford
(for Mark II safety seat)
Clayton Dewandre Company Ltd
(for load-sensitive brake control)

1967

Gold Medal   The Corporation of London
(for the Blackfriars Underpass)

Silver Medals   The Motoring Unit of the BBC
(for its motoring programme and information service for drivers)
Automobile and Industrial Developments Ltd
(for dual and hand control conversion equipment for handicapped drivers)
British Lighting Industries
(for twin-filament (dip-beam) tungsten halogen bulb developed by Mazda Division)

1968

Gold Medal   Dover Harbour Board
(for their efforts to facilitate the outward and inward passage of record numbers of motor vehicles)

Silver Medals   Corporation of Sheffield
(for the Arundel Gate Traffic Scheme)
British Leyland Motor Corporation
(for its gas turbine engine for commercial vehicles)

1969

Gold Medal   Britax (London) Ltd
(for their Centre-Lok car seat belt)

Silver Medals   The Motor Industry Research Ass.
(for its Impact Laboratory which allows tests on vehicle safety)
East Sussex County Council
(for the Lewes Traffic Management Scheme)

Durham County Council
(for its establishment of a number of roadside picnic sites and its work in the conservation of the countryside in general)

1970

Silver Medals   The London Borough of Croydon
(for the development of its town centre to facilitate passing traffic and to accommodate stationary vehicles)
The British Hovercraft Corporation Ltd
(for its highly successful work in the development of the *SRN 4* Hovercraft)
Shell International Petroleum Company Ltd
(for its development of 'Shellgrip' road surface dressing)

1971

Gold Medal   Sir William Lyons
(in recognition of his long and distinguished service to motoring in Great Britain and to mark his recent retirement)

Silver Medal   The North Riding Road Accident After Care Scheme
(for its pioneer work in establishing a pattern of 'flying doctor' schemes which now exist in other parts of the country)

1972

Gold Medal   National Motor Museum, Beaulieu

1973

Gold Medal: Dunlop Ltd
(for its Denovo Total Mobility Tyre)

Silver Medal   London Borough of Harrow
(for its Driver Training Centre)

1974

Gold Medal   The Forestry Commission
(for the advancement of conservation and leisure facilities in Scotland)

1975   No awards given

1976

Gold Medals   Leyland Cars
(for the new Rover 3500)
Triplex Safety Glass Company Ltd
(for the development of the Ten Twenty laminated windscreen)

Silver Medal   The British Insurance Association Repair Centre at Thatcham
(for its valuable research work particularly into economies of repair methods, repairability and insurance engineering training)

1977
Silver Medal   Road Safety Unit of the Greater London Council
(for its success in achieving a notable reduction in road accidents)

1978
Gold Medal   Quinton Hasell Automotive
(for the Underider safety device designed to minimise the effects of collisions between cars and lorries)

Silver Medal   Cornwall County Council, West Penwith District Council and British Rail
(for the St Ives park-and-ride scheme enabling motorists to park outside the town and catch a train to the centre)
Berm Optical Products
(for the Vanguard PVC rear view lens)

MOTOR RACING *(See also* Rallying)

World Drivers' Championship

Inaugurated in 1950, the world drivers' championship is made up of specified Formula One Grand Prix races each season. Winners:

1950	Giuseppe Farina (Ita)	1960	Jack Brabham (Aus)	1970	Jochen Rindt (Ger)
1951	Juan Manuel Fangio (Arg)	1961	Phil Hill (USA)	1971	Jackie Stewart (GB)
1952	Alberto Ascari (Ita)	1962	Graham Hill (GB)	1972	Emerson Fittipaldi (Bra)
1953	Alberto Ascari (Ita)	1963	Jim Clark (GB)	1973	Jackie Stewart (GB)
1954	Juan Manuel Fangio (Arg)	1964	John Surtees (GB)	1974	Emerson Fittipaldi (Bra)
1955	Juan Manuel Fangio (Arg)	1965	Jim Clark (GB)	1975	Niki Lauda (Aut)
1956	Juan Manuel Fangio (Arg)	1966	Jack Brabham (Aus)	1976	James Hunt (GB)
1957	Juan Manuel Fangio (Arg)	1967	Denny Hulme (NZ)	1977	Niki Lauda (Aut)
1958	Mike Hawthorn (GB)	1968	Graham Hill (GB)	1978	Mario Andretti (USA)
1959	Jack Brabham (Aus)	1969	Jackie Stewart (GB)		

Manufacturer's World Championship (Formula One)

1958	Vanwall	1965	Lotus-Climax	1972	J.P.S. Lotus
1959	Cooper-Climax	1966	Repco-Brabham	1973	J.P.S. Lotus
1960	Cooper-Climax	1967	Repco-Brabham	1974	McLaren
1961	Ferrari	1968	Lotus-Ford	1975	Ferrari
1962	BRM	1969	Matra-Ford	1976	Ferrari
1963	Lotus-Climax	1970	Lotus-Ford	1977	Ferrari
1964	Ferrari	1971	Tyrell-Ford	1978	J.P.S. Lotus

Juan Manuel Fangio won 24 Grand Prix races and the World Drivers' Championship a record five times. He narrowly failed to win also in 1950 and he is shown here in his Alfa Romeo in the Italian Grand Prix where shortage of fuel cost him the championship

Indianapolis 500

America's most famous motor race was first held in 1911. Anthony (A. J.) Foyt is the only man to have won on four occasions. Winners since 1946 (all USA except where stated):

	Driver	Car	Speed (mph)
1946	George Robson	Thorne Engineering	114.820
1947	Mauri Rose	Blue Crown Special	116.338
1948	Mauri Rose	Blue Crown Special	119.814
1949	Bill Holland	Blue Crown Special	121.327
1950	Johnny Parsons	Wynn Kurtis Kraft	124.002
1951	Lee Wallard	Belanger	126.224
1952	Troy Ruttman	Agajanian	128.922
1953	Bill Vukovich	Fuel Injection	128.740
1954	Bill Vukovich	Fuel Injection	130.840
1955	Bob Sweikert	John Zink Special	128.209
1956	Pat Flaherty	John Zink Special	128.490
1957	Sam Hanks	Belond Exhaust	135.601
1958	Jimmy Bryan	Belond A. P.	133.791
1959	Rodger Ward	Leader Card Special	135.857
1960	Jim Rathmann	Ken-Paul Special	138.767
1961	A. J. Foyt	Bowes Seal Fast	139.130
1962	Rodger Ward	Leader Card Special	140.293
1963	Parnelli Jones	Agajanian Special	143.137
1964	A. J. Foyt	Sheraton-Thompson Special	147.350
1965	Jim Clark (GB)	Lotus-Ford	150.686
1966	Graham Hill (GB)	American Red Ball	144.317
1967	A. J. Foyt	Sheraton-Thompson Special	151.207
1968	Bobby Unser	Rislone Special	152.882
1969	Mario Andretti	STP Oil Treatment Special	156.867
1970	Al Unser	Johnny Lightning Special	155.749
1971	Al Unser	Johnny Lightning Special	157.735
1972	Mark Donohue	Sunoco McLaren	162.962
1973	Gordon Johncock	STP Double Oil Filter	159.036
1974	Johnny Rutherford	McLaren	158.589
1975	Bobby Unser	Jorgensen Eagle	149.213
1976	Johnny Rutherford	Hygain McLaren	148.725
1977	A. J. Foyt	Gilmore Coyote-Foyt	161.331
1978	Al Unser	Lola-Chapparal Cosworth	161.363
1979	Rick Mears	Penske-Cosworth	158.899

Le Mans 24-Hour Race

The world's most important race for sports cars was first held in 1923. The most wins by one man is four by Olivier Gendebien (Bel) and Jackie Ickx (Bel). Winners since 1949 when the race was revived after the Second World War:

	Driver	Car	Speed (mph)
1949	Luigi Chinetti/Lord Peter Selsdon	Ferrari	82.27
1950	Louis Rosier/Jean-Louis Rosier	Talbot	89.73
1951	Peter Walker/Peter Whitehead	Jaguar	93.50
1952	Hermann Lang/Fritz Riess	Mercedes	96.67
1953	Anthony Rolt/Duncan Hamilton	Jaguar	105.85
1954	José Froilan Gonzalez/Maurice Trintignant	Ferrari	105.15
1955	Mike Hawthorn/Ivor Bueb	Jaguar	107.07
1956	Ron Flockhart/Ninian Sanderson	Jaguar	104.46
1957	Ron Flockhart/Ivor Bueb	Jaguar	113.85
1958	Phil Hill/Olivier Gendebien	Ferrari	106.20
1959	Roy Salvadori/Carroll Shelby	Aston Martin	112.57
1960	Paul Frère/Olivier Gendebien	Ferrari	109.19
1961	Phil Hill/Olivier Gendebien	Ferrari	115.90
1962	Phil Hill/Olivier Gendebien	Ferrari	115.24

1963	Ludovico Scarfiotti/Lorenzo Bandini	Ferrari	118.10
1964	Jean Guichet/Nino Vaccarella	Ferrari	121.55
1965	Masten Gregory/Jochen Rindt	Ferrari	121.09
1966	Bruce McLaren/Chris Amon	Ford	126.01
1967	Anthony Joseph Foyt/Dan Gurney	Ford	132.49
1968	Pedro Rodriguez/Lucien Bianchi	Ford	115.29
1969	Jackie Ickx/Jackie Oliver	Ford	125.44
1970	Hans Herrmann/Richard Attwood	Porsche	119.29
1971	Helmut Marko/Gijs van Lennep	Porsche	138.142
1972	Graham Hill/Henri Pescarolo	Matra-Simca	121.47
1973	Henri Pescarolo/Gerard Larrousse	Matra-Simca	125.68
1974	Henri Pescarolo/Gerard Larrousse	Matra-Simca	119.27
1975	Jackie Ickx/Derek Bell	Gulf Ford	118.99
1976	Jackie Ickx/Gijs van Lennep	Porsche	123.50
1977	Jackie Ickx/Jurgen Barth/Hurley Haywood	Porsche	120.95
1978	Didier Peroni/Jean-Pierre Jaussaud	Renault Alpine	130.60
1979	Klaus Ludwig/Bill and Don Whittington	Porsche	108.06

British Grand Prix

First run as the RAC Grand Prix at Brooklands in 1927, and later as the Donington Grand Prix in 1937 and 1938. The name British Grand Prix was first used in 1949. Full list of winners, circuits and distance:

	Driver	Car	Circuit	Distance (miles)	Speed (mph)
1926	Robert Sénéchal/Louis Wagner	Delage	Brooklands	287	71.61
1927	Robert Benoist	Delage	Brooklands	325	85.59
1935	Richard Shuttleworth	Alfa Romeo	Donington	306	63.97
1936	Hans Ruesch/Richard Seaman	Alfa Romeo	Donington	306	69.23
1937	Bernd Rosemeyer	Auto-Union	Donington	250	82.85
1938	Tazio Nuvolari	Auto-Union	Donington	250	80.49
1948	Luigi Villoresi	Maserati	Silverstone	250	72.28
1949	Baron Emmanuel de Graffenried	Maserati	Silverstone	300	77.31
1950	Giuseppe Farina	Alfa Romeo	Silverstone	202	90.95
1951	Froilan Gonzalez	Ferrari	Silverstone	253	96.11
1952	Alberto Ascari	Ferrari	Silverstone	249	90.92
1953	Alberto Ascari	Ferrari	Silverstone	263	92.97
1954	Froilan Gonzalez	Ferrari	Silverstone	270	89.69
1955	Stirling Moss	Mercedes-Benz	Aintree	270	86.47
1956	Juan Manual Fangio	Ferrari	Silverstone	300	98.65
1957	Tony Brooks/Stirling Moss	Vanwall	Aintree	270	86.80
1958	Peter Collins	Ferrari	Silverstone	225	102.05
1959	Jack Brabham	Cooper-Climax	Aintree	225	89.88
1960	Jack Brabham	Cooper-Climax	Silverstone	231	108.69
1961	Wolfgang von Trips	Ferrari	Aintree	225	83.91
1962	Jim Clark	Lotus-Climax	Aintree	225	92.25
1963	Jim Clark	Lotus-Climax	Silverstone	246	107.75
1964	Jim Clark	Lotus-Climax	Brands Hatch	212	94.14
1965	Jim Clark	Lotus-Climax	Silverstone	240	112.02
1966	Jack Brabham	Repco Brabham	Brands Hatch	212	95.48
1967	Jim Clark	Lotus-Ford	Silverstone	240	117.64
1968	Joseph Siffert	Lotus-Ford	Brands Hatch	212	104.83
1969	Jackie Stewart	Matra-Ford	Silverstone	246	127.25
1970	Jochen Rindt	Lotus-Ford	Brands Hatch	212	108.69
1971	Jackie Stewart	Tyrell-Ford	Silverstone	199	130.48
1972	Emerson Fittipaldi	JPS-Ford	Brands Hatch	201	112.06
1973	Peter Revson	McLaren-Ford	Silverstone	196	131.75
1974	Jody Scheckter	Tyrell-Ford	Brands Hatch	199	115.73
1975	Emerson Fittipaldi	McLaren-Ford	Silverstone	164	120.01
1976	Niki Lauda	Ferrari	Brands Hatch	198	114.24
1977	James Hunt	McLaren-Ford	Silverstone	199	130.36
1978	Carlos Reutemann	Ferrari	Brands Hatch	199	116.61
1979	'Clay' Regazzoni	Saudia Williams	Silverstone	199	138.80

THE RAC's HAWTHORN MEMORIAL TROPHY
To the highest placed British or Commonwealth driver
in the World Championship. Winners since foundation
in 1960:

1960	Jack Brabham			1973	Jackie Stewart
1961	Stirling Moss	1967	Denis Hulme	1974	Denis Hulme
1962	Graham Hill	1968	Graham Hill	1975	James Hunt
1963	Jim Clark	1969	Jackie Stewart	1976	James Hunt
1964	John Surtees	1970	Denis Hulme	1977	James Hunt
1965	Jim Clark	1971	Jackie Stewart	1978	John Watson
1966	Jack Brabham	1972	Jackie Stewart		

THE RAC's CAMPBELL MEMORIAL TROPHY
This is for 'the outstanding performance by the British
driver of a British car in any form of motor competition
during the calendar year'. Winners since foundation in
1950:

1950	Ian Appleyard	1960	No award	1969	Graham Hill
1951	Peter Walker and Peter Whitehead	1961	Stirling Moss	1970	Anthony Densham
1952	Sydney Allard	1962	Graham Hill	1971	No award
1953	Duncan Hamilton and Tony Rolt	1963	Jim Clark	1972	Roger Clark
1954	Peter Whitehead and Ken Wharton	1964	No award	1973	James Hunt
1955	Mike Hawthorn	1965	Jim Clark	1974	No award
1956	Ronnie Adams	1966	No award	1975	No award
1957	Stirling Moss	1967	Jim Clark	1976	James Hunt
1958	Stirling Moss	1968	Andrew Cowan, Brian Coyle	1977	James Hunt
1959	Jack Brabham		and Colin Malkin	1978	James Hunt

MUSEUMS

The Museum of the Year Award

The 1979 Museum of the Year Award went to the Guernsey Museum. This illustration shows 17th-century bronze measures in the section on 'Guernsey Life'

This is an annual award sponsored by the *Illustrated London News* in conjunction with National Heritage, a voluntary organisation set up to protect the interests of museums and galleries throughout the country. The *Illustrated London News* donates the first prize of not less than £2000, and the ILN Award, a Henry Moore porcelain sculpture called 'Moon Head'. The award began in 1973 to induce industry to promote the arts. The museums are judged for their enterprise, general improvements and improved facilities.

1973 Abbot Hall Museum of Lakeland Life and Industry, Kendal	1977 Ironbridge Gorge Museum, Telford, Salop
1974 National Motor Museum, Beaulieu, Hants	1978 *Joint winners:* Museum of London, and Erddig, a country house near Wrexham in Clwyd
1975 Weald and Downland Open Air Museum, Chichester	1979 Museum and Art Gallery of St Peter Port, Guernsey
1976 Gladstone Pottery Museum, Stoke on Trent	

MUSIC

Audio Awards

An annual presentation, organised by *Hi-Fi News & Record Review*, to musicians and others for their services to music via the gramophone record. This dates back to 1967, and is supported by the Composers' Guild of Great Britain, the Mechanical Copyright Protection Society, the National Federation of Gramophone Societies, the National Music Council, the Songwriters' Guild of GB and the Performing Rights Society. Those who have received this since 1970 have been:

1970	Neville Marriner	1974	Peter Pears	1977	John Williams
1971	Sir Adrian Boult		Kinloch Anderson		Julian Bream
1972	No award	1975	Colin Davis	1978	André Previn
1973	Raymond Leppard	1976	Dame Janet Baker	1979	Arthur Haddy
					Tony Griffith

BBC Radio Music Competitions

The BBC has organised a series of competitions for musicians, singers and conductors. The winners from 1965:

1965	Violin	Maurice Smith
1966	Violin	Haroutune Bedelian
1967	'Cello	No 1st prize
1968	Mozart Piano Concertos	Kathleen Jones
	Piano	Christian Blackshaw
1969	Beethoven Competition for Violin and Piano	Chilingirian Duo (Levon Chilingirian, Clifford Benson)
	'Cello and Piano	No 1st prize
	Piano Trio	Orion Trio (Peter Thomas, Sharon McKinley, Ian Brown)
1970	Composers	Nicola Le Fanu
1971	Piano	Anthony Peebles
1973	Orchestral work	Joint Prizewinners: Brian Chapple, Derek Bourgeois
	BBC Piano Competition	Yitkin Seow
1974	Rupert Foundation Conductors Competition	Marc Soustrot
1976	Rupert Foundation Conductors' Competition	Ivan Fischer
1978	Rupert Foundation Conductors' Competition	Gerard Akoka
	TV Young Musician of the Year Competition	Michael Hext

Capital Radio's Hall of Fame 1953—1978

The Best Single Records of the past 25 years according to the votes of Capital Radio listeners in 1978.

1	I'm Not in Love, 10 CC	6	Layla, Derek and The Dominoes
2	Bridge Over Troubled Water, Simon and Garfunkel	7	Hey Jude, Beatles
3	Nights in White Satin, Moody Blues	8	Maggie May, Rod Stewart
4	A Whiter Shade of Pale, Procul Harum	9	Jailhouse Rock, Elvis Presley
5	Bohemian Rhapsody, Queen	10	Stairway to Heaven, Led Zeppelin
		11	Without You, Nilsson

Bill Haley whose record 'Rock Around The Clock' was voted 25th best record of the past by Capital Radio listeners

12 House of the Rising Sun, Animals
13 All Right Now, Free
14 Brown Sugar, Rolling Stones
15 Albatross, Fleetwood Mac
16 Good Vibrations, Beach Boys
17 Lay Lady Lay, Bob Dylan
18 If You Leave Me Now, Chicago
19 Satisfaction, Rolling Stones
20 Hotel California, Eagles
21 Your Song, Elton John
22 Sailing, Rod Stewart
23 American Pie, Don McLean
24 River Deep, Mountain High, Ike and Tina Turner
25 Rock Around the Clock, Bill Haley
26 Like A Rolling Stone, Bob Dylan
27 Yesterday, Beatles
28 Let It Be, Beatles
29 The Sound of Silence, Simon and Garfunkel
30 Penny Lane/Strawberry Fields Forever, Beatles
31 You've Lost That Lovin' Feelin', The Righteous Brothers
32 Vincent, Don McLean
33 Space Oddity, David Bowie
34 Night Fever, Bee Gees
35 I Heard It Through the Grapevine, Marvin Gaye
36 The Air That I Breathe, Hollies
37 The First Time Ever I Saw Your Face, Roberta Flack
38 The Long and Winding Road, Beatles
39 Imagine, John Lennon
40 Samba Pa Ti, Santana
41 How Deep Is Your Love, Bee Gees
42 Blueberry Hill, Fats Domino
43 In the Ghetto, Elvis Presley
44 My Generation, The Who
45 Get Back, Beatles

46 Heartbreak Hotel, Elvis Presley
47 Easy, The Commodores
48 Dock of the Bay, Otis Redding
49 My Sweet Lord, George Harrison
50 Life On Mars, David Bowie
51 Angie, Rolling Stones
52 At The Hop, Danny and the Juniors
53 MacArthur Park, Richard Harris
54 God Only Knows, Beach Boys
55 San Francisco, Scott McKenzie
56 Nutbush City Limits, Ike and Tina Turner
57 All Along The Watch Tower, Jimi Hendrix
58 Where Do You Go To My Lovely, Peter Sarstedt
59 Blue Suede Shoes, Elvis Presley
60 Don't Be Cruel, Elvis Presley
61 Suspicious Minds, Elvis Presley
62 Honky Tonk Women, Rolling Stones
63 Riders On The Storm, The Doors
64 When A Man Loves A Woman, Percy Sledge
65 Go Now, Moody Blues
66 Desperado, Eagles
67 Born to Run, Bruce Springsteen
68 You Are The Sunshine Of My Life, Stevie Wonder
69 The Boxer, Simon and Garfunkel
70 She Loves You, Beatles
71 All You Need Is Love, Beatles
72 Something In The Air, Thunderclap Newman
73 Apache, Shadows
74 Walk On The Wild Side, Lou Reed
75 Young Girl, Gary Puckett and The Union Gap
76 I'm Mandy Fly Me, 10 CC
77 Killing Me Softly, Roberta Flack
78 Summertime Blues, Eddie Cochran
79 Goodbye Yellow Brick Road, Elton John
80 Lyin' Eyes, Eagles
81 All Shook Up, Elvis Presley
82 Free, Lynyrd Skynyrd
83 Mr Tambourine Man, Byrds
84 When I Need You, Leo Sayer
85 Mr Blue Sky, Electric Light Orchestra
86 Evergreen, Barbra Streisand
87 Hound Dog, Elvis Presley
88 Three Times A Lady, The Commodores
89 Candle in The Wind, Elton John
90 Peggy Sue, Buddy Holly
91 Whole Lotta Love, Led Zeppelin
92 All I Have To Do Is Dream, Everly Brothers

Capital Radio listeners voted 'Night Fever' and 'How Deep Is Your Love' by the Bee Gees as the 34th and 41st best records of the past, respectively

93   Superstition, Stevie Wonder
94   A Day in The Life, Beatles
95   Baby Love, Supremes
96   Band On The Run, Wings
97   The Way We Were, Gladys Knight and The Pips
98   Killer Queen, Queen
99   Eleanor Rigby, Beatles
100   Annie's Song, John Denver
101   Baker Street, Gerry Rafferty
102   Help, Beatles
103   Johnny B. Goode, Chuck Berry
104   Music, John Miles
105   It's Now Or Never, Elvis Presley
106   My Way, Frank Sinatra
107   Substitute, The Who
108   Itchycoo Park, The Small Faces
109   Summer Breeze, The Isley Brothers
110   December '63, The Four Seasons
111   Won't Get Fooled Again, The Who
112   Seasons In The Sun, Terry Jacks
113   See Emily Play, Pink Floyd
114   Cathy's Clown, Everly Brothers
115   Light My Fire, The Doors
116   Mull of Kintyre, Wings
117   I'm Still Waiting, Diana Ross
118   Don't Cry For Me Argentina, Julie Covington
119   Walk On By, Dionne Warwick
120   Pretty Vacant, The Sex Pistols
121   Jumping Jack Flash, Rolling Stones
122   Last Resort, Eagles
123   Anarchy in The UK, Sex Pistols
124   Lola, Kinks
125   She's Gone, Daryl Hall and John Oates
126   Isn't She Lovely, Stevie Wonder
127   No Woman No Cry, Bob Marley and The Wailers
128   Horse With No Name, America
129   Waterloo Sunset, Kinks
130   Rave On, Buddy Holly
131   Whiskey In The Jar, Thin Lizzy
132   One Of These Nights, Eagles
133   Dreams, Fleetwood Mac

Abba with 'Dancing Queen' achieved the 142nd place in the Capital Radio listeners' best records of the past

134   Tears Of A Clown, Smokey Robinson and The
         Miracles
135   Wooden Heart, Elvis Presley
136   Spirit In The Sky, Norman Greenbaum
137   Pinball Wizard, The Who
138   Runaway, Del Shannon
139   At 17, Janis Ian
140   Roll Over Beethoven, Electric Light Orchestra
141   Caroline, Status Quo
142   Dancing Queen, Abba
143   Love and Affection, Joan Armatrading
144   Return To Sender, Elvis Presley
145   Wishing Well, Free
146   Summer The First Time, Bobby Goldsboro
147   King Creole, Elvis Presley
148   Reach Out, I'll Be There, The Four Tops
149   Wishing On A Star, Rose Royce
150   Daniel, Elton John

Capital Radio Music Awards

Capital broadcasts in the Greater London area and has a listening audience of over 5 million each week. Listeners are asked to make nominations for the music awards and to vote for the winners. (The last four categories were newly introduced in 1978.)

BEST SINGLE
1976   Don't Go Breaking My Heart, Elton John and
          Kiki Dee
1977   Mull of Kintyre, Paul McCartney and Wings
1978   Night Fever, Bee Gees

BEST ALBUM
1976   How Dare You, 10 CC
1977   Out of the Blue, ELO
1978   A Single Man, Elton John

BEST MALE SINGER
1976   Elton John
1977   Elton John
1978   Elton John

BEST FEMALE SINGER
1976   Kiki Dee
1977   Julie Covington
1978   Kate Bush

BEST LONDON BAND
1976   Dr Feelgood
1977   Tom Robinson Band
          (After 1977 no longer held)

MOST PROMISING NEWCOMER
1976   Climax Blues Band
1977   Tom Robinson Band
1978   Kate Bush

BEST LONDON CONCERT
1976   Wings, Wembley
1977   Elton John, Wembley
       (After 1977 no longer held)

**MOST REQUESTED RECORD ON THE
CAPITAL HITLINE**
1976   I'm Mandy Fly Me, 10 CC
1977   We Are The Champions, Queen
1978   Night Fever, Bee Gees

BEST SONGWRITER OF THE YEAR
1978   The Gibb Brothers (Bee Gees)

BEST LONDON ARTIST
1978   Ian Dury

BEST INTERNATIONAL ARTIST
1978   Earth, Wind and Fire

BEST BRITISH GROUP
1978   The Bee Gees

Elton John receives the award for the Best Male Singer from Lord George-Brown at the 1978 Capital Radio Music Awards. Elton John also won the award in 1976 and again in 1977, achieving a hat-trick

Carl Flesch International Violin Competition

Carl Flesch was one of the major figures in the development of violin playing and teaching in the 20th century. During the 1930s he lived in London, and later Switzerland where he continued his teaching until his death there in 1944. His former assistant, Max Rostal, took Carl Flesch's place as the most important violin teacher in this country. It was the joint idea of Max Rostal, Edric Cundell (then Principal of the Guildhall School) and Carl F. Flesch (Carl Flesch's son) to commemorate the great man by instituting in 1945 the Carl Flesch Medal 'for excellence in violin playing', to be won as the result of a Competition held in the Guildhall School and open to violinists of any nationality. In 1968 the Carl Flesch Competition was presented in a new and expanded form: with four money prizes, an outstanding international jury and one final session with orchestra for the first three prizewinners. In 1970 the City Arts Trust, through the Festival, agreed to expand further the scope of the Competition into its present shape with all six finalists receiving prize money and playing with orchestra in two concerts. It is a major international competition and part of the biennial Festival of the City of London. List of winners:

1945	1st	Raymond Cohen (GB)
1946	1st	Norbert Brainin (GB)
1947	1st	Erich Gruenberg (Pal)
	2nd	Howard Leyton-Brown (GB)
1948	1st	Gabrielle Lengyel (Fra)
	2nd	Howard Leyton-Brown (GB)
1949	1st	John Glickman (Aus)
1950	1st	Eugene Prokop (Cze)
1951	1st	Igor Ozim (Yug)
1952	1st	Pierre Jetteur (Bel)
1953	1st	Betty-Jean Hagen (Can)
	2nd	Sandor Karolyi (Hun)
1954	1st	Maria Vischnia (Uru)
1955	1st	Denes Kovacs (Hun)
	2nd	Agnes Vadas (Hun)
1956	1st	Ladislav Jasek (Cze)
	2nd	Steven Staryk (Can)
1957	1st	Michael Davis (GB)
	2nd	Sylvia Rosenberg (USA)
	3rd	Leon Spierer (Arg)
1958	1st	Wilfred Lehmann (GB)

1959	1st	Ronald Thomas (Aus)
	2nd	Caroline Gundy (Can)
1960	1st	Antoine Goulard (Fra)
	2nd	Allan Schiller (USA)
1961	1st	Marie Renaudie (Fra)
	2nd	Marjeta Korosec (Yug)
1962	1st	Jean-Jacques Kantorow (Fra)
	2nd	Jennifer Nuttall (GB)
	3rd	André Delcourte (Bel)
1963	1st	Ana Chumachenco (Arg)
	2nd	Frances Mason (GB)
1964	1st	Eva Zurbruegg (Swi)
	2nd	Elizabeth Balmas (Fra)
1965	1st	Eszter Boda (Hun)
	2nd	Sylvie Gazeau (Fra)
	3rd	Marie-Françoise Coffard (Fra)
1966	1st	Andreas Rohn (Ger)
	2nd	Mariko Takagi (Jap)
	3rd	Peter Michalica (Cze)
1968	1st	Joshua Epstein (Isr)
	2nd	Sylvie Gazeau (Fra)
	3rd	Masako Yanagita (Jap)

1970 1st Stoika Milanova (Bul)
      2nd Luigi Bianchi (Ita)
      3rd Csaba Erdelyi (Hun) – viola
      4th Takayoshi Wanami (Jap)
      5th Roswitha Randacher (Aut)
      6th Mariana Sirbu (Rom)
      Audience Prize: Stoika Milanova
1972 1st Csaba Erdelyi (Hun) – viola
      2nd Atar Arad (Isr) – viola
      3rd Gonçal Comellas (Spa)
      4th Mincho Minchev (Bul)
      5th Michael Bochmann (GB)
      6th Otto Armin (Can)
      Audience Prize: Gonçal Comellas
1974 1st Mincho Minchev (Bul)
      2nd Donk-Suk Kang (Kor)
      3rd Isaac Shuldman (Isr)
      4th Gottfried Schneider (Ger)
      5th Tadeusz Gadzina (Pol)
      6th Serban Lupu (Rom)

      Audience Prize: Mincho Minchev
      Beethoven Sonata Prize: Mincho Minchev and
                             Donk-Suk Kang (joint)
1976 1st Dora Schwarzberg (Isr)
      2nd Andrew Watkinson (GB)
      3rd Magdalena Rezler-Niesiołowska (Pol)
      4th Eugene Sarbu (Rom)
      5th Isabelle Flory (Fra)
      6th Mihaela Martin (Rom)
      Audience Prize: Magdalena Rezler-Niesiolowska
      Beethoven Sonata Prize: Andrew Watkinson
1978 1st Eugene Sarbu (Rom)
      2nd Takashi Shimizu (Jap)
      3rd Fiona Vanderspar (GB)
      4th Vanya Milanova (Bul)
      5th Krzysztof Smietana (Pol)
      6th Valentin Stefanov (Bul)
      Audience Prize: Eugene Sarbu
      Beethoven Sonata Prize: Takashi Shimizu

Grammy Awards

The major music industry awards in the United States, the Grammys were founded in 1959 and are presented each year by the National Academy of Recording Arts and Sciences. Recent winners include:

1976

Record of the Year: This Masquerade, George Benson

Album of the Year: Songs in the Key of Life, Stevie Wonder

Song of the Year: I Write the Songs: songwriter, Bruce Johnson

Best new artist: Starland Vocal Band

Best instrumental arrangement: Leprechaun's Dream, Chick Corea

Best arrangement accompanying vocalist: If You Leave Me Now, Chicago

Best album package: Chicago X, Chicago

Best solo jazz: Basie and Zoot, Count Basie

Best group jazz: The Leprechaun, Chick Corea

Best big band jazz performance: The Ellington Suites, Duke Ellington

Best female pop vocal performance: Hasten Down the Wind. Linda Ronstadt

Best male pop vocal performance: Songs in the Key of Life, Stevie Wonder

Best pop vocal performance by a duo, group, or chorus: If You Leave Me Now, Chicago

Best pop instrumental performance: Breezin', George Benson

Best rhythm and blues female vocal: Sophisticated Lady (She's a Different Lady). Natalie Cole

Best rhythm and blues male vocal performance: I Wish, Stevie Wonder

Best rhythm and blues instrumental performance: Theme From Good King Bad, George Benson

Best rhythm and blues by duo, group, or chorus: You Don't Have to be a Star (To Be in My Show), Marilyn McCoo and Billy Davis Jr

Best rhythm and blues song: Lowdown, songwriters: Boz Scaggs, David Paich

Best soul gospel performance: How I Got Over, Mahalia Jackson

Best female country vocal performance: Elite Hotel, Emmylou Harris

Best male country vocal performance: (I'm a) Stand by My Woman Man, Ronnie Milsap

Best country vocal performance by a duo or group: The End is Not in Sight (The Cowboy Tune), Amazing Rhythm Aces

Best country instrumental performance: Chester & Lester, Chet Atkins and Les Paul

Best country song: Broken Lady, Larry Gatlin

Best inspirational performance: The Astonishing Outrageous, Amazing, Incredible, Unbelievable, Different World of Gary S. Paxton, Gary Paxton

Best gospel performance: Where the Soul Never Dies, Oak Ridge Boys

Best ethnic: Mark Twang, John Hartford

Best for Children: Peter and the Wolf, and Carnival of the Animals, Hermione Gingold, Karl Bohm

Best comedy recording: Bicentennial Nigger, Richard Pryor

Best spoken word recording: Great American Documents, Orson Welles, Henry Fonda, Helen Hayes, James Earl Jones

Best instrumental composition: Bellavia, Chuck Mangione

Best original score for a motion picture or television special: Car Wash, Norman Whitfield

Best cast show album: Bubbling Brown Sugar, Hugo and Luigi

Classical album of the year: Beethoven, The Five Piano Concertos, Arthur Rubinstein and Daniel Barenboim, conductors

Best opera recording: Porgy and Bess, Lorin Maazel, conductor

Best classical choral performance: Rachmaninoff, The Bells, André Previn, conductor

Best chamber music performance: The Art of Courtly Love, David Munrow, conducting
Best classical by soloist with orchestra: Beethoven, The Five Piano Concertos, Arthur Rubinstein, Daniel Barenboim, conductors
Best solo classical performance: Horowitz Concerts 1975–76, Vladimir Horowitz
Best classical vocal: Music of Victor Herbert, Beverly Sills
Best classical by orchestra: Strauss: Also Sprach Zarathustra, George Solti, conductor

1977
Record of the Year: Hotel California, The Eagles
Album of the Year: Rumours, Fleetwood Mac
Song of the Year: Evergreen, Barbra Streisand and Paul Williams; You Light Up My Life, Joe Brooks, writer
Best New Artist of the Year: Debby Boone
Best Pop Vocal Performance, Female: Evergreen, Barbra Streisand

Billy Joel won a Grammy Award for the best single record, with 'Just The Way You Are', in 1978

Best Pop Vocal Performance, Male: Handy Man, James Taylor
Best Pop Vocal Performance, Group: How Deep Is Your Love, Bee Gees
Best Pop Instrumental Performance: Star Wars, London Symphony Orchestra, John Williams
Best Jazz Vocal Performance: Look to the Rainbow, Al Jarreau
Best Jazz Performance by a Soloist: The Giants, Oscar Peterson
Best Jazz Performance, Group: The Phil Woods Six–Live From the Showboat, Phil Woods
Best Jazz Performance, Big Band: Prime Time, Count Basie & his orchestra
Best Rhythm and Blues Vocal Performance, Female: Don't Leave Me This Way, Thelma Houston
Best Rhythm and Blues Vocal Performance, Male: Unmistakably Lou, Lou Rawls
Best Rhythm and Blues Instrumental Performance: Q, Brothers Johnson
Best Rhythm and Blues Song: You Make Me Feel Like Dancing, Leo Sayer, Vini Poncia, songwriters
Best Gospel Performance, Contemporary or Traditional: Sail On, Imperials
Best Country Vocal Performance, Female: Don't It Make My Brown Eyes Blue, Crystal Gayle
Best Country Vocal Performance, Male: Lucille, Kenny Rogers
Best Country Vocal Performance, Group: Heaven's Just A Sin Away, The Kendalls
Best Country Instrumental Performance: Country Instrumentalist of the Year, Hargus [Pig] Robbins
Best Recording for Children: Aren't You Glad You're You, The Sesame Street Cast
Best Comedy Recording: Let's Get Small, Steve Martin
Best Cast Show Album: Annie, Charles Strouse, Martin Charnin, composers; Larry Morton and Charles Strouse, producers
Album of the Year, Classical: Concert of the Century, various artists, recorded live at Carnegie Hall, May 1976; Thomas Frost, producer
Best Opera Recording: Gershwin, Porgy and Bess, Houston Grand Opera production

1978
Best album: Saturday Night Fever, Bees Gees
Best vocal by a group: Bee Gees
Producers of the year: Bee Gees
Best arrangement for voices: Bee Gees, Stayin' Alive
Best single record: Billy Joel, Just the Way You Are
Best song: Billy Joel, Just the Way You Are
Best male pop singer: Barry Manilow
Best female pop singer: Anne Murray, You Needed Me
Best rhythm and blues female vocal: Donna Summer
Best rhythm and blues male vocal: George Benson
Best country and western female vocal: Dolly Parton
Best country and western male vocal: Willie Nelson
Best jazz soloist: Oscar Peterson
Best classical album: Brahms Concerto for Violin in D Major, Chicago Orchestra, conducted by Carlo Guilini; soloist Itzhak Perlman
Best spoken word recording: Orson Welles, Citizen Kane
Best new artists: A Taste of Honey
Best album for a film score: Close Encounters of the Third Kind

Llangollen International Musical Eisteddfod

The first eisteddfod was held in 1947, just two years after the Second World War. It was instituted by a small band of ordinary citizens and idealists of the small township of Llangollen who aimed, through the use of the international language of music, to bring about the beginnings of a measure of tolerance and understanding among the various nations of the world.

With the passage of 33 years its scope, influence and popularity has greatly increased; 30 to 35 countries are represented annually and the total number of competitors is in excess of 10 000. Each year upwards of 120 000 people attend to watch the numerous dancers in their national costumes and to listen to music. Thus, up to the present time, well over 3 000 000 people have visited the eisteddfod.

In 1979, the Eisteddfod Council through the auspices of the Welsh Arts Council announced the inclusion of an additional competition to its syllabus, for young composers. Prize winners and complete details are available from the Eisteddfod Council.

The 'Melody Maker' Jazz Awards

This poll by readers of the magazine was introduced in 1946, and separate British and international sections were operated from 1955 until 1974 when the poll was discontinued. A special poll for jazz critics on newspapers and magazines was also held, and in 1977 *Melody Maker* organised a poll of international jazz critics to find the world's best jazz musicians and artists.

The following are just a selection of some of the winners of the *Melody Maker* jazz poll:

1946

Bandleader	Geraldo
Trumpet	Kenny Baker
Alto Sax	Harry Hayes
Swing Band	Ted Heath
Male Vocal	Benny Lee
Female Vocal	Anne Shelton
Drums	Jack Parnell
Trombone	George Chisholm
Small Combo	Jack Parnell
Sweet Band	Geraldo
Tenor Sax	Johnny Gray
Piano	Norman Stenfalt
Bass	Charlie Short
Guitar	Ivor Mairants
Clarinet	Carl Barmtean

1947

Swing Band	Ted Heath
Sweet Band	Geraldo
Small Combo	Jack Parnell
Female Vocal	Anne Shelton
Male Vocal	Benny Lee
Favourite Bandleader	Ted Heath

1948

(Details not available)

1949

Sweet Band	Geraldo
Latin American	Edmundo Ross
Swing Band	Ted Heath
Small Combo	Ray Ellington
Male Vocal	Alan Dean
Female Vocal	Terry Devon
Musician of the Year	Johnny Dankworth

1950–51

Musician of the Year	Johnny Dankworth
Swing Band	Ted Heath
Latin American	Edmundo Ross
Small Combo	Johnny Dankworth
Male Vocal	Alan Dean
Female Vocal	Pearl Carr
Vocal Group	Keynotes
Sweet Band	Geraldo

1951–52

Musician of the Year	Johnny Dankworth
Swing Band	Ted Heath
Modern Group	Johnny Dankworth
Latin American	Edmundo Ross
Arranger	Johnny Dankworth
Trad Group	Humphrey Lyttelton
Commercial Band	Geraldo
Male Singer	Alan Dean
Girl Singer	Lita Roza
Vocal Group	Stargazers

1953

Band of the Year	Ted Heath
Modern Group	Johnny Dankworth
Latin American	Edmundo Ross
Trad	Humphrey Lyttelton
Tenor Sax	Ronnie Scott
Musician of the Year	Jack Parnell
Male Singer	Dickie Valentine
Girl Singer	Lita Roza
Vocal Group	Stargazers

1954

Band of the Year	Ted Heath
Musician of the Year	Johnny Dankworth

Small Group	Ronnie Scott (modern)
	Humphrey Lyttelton (trad)
Male Singer	Dickie Valentine
Girl Singer	Lita Roza

1955
British Section

Band of the Year	Ted Heath
Modern Group	Ronnie Scott
Traditional Group	Humphrey Lyttelton
Guitar	Bert Weedon
Vibes	Vic Feldman
Trumpet	Kenny Baker
Trombone	Don Lusher
Clarinet	Vic Ash
Male Singer	Dickie Valentine
Piano	Bill McGuffie
Drums	Eric Delaney
Tenor Sax	Tommy Whittle
Musician of the Year	Eric Delaney
Violin	Freddy Ballerini
Vocal Group	Stargazers
Baritone Sax	Harry Klein
Bass	Johnny Hawksworth
Girl Singer	Lita Roza
Accordion	Tito Burns
Arranger	Johnny Dankworth
Alto Sax	Johnny Dankworth
Organ	Harold Smart
Soprano Sax	Frank Weir

World Section (as introduced that year)

Musician of the Year	Gerry Mulligan
Traditional Group	Louis Armstrong
Vibes	Lionel Hampton
Alto Sax	Lee Konitz
Band of the Year	Stan Kenton
Tenor Sax	Stan Getz
Baritone Sax	Gerry Mulligan
Soprano Sax	Sidney Bechet
Clarinet	Buddy de Franco
Piano	Oscar Peterson
Modern Group	Gerry Mulligan
Trumpet	Chet Baker
Arranger	Shorty Rogers
Accordion	Tito Burns
Girl Singer	Sarah Vaughan
Male Singer	Frank Sinatra
Bass	Johnny Hawksworth
Trombone	Frank Rosolino
Violin	Stephane Grappelly
Vocal Group	Four Aces
Organ	Harold Smart
Guitar	Barney Kessel
Drums	Shelly Manne

1956
(Details not available)

1957
British Section

Musician of the Year	Johnny Dankworth
Big Band	Johnny Dankworth
Small Combo	Tony Kinsey

Male Singer	Dennis Lotis
Female Singer	Cleo Laine
Vocal Group	Stargazers

World Section

Musician of the Year	Count Basie
Big Band	Count Basie
Small Combination	Modern Jazz Quartet
Trumpet	Louis Armstrong
Male Singer	Frank Sinatra
Female Singer	Ella Fitzgerald
Vocal Groups	Hi-lo's
Arranger	Peter Rugolo
Composer	Duke Ellington

1958–1960
(Details not available)

1961
Critics' Awards

Musician of the Year	Miles Davis
Small Combo	Miles Davis
New Star	Ray Bryant
Big Band	Duke Ellington
Male Singer	Jimmy Rushing
Female Singer	Ella Fitzgerald
Vocal Group	Lambert, Hendricks and Ross

Readers' Awards, British Section

Musician of the Year	Johnny Dankworth
Small Combo	Tubby Hayes
Big Band	Johnny Dankworth
Trumpet	Humphrey Lyttelton
Guitar	Diz Disley
Male Singer	George Melly (third year in succession)
Female Singer	Cleo Laine
Vocal Group	The Polka Dots (79.1 per cent of votes cast)

Readers' Awards, World Section

Musician of the Year	Miles Davis
Small Combo	Modern Jazz Quartet
Big Band	Count Basie
Male Singer	Frank Sinatra
Female Singer	Ella Fitzgerald
Vocal Group	Four Freshmen

1962
British Section, Trad Awards

Band	Chris Barber
Male Singer	George Melly
Female Singer	Ottilie Patterson
Clarinet	Acker Bilk

British Section, Other Awards

Musician of the Year/ Small Combo	Tubby Hayes
Female Singer	Cleo Laine
Vocal Group	The Polka Dots
Big Band	Johnny Dankworth
Male Singer	Matt Monro
New Star	Dick Morrissey

World Section

Musician of the Year	Duke Ellington
Big Band	Count Basie
Combo	Dave Brubeck
Male Singer	Frank Sinatra
Female Singer	Ella Fitzgerald
Vocal Group	Four Freshmen
Arranger	Duke Ellington
Composer	Duke Ellington
New Star	Leo Wright

1963

British Section

Musician of the Year	Tubby Hayes
Big Band	Johnny Dankworth
Combo	Tubby Hayes
Male Singer	Matt Monro
Female Singer	Cleo Laine
Arranger/Composer	Johnny Dankworth

British Section, Trad

Top Band	Chris Barber
Male Singer	George Melly
Female Singer	Ottilie Patterson

World Section

Musician of the Year	Duke Ellington
Big Band	Count Basie
Combo	Dave Brubeck
Male Singer	Frank Sinatra
Female Singer	Ella Fitzgerald
Vocal Group	Lambert, Hendricks and Ross

Critics' Section

Musician of the Year	Duke Ellington
Big Band	Duke Ellington
Combo	Miles Davis
Male Singer	Louis Armstrong
Female Singer	Sarah Vaughan

1964

Critics' Section

Musician of the Year	Duke Ellington
Big Band	Duke Ellington
Combo	Charlie Mingus
Arranger/Composer	Duke Ellington
Male Singer	Louis Armstrong
Female Singer	Sarah Vaughan
Blues/Gospel	Marion Williams
New Star	Anthony Williams

British Section

Musician of the Year	Tubby Hayes
Big Band	Johnny Dankworth
Small Group	Tubby Hayes
Male Singer	Matt Monro
Female Singer	Cleo Laine
Vocal Group	Polka Dots
Arranger/Composer	Johnny Dankworth
New Star	Brian Auger

World Section

Musician of the Year	Duke Ellington
Big Band	Duke Ellington
Small Group	Modern Jazz Quartet
Male Singer	Frank Sinatra
Female Singer	Ella Fitzgerald
Vocal Group	Four Freshmen

1965

British Section

Musician of the Year	Tubby Hayes
Big Band	Johnny Dankworth
Small Group	Tubby Hayes
R & B Group	Georgie Fame
Male Singer	Matt Monro
Female Singer	Cleo Laine
Vocal Group	Polka Dots
Trumpet	Jimmy Deuchar
Trombone	Keith Christie
Clarinet	Sandy Brown
Alto	Joe Harmott
Tenor	Tubby Hayes
Baritone	Ronnie Ross
Flute	Tubby Hayes
Piano	Stan Tracey
Organ	Alan Haven
Guitar	Ernest Ranglin
Bass	Spike Heatley
Drums	Allan Ganley
Vibes	Tubby Hayes
Misc. Instruments	Shake Keane
Arranger/Composer	Johnny Dankworth
New Star	Ernest Ranglin

World Section

Musician of the Year	Duke Ellington
Big Band	Duke Ellington
Small Group	Modern Jazz Quartet
R & B Group	Rolling Stones
Male Singer	Frank Sinatra
Female Singer	Ella Fitzgerald
Vocal Group	Les Swingle Singers
Blues Artist	Jimmy Witherspoon
Trumpet	Miles Davis
Trombone	J. J. Johnson
Clarinet	Pee Wee Russell
Alto	Johnny Hodges
Tenor	John Coltrane
Baritone	Gerry Mulligan
Flute	Roland Kirk
Piano	Thelonious Monk
Organ	Jimmy Smith
Guitar	Wes Montgomery
Bass	Ray Brown
Drums	Joe Morello
Vibes	Milt Jackson
Misc. Instruments	Roland Kirk
Arranger/Composer	Duke Ellington
New Star	Tony Williams

1966

British Section

Musician of the Year	Tubby Hayes
Big Band	Johnny Dankworth
Small Group	Freddy Randall
Composer	Johnny Dankworth
Arranger	Johnny Dankworth
New Star	Roy Budd
Male Singer	Georgie Fame

Female Singer — Cleo Laine
Vocal Group — Morgan James Duo
Blues Artist — Georgie Fame

World Section
Musician of the Year — Duke Ellington
Big Band — Duke Ellington
Small Group — Modern Jazz Quartet
Composer — Duke Ellington
Arranger — Duke Ellington
New Star — Albert Ayler
Male Singer — Frank Sinatra
Female Singer — Ella Fitzgerald
Vocal Group — Les Swingle Singers
Blues Artist — Jimmy Witherspoon

Critics' Poll
Musician of the Year — Ornette Coleman
Big Band — Duke Ellington
Small Group — Clark Terry/Bob Brookmeyer

1967
British Section
Top Musician — Tubby Hayes
Big Band — Harry South
Small Group — Don Rendell/Ian Carr
Male Singer — Georgie Fame
Female Singer — Cleo Laine
Vocal Group — Morgan James Duo
Blues Artist — Georgie Fame
LP of the Year — Indo-Jazz Suite, Joe Harriott and John Mayer

World Section
Top Musician — Duke Ellington
Big Band — Duke Ellington
Small Group — Modern Jazz Quartet
Male Singer — Frank Sinatra
Female Singer — Ella Fitzgerald
Vocal Group — Les Swingle Singers
LP of the Year — Ornette Coleman at the Golden Circle, Stockholm Vol. 1

1968
(Details not available)

1969
British Section
Top Musician — Tubby Hayes
Big Band — Mike Westbrook
Small Group — Don Rendell/Ian Carr
Male Singer — Georgie Fame
Female Singer — Cleo Laine
Blues Artist — John Mayall
Arranger — Johnny Dankworth
Composer — Stan Tracey
New Star — Dave Holland
LP of the Year — Little Klunk, Stan Tracey

World Section
Top Musician — Duke Ellington
Big Band — Duke Ellington
Small Group — Miles Davis
Male Singer — Jon Hendricks
Female Singer — Ella Fitzgerald
Blues Artist — Muddy Waters
Arranger/Composer — Duke Ellington
New Star — Joe Farrell
LP of the Year — Mama Too Tight, Archie Shepp

Critics' Section
Top Musician — John Surman
Big Band — Duke Ellington
Small Group — Miles Davis
Male Singer — Louis Armstrong
Female Singer — Sarah Vaughan

1970
British Section
Top Musician — John Surman
Big Band — Mike Westbrook
Small Group — Alex Welsh
Male Singer — Georgie Fame
Female Singer — Cleo Laine
Blues Artist — John Mayall
Arranger/Composer — Mike Westbrook
New Star — Keith Tippett
LP of the Year — Extrapolation, John McLaughlin

World Section
Top Musician — Miles Davis
Big Band — Duke Ellington
Small Group — Miles Davis
Male Singer — Jon Hendricks
Female Singer — Ella Fitzgerald
Blues Artist — Jimmy Witherspoon
Arranger/Composer — Duke Ellington
New Star — Chick Corea
LP of the Year — Filles de Kilimanjaro, Miles Davis

1971
British Section
Top Musician — John Surman
Big Band — Mike Westbrook
Small Group — Nucleus
Male Singer — Georgie Fame
Female Singer — Norma Winstone
Blues Artist — John Mayall
LP of the Year — The Trio

World Section
Top Musician — Miles Davis
Big Band — Sun Ra
Small Group — Miles Davis
Male Singer — Leon Thomas
Female Singer — Norma Winstone
Blues Artist — Muddy Waters
Arranger/Composer — Duke Ellington
New Star — John McLaughlin
LP of the Year — Bitches Brew, Miles Davis

1972
British Section
Musician of the Year — John Surman
Big Band — Centipede
Small Group — Nucleus
Male Singer — Jack Bruce
Female Singer — Norma Winstone

Blues Artist	John Mayall	Small Group	Soft Machine
Composer/Arranger	Mike Gibbs	Male Singer	George Melly
New Star	Stan Sulzmann	Female Singer	Cleo Laine
LP of the Year	Septober Energy, Centipede	Blues Artist	John Mayall
		Arranger/Composer	Mike Gibbs
		New Star	Gary Boyle
		LP of the Year	In the Public Interest, Mike Gibbs

World Section

Top Musician	Miles Davis
Big Band	Duke Ellington
Small Group	Miles Davis
Male Singer	Leon Thomas
Female Singer	Ella Fitzgerald
Blues Artist	BB King
Trumpet	Miles Davis
Clarinet	Benny Goodman
Composer	Duke Ellington
Arranger	Mike Gibbs
New Star	Gary Bartz
LP of the Year	Zawinul, Joe Jawinul

World Section

Musician	Duke Ellington
Big Band	Duke Ellington
Small Group	Mahavishnu Orchestra
Male Singer	Leon Thomas
Female Singer	Ella Fitzgerald
Blues Artist	BB King
New Star	Billy Cobham
LP of the Year	Spectrum, Billy Cobham

There were no *Melody Maker* **readers' polls after 1974**

1973
British Section

Musician	John McLaughlin and Mike Gibbs
Big Band	Mike Gibbs
Small Group	Nucleus
Male Singer	George Melly
Female Singer	Norma Winstone
Blues Artist	John Mayall
Composer/Arranger	Mike Gibbs
New Star	Alan Holdsworth
LP of the Year	Soft Machine 6 Iskra 1903

1977
International Jazz Critics' Awards

Big Band	Thad Jones/Mel Lewis
Ensemble	McCoy Tyner
Composer	Keith Jarrett
Arranger	Gil Evans
Trumpet	Dizzy Gillespie
Soprano Sax	Steve Lacy
Alto Sax	Anthony Braxton
Tenor Sax	Sonny Rollins
Baritone Sax	Gerry Mulligan
Clarinet	Anthony Braxton
Flute	Hubert Laws
Trombone	Albert Mangelsdorff
Piano	Cecil Taylor
Organ	Jimmy Smith
Synthesiser	Joe Zawinul
Guitar	Jim Hall
Violin	Jean-luc Ponty
Acoustic Bass	Niels-Henning Orsted-Pedersen
Electric Bass	Stanley Clarke
Vibes	Gary Burton
Drums	Elvin Jones
Percussion	Airto Moreira
Misc. Instruments	Roland Kirk
Male Vocal	Joe Williams
Female Vocal	Sarah Vaughan

World Section

Musician	Miles Davis
Big Band	Duke Ellington
Small Group	Mahavishnu Orchestra
Male Singer	Leon Thomas
Female Singer	Norma Winstone
Blues Artist	BB King
Arranger	Mike Gibbs
Composer	Duke Ellington
New Star	Stanley Clarke
LP of the Year	Escalator over the Hill, Carla Bley

1974
British Section

Musician	Mike Gibbs
Big Band	Mike Gibbs

'Melody Maker' Readers' Pop Poll and Annual Awards

This annual poll by readers of the magazine was inaugurated in 1960. The separate British (B) and World (W) Sections, introduced in 1963, were abandoned in 1978.

TOP MALE SINGER OF THE YEAR

1960	Cliff Richard	1967	Cliff Richard (B) and Otis Redding (W)
1961	Cliff Richard	1968	Scott Walker (B) and Bob Dylan (W)
1962	Cliff Richard	1969	Tom Jones (B) and Bob Dylan (W)
1963	Cliff Richard (B) and Elvis Presley (W)	1970	Robert Plant (B) and Bob Dylan (W)
1964	Cliff Richard (B) and Elvis Presley (W)	1971	Rod Stewart (B) and Neil Young (W)
1965	Cliff Richard (B) and Elvis Presley (W)	1972	Rod Stewart (B) and Neil Young (W)
1966	Tom Jones (B) and Elvis Presley (W)	1973	David Bowie (B) and Robert Plant (W)
		1974	Paul Rodgers (B) and David Bowie (W)

Cliff Richard (*left*) won the Top Male Singer of the Year Award in the Melody Maker Readers Pop Poll seven times (British section) and **Elvis Presley** (*centre*) won it four times (World section) in the 1960s. **Kate Bush** (*right*) won various awards in 1978, including the Melody Maker Readers Pop Poll Award for the Brightest Hope of the Year and Female Singer of the Year, and the 1978 Capital Radio Best Female Singer of the Year Award

1975   Robert Plant (B and W)
1976   Jon Anderson (B) and Robert Plant (W)
1977   Jon Anderson (B and W)
1978   Jon Anderson

FEMALE SINGER OF THE YEAR
1960   Shirley Bassey
1961   Shirley Bassey
1962   Helen Shapiro
1963   Susan Maughan (B) and Brenda Lee (W)
1964   Cilla Black (B) and Mary Wells (W)
1965   Sandie Shaw (B) and Brenda Lee (W)
1966   Dusty Springfield (B and W)
1967   Dusty Springfield (B and W)
1968   Julie Driscoll (B) and Aretha Franklin (W)
1969   Christine Perfect (B) and Janis Joplin (W)
1970   Sandy Denny (B) and Joni Mitchell (W)
1971   Sandy Denny (B) and Joni Mitchell (W)
1972   Maggie Bell (B) and Joni Mitchell (W)
1973   Maggie Bell (B) and Carly Simon (W)
1974   Maggie Bell (B) and Joni Mitchell (W)
1975   Maggie Bell (B) and Joni Mitchell (W)
1976   Kiki Dee (B) and Joni Mitchell (W)
1977   Kiki Dee (B) and Joni Mitchell (W)
1978   Kate Bush

BRIGHTEST HOPE OF THE YEAR
1960   Emile Ford
1961   The Allisons
1962   Helen Shapiro
1963   Billy J. Kramer (B) and Lesley Gore (W)
1964   Lulu and the Lovers (B) and P.J. Proby (W)
1965   Donovan (B) and Walker Bros (W)
1966   The Troggs (B) and Mama's and Papa's (W)
1967   Procol Harum (B and W)
1968   Julie Driscoll and Brian Auger Trinity (B and W)
1969   Blind Faith (B and W)
1970   Mungo Jerry (B) and Emerson, Lake and Palmer (W)
1971   Wishbone Ash (B) and Mountain (W)
1972   Roxy Music (B) and Focus (W)
1973   Nazareth (B) and Beck, Bogert and Appice (W)
1974   Bad Company (B) and Sparks (W)
1975   Camel (B and W)
1976   Thin Lizzy (B) and Peter Frampton (W)

1977   Stranglers (B) and Television (W)
1978   Kate Bush

INSTRUMENTALIST OF THE YEAR
1960   Russ Conway
1961   Bert Weedon
1962   Acker Bilk
1963   Jet Harris (B) and Duane Eddy (W)
Discontinued

MALE TV ARTIST OF THE YEAR
1960   Bruce Forsyth
1961   Anthony Newley
1962   Bruce Forsyth
1963   Norman Vaughan
1964   Cliff Richard
1965   Cliff Richard
1966   Barry Fantoni
1967   Simon Dee
1968   Simon Dee
1969   Tom Jones
Discontinued

FEMALE TV ARTIST OF THE YEAR
1960   Alma Cogan
1961   Alma Cogan
1962   Helen Shapiro
1963   Millicent Martin
1964   Kathy Kirby
1965   Cathy McGowan
1966   Cathy McGowan
1967   Lulu
1968   Lulu
1969   Lulu
Discontinued

RADIO SHOW OF THE YEAR
1960   Saturday Club
1961   Saturday Club
1962   Saturday Club
1963   Pick of the Pops
1964   Saturday Club
1965   Saturday Club
1966   Saturday Club
1967   Radio London Fab 40

1968	Top Gear, John Peel
1969	Top Gear, John Peel
1970	Top Gear, John Peel
1971	John Peel's In Concert Sunday Show
1972	Sounds of the Seventies
1973	Sounds of the Seventies
1974	Alan Freeman's Saturday Show
1975	Alan Freeman's Saturday Show
1976	Alan Freeman's Saturday Show
1977	Alan Freeman's Saturday Show
1978	Alan Freeman's Saturday Show

TV SHOW OF THE YEAR

1960	Boy Meets Girl (ITV)
1961	Juke Box Jury (BBC)
1962	Thank Your Lucky Stars (ITV)
1963	Lucky Stars – Summer Spin (ITV)
1964	Ready Steady Go (ITV)
1965	Ready Steady Go (ITV)
1966	Top of the Pops (BBC)
1967	Top of the Pops (BBC)
1968	Top of the Pops (BBC)
1969	Colour Me Pop
1970	Disco 2
1971	Disco 2
1972	Old Grey Whistle Test (BBC2)
1973	Old Grey Whistle Test (BBC2)
1974	Old Grey Whistle Test (BBC2)
1975	Old Grey Whistle Test (BBC2)
1976	Old Grey Whistle Test (BBC2)
1977	Old Grey Whistle Test (BBC2)
1978	Revolver

VOCAL DISC OF THE YEAR
(British Section)

1960	Living Doll, Cliff Richard
1961	Portrait of my Love, Matt Monro
1962	The Young Ones, Cliff Richard
1963	From Me to You, Beatles
1964	Not Fade Away, Rolling Stones
1965	Ticket to Ride, Beatles
1966	Paperback Writer, Beatles
Discontinued	

INSTRUMENTAL DISC OF THE YEAR
(British Section)

1960	Petite Fleur, Chris Barber
1961	Apache, The Shadows
1962	Stranger on the Shore, Acker Bilk
1963	Diamonds, Jet Harris and Tony Meeham
1964	Rise and Fall of Flingel Bunt, Shadows
1965	Cast Your Fate to the Winds, Sounds Orchestral
1966	The War Lord, Shadows
Discontinued	

VOCAL GROUP OF THE YEAR

1960	Polka Dots
1961	King Brothers
1962	Springfields
1963	Beatles (B) and Four Seasons (W)
1964	Rolling Stones (B) and Beatles (W)
1965	Beatles (B and W)
1966	Beatles (B and W)
1967	Beatles (B and W)
1968	Beatles (B and W)

1969	Beatles (B and W)
1970	Led Zeppelin (B and W)
1971	Emerson, Lake and Palmer (B) and Crosby, Stills, Nash and Young (W)
1972	Emerson, Lake and Palmer (B and W)
1973	Emerson, Lake and Palmer (B and W)
Discontinued	

DISC JOCKEY OF THE YEAR

1960	David Jacobs
1961	David Jacobs
1962	David Jacobs
1963	David Jacobs
1964	Jimmy Savile
1965	Jimmy Savile
1966	Jimmy Savile
1967	Jimmy Savile
1968	John Peel
1969	John Peel
1970	John Peel
1971	John Peel
1972	John Peel
1973	John Peel
1974	John Peel
1975	John Peel
1976	John Peel
1977	John Peel
1978	John Peel

MUSICIAN OF THE YEAR (British Section)

1964	Hank Marvin
1965	Hank Marvin
1966	Hank Marvin
1967	Eric Clapton
1968	Eric Clapton
1969	Eric Clapton
Discontinued	

TOP MUSICIAN (World Section)

1964	Chuck Berry
1965	Burt Bacharach
1966	Herb Alpert
1967	Jimi Hendrix
1968	Eric Clapton
1969	Eric Clapton
Discontinued	

TOP GUITARIST (World Section)

1970	Eric Clapton
1971	Eric Clapton
1972	Rory Gallagher
1973	Jan Akkerman
1974	Eric Clapton
1975	Jimmy Page
1976	Steve Howe
1977	Jimmy Page
1978	Steve Howe

TOP KEYBOARDS (World Section)

1970	Keith Emerson
1971	Keith Emerson
1972	Keith Emerson
1973	Rick Wakeman
1974	Rick Wakeman
1975	Rick Wakeman

1976   Rick Wakeman
1977   Keith Emerson
1978   Rick Wakeman

VOCAL DISC OF THE YEAR (World Section)
1963   Can't Get Used to Losing You, Andy Williams
1964   It's Over, Roy Orbison
1965   Crying in the Chapel, Elvis Presley
1966   Paperback Writer, Beatles
Discontinued

INSTRUMENTAL DISC OF THE YEAR (World Section)
1963   Pipeline, Chantays
1964   Rise and Fall of Flingel Bunt, Shadows
1965   Cast Your Fate to the Winds, Sounds Orchestral
1966   Spanish Flea, Herb Alpert
Discontinued

SINGLE DISC OF THE YEAR (British Section)
1967   Whiter Shade of Pale, Procol Harum
1968   Jumpin' Jack Flash, Rolling Stones
1969   Get Back, Beatles
1970   All Right Now, Free
1971   My Sweet Lord, George Harrison
1972   Lady Eleanor, Lindisfarne
1973   Jean Genie, David Bowie
1974   Can't Get Enough, Bad Company
1975   I'm Not in Love, 10cc
1976   Bohemian Rhapsody, Queen
1977   Fanfare for the Common Man, Emerson, Lake
        and Palmer
Discontinued

LP/ALBUM OF THE YEAR (British Section)
1967   Sgt Pepper's Lonely Hearts Club Band, Beatles
1968   Scott 2, Scott Walker
1969   Goodbye, Cream
1970   Led Zeppelin II
1971   Tarkus, Emerson, Lake and Palmer
1972   Argus, Wishbone Ash
1973   Dark Side of the Moon, Pink Floyd
1974   Tubular Bells, Mike Oldfield
1975   Physical Graffiti, Led Zeppelin
1976   A Trick of the Tail, Genesis
1977   Works, ELO
Discontinued

BEST LIVE ACT OF THE YEAR (British Section)
1973   Emerson, Lake and Palmer
1974   Genesis
1975   Genesis
1976   Genesis
1977   Genesis
Discontinued

SINGLE DISC OF THE YEAR (World Section)
1967   Whiter Shade of Pale, Procol Harum
1968   US Male, Elvis Presley
1969   The Boxer, Simon and Garfunkel
1970   Bridge Over Troubled Water, Simon and Gar-
        funkel
1971   My Sweet Lord, George Harrison
1972   American Pie, Don McLean
1973   Walk on the Wild Side, Lou Reed
1974   This Town Ain't Big Enough for Both of Us,
        Sparks

1975   I'm Not in Love, 10cc
1976   Bohemian Rhapsody, Queen
1977   Fanfare for the Common Man, Emerson, Lake
        and Palmer
1978   Baker Street, Gerry Rafferty

LP/ALBUM OF THE YEAR (World Section)
1967   Sgt Pepper's Lonely Hearts Club Band, Beatles
1968   John Wesley Harding, Bob Dylan
1969   Nashville Skyline, Bob Dylan
1970   Hot Rats, Frank Zappa
1971   After the Gold Rush, Neil Young
1972   Harvest, Neil Young
1973   Dark Side of the Moon, Pink Floyd
1974   Tubular Bells, Mike Oldfield
1975   Physical Graffiti, Led Zeppelin
1976   A Trick of the Tail, Genesis
1977   Works, Emerson, Lake and Palmer
1978   Live and Dangerous, Thin Lizzy

TOP BAND OF THE YEAR (British Section)
1973   Yes
1974   Yes
1975   Yes
1976   Yes
1977   Genesis
Discontinued

TOP RECORD PRODUCER (World Section)
1970   Frank Zappa
1971   Bob Johnson
1972   Greg Lake
1973   David Bowie
1974   Eddie Offord
1975   Eddie Offord
1976   Jimmy Page
1977   Jimmy Page
1978   David Hentschell

TOP COMPOSER (World Section)
1971   Neil Young
1972   Keith Emerson/Greg Lake
1973   David Bowie
1974   Jon Anderson/Steve Howe
1975   Jon Anderson
1976   Jon Anderson
1977   Jimmy Page/Robert Plant
1978   Genesis

TOP ARRANGER (World Section)
1971   Paul Buckmaster
1972   Emerson, Lake, Palmer
1973   Emerson, Lake, Palmer
1974   David Bowie
1975   Yes
1976   Yes
1977   Genesis
1978   Genesis

TOP BAND (World Section)
1973   Yes
1974   Yes
1975   Led Zeppelin
1976   Yes
1977   Yes
1978   Genesis

TOP LIVE ACT (World Section)
1973   Alice Cooper
1974   Emerson, Lake and Palmer
1975   Led Zeppelin
1976   Genesis
1977   Genesis
1978   Genesis

BEST DISCO RECORD
1978   Night Fever, Bee Gees

BEST JAZZ ACT
1978   Brand X

BEST REGGAE ACT
1978   Bob Marley and the Wailers

Pulitzer Prizes

(*See* Pulitzer Prizes.) This music award, instituted in 1943, carries a prize of $1000.

1943 *Secular Cantata No. 2*, William Schuman	1962 *The Crucible*, Robert Ward
1944 *Symphony No. 4, opus 34*, Howard Hanson	1963 *Piano Concerto No. 1*, Samuel Barber
1945 *Appalachian Spring*, Aaron Copland	1964 No award
1946 *The Canticle of the Sun*, Leo Sowerby	1965 No award
1947 *Symphony No. 3*, Charles Ives	1966 *Variations for Orchestra*, Leslie Bassett
1948 *Symphony No. 3*, Walter Piston	1967 *Quartet No. 3*, Leon Kirchner
1949 *Louisiana Story*, Virgil Thomson	1968 *Echoes of Time and the River*, George Crumb
1950 *The Consul*, Gian-Carlo Menotti	1969 *String Quartet No. 3*, Karel Husa
1951 *Giants in the Earth*, Douglas S. Moore	1970 *Time's Economium*, Charles W. Wuorinen
1952 *Symphony Concertante*, Gail Kubik	1971 *Synchronisms No. 6*, Mario Davidovsky
1953 No award	1972 *Windows*, Jacob Druckman
1954 *Concerto for Two Pianos and Orchestra*, Quincy Porter	1973 *String Quartet No. 3*, Elliott Carter
	1974 *Notturno*, Donald Martino; special citation to Roger Sessions
1955 *The Saint of Bleecker Street*, Gian-Carlo Menotti	
1956 *Symphony No. 3*, Ernst Toch	1975 *From the Diary of Virginia Woolf*, Dominick Argento
1957 *Meditations on Ecclesiastes*, Norman Dello Joio	
1958 *The Score of Vanessa*, Samuel Barber	1976 *Air Music, 10 études for orchestra*, Ned Rorem
1959 *Concerto for Piano and Orchestra*, John La Montaine	1977 *Visions of Terror and Wonder*, Richard Wernick
1960 *Second String Quartet*, Elliott C. Carter Jr.	1978 *Déjà Vu for Percussion Quartet and Orchestra*, Michael Colgrass
1961 *Symphony No. 7*, Walter Piston	

NETBALL

World Championships

World Championships for women's netball teams were first held in 1963. Winners:

1963	Australia	1971	Australia
1967	New Zealand	1975	Australia

NOBEL PRIZES

Nobel Prizes are awarded each year to persons who have made important contributions for the good of humanity.

The awards were established in the will of Alfred Bernhard Nobel (1833–96), a Swedish chemist who became wealthy from his invention of dynamite in 1867. He regretted that dynamite had been used as an instrument of war, and left a fund of about $9 million to establish the Nobel Prizes to encourage peace and progress.

Six prizes are awarded each year in chemistry, economics, literature, peace, physics and physiology or medicine. The first prizes were awarded in 1901. The economics prize was added in 1969. Each prize in 1977 carried a monetary award of about $145 000, divided when there was more than one recipient.

The Royal Academy of Science in Sweden picks the prizewinners in physics, chemistry, and economics. The medical faculty of Stockholm's Caroline Institute chooses the winner in the field of physiology or medicine. The Swedish Academy of Literature names the winner in the field of literature. The Norwegian parliament elects a committee of five persons to select the winner of the prize for peace.

(*See* under Chemistry, Economics, Literature, Medicine, Peace and Physics for details of winners.)

NURSING

National Nursing Awards

These are organised annually by the Royal College of Nursing and sponsored by Reckitt and Colman. The competition began in 1974, and there was a separate category for students in 1976 and 1977. The awards for 1979 were directed towards nurses engaged in occupational health, to mark the centenary of the appointment of Britain's first industrial community nurse, Philippa Flowerday, by J. J. Colman Ltd of Norwich.

1974   Alison Cumming, Western Infirmary, Glasgow
1975   Mary Fearon, Musgrave Park Hospital, Belfast
1976   Margaret Height, Royal Victoria Hospital, Edinburgh
1977   Betty Earnshaw, Royal Ordnance Factory, Crewe
1978–79 Renee Hartley, Cheshire County Council

Students' awards
1976   Eileen Birch, Harlow District School of Nursing, Harlow, Essex
1977   Rhonda Eileen Wright, Magherafelt, Co Londonderry

Mary Fearon (*left*) 1975 winner of the National Nursing Award, holding the Dettol Sword Trophy with the 1976 winner (*right*) Margaret Height of the Royal Victoria Hospital, Edinburgh (*Keystone*)

Nurse of the Year

This competition is organised each year by the *Daily Express* and featured on BBC television's Nationwide. Readers vote to give their favourite nurse a chance to win the title of 'The Nurse of the Year' and a cruise for two in the Canaries in the QE2 with £200 pocket money, presented by Cunard.

Anyone can nominate a nurse for the title – patients, colleagues, relatives and friends. Academic achievement and experience are not the main criteria -- kindness, efficiency, manner, general disposition and aspirations are more likely to influence the independent panel of judges.

The contest is open to all qualified nurses, female and male, in the National Health Service, Queen Alexandra's Royal Naval Nursing Service, Princess Mary's Royal Air Force Nursing Service and the Queen Alexandra's Royal Army Nursing Corps. It is also open to nurses in the NHS or Services who are studying for nursing qualifications and in full-time employment. The winners to date are:

1970	Madeline Ambrose	1975	Joy Dyer
1971	Dilys Owen	1976	Tessa Dodds
1972	Patricia Henry	1977	Nancy Farley
1973	Barbara Murray	1978	Cecilia Holden
1974	Jenny Denham	1979	Susan Hemming

NUTRITION

Rank Prize in Nutrition

The Rank Prize Funds were established in 1972, shortly before the death of Lord Rank, to encourage research and provide awards to scholars. The prize was awarded in 1976, but the awards are not given annually and they are not of a fixed sum.

1976   Norman Wingate Pirie, Rothamsted Experimental Station, Harpenden. £15 000 for 'his outstanding contribution to the development of the technology for the isolation of protein food from the herbage'.

OLYMPIC GAMES

The first Olympic Games of the modern era were held in Athens, Greece in 1896. Since then, with the exception of the war years (1916, 1940 and 1944), Games have been held every four years, and additionally in Athens in 1906. Separate Winter Olympics were first held in 1924.

Most individual gold medals:
Men: 10   Ray Ewry (USA): Track and Field Athletics 1900–08
Women: 7   Vera Caslavska (Cze): Gymnastics 1964–68
The dates and venues have been allocated as follows:

I	Athens	6–15 Apr 1896
II	Paris	20 May–28 Oct 1900
III	St. Louis	1 Jul–23 Nov 1904
†	Athens	22 Apr–2 May 1906
IV	London	27 Apr–31 Oct 1908
V	Stockholm	5 May–22 Jul 1912
VI	*Berlin	1916
VII	Antwerp	20 Apr–12 Sep 1920
VIII	Paris	4 May–27 Jul 1924
IX	Amsterdam	17 May–12 Aug 1928
X	Los Angeles	30 Jul–14 Aug 1932
XI	Berlin	1–16 Aug 1936
XII	*Tokyo, then Helsinki	1940
XIII	*London	1944
XIV	London	29 Jul–14 Aug 1948
XV	Helsinki	19 Jul–3 Aug 1952
XVI	‡Melbourne	22 Nov–8 Dec 1956
XVII	Rome	25 Aug–11 Sep 1960
XVIII	Tokyo	10–24 Oct 1964
XIX	Mexico City	12–27 Oct 1968
XX	Munich	26 Aug–10 Sep 1972
XXI	Montreal	17 Jul–1 Aug 1976
XXII	Moscow	19 Jul–3 Aug 1980
XXIII	Los Angeles	1984

The Winter Olympics were inaugurated in 1924 and have been allocated as follows:

I	Chamonix, France	25 Jan–4 Feb 1924
II	St. Moritz, Switzerland	11–19 Feb 1928
III	Lake Placid, USA	4–15 Feb 1932
IV	Garmisch-Partenkirchen Germany	6–16 Feb 1936
V	St. Moritz, Switzerland	30 Jan–8 Feb 1948
VI	Oslo, Norway	14–25 Feb 1952
VII	Cortina d'Ampezzo, Italy	26 Jan–5 Feb 1956
VIII	Squaw Valley, California	18–28 Feb 1960
IX	Innsbruck, Austria	29 Jan–9 Feb 1964
X	Grenoble, France	6–18 Feb 1968
XI	Sapporo, Japan	3–13 Feb 1972
XII	Innsbruck, Austria	4–15 Feb 1976
XIII	Lake Placid, USA	14–23 Feb 1980
XIV	Sarajevo, Yugoslavia	1–12 Feb 1984 (prov.)

* Cancelled due to World Wars
† Intercalated Celebration not numbered but officially organised by the IOC (International Olympic Committee)
‡ Equestrian events held in Stockholm, Sweden 10–17 Jun 1956

See the following sports for additional details:
Archery, Association Football, Athletics, Basketball, Bobsleigh and Tobogganing, Boxing, Canoeing, Cycling, Equestrian Events, Fencing, Gymnastics, Hockey, Ice Hockey, Ice Skating, Judo, Modern Pentathlon, Rowing, Shooting, Skiing (and Biathlon), Swimming, Volleyball, Water Polo, Weightlifting, Wrestling, Yachting

ORCHIDS

The British Orchid Growers' Association Championship

The association holds an annual show in London, and various awards are made to professional growers. In 1979, Gloria Cotton from Birmingham, who cultivates 1000 orchid plants in two large greenhouses, without professional help, was declared amateur champion. She was awarded the association's own trophy and a gold medal from the Royal Horticultural Society.

The other star grower on this occasion was Eric Young, a Jersey-based amateur orchid grower who won the trophy for the finest set of cymbidiums put up for competition. An unnamed seedling in Mr Young's collection, a four-year-old plant with nine flower stems each bearing a dozen green and maroon blooms, was declared 'best in show'.

ORIENTEERING

World Champions

World Championships were first held in 1966.

	Men's Individual	Women's Individual	Men's Relay	Women's Relay
1966	Aage Hadler (Nor)	Ulla Lindqvist (Swe)	Sweden	Sweden
1968	Karl Johansson (Swe)	Ulla Lindqvist (Swe)	Sweden	Norway
1970	Stig Berge (Nor)	Ingrid Hadler (Nor)	Norway	Sweden
1972	Aage Hadler (Nor)	Sarolta Monspart (Fin)	Sweden	Finland
1974	Bernt Frilen (Swe)	Mona Norgaard (Den)	Sweden	Sweden
1976	Egil Johansen (Nor)	Liisa Veijalainen (Fin)	Sweden	Sweden
1978	Egil Johansen (Nor)	Anne Berit Eid (Nor)	Norway	Finland

PEACE

Nobel Prize for Peace (*See* Nobel Prizes.)

1901	Jean H. Dunant (Swi)		1930	Lårs O. N. Söderblom (Swe)
	Frederic Passy (Fra)		1931	Jane Addams (USA)
1902	Elie Ducommun (Swi)			Nicholas Murray Butler (USA)
	Charles A. Gobat (Swi)		1932	No award
1903	Sir William R. Cremer (GB)		1933	Sir Norman Angell (GB)
1904	Institute of International Law		1934	Arthur Henderson (GB)
1905	Baroness Bertha von Suttner (Aut)		1935	Carl von Ossietzky (Ger)
1906	Theodore Roosevelt (USA)		1936	Carlos Saavedra Lamas (Arg)
1907	Ernesto T. Moneta (Ita)		1937	Viscount Cecil of Chelwood (GB)
	Louis Renault (Fra)		1938	International Office for Refugees
1908	Klas P. Arnoldson (Swe)		1939–43	No award
	Fredrik Bajer (Den)		1944	International Committee of the Red Cross
1909	Auguste M. F. Beernaert (Bel)		1945	Cordell Hull (USA)
	Paul H. B. B. d'Estournelles de Constant (Fra)		1946	Emily G. Balch (USA)
1910	Permanent International Peace Bureau			John R. Mott (USA)
1911	Tobias M. C. Asser (Hol)		1947	Friends Service Council (GB)
	Alfred H. Fried (Aut)			American Friends Service Committee
1912	Alihu Root (USA)		1948	No award
1913	Henri Lafontaine (Bel)		1949	Lord John Boyd Orr of Brechin (GB)
1914–16	No award		1950	Ralph J. Bunche (USA)
1917	International Committee of the Red Cross		1951	Léon Jouhaux (Fra)
1918	No award		1952	Albert Schweitzer (Fra) (German-born)
1919	Woodrow Wilson (USA)		1953	George C. Marshall (USA)
1920	Léon V. A. Bourgeois (Fra)		1954	Office of UN High Commissioner for Refugees
1921	Karl H. Branting (Swe)		1955–56	No award
	Christian L. Lange (Nor)		1957	Lester B. Pearson (Can)
1922	Fridtjof Nansen (Nor)		1958	Georges Pire (Bel)
1923–24	No award		1959	Philip J. Noel-Baker (GB)
1925	Sir J. Austen Chamberlain (GB)		1960	Albert J. Luthuli (SA)
	Charles G. Dawes (USA)		1961	Dag Hammarskjöld (Swe) posthumous
1926	Aristide Briand (Fra)		1962	Linus C. Pauling (USA)
	Gustav Stresemann (Ger)		1963	International Committee of the Red Cross
1927	Ferdinand Buisson (Fra)			Red Cross Societies League
	Ludwig Quidde (Ger)		1964	Martin Luther King Jr (USA)
1928	No award		1965	United Nations Children's Fund (UNICEF)
1929	Frank B. Kellogg (USA)		1966–67	No award

1968	René Cassin (Fra)	1975	Andrei D. Sakharov (USSR)
1969	International Labour Organisation (ILO)	1976	Betty Williams and Mairead Corrigan (GB), organisers of peace movement to resist terrorist violence in Northern Ireland
1970	Norman E. Borlaug (USA)		
1971	Willy Brandt (Ger)		
1972	No award	1977	Amnesty International, organisation that exposes governmental violations of human rights
1973	Henry A. Kissinger (USA) (German-born) Le Duc Tho (N. Viet)		
1974	Eisaku Sato (Jap) Sean MacBride (Ire)	1978	Anwar el Sadat (Egy) Menachem Begin (Isr)

PELOTA (*See* Jai Alai)

PENTATHLON (*See* Modern Pentathlon)

PETS

Pet of the Year

The Pet of the Year award was first presented in 1978. Organised by the Junglies Club – an off-shoot of the World Wildlife Fund's Wildlife Youth Service – the competition is open to any child who has a pet of any description.

Entrants are invited to send a photograph of their pet together with, in no more than 100 words, their reasons why they think their animal should be the Pet of the Year. The winner's owner is presented with a cash prize and various other Junglies products, together with a brass plaque commemorating the Pet of the Year award.

1978   Alsatian called Sherry, owned by two sisters, Julie and Gina Wilding from Bolton, Lancs

Below: **The 1978 'Pet of the Year' was an Alsatian called Sherry, owned by two sisters, Julie and Gina Wilding, shown here**

PHOTOGRAPHY

British Photography Competition

The competition, held annually since 1975, is organised by the *Telegraph Sunday Magazine* with British Airways and Kodak, and is open to all photographers resident in the UK. The National Trust and BBC television are also associated with the awards.

1975
Theme:
The British Weekend
Winner:
Rosemary Drayson
£1000 and two weeks in Bangkok

1976
Theme:
The British on Holiday
Winners: Professional Category
G. P. Eisen, LRPS
£500 and Sovereign Holiday for two in Istanbul
Amateur Category
Andrew Polakowski
£500 and Sovereign Holiday for two in Tenerife

1977
Theme:
Britain '77
Winners:
Section 1 – On The Move
John Eyett (Two Hurdlers)
£250

Section 2 – National Trust and British Heritage (open to amateur and professional photographers)
P. Lacey (West Clandon)
£250 plus life membership of National Trust
Section 3 – A Sense of Community (open to amateur photographers only)
Clive B. Harrison
£250

Overall Winner:
John Eyett
£1000 and 14 days in Hong Kong for two

1978
Theme:
A Sense of Beauty

Winners:
People
Barney Edwards (Man and Dog in Mist)
£500
Places
K. Taylor (St. Kilda)
£500

'A Sense of Beauty'—the theme for the 1978 British Photography Competition. First prize in the 'Things' section was awarded to J. G. Corbett for his picture of Sun Clocks

Things
J. G. Corbett (Sun Clocks)
£500
National Trust
Patricio Goycolea (Glastonbury Tor)
£500 plus life membership of the National Trust

Overall winner:
Barney Edwards
£1000 and 14-day holiday for two in Mauritius

Kodak Under Fives Portrait Awards

In this annual competition, which dates from 1976, parents are invited to have their young children (five years or under) photographed in colour by a professional photographer. Two cash prizes of £100 are awarded each month for the photographs of the girl and boy judged to look 'the most lovable and appealing'. There is an annual prize of £500 each for the two overall winners.

    1976   Helen Ann Clark
    1977   Twins Wendy and Amanda Henoq
    1978   Robb Halley, and Rhiannon James

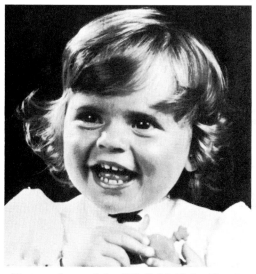 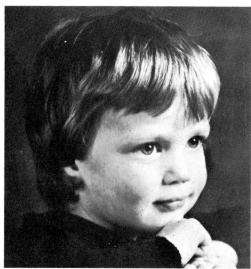

The two winners of the 1978 Kodak Under Fives Portrait Award. *Left:* **two-year-old Rhiannon James;** and *right:* **four-year-old Robb Halley**

PHYSICS

Nobel Prize for Physics
(*See* Nobel Prizes)

1901	Wilhelm C. Roentgen (Ger)
1902	Hendrik A. Lorentz (Hol)
	Pieter Zeeman (Hol)
1903	Antoine Henri Becquerel (Fra)
	Marie Curie (Fra) (Polish-born)
	Pierre Curie (Fra)
1904	Lord Rayleigh (John W. Strutt) (GB)
1905	Philipp E. A. von Lenard (Ger)(Hungarian-born)
1906	Sir Joseph John Thomson (GB)
1907	Albert A. Michelson (USA) (German-born)
1908	Gabriel Lippmann (Fra) (Lux-born)
1909	Guglielmo Marconi (Ita)
	Carl F. Braun (Ger)

1910	Johannes D. van der Waals (Hol)
1911	Wilhelm Wien (Ger)
1912	Nils G. Dalén (Swe)
1913	Heike Kamerlingh-Onnes (Hol)
1914	Max von Laue (Ger)
1915	Sir William H. Bragg (GB)
1916	No award
1917	Charles G. Barkla (GB)
1918	Max K. E. L. Planck (Ger)
1919	Johannes Stark (Ger)
1920	Charles E. Guillaume (Fra) (Swiss-born)
1921	Albert Einstein (USA) (German-born)
1922	Niels Bohr (Den)

1923	Robert A. Millikan (USA)	1957	Tsung-Dao Lee (USA) (Chinese-born)
1924	Karl M. G. Siegbahn (Swe)		Chen Ning Yang (USA) (Chinese-born)
1925	James Franck (Ger)	1958	Paval A. Cherenkov (USSR)
	Gustav Hertz (Ger)		Ilya M. Frank (USSR)
1926	Jean B. Perrin (Fra)		Igor J. Tamm (USSR)
1927	Arthur H. Compton (USA)	1959	Owen Chamberlain (USA)
	Charles T. R. Wilson (GB)		Emilio G. Segrè (USA) (Italian-born)
1928	Owen W. Richardson (GB)	1960	Donald A. Glaser (USA)
1929	Prince Louis-Victor de Broglie (Fra)	1961	Robert Hofstadter (USA)
1930	Sir Chandrasekhara V. Raman (Ind)		Rudolf L. Mössbauer (Ger)
1931	No award	1962	Lev D. Landau (USSR)
1932	Werner Heisenberg (Ger)	1963	Maria Goeppert-Mayer (USA)
1933	Paul A. M. Dirac (GB)		J. Hans D. Jensen (Ger)
	Erwin Schrödinger (Aut)		Eugene P. Wigner (USA)
1934	No award	1964	Nikolai G. Basov (USSR)
1935	Sir James Chadwick (GB)		Aleksandr M. Prokhorov (USSR)
1936	Carl D. Anderson (USA)		Charles H. Townes (USA)
	Victor F. Hess (Aut)	1965	Richard P. Feynman (USA)
1937	Clinton J. Davisson (USA)		Julian S. Schwinger (USA)
	George P. Thomson (GB)		Sin-itiro Tomonaga (Jap)
1938	Enrico Fermi (USA) (Italian-born)	1966	Alfred Kastler (Fra)
1939	Ernst O. Lawrence (USA)	1967	Hans A. Bethe (USA) (German-born)
1940	No award	1968	Luis W. Alvarez (USA)
1941	No award	1969	Murray Gell-Mann (USA)
1942	No award	1970	Hannes O. G. Alfven (Swe)
1943	Otto Stern (USA) (German-born)		Louis E. F. Néel (Fra)
1944	Isidor Isaac Rabi (USA)	1971	Dennis Gabor (GB) (Hungarian-born)
1945	Wolfgang Pauli (USA)	1972	John Bardeen (USA)
1946	Percy Williams Bridgman (USA)		Leon N. Cooper (USA)
1947	Sir Edward V. Appleton (GB)		John R. Schrieffer (USA)
1948	Patrick M. S. Blackett (GB)	1973	Ivar Giaever (USA) (Norwegian-born)
1949	Hideki Yukawa (Jap)		Leo Esaki (Jap)
1950	Cecil F. Powell (GB)		Brian D. Josephson (GB)
1951	Sir John D. Cockroft (GB)	1974	Antony Hewish (GB)
	Ernest T. S. Walton (Ire)		Sir Martin Ryle (GB)
1952	Felix Bloch (USA) (Swiss-born)	1975	L. James Rainwater (USA)
	Edward M. Purcell (USA)		Aage Bohr (Den)
1953	Fritz Zernike (Hol)		Ben Roy Mottelson (Den) (USA-born)
1954	Max Born (GB) (German-born)	1976	Burton Richter (USA)
	Walther Bothe (Ger)		Samuel C. C. Ting (USA)
1955	Polykarp Kusch (USA) (German-born)	1977	John H. Van Vleck (USA)
	Willis E. Lamb (USA)		Philip W. Anderson (USA)
1956	John Bardeen (USA)		Sir Nevill F. Mott (GB)
	Walter H. Brattain (USA)	1978	Piotr Leontevich Kapitsa (USSR)
	William Shockley (USA)		Arno A. Penzias (USA) (German-born)
			Robert W. Wilson (USA)

PIGEONS

The Royal Pigeon Racing Association's affiliates hold various annual championship races, of which two principal events are detailed below.

The British Barcelona Club Annual Race from Palomos in Spain

This is one of the longest distance races held by clubs in Britain. The winning details include the name of the owner, the bird's number, the velocity in yards per minute, the number of birds and the distance flown.

1967 A. G. M. Stevens, Colerne, Wilts
Blue Hen. NU 63 N 43025. Vel. 849. 296 Birds.
707 miles

1968 L. S. Bunn, Folkestone, Kent
Blue Hen. NU 65 N 29272. Vel. 886. 425 Birds.
643 miles

1969 A. Hustler, Poole, Dorset
Mealy Cock. NU 66 N 18473. Vel. 785. 565 Birds.
657 miles

1970 W. J. Challen, Cookham Dean, Berks
Blue Ch. Cock. NU 66 A 68713. Vel. 898. 507
Birds. 691 miles

1971 J. & J. G. Paley, Keighley, Yorks
Mealy Cock. NU 64 L 45003. Vel. 788. 615 Birds.
861 miles

1972 C. R. Medway, Sholing, Southampton
Blue Cock. NU 65 N 51310. Vel. 637. 693 Birds.
661 miles

1973 R. Churchill, Weymouth, Dorset
Dark Ch Hen. NU 66 N 28449. Vel. 627. 702
Birds. 657 miles

1974 T. W. Hodges, Taunton, Somerset
Blue Hen. NU 69 N 11627. Vel. 1007. 1023 Birds.
694 miles

1975 T. Dodd, Taunton, Somerset
Blue Cock. NU 70 N 79801. Vel. 860. 923 Birds.
694 miles

1976 T. J. Perrett, Mere, Wilts
Blue Ch Pied Hen. NU 73 J 86506. Vel. 741. 1144
Birds. 684 miles

1977 W. J. Bradford, Sutton, Surrey
Blue Hen. NU 72 C 49867. Vel. 844. 1040 Birds.
672 miles

1978 R. Dowden, Paulsgrove, Portsmouth
Blue Ch Hen. NU 75 S 3876. Vel. 863. 848 Birds.
649 miles

King's Cup
The North Road Championship Club Race from Lerwick.

	Owners	Town	Race Point	Miles	Entry	Velocity
1932	F. Stevenson	Skegness	Lerwick	488	489	928
1933	Branstone, Son & Smith	Mansfield	Lerwick	485	716	849
1934	S. R. Atkins	Ipswich	Lerwick	566	967	1257
1935	J. R. Marriott	Derby	Lerwick	502	1043	784
1936	D. Robotham & Sons	Leicester	Lerwick	524	917	1035
1937	R. F. Towle	Toton	Lerwick	501	782	1390
1938	Major G. S. Rogers	Sheringham	Lerwick	507	885	1279
1939	Jepson Bros. & Curtis	Peterborough	Lerwick	525	700	1875
1940	North & Son	Skegness	Fraserburgh	327	912	1786
1941	H.M. King George VI	Sandringham	Banff	356	770	1199
1942	W. J. Smith	Leicester	Banff	352	1031	794
1943	W. L. Thackery	Malton	Banff	253	1289	1601
1944	A. Bush	Tibshelf	Banff	317	1408	867
1945	Jepson Bros. & Curtis	Peterborough	Thurso	435	1750	1204
1946	Perry, Morgan & Heardman Bros.	Clay Cross	Lerwick	482	1360	938
1947	R. Preston	Ellistown	Lerwick	515	1318	1466
1948	A. Bush	Tibshelf	Lerwick	485	1365	913
1949	S. Powling	Ipswich	Lerwick	568	1461	1800
1950	E. Stevenson	Mansfield	Lerwick	485	1518	955
1951	H.M. King George VI	Sandringham	Lerwick	511	1414	1364
1952	V. Divit	Mansfield	Lerwick	485	1564	1157
1953	H. Harding	Spalding	Lerwick	511	1554	793
1954	Mrs H. A. Bridge	Thundersley	Lerwick	598	1293	1370
1955	A. W. Keeble	Ipswich	Lerwick	566	1575	1221
1956	H. A. Bridge	Thundersley	Lerwick	598	1872	1698
1957	Marsh & Bailey	Swanwick	Lerwick	490	1467	1786
1958	A. Smith	Mansfield	Lerwick	485	1244	1165
1959	Mrs H. A. Bridge	Thundersley	Lerwick	598	1440	1068
1960	Carter & Son	Thorney	Lerwick	523	1502	1427
1961	E. F. Soames	Manningtree	Lerwick	576	1776	1219
1962	Caston & Son	Norwich	Lerwick	530	1459	1233
1963	G. Breuninger	Radcliffe-on-Trent	Lerwick	498	1350	1169
1964	F. H. Perkins	Boston	Lerwick	498	1471	1892
1965	J. H. Lovell	Donington	Lerwick	502	1507	752
1966	Springthorpe Bros.	Hucknall	Thurso	394	1554	1019
1967	Waldram & Young	Alfreton	Lerwick	488	1732	874
1968	F. C. Hudson	Lincoln	Lerwick	481	1720	1237
1969	N. Springthorpe	Hucknall	Lerwick	492	1672	947
1970	J. & R. Brill	Ipswich	Lerwick	566	1896	731
1971	Smith & Coupland	Alford	Lerwick	479	1603	1235
1972	J. H. Lovell	Donington	Lerwick	502	1725	841
1973	W. A. Lawson	Ravenstone	Lerwick	514	1688	868
1974	Mr and Mrs C. W. R. Wright	Bourne	Lerwick	512	1593	789
1975	Wigg Bros.	Knodishall	Lerwick	560	2019	1678
1976	C. R. Brunt	Walesby	Lerwick	479	1769	1085
1977	Mr and Mrs J. Brand	Ely	Thurso	453	1663	1118
1978	Bates, Son & Burley	Langley Mill	Lerwick	493	1473	1389

PLOUGHING

British National Ploughing Championships

The following list of British competitors in the World Ploughing Contest was supplied by the Society of Ploughing, which was formed in 1951. From 1968, Britain's international representatives were also the winners and runners up of the British National Ploughing Championship. The winners from 1951, and location of contest:

1951 } 1952 } Class Winners Only	
1953 (Canada) Leslie Dixon and R. A. Hogg	1967 (New Zealand) Raymond Goodwin and Philip Skyrme
1954 (Ireland) R. L. Roberts and Leslie Dixon	1968 (Rhodesia) Robert Anderson and Ken Chappell
1955 (Sweden) E. J. Walker and T. C. Watkins	1969 (Yugoslavia) Gerald I. Smith and Geo. F. Allwood
1956 (England) E. J. Walker and J. D. Lomas	1970 (Denmark) Raymond H. Robson and David Dick
1957 (USA) John Mason and R. J. Miller	1971 (England) J. J. Metcalfe and F. H. Millington
1958 (Germany) T. L. Goodwin and John Dixon	1972 (USA) J. B. Smith and Philip Skyrme
1959 (N. Ireland) J. H. Nott and E. S. Davies	1973 (Ireland) J. Milnes and D. W. J. Bonning
1960 (Italy) J. A. Gwilliam and H. R. Jones	1974 (Finland) L. F. Waudby and L. Iredale
1961 (France) W. T. Phillips and G. W. Hoskins	1975 (Canada) Robert Anderson and V. E. Samuel
1962 (Holland) H. R. Jones and J. W. Sandford	1976 (Sweden) J. T. Smith and Raymond Goodwin
1963 (Canada) L. J. Williams and D. W. J. Bonning	1977 (Netherlands) J. T. Smith and David Chappell
1964 (Austria) J. W. Cole and J. Mason	1978 (West Germany) V. E. Samuel and C. T. W. Potter
1965 (Norway) J. L. Nixon and D. W. J. Bonning	1979 (N. Ireland) V. E. Samuel and F. H. Millington

POETRY

Poets Laureate

The office of poet laureate is one of great honour, conferred on a poet of distinction. In 1616, James I granted a pension to the poet Ben Jonson, but it was not until 1668 that the laureateship was created as a royal office. When the position of poet laureate falls vacant, the prime minister is responsible for putting forth names for a new laureate, to be chosen by the sovereign. The sovereign then commands the Lord Chamberlain to appoint the poet laureate, and he does so by issuing a warrant to the laureate-elect. The Lord Chamberlain also arranges for the appointment – for life – to be announced in the *London Gazette*.

John Dryden (1631–1700; laureate 1668–88)
Thomas Shadwell (1642?–92; laureate 1688–92)
Nahum Tate (1652–1715; laureate 1692–1715)
Nicholas Rowe (1674–1718; laureate 1715–18)
Laurence Eusden (1688–1730; laureate 1718–30)
Colley Cibber (1671–1757; laureate 1730–57)
William Whitehead (1715–85; laureate 1757–85)
    (Appointed after Thomas Gray declined the offer)
Thomas Warton (1728–90; laureate 1785–90)
Henry James Pye (1745–1813; laureate 1790–1813)

Robert Southey (1774–1843; laureate 1813–43)
William Wordsworth (1770–1850; laureate 1843–50)
Alfred, Lord Tennyson (1809–92; laureate 1850–92)
    (Appointed after Samuel Russell declined the offer)
Alfred Austin (1835–1913; laureate 1896–1913)
Robert Bridges (1844–1930; laureate 1913–30)
John Masefield (1878–1967; laureate 1930–67)
Cecil Day-Lewis (1904–72; laureate 1968–72)
Sir John Betjeman (1906– ; laureate 1972–   )

Pulitzer Prizes
(*See* Pulitzer Prizes)

1918 *Love Songs*, Sara Teasdale	1924 *New Hampshire: A Poem with Notes and Grace Notes*, Robert Frost
1919 *Corn Huskers*, Carl Sandburg *Old Road to Paradise*, Margaret Widdemer	1925 *The Man Who Died Twice*, Edwin Arlington Robinson
1920 No award	1926 *What's O'Clock*, Amy Lowell
1921 No award	1927 *Fiddler's Farewell*, Leonora Speyer
1922 *Collected Poems*, Edwin Arlington Robinson	1928 *Tristram*, Edwin Arlington Robinson
1923 *The Ballad of the Harp-Weaver; A Few Figs from Thistles;* eight sonnets in *American Poetry, 1922, A Miscellany*, Edna St. Vincent Millay	1929 *John Brown's Body*, Stephen Vincent Benet
	1930 *Selected Poems*, Conrad Aiken

1931	*Collected Poems*, Robert Frost	1956	*Poems – North & South*, Elizabeth Bishop
1932	*The Flowering Stone*, George Dillon	1957	*Things of This World*, Richard Wilbur
1933	*Conquistador*, Archibald MacLeish	1958	*Promises: Poems 1954–56*, Robert Penn Warren
1934	*Collected Verse*, Robert Hillyer	1959	*Selected Poems 1928–1958*, Stanley Kunitz
1935	*Bright Ambush*, Audrey Wurdemann	1960	*Heart's Needle*, W. D. Snodgrass
1936	*Strange Holiness*, R. P. Tristram Coffin	1961	*Times Three: Selected Verse from Three Decades*, Phyllis McGinley
1937	*A Further Range*, Robert Frost		
1938	*Cold Morning Sky*, Marya Zaturenska	1962	*Poems*, Alan Dugan
1939	*Selected Poems*, John Gould Fletcher	1963	*Pictures from Breughel*, William Carlos Williams
1940	*Collected Poems*, Mark Van Doren	1964	*At the End of the Open Road*, Louis Simpson
1941	*Sunderland Capture*, Leonard Bacon	1965	*77 Dream Songs*, John Berryman
1942	*The Dust Which is God*, William Benet	1966	*Selected Poems*, Richard Eberhart
1943	*A Witness Tree*, Robert Frost	1967	*Live or Die*, Anne Sexton
1944	*Western Star*, Stephen Vincent Benet	1968	*The Hard Hours*, Anthony Hecht
1945	*V-Letter and Other Poems*, Karl Shapiro	1969	*Of Being Numerous*, George Oppen
1946	No award	1970	*Untitled Subjects*, Richard Howard
1947	*Lord Weary's Castle*, Robert Lowell	1971	*The Carrier of Ladders*, W. S. Merwin
1948	*The Age of Anxiety*, W. H. Auden	1972	*Collected Poems*, James Wright
1949	*Terror and Decorum*, Peter Viereck	1973	*Up Country*, Maxine Winokur Kumin
1950	*Annie Allen*, Gwendolyn Brooks	1974	*The Dolphin*, Robert Lowell
1951	*Complete Poems*, Carl Sandburg	1975	*Turtle Island*, Gary Snyder
1952	*Collected Poems*, Marianne Moore	1976	*Self-Portrait in a Convex Mirror*, John Ashbery
1953	*Collected Poems 1917–1952*, Archibald MacLeish	1977	*Divine Comedies*, James Merrill
1954	*The Waking*, Theodore Roethke	1978	*Collected Poems*, Howard Nemerov
1955	*Collected Poems*, Wallace Stevens		

POPULARITY

Each year at the Madam Tussaud's wax museums in London and Amsterdam a questionnaire is handed out to visitors to discover their favourite heroes and heroines. Full lists are available from Madam Tussaud's, and recent results appear below.

POLITICS

1973
1 Dr Kissinger
2 Mrs Meir
3 Sir Robert Menzies
4 Richard Nixon
5 Edward Heath

1974
1 Dr Kissinger
2 Edward Heath
3 Jeremy Thorpe
  Enoch Powell
5 Richard Nixon

1975
1 Dr Kissinger
2 Amin
3 Harold Wilson
4 Edward Heath
5 Enoch Powell

1976
1 Churchill
  J. F. Kennedy
3 Edward Heath
  Dr Kissinger
5 Mrs Thatcher

1977
1 Mrs Thatcher
2 Jimmy Carter

3 Edward Heath
4 Sir Harold Wilson
5 Denis Healey

1978
1 Jimmy Carter
2 Mrs Thatcher
3 Sadat
  Churchill
5 Edward Heath

SPORTING FAVOURITES

1973
1 Pele
2 Yvonne Goolagong
3 Billie Jean King
4 George Best
5 Joe Namath

1974
1 Muhammad Ali
2 Pele
3 John Conteh
  Barry John
5 Babe Ruth

1975
1 Muhammad Ali
2 Bjorn Borg
3 Arthur Ashe
4 Ilie Nastase

5 Gary Player

1976
1 Kevin Keegan
2 Muhammad Ali
3 Johann Cruyff
4 Pele
  James Hunt

1977
1 Kevin Keegan
2 Virginia Wade
3 Bjorn Borg
4 Pele
5 Ilie Nastase

1978
1 Muhammad Ali
2 Pele
3 Kevin Keegan
4 Bjorn Borg
5 Ilie Nastase

ENTERTAINMENT

1973
1 Tom Jones
2 Woody Allen
3 Frank Sinatra
4 Julie Andrews
5 Richard Burton

1974
1 Charlie Chaplin
  Morecambe and Wise
3 Elton John
  Sammy Davis Jnr
  Frank Sinatra

1975
1 Morecambe and Wise
2 Frank Sinatra
3 Elton John
4 Liza Minnelli
5 Benny Hill

1976
1 Liza Minnelli
2 Mike Yarwood
3 Dave Allen
4 Frank Sinatra
5 Elton John

1977
1 Elton John
2 Two Ronnies
3 Morecambe and Wise
4 Liza Minnelli
5 Bruce Forsyth

1978
1 Bruce Forsyth
2 Elton John

3   Charlie Chaplin
    Liza Minnelli
5   Frank Sinatra

ARTS

1973
1   Picasso
2   Nureyev
3   Leonard Bernstein
4   Salvador Dali
5   Rembrandt

1974
1   Picasso
2   Nureyev
3   van Gogh
    Salvador Dali
    Margot Fonteyn

1975
1   Picasso
2   Margot Fonteyn
3   Salvador Dali
4   Nureyev
5   van Gogh

1976
1   Picasso
2   Rembrandt
3   Salvador Dali
    Margot Fonteyn
    Leonardo da Vinci

1977
1   Picasso
2   Nureyev
3   André Previn
4   Margot Fonteyn
5   Elton John

The wax portrait of Hitler at Madame Tussaud's in London. He was voted the most hated and feared person in 1974, 1975, 1976 and 1978

1978
1   Picasso
2   Margot Fonteyn
3   Salvador Dali
    Rembrandt
5   Nureyev

BEAUTY

1973
1   Sophia Loren
2   Elizabeth Taylor
3   Raquel Welch
4   Brigitte Bardot
5   Princess Grace

1974
1   Sophia Loren
2   Raquel Welch
3   Twiggy
    Elizabeth Taylor
    Brigitte Bardot

1975
1   Elizabeth Taylor
2   Sophia Loren
3   Raquel Welch
4   Twiggy
5   Brigitte Bardot

1976
1   Twiggy
2   Brigitte Bardot
3   Marilyn Monroe
4   Elizabeth Taylor
5   Raquel Welch

1977
1   Brigitte Bardot

2   Sophia Loren
3   Twiggy
4   Marilyn Monroe
5   F. Fawcett-Majors

1978
1   Sophia Loren
    Marilyn Monroe
    Elizabeth Taylor
4   Liza Minnelli
5   Raquel Welch

HATE AND FEAR

1973
1   Richard Nixon
2   Hitler
3   Jack the Ripper
4   Dayan
5   Gadaffi

1974
1   Hitler
2   Harold Wilson
3   Richard Nixon
4   Jack the Ripper
5   Dracula

1975
1   Hitler
2   General Amin
3   Dracula
4   Richard Nixon
5   Jack the Ripper

1976
1   Hitler
2   General Amin
3   Christie
4   Jimmy Carter
    Dracula

1977
1   General Amin
2   Hitler
3   Dracula
4   Dr Crippen
5   Denis Healey

1978
1   Hitler
2   General Amin
3   Mrs Thatcher
4   Dracula
5   Jack the Ripper

HERO OR HEROINE IN MADAME TUSSAUD'S
1973
1   Picasso
2   Agatha Christie
3   J. F. Kennedy
4   Churchill
5   Gandhi

1974
1   Agatha Christie
2   Picasso
    Muhammad Ali
4   Charlie Chaplin
    Humphrey Bogart

1975
1   Henry VIII
2   Muhammad Ali
3   Agatha Christie
4   Gandhi
5   Picasso

1976
1   Gandhi
2   Picasso
3   Agatha Christie
4   Kevin Keegan
5   The Queen

1977
1   Gandhi
2   Kojak
3   The Queen
4   Picasso
5   Henry VIII

1978
1   Agatha Christie
2   Kojak
3   Elton John
4   Elvis Presley
5   The Queen

HERO OR HEROINE OF ALL TIME

1973
1   Jesus
2   Churchill
3   J. F. Kennedy
4   Joan of Arc
5   Dayan

1974
1   Churchill
    Nelson
    Florence Nightingale
4   Joan of Arc
5   J. F. Kennedy

1975
1   Churchill
2   J. F. Kennedy
3   Joan of Arc
4   Robin Hood
5   Napoleon

1976
1   Joan of Arc
2   Churchill
3   Jesus
    J. F. Kennedy
    Nelson

1977		**1978**	
1	Elvis Presley	1	Churchill
2	Churchill		Superman
3	Nelson	3	Muhammad Ali
4	Florence Nightingale	4	Nelson
5	J. F. Kennedy		J. F. Kennedy

PUBLISHERS

Publisher of the Year

The Booksellers' Association instituted this award in 1979. The winner is chosen through a poll of the Association's 3150 members, who are asked to nominate candidates for the award on the basis of four criteria: editorial quality, terms and conditions, distribution (including accuracy of invoicing, returns policy, etc.), and promotion and publicity. This will be an annual award. The winner in 1979 was Thames & Hudson.

PUBS

The 'Evening Standard' 'Pub of the Year

The London *Evening Standard* has organised this annual competition since 1967 to find the best pub in London. The judges are sent to inspect all the pubs nominated by readers, and the winning landlord, his wife and the nominator all get a free holiday. In 1978–79 these prizes were given by Olympic Holidays and Singapore Airlines.

1967	The Red Lion, Brentford (Fullers)	1973	Pied Bull, Streatham (Youngs)
	The White Hart, Newenden (Courage)	1974	Flask, Highgate (Ind Coope)
1968	The Jolly Millers, Bexleyheath (Charrington)	1975	Greyhound, Kensington Square (Watneys)
	The Swan, West Peckham (Courage)	1976	Orange Tree, Richmond (Youngs)
1969	The White Lion, Selling (Shepherd Neame)	1977	The Angel, Bermondsey (Courage)
1970	The Rose and Crown, Wimbledon (Youngs)		(River Pub of the Year – Jubilee Year)
1971	Duke of Cumberland, Parsons Green (Youngs)	1978	The Old Ship, Hammersmith (Watneys)
1972	The Victoria, Bermondsey (Trumans)		

PULITZER PRIZES

The Pulitzer Prizes are the most prestigious awards made each year in the United States for journalism, literature, and music. The prizes are established under the terms of the will of Joseph Pulitzer (1847–1911), a Hungarian immigrant who in 1878 founded one of America's great newspapers, the *St. Louis Post-Dispatch*, and then in 1883 purchased New York City's *The World*, making it into a crusading newspaper with the largest circulation in the United States.

Upon his death in 1911, Pulitzer left $2 million to found a graduate school of journalism at Columbia University in New York City with the provision that after the school had operated for at least three years prizes should be awarded annually for the advancement of journalism, literature, music, and public service. The Columbia University School of Journalism was founded in 1912. The first Pulitzer Prizes began to be awarded in 1917.

Each prize carries an award of $1000 except for the gold medal award to a newspaper for meritorious public service.

Prizes in journalism are awarded in 11 categories. Prizes in literature, drama, and music are awarded in seven areas. In addition, special awards are made from time to time. (For further details see entries under Journalism, Literature, Music and Poetry.)

PURCHASING

Buyer of the Year

This event was started in 1977 to give a boost to the purchasing function and to promote awareness of the range of economies which can be achieved if greater priority is given to controlling the activities of buying departments and to their monitoring by senior management. Sponsored by the Ravensdown Metals Group and the magazine *Modern Purchasing*, the competition begins with a series of written questions concerning aspects of a buyer's business that he or she might face at any time. Three qualifying rounds whittle down the number to six finalists who then have a face-to-face confrontation with the judges.

WINNERS

1977
Paul Walker, 24, senior section buyer for 3½ years, married, from Belfast. Buyer for Short Bros. and Harland, Belfast aircraft manufacturers.

1978
Geoffrey Collier, Purchasing Manager, Diversey, Northampton.

1979
John B. A. Beck, Engineering Buyer, Imperial Chemical Industries, London

QUIZ

Brain of Britain

BBC Radio organises this annual nationwide general knowledge quiz. The winners have been:

1953–54	Martin Dakin	1963	Ian Barton
1955	Arthur Maddocks	1964	Ian Gillies
1956	Anthony Carr	1965	Robert Crampsey
1957	Rosemary Watson	1966	Richard Best
1958	David Keys	1967	Lieut.-Commander Julian Loring
1959	Dr Reginald Webster	1968	Ralph Raby
1960	Patrick Bowles	1969	T. D. Thomson
1961	Irene Thomas	1970	Iain Matheson
1962	Henry Button	1971	Fred Morgan

Dr Roger Pritchard was the 1974 Brain of Britain. He won the final of BBC Radio 4's nationwide contest by a single vote. *Left to right:* **Bill Bent, Philip Hardingham, Group Captain David Rhodes, and Dr Roger Pritchard** (*BBC Copyright*)

1972	Aubrey Lawrence
1973	Dr Glyn Court
1974	Dr Roger Pritchard
1975	Winifred Lawson
1976	Thomas Dyer
1977	Martin Costelow
1978	James Nesbitt

BRAIN OF BRAINS

This is competed for every three years.

1956	Anthony Carr	1968	Ralph Raby
1959	Dr Reginald Webster	1971	Iain Matheson
1962	Irene Thomas	1974	Dr Roger Pritchard
1965	Ian Gillies	1977	Thomas Dyer

Brain of Sport

'Brain of Sport' is transmitted on BBC Radio 2, and the first competition in the series was held in 1975.

The competition is open to anyone in the UK over the age of 16. All applicants are required to take part in an eliminating test and the 24 contestants with the highest marks take part in the quiz.

The 'Brain of Sport' since the start of the programmes have been as follows:

| 1975 | Patricia Arthur | 1977 | David Ball |
| 1976 | Paul Hewett | 1978 | Julian Pincher |

Mastermind

This popular competition is organised each year by BBC Television. The entrants answer detailed questions on a special subject of their own choice, and then face further questions on general knowledge. If unsure of an answer the competitor may 'pass', rather than lose time whilst the compère Magnus Magnusson corrects a mistake. The top scorers in each round go forward to the semi-finals and finals, and the eventual winner is awarded the Mastermind trophy. Winners since the competition began:

1972	Nancy Wilkinson
1973	Patricia Owen
1974	Elizabeth Horrocks
1975	John Hart
1976	Roger Pritchard
1977	Sir David Hunt
1978	Rosemary James

Supermind winners since the competition began:

1975	Nancy Wilkinson (1972 Mastermind)
1976	Walter Dobson (1976 Brain of Mensa)
1977	David Shenkin (1977 Brain of Mensa)
	Not held since

Sir David Hunt receiving the specially created Caithness Glass Trophy from Bill Cotton (*left*), controller of BBC 1, after his victory in the 1977 Mastermind finals. With them is Magnus Magnusson. Sir David's score of 37 was the highest ever recorded at that time in a final. (*BBC Copyright*)

Mastermind International

The British competition has been copied in many countries round the world, and in 1978 the winners were:

Australia: John Bond	Ireland ('Top Score' Winner): John Mulcahy
New Zealand: Mark Allan	Canada ('$128,000 Quiz' winner): Barbara Eddy
Nigeria: Godwin Anaba	

In 1979 all these winners, together with Rosemary James, the UK Mastermind, and Sir David Hunt, winner of the 'Jubilee Mastermind', took part in the first International Mastermind competition. The specialist subjects chosen included: the Life and Works of Shakespeare; Egypt and the Sudan; Bushranging; Rock Music; Norse Mythology; Irish History; and the Roman Revolution.

The winner was John Mulcahy from Ireland.

Top of The Form

One of BBC Radio's long-established and popular annual competitions for teams of children representing secondary schools throughout the country. The teams, each made up of four members with ages ranging from 11 to 18, are tested on general knowledge. The winners have been:

1948	Royal High School, Edinburgh	1964	The Academy, Montrose
1949	Elgin Academy, Scotland	1965	The High School, Falkirk
1950	Robert Gordon's College, Aberdeen	1966	St Martin-in-the-Fields High School, London
1951	Morgan Academy, Dundee	1967	Greenock Academy
1952	Bangor Grammar School, North Wales	1968	Grove Park School, Wrexham
1953	Nicholson Institute, Stornoway	1969	Queen Elizabeth Grammar School for Girls, Carmarthen
1954	Grove Park School, Wrexham		
1955	Newtown Girls' County Grammar School, Wales	1970	Wyggeston Boys' School, Leicester
1956	Sutton Coldfield High School	1971	Cheadle Hulme School, Cheadle, Cheshire
1957	Wycombe High School for Girls, High Wycombe	1972	The County Girls' Grammar School, Newbury
1958	Gordon Schools, Huntly, Aberdeenshire	1973	Kirkcudbright Academy, Kirkcudbright
1959	Mackie Academy, Stonehaven, Kincardine	1974	The Grammar School, Cheltenham
1960	Grove Park Grammar School for Girls, Wrexham	1975	King William's College, Isle of Man
1961	Archbishop Holgate's Grammar School, York	1976	County High School for Girls, Macclesfield
1962	Hull Grammar School	1977	Wellington School, Somerset
1963	Cambridgeshire High School for Boys, Cambridge	1978	Brinkburn School, Hartlepool

University Challenge

Granada Television has organised since 1964 this competition between teams from British universities, which calls for a very detailed and wide general knowledge and speed in answering the questions put by compère, Bamber Gascoigne. Each year there is a final knock-out competition between all the teams who have won three games. The winners are:

1964	Leicester University	1969	University of Sussex	1974	Trinity College, Cambridge
1965	New College, Oxford	1970	Churchill College, Cambridge	1975	Keble College, Oxford
1966	Oriel College, Oxford	1971	Sidney Sussex College, Cambridge	1976	University College, Oxford
1967	University of Sussex	1972	University College, Oxford	1977	University of Durham
1968	Keble College, Oxford	1973	Fitzwilliam College, Cambridge	1978	Sidney Sussex College, Cambridge

Members of the 1978 University Challenge Champion Team from Sidney Sussex College, Cambridge represented the UK in the second World Championship between student quiz teams, when they met a team from Davidson College, North Carolina—current American 'College Bowl' champions. Winners of the contest were the UK team—by 215 points to 210 (Granada Television)

RACING (*See* Horse Racing)

RACKETS

World Championships

The first recognised World Champion was Robert Mackay in 1820, since when champions have been:

1820	Robert Mackay (GB)	1878–87	Joseph Gray (GB)
1825–34	Thomas Pittman (GB)	1887–1902	Peter Latham (GB)
1834–38	John Pittman (GB)	1903–11	J. Jamsetji (Ind)
1838–46	John Lamb (GB)	1911–14	Charles Williams (GB)
1846–60	L. C. Mitchell (GB)	1914–28	Jock Souter (USA)
1860	Francis Erwood (GB)	1928–35	Charles Williams (GB)
1860–63	Sir William Hart-Dyke (GB)	1937–47	David Milford (GB)
1863–66	Henry Gray (GB)	1947–52	James Dear (GB)
1866–75	William Gray (GB)	1952–71	Geoffrey Atkins (GB)
1876–77	H. B. Fairs (GB)	1972–	William Surtees (USA)

RADIO

Miscellaneous Awards in the 1970s

1973
Brno Radio Prize: The Dance of Albion, BBC

1974
Italia Prize, Best Radio Play: The Pump, by James Cameron (BBC)

Japan Prize, Jury Prize: Everything New, a radiovision schools programme in the series Stories and Rhymes (BBC)

Radio Industries Club of Scotland, Radio Personality of the Year: Mary Marquis

Ivor Novello Award: Made in Britain

Hungarian Radio's Pro Musica Competition: Summertime on Bredon won first prize

ITT Creed Award: Chris Denham, BBC Radio Bristol, for his reporting of the Basle air disaster

Nordring Radio Festival, Holland, Top Arranger's Prize: Les Reed, BBC

Slovene Song Festival, Ljubljana, Grand Prix winning song: sung by Frank Ifield, entered by the BBC

Billboard International Country Music Awards, Programme of the Year: Country Club.

1975
Italia Prize, Guy Vaesen's production of Bill Naughton's play, The Mystery, won the Italia Prize for radio drama

Radio Industries Club of Scotland, New Personality of the year: Anne Lorne Gillies

Nordring Radio Prize, Holland: All three prizes went to the BBC Radio 2 production, A Tourist View of Britain, David Rayvern Allen winning the producer's prize, Robert Farnon the arranger's prize and Rita Morris the performer's prize

The Prix Jean-Antoine Variété Trophy, Monte Carlo: London by Music, produced by Derek Mills.

The Prix Musical de Radio Brno, Czechoslovakia: The English Renascence, produced by Elaine Padmore.

1976
UNDA International Festival of Religious Broadcasting: Awards won by the People's Service for Easter Day (broadcast on BBC, Radio 2) and by BBC Radio Manchester in the category of religious songs.

Music Trade Association: Award for the best speech record for 1975 went to the BBC in association with Argo for T. S. Eliot read by Alec Guinness

The British Racing and Sports Car Club: The Roy James Trophy for the most significant contribution to the furtherance of motor sport went to Radio Sport. The same department also won the Lombard-RAC Trophy for the most outstanding coverage of the RAC Rally

Awards for Local Radio: BBC Radio Medway won the Conoco Jet Trophy for its motoring programme, Wheels; Dhramendra Gautam, one of the presenters of BBC Radio London's Hindi/Urdu programme Jharoka was presented with the Sikh Siropa for his services in improving community relations in the London Borough of Ealing; Susan Davis of BBC Radio Stoke was runner-up in the ITT Creed competition for local radio journalists and also gained second place in the Catherine Pakenham Memorial Award Contest for women journalists

1977
The Japan Prize, The Minister of Education Prize went to The Deep Blue Sea, a BBC Schools programme produced by John Parry

The Governor of Tokyo Prize went to The Handicapped Person in the Community, an Open University BBC programme produced by Donald Holms

UNDA International Festival of Religious Broadcasting Category A: BBC Radio Medway won first prize with A

Question of Obedience by Father Wilfried McGreal, produced by Father Patrick O'Leary

Category B: Radio London came joint first with Underneath the Arches, produced by Owen Spencer Thomas

Category C: Radio Leeds came first with a song called And Then You Came by Mrs Christine Bovim

Awards for Local Radio:

Sue Davies of Radio Stoke on Trent was named ITT Creed Local Radio Journalist of the Year

Tony Adamson of Radio Oxford was chosen by the Country Music Association (Great Britain) Ltd as Country Music DJ of the Year

1978

Festival of Wales Trophy Awards: BBC Wales was awarded a Certificate of Special Commendation for extending the appreciation of Wales and enhancing its prestige in other countries

Overseas Festival Awards, Slovene Song Festival at Celje, Yugoslavia – Vince Hill, BBC. Nordring Festival, Copenhagen: the BBC representative, Keeley Ford, won the soloist's prize

Awards for Local Radio:

Geoff Griffiths, presenter of First Thing on Radio Newcastle, won the *Newcastle Journal* award for Disc Jockey of the Year, 1977–78

The Publicity Association of Leicester awarded Radio Leicester the City and County Publicity Achievement Award for 1977

Radio London won three out of the first five places in *Black Echoes* magazine's national poll. The first prize went to Robbie Vincent for his Saturday Show, the third to David Simmons for Soul 77, and the fourth to the programme Reggae Time

Radio Music Shows and Disc Jockeys

(*See also* Disc Jockeys)

Tony Blackburn was voted top Radio 1 DJ in a *Reveille* **poll in both 1974 and 1975**

1974

Polls in the *New Musical Express, Melody Maker* and *Sounds* voted BBC Radio I's 'Sounds of the 70s' as the top radio programme. Polls in *Disc* and *Record Mirror* voted the 'Noel Edmonds show' on Radio I the top radio show, and they also voted Noel Edmonds the top DJ. A *Reveille* poll voted Tony Blackburn the top Radio 1 DJ and Terry Wogan top Radio 2 DJ. Polls in the *New Musical Express* and *Melody Maker* voted John Peel as top DJ.

1975

Noel Edmonds was voted top DJ by polls in the *New Musical Express* and *Record Mirror*, and won the Carl Alan award. Polls in *Disc* and the *Melody Maker* voted John Peel the top DJ. Polls in *Disc, Melody Maker, New Musical Express* and *Sounds* voted the Alan Freeman Show the top BBC Radio 1 show. A poll in the *Record Mirror* voted the Noel Edmonds show the top Radio 1 show. Polls in *Reveille* voted Tony Blackburn the top Radio 1 DJ, Terry Wogan the top Radio 2 DJ and Open House the favourite Radio 1 and 2 programme

1976

Noel Edmonds was voted top DJ by readers of the *Sun* newspaper and the *Record Mirror*, and he also won the Carl Alan award for the second year running. John Peel was voted top DJ by polls in the *Melody Maker*, the *New Musical Express* and *Sounds*. Alan Freeman's Saturday afternoon programme on BBC Radio I was voted top radio show by readers of the *Melody Maker* and the *New Musical Express*; Johnnie Walker was given an award as top international DJ at a *Billboard* forum in New York.

1977

Noel Edmonds was voted top DJ in *Daily Mirror* and *Record Mirror* polls. He also won the Carl Alan Award for the third year running. John Peel was voted top DJ and Alan Freeman's Saturday Show the top show in both the *Melody Maker* and the *New Musical Express*. Readers of *Sounds* also voted for Alan Freeman's programme as the top radio show.

1978
John Peel was voted top DJ for the 10th year running by readers of *Melody Maker*, readers of *Sounds* and readers

of *New Musical Express*, who also voted his the top radio show. Alan Freeman's show was voted the top radio show by readers of *Melody Maker*; David Allen won the DJ of the Year Award for the best Network Country Music Show (Country Club Radio 2) given by the Country Music Association of Great Britain; Terry Wogan won a Carl Alan Award. Noel Edmonds won the Carl Alan Award for the fourth year running.

The Radio Industries Club Awards
Recent prizewinners include:

RADIO PERSONALITY OF THE YEAR
1972   John Dunn
1973   Pete Murray
1974   Robert Robinson
1975   Terry Wogan
1976   Pete Murray
1977   Terry Wogan
1978   Terry Wogan

RADIO PROGRAMME OF THE YEAR
1972   Today, BBC Radio 4
1973   Today, BBC Radio 4
1974   Today, BBC Radio 4
1975   Today, BBC Radio 4
1976   The World At One, BBC Radio 4
1977   Today, BBC Radio 4
1978   Noel Edmonds' Breakfast Show, BBC Radio 1

RAILWAYS

London Transport's Top Stations and Underground Proficiency Awards

In 1977 and 1978 fifteen London Transport Underground stations won awards for their proficiency and general high standards. Top honours went to Victoria and Golders Green stations, which have been among the winners four times in the last six years.

In addition to marks for the standard of service to the public, account is taken of commendations to staff from passengers, economy in the use of stores, and the condition of equipment. Marks are deducted for public complaints and for delays caused by the actions of station staff.

All station staff at winning stations receive a small cash payment and a framed certificate is displayed in the station booking hall for a year. The award-winning stations are:

1977
Acton Town
Becontree
Belsize Park
Eastcote
Golders Green
Hanger Lane
Holland Park
Leyton
Northwood Hills
Osterley

Paddington
   (Metropolitan Line)
Royal Oak
Upney
Victoria
Walthamstow Central

1978
Burnt Oak
Chancery Lane
East Acton

Edgware
Finsbury Park
Heathrow Central
Moor Park
Russell Square
St John's Wood
St Paul's
Stepney Green
Trafalgar Square
Walthamstow Central
Willesden Green
Wood Green

BEST UNDERGROUND STATION GARDEN
1977   Devdatt Sethi, Rayners Lane Station
1978   Fred Pearce, Totteridge

RALLYING

Monte Carlo Rally

The world's most famous car rally event is held annually, the drivers converging on Monte Carlo from all over Europe.

MONTE CARLO RALLY

Year	Driver	Car
1911	Henri Rougier	Turcat-Mery 25hp
1912	J. Beutler	Berliet 16hp
1924	Jean Ledure	Bignan 2 litre
1925	Francois Repusseau	Renault 40 CV
1926	Hon Victor Bruce	AC Bristol
1927	Lefebvre	Amilcar 1100cc
1928	Jacques Bignan	Fiat 990cc
1929	Dr Sprenger Van Eijk	Graham-Paige 4.7 litre
1930	Hector Petit	Licorne 904cc
1931	Donald Healey	Invicta 4.5 litre
1932	M. Vasselle	Hotchkiss 2.5 litre
1933	M. Vasselle	Hotchkiss 3.5 litre
1934	Gas	Hotchkiss 3.5 litre
1935	Christian Lahaye	Renault Nervasport 5.6 litre
1936	I. Zamfirescu	Ford 3.6 litre
1937	René le Begue	Delahaye 3.6 litre
1938	Bakker Schut	Ford 3.6 litre
1939	{ Jean Trevoux	Hotchkiss 3.5 litre
	{ Paul	Delahaye 3.6 litre
1949	Jean Trevoux	Hotchkiss 3.5 litre
1950	Marcel Becquart	Hotchkiss 3.5 litre
1951	Jean Trevoux	Delahaye 4.6 litre
1952	Sidney Allard	Allard P2 4.4 litre
1953	Maurice Gatsonides	Ford Zephyr 2.3 litre
1954	Louis Chiron	Lancia-Aurelia 2.5 litre
1955	Per Malling	Sunbeam-Talbot 2.3 litre
1956	Ronnie Adams	Jaguar Mk VII 3.4 litre
1957	No rally held due to Suez Crisis	
1958	Guy Monraisse	Renault Dauphine 845cc
1959	Paul Coltelloni	Citroen ID 19 1.9 litre
1960	Walter Schock	Mercedes 220 SE
1961	Maurice Martin	Panhard PL17 848cc
1962	Erik Carlsson/Gunnar Haggbom	Saab 96 848cc
1963	Erik Carlsson/Gunnar Palm	Saab 96 848cc
1964	Paddy Hopkirk/Henry Liddon	Mini-Cooper 'S' 1071cc
1965	Timo Makinen/Paul Easter	Mini-Cooper 'S' 1275cc
1966	Pauli Toivonen/Ensio Mikander	Citroen DS 21
1967	Rauno Aaltonen/Henry Liddon	Mini-Cooper 'S' 1275cc
1968	Vic Elford/David Stone	Porsche 911T
1969	Bjorn Waldegaard/Lars Helmer	Porsche 911
1970	Bjorn Waldegaard/Lars Helmer	Porsche 911 S
1971	Ove Andersson/David Stone	Alpine Renault A110
1972	Sandro Munari/Mario Manucci	Lancia Fulvia 1.6
1973	Jean-Claude Andruet/'Biche'	Alpine Renault A110
1974	No rally due to fuel crisis	
1975	Sandro Munari/Mario Manucci	Lancia Stratos
1976	Sandro Munari/Silvio Maiga	Lancia Stratos
1977	Sandro Munari/Mario Manucci	Lancia Stratos
1978	Jean-Pierre Nicolas/Vincent Laverne	Porsche Carrera
1979	Bernard Darniche/Alain Mahe	Lancia Stratos

(Co-drivers names included after 1962 when special stages and pace notes used for first time)

World Rallying Championship

For makes of car.

Year	Make	Year	Make
1968	Ford GB	1974	Lancia
1969	Ford Europe	1975	Lancia
1970	Porsche	1976	Lancia
1971	Renault Alpine	1977	Fiat
1972	Lancia	1978	Fiat
1973	Renault Alpine		

RAC International Rally of Great Britain

The first RAC Rally was held in 1927, and in 1951 this event was recognised by the Fédération International de l'Automobile as of international status. Since then the winning drivers and cars have been:

1951	Ian Appleyard	Jaguar XK	1965	Rauno Aaltonen	Mini Cooper S 1275
1952	Goff Imhof	Cadillac-Allard	1966	Bengt Soderstrom	Ford Cortina Lotus
1953	Ian Appleyard	Jaguar XK	1967	*Rally cancelled owing to foot and mouth epidemic*	
1954	Johnny Wallwork	Triumph	1968	Simo Lampinen	Saab 96 V4
1955	Jimmy Ray	Standard	1969	Harry Kallstrom	Lancia Fulvia
1956	Lyndon Sims	Aston-Martin	1970	Harry Kallstrom	Lancia Fulvia
1957	*Rally cancelled owing to petrol rationing*		1971	Stig Blomqvist	Saab 96 V4
1958	Peter Harper	Sunbeam Rapier	1972	Roger Clark	Ford Escort
1959	Gerry Burgess	Ford Zephyr	1973	Timo Mäkinen	Ford Escort
1960	Erik Carlsson	Saab 96	1974	Timo Mäkinen	Ford Escort
1961	Erik Carlsson	Saab 96	1975	Timo Mäkinen	Ford Escort
1962	Erik Carlsson	Saab 96	1976	Roger Clark	Ford Escort
1963	Tom Trana	Volvo PV 544	1977	Bjorn Waldegaard	Ford Escort
1964	Tom Trana	Volvo 122 S	1978	Hannu Mikkola	Ford Escort

REAL TENNIS

World Championship

The list of world champions at Real Tennis extends further back than just about any sport, as it begins with Clergé of France in 1740. Since then:

1765–85	Raymond Masson (Fra)	1908–12	Cecil Fairs (GB)
1785–1816	Joseph Barcellon (Fra)	1912–14	George Covey (GB)
1816–19	Marchesio (Ita)	1914–16	Jay Gould (USA)
1819–29	Philip Cox (GB)	1916–28	George Covey (GB)
1829–62	Edmond Barre (Fra)	1928–55	Pierre Etchebaster (Fra)
1862–71	Edmund Tomkins (GB)	1955–57	James Dear (GB)
1871–85	George Lambert (GB)	1957–59	Albert Johnson (GB)
1885–90	Tom Pettitt (USA)	1959–69	Northrup Knox (USA)
1890–95	Charles Saunders (GB)	1969–72	George 'Pete' Bostwick (USA)
1895–1905	Peter Latham (GB)	1972–75	Jimmy Bostwick (USA)
1905–07	Cecil Fairs (GB)	1976–	Howard Angus (GB)
1907–08	Peter Latham (GB)		

REFERENDA

Common Market

The first national referendum ever held in the UK took place on 5 June 1975. It was held to decide whether Britain should remain in the Common Market (the European Economic Community). The voters were asked the simple question 'Do you think that the United Kingdom should stay in the European Economic Community?'

The voting was as follows:

'Yes' votes 17 378 581 (67.2 per cent)
'No' votes 8 470 073 (32.8 per cent)

The only two areas of the country to say 'No' were the Shetland Isles and the Western Isles.

Devolution

On 1 March 1979 the voters of Scotland and Wales went to the polls over the question of the establishment of assemblies for Scotland and Wales. The results were as follows:

'Yes' votes, Scotland 1 230 937 (32.85 per cent)   'No' votes, Scotland 1 153 502 (30.78 per cent)
          Wales   243 048 (11.9 per cent)   Wales   956 330 (46.9 per cent)

Not voting, Scotland 36.37 per cent
           Wales   41.2 per cent

RESTAURANTS

Egon Ronay Restaurant of the Year

The premier award in Britain for the best restaurant, given by the famous gourmet and critic.

1969 Thornbury Castle, Thornbury (Avon)	1974 Shezan, London SW7
1970 Le Poulbot, London EC2	1975 Wilton's, London SW1
1971 Box Tree Cottage, Ilkley (West Yorkshire)	1976 Horn of Plenty, Gulworthy (Devon)
1972 Le Gavroche, London SW1	1977 Carrier's, Islington, London N1
1973 Kildwick Hall, Kildwick (West Yorkshire)	1978 McCoy's Restaurant, Staddle Bridge (Yorkshire)

RODEO

Professional Rodeo Cowboys Association All-round Champions

The title goes to the biggest money winner in America in two or more events. Winners since 1960:

1960	Harry Tompkins	$32 522
1961	Benny Reynolds	$31 309
1962	Tom Nesmith	$32 611
1963	Dean Oliver	$31 329
1964	Dean Oliver	$31 150
1965	Dean Oliver	$33 163
1966	Larry Mahan	$40 358
1967	Larry Mahan	$51 996
1968	Larry Mahan	$49 129
1969	Larry Mahan	$57 726
1970	Larry Mahan	$41 493
1971	Phil Lyne	$49 245
1972	Phil Lyne	$60 852
1973	Larry Mahan	$64 447
1974	Tom Ferguson	$66 929
1975	Leo Camarillo	$50 830
1976	Tom Ferguson	$87 908
1977	Tom Ferguson	$100 080
1978	Tom Ferguson	$128 434

Larry Mahan, from Brooks, Oregon, won a record six All-round Rodeo Cowboys world championships (*Jack de Lorme*)

There are also champions in the individual events of calf roping, steer wrestling, saddle bronc riding, bull riding, bareback riding and team riding.

ROLLER SKATING

World Champions

World Championships were first held in 1947. Just as in Ice Skating both speed skating and figure skating events are held.

FIGURE SKATING

Men

Winners since 1972:

1972 Michael Obrecht (Ger)
1973 Randy Dayney (USA)
1974 Michael Obrecht (Ger)
1975 Leonardo Lienhard (Swi)
1976 Thomas Nieder (Ger)
1977 Thomas Nieder (Ger)
1978 Thomas Nieder (Ger)

Most titles: 5 Karl-Heinz Losch (Ger) 1958, 1959, 1961, 1962, 1966

Women

Winners since 1972:

1972 Petra Hausler (Ger)
1973 Sigrid Mullenbach (Ger)
1974 Sigrid Mullenbach (Ger)
1975 Sigrid Mullenbach (Ger)
1976 Natalie Dunn (USA)
1977 Natalie Dunn (USA)
1978 Natalie Dunn (USA)

Most titles: 4 Astrid Bader (Ger) 1965–68

Pairs

Winners since 1972:

1972 Ronald Robovitsky and Gail Robovitsky (USA)
1973 Louis Stovel and Vicki Handyside (USA)
1974 Ron Sabo and Susan McDonald (USA)
1975 Ron Sabo and Darlene Waters (USA)
1976 Ron Sabo and Darlene Waters (USA)
1977 Ray Chapatta and Karen Mejia (USA)
1978 Pat Jones and Rooie Coleman (USA)

Most titles: 3 Dieter Fingerle and Ute Keller (Ger) 1965–67 (Fingerle also won in 1959 with S. Schneider)

Dance

Winners since 1972:

1972 Tom Straker and Bonnie Lambert (USA)
1973 James Stephens and Jane Puracchio (USA)
1974 Udo Donsdorf and Christine Henke (Ger)
1975 Kerry Cavazzi and Jane Puracchio (USA)
1976 Kerry Cavazzi and Jane Puracchio (USA)
1977 Dan Littel and Fleurette Arsenault (USA)
1978 Dan Littel and Fleurette Arsenault (USA)

ROWING

World Championships

World Championships were first held in 1962 at Lucerne and have subsequently been held in 1966 at Bled, 1970 at St. Catherines, Canada, 1974 at Lucerne, 1975 at Nottingham, 1977 at Amsterdam and 1978 at Lake Karipiro, New Zealand. Women's world championships were first held in 1974.

Winners (*note*—in all coxed events, the name of the cox is shown last):

MEN

Single Sculls

1962 Vyacheslav Ivanov (USSR)
1966 Don Spero (USA)
1970 Alberto Demiddi (Arg)
1974 Wolfgang Honig (GDR)
1975 Peter-Michael Kolbe (Ger)
1977 Joachim Dreifke (GDR)
1978 Peter-Michael Kolbe (Ger)

Double Sculls

1962 Fra (René Duhamel and Bernard Monnereau)
1966 Swi (Melchior Buergin and Martin Studach)
1970 Den (J. Engelbrecht and N. Secher)
1974 GDR (Hans-Ulrich Schmied and Christof Kreuziger)
1975 Nor (Frank Hansen and Alf Hansen)
1977 GB (Chris Baillieu and Michael Hart)
1978 Nor (Frank Hansen and Alf Hansen)

Coxless Pairs

1962 Ger (Bander, Z. Keller)
1966 GDR (P. Kremitz, A. Göhler)
1970 Ger (W. Klatt, P. Gorniv)
1974 GDR (B. Landvoigt, J. Landvoigt)
1975 GDR (B. Landvoigt, J. Landvoigt)
1977 USSR (V. Elisev, A. Kulagine)
1978 GDR (B. Landvoigt, J. Landvoigt)

Coxed Pairs

1962 Ger (Jordan, Neuss)
1966 Hol (H. van Nes, J. van de Graaf)
1970 Rom (S. Tudor, P. Ceapura)
1974 USSR (V. Ivanov, V. Eshinov)
1975 GDR (J. Lucke, W. Gunkel, B. Fritsch)
1977 Bul (T. Mrankov, S. Yanakiev, S. Stoykov)
1978 GDR (J. Pfieffer, G. Uebeler, O. Beyer)

Coxless Fours

| 1962 | Ger | 1970 | GDR |
| 1966 | GDR | 1974 | GDR |

1975 GDR (S. Brietzke, A. Decker, S. Semmler, W. Mager)
1977 GDR (S. Brietzke, A. Decker, S. Semmler, W. Mager)
1978 USSR (V. Preobrazenski, N. Kuznyetsov, V. Dolinin, A. Nemtirjov)

Coxed Fours

1962	Ger	1970	Ger
1966	GDR	1974	GDR

1975 USSR (V. Eshiniv, N. Ivanov, A. Sema, A. Klepikov, A. Lukianov)
1977 GDR (U. Diessner, G. Döhn, W. Diessner, D. Wendisch, A. Gregor)
1978 GDR (U. Diessner, G. Döhn, W. Diessner, D. Wendisch, A. Gregor)

Quadruple Sculls

1974 GDR
1975 GDR (S. Weisse, W. Guldenpfennig, W. Hönig, C. Kreuziger)
1977 GDR (W. Guldenpfennig, K-H. Bussert, M. Winter, F. Dundr)
1978 GDR (J. Dreifke, K-H. Bussert, M. Winter, F. Dundr)

Eights

1962	Ger	1974	USA
1966	Ger	1975	GDR
1970	GDR	1977	GDR
		1978	GDR

WOMEN

Single Sculls

1974 Christine Scheiblich (GDR)
1975 Christine Scheiblich (GDR)
1977 Christine Scheiblich (GDR)
1978 Christine Hann (GDR)
      (née Scheiblich)

Double Sculls

1974 USSR (G. Yermoleyeva, E. Antonova)
1975 USSR (G. Yermoleyeva, E. Antonova)
1977 GDR (R. Zobelt, A. Borchmann)
1978 Bul (S. Olzetova, Z. Yordanova)

Coxless Pairs

1974 Rom (C. Neascu, M. Ghita)
1975 GDR (A. Noack, S. Dähne)
1977 GDR (A. Noack, S. Dähne)
1978 GDR (C. Bugel, U. Steindord)

Quadruple Sculls		**Coxed Fours**		**Eights**	
1974	GDR	1974	GDR	1974	GDR
1975	GDR	1975	GDR	1975	GDR
1977	GDR	1977	GDR	1977	GDR
1978	Bul	1978	GDR	1978	USSR

Olympic Games

Rowing has been included in each Olympic Games since 1900. Winners at each event since 1964 have been:

Single Sculls

1964 Vyacheslav Ivanov (USSR)
1968 Henri Wienese (Hol)
1972 Yuriy Malishev (USSR)
1976 Pertti Karppinen (Fin)

Double Sculls

1964 USSR (Oleg Tyurin and Boris Dubrovsky)
1968 USSR (Anatoliy Sass and Aleksandr Timoshinin)
1972 USSR (Aleksandr Timoshinin and Gennadiy Korshikov)
1976 Nor (Frank Hansen and Alf Hansen)

Coxless Pairs

1964 Can (G. Hungerford, R. Jackson)
1968 GDR (J. Lucke, H-J. Bothe)
1972 GDR (S. Brietzke, W. Mager)
1976 GDR (J. Landvoigt, B. Landvoigt)

Coxed Pairs

1964 USA (E. Ferry, C. Findlay, K. Mitchell)
1968 Ita (P. Baron, R. Sambo, B. Cipolla)
1972 GDR (W. Gunkel, J. Lucke, K-D. Neubert)
1976 GDR (H. Jahrling, F. Ulrich, G. Spohr)

Coxless Fours

1964 Den (J. O. Hansen, B. Haslöv, E. Petersen, K. Helmudt)
1968 GDR (F. Forberger, D. Grahn, F. Rühle, D. Schubert)
1972 GDR (F. Forberger, F. Rühle, D. Grahn, D. Schubert)
1976 GDR (S. Brietzke, A. Decker, S. Semmler, W. Mager)

Coxed Fours

1964 Ger (P. Neusel, B. Britting, J. Werner, E. Hirschfelder, J. Oelke)
1968 NZ (R. Joyce, D. Storey, W. Cole, R. Collinge, S. Dickie)
1972 Ger (P. Berger, H-J. Faerber, G. Auer, A. Bierl, U. Benter)
1976 USSR (V. Eshinov, N. Ivanov, M. Kuznyetsov, A. Klepikov, A. Lukianov)

Quadruple Sculls

1976 GDR (W. Guldenpfennig, R. Reiche, K.-H. Bussert, M. Wolfgramm)

Eights

1964	USA	1972	NZ
1968	Ger	1976	GDR

Henley Royal Regatta

The annual regatta on the Thames at Henley was first held in 1839. Many events are held, but perhaps the two most famous are the Grand Challenge Cup for Eights, first held 1839 and the Diamond Challenge Sculls, first held 1844. Winners of these events since 1965 have been:

GRAND CHALLENGE CUP

1965	Ratzeburg, Germany
1966	TSC Berlin
1967	SCW Leipzig
1968	Univ. of London
1969	SC Einheit, Dresden
1970	ASK Rostock
1971	Tideway Scullers
1972	WMF Moscow
1973	Trud Kolomna, USSR
1974	Trud Kolomna, USSR
1975	Leander/Thames Tradesmen
1976	Thames Tradesmen
1977	Univ. of Washington
1978	Trakia Club, Bulgaria
1979	Thames Tradesmen, London

DIAMOND CHALLENGE SCULLS

1965	Don Spero (USA)
1966	Achim Hill (Ger)
1967	Martin Studach (Swi)
1968	Hugh Wardell-Yerburgh (GB)
1969	Hans-Joachim Böhmer (GDR)
1970	Jochen Meissner (Ger)
1971	Alberto Demiddi (Arg)
1972	Aleksandr Timoshinin (USSR)
1973	Sean Drea (Ire)
1974	Sean Drea (Ire)
1975	Sean Drea (Ire)
1976	Edward Hale (Aus)
1977	Tim Crooks (GB)
1978	Tim Crooks (GB)
1979	Hugh Matheron (GB)

Most wins: 6 Stuart Mackenzie (Aus) 1957–62

University Boat Race

The Boat Race between the Universities of Oxford and Cambridge is rowed annually on the Thames from Putney to Mortlake over a distance of 4 miles 374 yards. It was first contested in 1829 at Henley. Winners have been:

OXFORD
1829, 1842, 1849, 1852, 1854, 1857, 1859, 1861–69, 1875, 1878, 1880–83, 1885, 1890–98, 1901, 1905, 1909–13, 1923, 1937–38, 1946, 1952, 1954, 1959–60, 1963, 1965–67, 1974, 1976–79

CAMBRIDGE
1836, 1839–41, 1845–46, 1849, 1856, 1858, 1860, 1870–74, 1876, 1879, 1884, 1886–89, 1899–1900, 1902–04, 1906–08, 1914, 1920–22, 1924–36, 1939, 1947–51, 1953, 1955–58, 1961–62, 1964, 1968–73, 1975

RUGBY LEAGUE

World Cup

First held in 1954. Winners:

1954	England	1968	Australia
1957	Australia	1970	Australia
1960	England	1972	Great Britain

International Championship

Replaced the World Cup in 1975:

1975	Australia	1977	Australia

Challenge Cup

First held in 1897; since 1929, with the exception of 1932, all finals have been at Wembley (except for the war-time finals, 1941–45). Winners:

1897	Batley	1907	Warrington	1921	Leigh	1931	Halifax
1898	Batley	1908	Hunslet	1922	Rochdale R.	1932	Leeds
1899	Oldham	1909	Wakefield Trinity	1923	Leeds	1933	Huddersfield
1900	Swinton	1910	Leeds	1924	Wigan	1934	Hunslet
1901	Batley	1911	Broughton R.	1925	Oldham	1935	Castleford
1902	Broughton R.	1912	Dewsbury	1926	Swinton	1936	Leeds
1903	Halifax	1913	Huddersfield	1927	Oldham	1937	Widnes
1904	Halifax	1914	Hull	1928	Swinton	1938	Salford
1905	Warrington	1915	Huddersfield	1929	Wigan	1939	Halifax
1906	Bradford	1920	Huddersfield	1930	Widnes	1940	No competition

1941	Leeds	1951	Wigan	1961	St Helens	1971	Leigh
1942	Leeds	1952	Workington Town	1962	Wakefield Trinity	1972	St Helens
1943	Dewsbury	1953	Huddersfield	1963	Wakefield Trinity	1973	Featherstone R.
1944	Bradford Northern	1954	Warrington	1964	Widnes	1974	Warrington
1945	Huddersfield	1955	Barrow	1965	Wigan	1975	Widnes
1946	Wakefield Trinity	1956	St Helens	1966	St Helens	1976	St Helens
1947	Bradford Northern	1957	Leeds	1967	Featherstone R.	1977	Leeds
1948	Wigan	1958	Wigan	1968	Leeds	1978	Leeds
1949	Bradford Northern	1959	Wigan	1969	Castleford	1979	Widnes
1950	Warrington	1960	Wakefield Trinity	1970	Castleford		

League Champions

From 1907 the first four teams in the Northern League played off for the title of league champions. For two seasons, 1962–63 and 1963–64 there were two divisions and no play-off. From 1964 to 1973 the top clubs again played off for the title and from 1973–74 there were again two divisions.

1906–07 Halifax	1931–32 St Helens	1958–59 St Helens
1907–08 Hunslet	1932–33 Salford	1959–60 Wigan
1908–09 Wigan	1933–34 Wigan	1960–61 Leeds
1909–10 Oldham	1934–35 Swinton	1961–62 Huddersfield
1910–11 Oldham	1935–36 Hull	1962–63 Swinton (Div. 1)
1911–12 Huddersfield	1936–37 Salford	1963–64 Swinton (Div. 1)
1912–13 Huddersfield	1937–38 Hunslet	1964–65 Halifax
1913–14 Salford	1938–39 Salford	1965–66 St Helens
1914–15 Huddersfield	1945–46 Wigan	1966–67 Wakefield Trinity
1919–20 Hull	1946–47 Wigan	1967–68 Wakefield Trinity
1920–21 Hull	1947–48 Warrington	1968–69 Leeds
1921–22 Wigan	1948–49 Huddersfield	1969–70 St Helens
1922–23 Hull K.R.	1949–50 Wigan	1970–71 St Helens
1923–24 Batley	1950–51 Workington Town	1971–72 Leeds
1924–25 Hull K.R.	1951–52 Wigan	1972–73 Dewsbury
1925–26 Wigan	1952–53 St Helens	1973–74 Salford (Div. 1)
1926–27 Swinton	1953–54 Warrington	1974–75 St Helens (Div. 1)
1927–28 Swinton	1954–55 Warrington	1975–76 Salford (Div. 1)
1928–29 Huddersfield	1955–56 Hull	1976–77 Featherstone Rovers (Div. 1)
1929–30 Huddersfield	1956–57 Oldham	1977–78 Widnes (Div. 1)
1930–31 Swinton	1957–58 Hull	1978–79 Hull K.R. (Div. 1)

Premiership Trophy

First held in the 1974–75 season, and contested by the leading teams in the League. Winners:

1975	Leeds	1976	St Helens	1977	St Helens	1978	Bradford Northern	1979	Leeds

Lancashire Cup

First held in 1905 and now sponsored by Forshaws.

1905	Wigan	1920	Broughton R.	1933	Oldham
1906	Broughton R.	1921	Warrington	1934	Salford
1907	Oldham	1922	Wigan	1935	Salford
1908	Wigan	1923	St Helens	1936	Salford
1909	Wigan	1924	Oldham	1937	Warrington
1910	Oldham	1925	Swinton	1938	Wigan
1911	Rochdale H.	1926	St Helens	1939	Swinton
1912	Wigan	1927	Swinton	1940–44	No competition
1913	Oldham	1928	Wigan	1945	Widnes
1914	Rochdale H.	1929	Warrington	1946	Wigan
1915–17	No competition	1930	St Helens	1947	Wigan
1918	Rochdale H.	1931	Salford	1948	Wigan
1919	Oldham	1932	Warrington	1949	Wigan

1950	Wigan	1960	St Helens	1970	Leigh
1951	Wigan	1961	St Helens	1971	Wigan
1952	Leigh	1962	St Helens	1972	Salford
1953	St Helens	1963	St Helens	1973	Wigan
1954	Barrow	1964	St Helens	1974	Wigan
1955	Leigh	1965	Warrington	1975	Widnes
1956	Oldham	1966	Wigan	1976	Widnes
1957	Oldham	1967	St Helens	1977	Widnes
1958	Oldham	1968	St Helens	1978	Workington Town
1959	Warrington	1969	Swinton	1979	Widnes

Yorkshire Cup

First held in 1905 and now sponsored by Esso.

1905	Hunslet	1932	Leeds	1956	Wakefield T.
1906	Bradford	1933	York	1957	Huddersfield
1907	Hunslet	1934	Leeds	1958	Leeds
1908	Halifax	1935	Leeds	1959	Featherstone R.
1909	Huddersfield	1936	York	1960	Wakefield T.
1910	Wakefield T.	1937	Leeds	1961	Wakefield T.
1911	Huddersfield	1938	Huddersfield	1962	Hunslet
1912	Batley	1939	Featherstone R.	1963	Halifax
1913	Huddersfield	1940	Bradford N.	1964	Wakefield T.
1914	Huddersfield	1941	Bradford N.	1965	Bradford N.
1919	(May) Huddersfield	1942	Dewsbury	1966	Hull K.R.
1919	(Nov) Huddersfield	1943	Bradford N.	1967	Hull K.R.
1920	Hull K.R.	1944	Halifax	1968	Leeds
1921	Leeds	1945	Bradford N.	1969	Hull
1922	York	1946	Wakefield T.	1970	Leeds
1923	Hull	1947	Wakefield T.	1971	Hull K.R.
1924	Wakefield T.	1948	Bradford N.	1972	Leeds
1925	Dewsbury	1949	Bradford N.	1973	Leeds
1926	Huddersfield	1950	Huddersfield	1974	Leeds
1927	Dewsbury	1951	Wakefield T.	1975	Hull K.R.
1928	Leeds	1952	Huddersfield	1976	Leeds
1929	Hull K.R.	1953	Bradford N.	1977	Leeds
1930	Leeds	1954	Halifax	1978	Castleford
1931	Huddersfield	1955	Halifax	1979	Bradford N.

Players No. 6 Trophy

First contested in the 1971–72 season.

1972	Halifax	1974	Warrington	1976	Widnes	1978	Warrington
1973	Leeds	1975	Bradford Northern	1977	Castleford	1979	Widnes

RUGBY UNION

The International Championship

Contested annually by England, France, Ireland, Scotland and Wales. First decided in 1884, France entered for the first time in 1910. In 1885, 1888, 1889, 1897, 1898, and 1972 not all matches were completed, but winners in the other years have been:

1884	England	1893	Wales	1901	Scotland
1886	England, Scotland	1894	Ireland	1902	Wales
1887	Scotland	1895	Scotland	1903	Scotland
1890	England, Scotland	1896	Ireland	1904	Scotland
1891	Scotland	1899	Ireland	1905	Wales
1892	England	1900	Wales	1906	Ireland, Wales

1907	Scotland	1932	England, Wales, Ireland	1959	France	
1908	Wales	1933	Scotland	1960	France, England	
1909	Wales	1934	England	1961	France	
1910	England	1935	Ireland	1962	France	
1911	Wales	1936	Wales	1963	England	
1912	England, Ireland	1937	England	1964	Scotland, Wales	
1913	England	1938	Scotland	1965	Wales	
1914	England	1939	England, Wales, Ireland	1966	Wales	
1920	England, Scotland, Wales	1947	Wales, England	1967	France	
1921	England	1948	Ireland	1968	France	
1922	Wales	1949	Ireland	1969	Wales	
1923	England	1950	Wales	1970	France, Wales	
1924	England	1951	Ireland	1971	Wales	
1925	Scotland	1952	Wales	1973	Quintuple tie	
1926	Scotland, Ireland	1953	England	1974	Ireland	
1927	Scotland, Ireland	1954	England, France, Wales	1975	Wales	
1928	England	1955	France, Wales	1976	Wales	
1929	Scotland	1956	Wales	1977	France	
1930	England	1957	England	1978	Wales	
1931	Wales	1958	England	1979	Wales	

Triple Crown

Won when one of the four British countries beats the other three in the same season. Winners have been:

England: 1884, 1892, 1913, 1914, 1921, 1923, 1924, 1928, 1934, 1937, 1954, 1957, 1960

Wales: 1893, 1900, 1902, 1905, 1908, 1909, 1911, 1950, 1952, 1965, 1969, 1971, 1976, 1977, 1978, 1979

Scotland: 1891, 1895, 1901, 1903, 1907, 1925, 1933, 1938
Ireland: 1894, 1899, 1948, 1949

Calcutta Cup

The annual contest between England and Scotland. To the end of the 1979 season, England have won 45 times, Scotland 34 and 15 have been drawn.

English County Championship

First held in 1889, the county championship is contested annually, firstly on a regional league basis and then by knock-out. Winners since 1965 have been:

1965	Warwickshire	1971	Surrey	1977	Lancashire
1966	Middlesex	1972	Gloucestershire	1978	East Midlands
1967	Durham & Surrey	1973	Lancashire	1979	Middlesex (played 31 Dec 1978)
1968	Middlesex	1974	Gloucestershire		
1969	Lancashire	1975	Gloucestershire		
1970	Staffordshire	1976	Gloucestershire		

Most wins: 13   Gloucestershire – 1910, 1913, 1920–22, 1930–32, 1937, 1972, 1974–76

Rugby Football Union Knock-out Cup

First held in the 1971–72 season. Contested by English clubs.

1972	Gloucester	1976	Gosforth
1973	Coventry	1977	Gosforth
1974	Coventry	1978	Gloucester
1975	Bedford	1979	Leicester

Welsh Rugby Union Challenge Cup

First held in the 1971–72 season. Contested by Welsh clubs.

1972	Neath	1976	Llanelli
1973	Llanelli	1977	Newport
1974	Llanelli	1978	Swansea
1975	Llanelli	1979	Bridgend

British Lions

The four home countries – England, Ireland, Scotland and Wales – come together to provide players for the British Isles touring teams (The Lions). Summarised results of internationals are:

Australia: British Isles 6, Australia 1, Drawn 0
New Zealand: British Isles 5, New Zealand 17, Drawn 2
South Africa: British Isles 7, South Africa 15, Drawn 4

Scottish Club Championship

Won by Hawick for the competition's first five seasons, from 1973–74 to 1977–78.

RUNNING (*See* Athletics, Cross-Country Running)

SAILING (*See* Yachting)

SCIENCE

Enrico Fermi Prize

Named in honour of Enrico Fermi, the atomic pioneer, the $25 000 award is given in recognition of 'exceptional or altogether outstanding' scientific and technical achievement in atomic energy.

1954	Enrico Fermi	1964	Hyman G. Rickover
1956	John von Neumann	1966	Otto Hahn, Lise Meitner and Fritz Strassman
1957	Ernest O. Lawrence	1968	John A. Wheeler
1958	Eugene P. Wigner	1969	Walter H. Zinn
1959	Glenn T. Seaborg	1970	Norris E. Bradbury
1961	Hans A. Bethe	1971	Shields Warren and Stafford L. Warren
1962	Edward Teller	1972	Manson Benedict
1963	J. Robert Oppenheimer	1976	William L. Russell

Young Scientists of the Year

This is the annual competition organised by BBC Television

1966   *Team:*   Michael Breton   Bexley Erith Technical High School
                Barry Lewis
        Subject: Measuring water in moulding sand

1967   *Team:*   Nicholas Pickvance   Heywood Grammar School
                David Lord
                Marilyn Hadfield
                Neil Brocklehurst
                Susan Blackburn
                Jose England
        Subject: Peat

1968   *Team:* Linda Hodgets   Janice Checketts   Erdington Girls Grammar School
                     Marilyn Cook   Christine Scoins
                     June Carrington   Camilla Wickins
                     June Harvey   Jennifer Dowsett
                     Pauline Jones
         Subject: Crease Resistance in the Family Wash

1969   *Team:* Sarah Mackay   Golspie High School
                     Katie McLellan
                     Walter Sutherland
         Subject: Trout in Scottish Lochs

1970   *Team:* David May   Gateway School, Leicester
                     Peter Hall
                     Peter Kitson
                     Mervyn Hall
         Subject: Fingerprints

1971   *Team:* Judith Greaves   Sittingbourne Girls Grammar School
                     Rosemary Underdown
                     Susan Whitesman
                     Susan Jury
         Subject: Difference in Eye Colour

1972   *Team:* Christopher O'Brien   Lincoln School
                     David Smith
                     Christopher Dennison
         Subject: Sowing Wild Oats

1973   *Team:* Keith Jones   Neath Grammar School, Glamorgan
                     Hugh Jones
         Subject: Runner Beans and Fungicide

1974   *Team:* Kings Dobson   Ifield School, Crawley, Sussex
                     Malcolm MacGarvin
                     David Law
         Subject: Magnetism Affecting Plant Growth

1975   *Team:* Wendy Heath   Codsall Comprehensive School, Codsall, Staffs.
                     Jane Darling
         Subject: Kinks caused by reaction between Magnesium and Hydrochloric acid

1976   *Team:* Nick Ramsden   Pocklington School, Pocklington, Yorks
                     Nick Pollard
                     Andrew Blacker
                     David Quarton
         Subject: Oscillating Aerofoil

1977   *Team:* Ben Holt   Yeovil College, Yeovil
                     Jonathan Stagg
                     Alyson Wreford
                     Anthony Brown
         Subject: Wool De-crimping

1978   *Team:* Paul Brown   Royal Grammar School, Newcastle upon Tyne
                     Alistair Wolf
         Subject: Hovercraft Crop Sprayer

1979   *Subject:* Psychology of Blushing   Madras College, St Andrews

SCOUTS

National Scoutcar Races

Introduced in Britain in 1939 by The Scout Association, these races are a test for Scouts in

National Scoutcar Races, 1976

designing, building and racing pedal-driven cars. Each team is allowed to spend a small sum (currently £25) on materials and so they are largely dependent on obtaining bicycle parts and miscellaneous spares.

The races are run annually over a flat 325 metre (one-fifth mile) course. Strict rules govern the dimensions of vehicles and safety factors.

There are three competition classes:

Novice – for groups which have never previously entered or, having entered in either of the two preceding years, were not placed in the first four in a final.

Premier – for groups which competed in either of the two preceding years and were placed in the first four in a final.

Championship – for Venture Scout Units entering cars built in the current or two preceding years.

There are separate events for Cub Scouts (8–11 years), Scouts (11–16 years and competing in two age groups – Section A and B) and Venture Scouts (16–20 years).

Full details of all the winners since 1939 are available from the Scout Association. Recent winners are:

1978	Driver	Scout Group	Name of Car	Speed(mph)
Fastest Cub Scout	C. Purchase	1st Fairfield	Fair-E-Zee	17.96
Fastest Scout (A)	J. Constable	1st Tonbridge	One Ton Wedge	20.45
Fastest Scout (B)	S. Allport	6th Holme Valley	Thor III	20.22
Fastest Venture Scout	T. Byrne	68th Coventry	Lazybones XI	21.82

Queen's Scout Award

The Queen's Scout Award, the highest Training Award of The Scout Association, was introduced as the King's Scout Award by King Edward VII in 1909. Originally it was an award for Scouts of any age but, today, it is available only to Venture Scouts aged 16–20.

The Award is given in recognition of exceptional qualities of character and self-reliance, a high standard of proficiency in a practical or creative skill and a substantial period of community service.

About 2000 young men and women qualify for the Award each year and full details can be obtained direct from the Scout Association.

SCRABBLE

British National Championships

These were inaugurated in 1971. The list of winners and scores is as follows:

1971	Stephen Haskell, 1345
1972	Olive Behan, 1215
1973	Anne Bradford, 1266
1974	Richard Sharp, 1288
1975	Olive Behan, 1363
1976	Alan Richter, 1359
1977	Michael Goldman, 1478
1978	Philip Nelkon, 1521
1979	Christine Jones, 1453

A past national champion, Anne Bradford (*left*) **playing in the grand finals of the National Scrabble Championship**

SECRETARIES

The Top Secretary Award

This has been given each year since 1956 to the candidate who obtains the highest marks in the Private Secretary's Diploma Examination offered by the Commercial Education Scheme of the London Chamber of Commerce and Industry as a professional secretarial qualification. It is generally regarded as the highest award of its kind and is designed for the secretary at top management level. The winners have been:

1956	Miss E. J. Phillips	British Transport Commission
1957	Miss S. A. Mitcher	Private Tuition
1958	Mrs E. I. Phillips	Liverpool College of Commerce
1959	Miss R. M. Anderson	Municipal College of Commerce – Newcastle
1960	Miss D. M. Moore	Ealing Technical College
1961	Mrs A. M. Billingsley	Secretary to the Borough Treasurer – Solihull
1962	M. J. Newton	Westminster College
1963	Mrs C. F. McClaren	Holborn College of Law, Languages and Commerce
1964	Susan Darwin	College of Technology, Sheffield
1965	Nancy Hall	West London College of Commerce
1966	Jennifer Tattersall	Ealing Technical College
1967	Gwen Weightman	Municipal College of Commerce – Newcastle
1968	Jacqueline Barlow	College of Technology – Slough
	Judith Fairhurst	College of Commerce – Liverpool
1969	Jeanne Priddle	Private Tuition
1970	Thelma Jenkins	Private Tuition
1971	Ruth A. Jarman	James Neill (Sheffield) Ltd
	Diana P. Tidd	Croydon Technical College
1972	Judith Wilkinson	Calder Water Board

1973	Jane Morrison	Birmingham Polytechnic
1974	Patricia Gibson	Croydon Technical College
1975	Christina Eveleigh	Highbury College – Portsmouth
1976	Heather Paterson	South East London College
1977	Jean Anderson	Westminster College
1978	Andrea Mullaney	South East Derbyshire College – Ilkeston

SEWING

Dressmaker of the Realm

A competition sponsored by *Women's Realm* and Singer in 1978 to find Britain's best dressmaker. There were two classes, for professionals and non professionals, and the winners in each class received £1000 in cash. Other prizes went to regional winners.

1978 WINNERS
Professional: Shirley Mackrill, Grimsby
Non professional: Janet Lockett, Newcastle region

SHEEPDOGS

The skills of the shepherd and his dog are tested each year at various competitive 'trials'.

The 'James A. Reid' Championship Shield

	Venue	*Handler and Dog*
1922	Criccieth	Wm. Wallace, East Otterburn, with 'Meg'
1923	York	G. P. Brown, Shepherd, Oxton, Berwickshire with 'Spot'
1924	Ayr	Thomas Roberts, Farmer, Corwen, with 'Jaff'
1925	Criccieth	A. Millar, Highbowhill, Newmilns, Ayrshire, with 'Spot'
1926	York	Mark Hayton, Clifton, Otley, Yorkshire, with 'Glen'
1927	Stirling	J. B. Bagshaw, The Mantles, Blyth, Rotherham, with 'Lad'
1928	Llandudno	James M. Wilson, Holmshaw, Moffat, with 'Fly'
1929	Morecambe	S. E. Batty, Letwell, Worksop, with 'Corby'
1930	Ayr	James M. Wilson, Holmshaw, Moffat, with 'Craig'
1931	Llandudno	John Thorp, Old House Derwent, Sheffield, with 'Jess'
1932	Scarborough	W. B. Telfer, Fairnley, Cambo, Morpeth, with 'Queen'
1933	Ayr	George Whiting, Tir Mawr, Aberdare, with 'Chip'
1934	Cardiff	James M. Wilson, Holmshaw, Moffat, with 'Roy'
1935	Blackpool	John Jones, Tany-y-gaer, Corwen with 'Jaff'
1936	Ayr	James M. Wilson, Whitehope, Innerleithen, with 'Roy'
1937	Cardiff	James M. Wilson, Whitehope, Innerleithen, with 'Roy'
1938	Southport	W. J. Wallace Jr, East Otterburn, Otterburn, with 'Jed 1'
1939–1945		Cancelled
1946	Edinburgh	J. M. Wilson, Whitehope, Innerleithen, with 'Glen'
1947	Cardiff	J. Gilchrist, Haddington, with 'Spot'
1948	Worcester	J. M. Wilson, Innerleithen, with 'Glen'
1949	Ayr	D. W. Daniel, Ystradgynlais, with 'Chip'
1950	Ruthin	J. M. Wilson, Innerleithen, with 'Mirk'
1951	Blackpool	E. A. Priestley, Bamford, with 'Pat'
1952	Inverness	D. W. Daniel, Ystradgynlais, with 'Chip'
1953	Cardiff	W. J. Evans, Magor, with 'Roy'
1954	Worcester	J. McDonald, Lauder, Berwicks, with 'Mirk'
1955	Edinburgh	J. M. Wilson, Innerleithen, with 'Bill'
1956	Llandudno	G. R. Redpath, Jedburgh, with 'Moss'
1957	Loughborough	J. H. Holliday, Pateley Bridge, with 'Moss'
1958	Dundee	W. J. Evans, Tidenham, Glos., with 'Tweed'
1959	Cardiff	Meirion Jones, Llandrillo, with 'Ben'
1960	Blackpool	E. L. Daniel, Ystradgynlais, with 'Ken'
1961	Ayr	Alan Jones, Pontllyfni, with 'Roy'

1962	Beaumaris	A. T. Lloyd, Builth Wells, with 'Garry'
1963	York	H. J. Worthington, Abergavenny, with 'Juno'
1964	Drymen	L. R. Suter, Cross Keys, with 'Craig'
1965	Cardiff	J. Richardson, Peebles, with 'Wiston Cap'
1966	Chester	Tim Longton, Quernmore, with 'Ken'
1967	Stirling	T. T. McKnight, Canonbie, with 'Gael'
1968	Towyn	Llyr Evans, Towcester, with 'Bosworth Coon'
1969	Chester	H. Huddleston, Carnforth, with 'Bet'
1970	Kilmartin	D. McTier, Peebles, with 'Wiston Bill'
1971	Cardiff	J. Murray, Sanquhar, with 'Glen'
1972	Newcastle	J. J. Templeton, Kilmarnock, with 'Cap'
1973	Bala	H. G. Jones, Bodfari, with 'Gel'
1974	Kilmartin	G. Jones, Penmachno, with 'Bill'
1975	York	R. C. MacPherson, Brampton, with 'Zac'
1976	Lockerbie	G. Jones, Penmachno, with 'Shep'
1977	Libanus	J. R. Thomas, Llandovery, with 'Craig'
1978	Chatsworth	R. J. Shennan, Girvan, with 'Mirk'

The skill of the shepherd and his dog being tested during one of the competitive trials (*Mark Henrie*)

One Man and His Dog

This BBC television programme organises its own championship, of which the winners are:

1976
Singles: David Shennan and 'Maid'
Doubles: Glyn Jones with 'Gel' and 'Bracken'

1977
Singles: Martin O'Neill and 'Risp'
Doubles: Tot Longton and 'Jed' and 'Kerry'

1978
Singles: Alan Jones and 'Spot'
Dougles: Alan Jones and 'Spot' and 'Craig'

SHOOTING

Olympic Games

Seven men have won five Gold medals at the Olympic Games at Shooting, including Carl Townsend Osburn (USA), who also won four Silver and two Bronze medals for a record total of 11 medals.

The events in the Olympics have varied considerably since Shooting was first included in 1908, and all events are now for individuals. The most individual Gold medals won is three by Gulbrandsen Skatteboe (Nor) in 1906, 1908, 1912. Winners in 1976 were:

Free Pistol (50m):   Uwe Potteck (GDR) 573/600
Small-Bore Rifle – Prone (50m):   Karl Heinz Smieszek (Ger) 599/600
Small-Bore Rifle – 3 Positions (50m):   Lanny Bassham (USA) 1162/1200
Rapid-Fire Pistol (25m):   Norbert Klaar (GDR) 597/600
Trap Shooting: Donald Haldeman (USA) 190/200
Skeet Shooting: Josef Panacek (Cze) 198/200
Running Game Target (50m):   Aleksandr Gazov (USSR) 579/600

World Championships

World Champions at the 1978 championships held in Seoul, South Korea, were:

MEN

Free Pistol (50m):   Moritz Minder (Swi) 577/600
Small-Bore Rifle – Prone (50m):   Alister Allan (GB) 599/600
Small-Bore Rifle – 3 Positions (50m):   Lanny Bassham (USA) 1165/1200
Rapid Fire Pistol (25m):   Ove Gunnarsson (Swe) 595/600
Trap Shooting: Eladio Vallduvi (Spa) 198/200
Skeet Shooting: Luciano Brunetti (Ita) 197/200
Running Game Target: Guha Rannikko (Fin) 572/600

WOMEN

Small-Bore Rifle – Prone (50m):   Sue-Ann Sandusky (USA) 596/600
Small-Bore Rifle – 3 Positions (50m):   Wanda Oliver (USA) 580/600
Trap Shooting: Susan Nattrass (Can) 195/200
Skeet Shooting: Bianca Hansberg (Ita) 189/200
(*Note:* in all cases the total possible score is shown last)

SHOW JUMPING (*See* Equestrian Events)

SKATEBOARDING

This sporting activity boomed in 1977, and BBC Television's Nationwide organised a national championship. The young people found to be the country's top skateboarders were:

Overall Winner – Jock Paterson   Intermediate Winner – John Shayer
Senior Winner – Jock Paterson   Junior Winner – Steven Kellner

SKATING (*See* Ice Skating and Roller Skating)

SKIING

World and Olympic Champions — Alpine Skiing

Alpine Skiing has been included in the winter Olympic Games since 1948, and World Championships were first held in 1932. Winners at World and Olympic (*) events since 1948 have been:

MEN

Alpine Combination					
1948	Henri Oreiller (Fra)	1966	Jean-Claude Killy (Fra)	1950	Zeno Colo (Ita)
1950	—	1968	Jean-Claude Killy (Fra)	1952*	Zeno Colo (Ita)
1952	—	1970	William Kidd (USA)	1954	Christian Pravda (Aut)
1954	Stein Eriksen (Nor)	1972	Gustavo Thoeni (Ita)	1956*	Toni Sailer (Aut)
1956	Toni Sailer (Aut)	1974	Franz Klammer (Aut)	1958	Toni Sailer (Aut)
1958	Toni Sailer (Aut)	1976	Gustavo Thoeni (Ita)	1960*	Jean Vuarnet (Fra)
1960	Guy Perillat (Fra)	1978	Andreas Wenzel (Lie)	1962	Karl Schranz (Aut)
1962	Karl Schranz (Aut)			1964*	Egon Zimmermann (Aut)
1964	Ludwig Leitner (Ger)	**Downhill**		1966	Jean-Claude Killy (Fra)
		1948*	Henri Oreiller (Fra)	1968*	Jean-Claude Killy (Fra)

1970	Bernhard Russi (Swi)
1972*	Bernhard Russi (Swi)
1974	David Zwilling (Aut)
1976*	Franz Klammer (Aut)
1978	Joseph Walcher (Aut)

Slalom

1948*	Edi Reinalter (Swi)
1950	Georges Schneider (Swi)
1952*	Othmar Schneider (Aut)
1954	Stein Eriksen (Nor)
1956*	Toni Sailer (Aut)
1958	Josl Rieder (Aut)
1960*	Ernst Hinterseer (Aut)
1962	Charles Bozon (Fra)
1964*	Josef Stiegler (Aut)
1966	Carlo Senoner (Ita)
1968*	Jean-Claude Killy (Fra)
1970	Jean-Noel Augert (Fra)
1972*	Francesco Ochoa (Spa)
1974	Gustavo Thoeni (Ita)
1976*	Piero Gros (Ita)
1978	Ingemar Stenmark (Swe)

Giant Slalom

1948*	—
1950	Zeno Colo (Ita)
1952*	Stein Eriksen (Nor)
1954	Stein Eriksen (Nor)
1956*	Toni Sailer (Aut)
1958	Toni Sailer (Aut)
1960*	Roger Staub (Swi)
1962	Egon Zimmermann (Aut)
1964*	Francois Bonlieu (Fra)
1966	Guy Perillat (Fra)
1968*	Jean-Claude Killy (Fra)
1970	Karl Schranz (Aut)
1972*	Gustavo Thoeni (Ita)
1974	Gustavo Thoeni (Ita)

| 1976* | Heini Hemmi (Swi) |
| 1978 | Ingemar Stenmark (Swe) |

WOMEN

Alpine Combination

1948	Trude Jochum/Beiser (Aut)
1950	—
1952	—
1954	Ida Schöpfer (Swi)
1956	Madeleine Berthod (Swi)
1958	Frieda Danzer (Swi)
1960	Anne Heggtveit (Can)
1962	Marielle Goitschel (Fra)
1964	Marielle Goitschel (Fra)
1966	Marielle Goitschel (Fra)
1968	Nancy Greene (Can)
1970	Michele Jacot (Fra)
1972	Annemarie Pröll (Aut)
1974	Fabienne Serrat (Fra)
1976	Rosi Mittermaier (Ger)
1978	Annemarie Moser (née Pröll) (Aut)

Downhill

1948*	Hedy Schlunegger (Swi)
1950	Trude Jochum/Beiser (Aut)
1952*	Trude Jochum/Beiser (Aut)
1954	Ida Schöpfer (Aut)
1956*	Madeleine Berthod (Swi)
1958	Lucille Wheeler (Can)
1960*	Heidi Biebl (Ger)
1962	Christl Haas (Aut)
1964*	Christl Haas (Aut)
1966	Erika Schinegger (Aut)
1968*	Olga Pall (Aut)
1970	Anneroesli Zyrd (Swi)
1972*	Marie-Therese Nadig (Swi)
1974	Annemarie Pröll (Aut)

| 1976* | Rosi Mittermaier (Ger) |
| 1978 | Annemarie Moser (née Pröll) (Aut) |

Slalom

1948*	Gretchen Fraser (USA)
1950	Dagmar Rom (Aut)
1952*	Andrea Mead Lawrence (USA)
1954	Trude Klecker (Aut)
1956*	Renée Colliard (Swi)
1958	Inger Björnbakken (Nor)
1960*	Anne Heggtveit (Can)
1962	Marianne Jahn (Aut)
1964*	Christine Goitschel (Fra)
1966	Annie Famose (Fra)
1968*	Marielle Goitschel (Fra)
1970	Ingrid Lafforgue (Fra)
1972*	Barbara Cochran (USA)
1974	Hanni Wenzel (Lie)
1976*	Rosi Mittermaier (Ger)
1978	Lea Sölkner (Aut)

Giant Slalom

1948*	—
1950	Dagmar Rom (Aut)
1952*	Andrea Mead Lawrence (USA)
1954	Lucienne Schmith (Fra)
1956*	Ossi Reichert (Ger)
1958	Lucille Wheeler (Can)
1960*	Yvonne Rüegg (Swi)
1962	Marianne Jahn (Aut)
1964*	Marielle Goitschel (Fra)
1966	Marielle Goitschel (Fra)
1968*	Nancy Greene (Can)
1970	Betsy Clifford (Can)
1972*	Marie-Therese Nadig (Swi)
1974	Fabienne Serrat (Fra)
1976*	Kathy Kreiner (Can)
1978	Maria Epple (Ger)

Alpine World Cup

The Alpine World Cup, a points competition involving the season's major events, was introduced in 1967.

MEN

1967	Jean-Claude Killy (Fra)
1968	Jean-Claude Killy (Fra)
1969	Karl Schranz (Aut)
1970	Karl Schranz (Aut)
1971	Gustavo Thoeni (Ita)
1972	Gustavo Thoeni (Ita)
1973	Gustavo Thoeni (Ita)
1974	Piero Gros (Ita)
1975	Gustavo Thoeni (Ita)

1976	Ingemar Stenmark (Swe)
1977	Ingemar Stenmark (Swe)
1978	Ingemar Stenmark (Swe)
1979	Peter Luescher (Swi)

WOMEN

1967	Nancy Greene (Can)
1968	Nancy Greene (Can)
1969	Gertrud Gabl (Aut)
1970	Michele Jacot (Fra)

1971	Annemarie Pröll (Aut)
1972	Annemarie Pröll (Aut)
1973	Annemarie Pröll (Aut)
1974	Annemarie Pröll (Aut)
1975	Annemarie Moser (née Pröll) (Aut)
1976	Rosi Mittermaier (Ger)
1977	Lise-Marie Morerod (Swi)
1978	Hanni Wenzel (Lie)
1979	Annemarie Moser (Aut)

World and Olympic Champions — Nordic Skiing

Nordic Skiing – Jumping and Cross-Country – was first included in the Olympic Games in 1924 and separate World Championships were first held in 1929. The *Nordic Combination* is for 15 kilometres cross-country and jumping. Winners since 1948 (* = Olympics):

MEN

| 1948* | Heikki Hasu (Fin) | 1950 | Heikki Hasu (Fin) | 1952* | Simon Slättvik (Nor) |

1954	Sverre Stenersen (Nor)	1964*	Tormod Knutsen (Nor)	1972*	Ulrich Wehling (GDR)
1956*	Sverre Stenersen (Nor)	1966	Georg Thoma (Ger)	1974	Ulrich Wehling (GDR)
1958	Paavo Korhonen (Fin)	1968*	Franz Keller (Ger)	1976*	Ulrich Wehling (GDR)
1960*	Georg Thoma (Ger)	1970	Ladislav Rygl (Cze)	1978	Konrad Winkler (GDR)
1962	Arne Larsen (Nor)				

CROSS-COUNTRY (MEN)

The current Olympic cross-country events are 15, 30 and 50 kilometres for individuals as well as a 4 × 10 kilometre relay.

Winner of the **most titles** is Sixten Jernberg (Swe) with 8 (5 individual and 3 relay) between 1956 and 1964. **Most individual titles** have been won by Johan Grøttumsbraaten (Nor) with 6 between 1926 and 1932.

CROSS-COUNTRY (WOMEN)

Women's Olympic events are at 5 and 10 kilometres for individuals and 4 × 5 kilometres relay.

Winner of the **most World and Olympic titles** is Galina Koulakova (USSR) with 9 between 1968 and 1978.

Annemarie Pröll in 1973 when at the age of 19 she completed a record sequence of 11 consecutive downhill wins in the World Cup series. In 1979 she won a record sixth World Cup title (*Keystone Press*)

SKI-JUMPING

Since 1964 men have competed at the Olympic Games at Ski-Jumping on a 70-metres hill and on a 90-metres hill. Champions have been:

70-metres hill
1964	Veikko Kankkonen (Fin) 229.90
1968	Jiri Raska (Cze) 216.5
1972	Yukio Kasaya (Jap) 244.2
1976	Hans-Georg Aschenbach (GDR) 252.0

90-metres hill
1964	Toralf Engen (Nor) 230.70
1968	Vladimir Beloussov (USSR) 231.3
1972	Wojciech Fortuna (Pol) 219.9
1976	Karl Schnabl (Aut) 234.8

World Champions
World ski-jumping championships were first held in 1929. Winners since 1966:
1966	Björn Wirkola (Nor) (70m and 90m)
1970	Gurij Napalkov (USSR) (70m and 90m)
1974	Hans-Georg Aschenbach (GDR) (70m and 90m)
1978	Mathias Buse (GDR) (70m)
	Tapio Räisänen (Fin) (90m)

BIATHLON

The Biathlon is a combination of Skiing and Shooting. World championships were first held in 1958 and Olympic championships in 1960. Champions (* = Olympics):
1958	Adolf Wiklund (Swe)
1959	Vladimir Melanin (USSR)
1960*	Klas Lestander (Swe)
1961	Kalevi Huuskonen (Fin)
1962	Vladimir Melanin (USSR)
1963	Vladimir Melanin (USSR)

1964*	Vladimir Melanin (USSR)
1965	Olav Jordet (Nor)
1966	Jon Istad (Nor)
1967	Viktor Mamatov (USSR)
1968*	Maganr Solberg (Nor)
1969	Aleksandr Tikhonov (USSR)
1970	Aleksandr Tikhonov (USSR)
1971	Heinz Dieter Speer (GDR)
1972*	Magnar Solberg (Nor)
1973	Aleksandr Tikhonov (USSR)
1974	Juhani Suutarinen (Fin) (10km and 20km)
1975	Aleksandr Elisarov (USSR) (10km)
	Heikki Ikola (Fin) (20km)
1976*	Nikolay Kruglov (USSR) (20km)
	Juhani Suutarinen (Fin) (10km)
1977	Heikki Ikola (Fin) (20km)
	Aleksandr Tikhonov (USSR) (10km)
1978	Odd Lirhus (Nor) (20km)
	Frank Ullrich (GDR) (10km)
1979	Klaus Siebert (GDR) (20km)
	Frank Ullrich (GDR) (10km)

Biathlon Team (Relay (3 × 7.5km) competition)
1958	Sweden	1973	USSR
1959	USSR	1974	USSR
1961	Finland	1975	Finland
1962	USSR	1976*	USSR
1963	USSR	1977	USSR
1965	Norway	1978	GDR
1966	Norway	1979	GDR
1967	Norway		
1968*	USSR		
1969	USSR		
1970	Norway		
1971	USSR		
1972*	USSR		

SLIMMING

Slimmer of the Year

Slimmer Magazine's 'Slimmer of the Year' contest was established in 1971. The contest winner is announced each year at a press reception held in September.

The winner is selected on the basis of physical weight-loss achieved to reach target weight, and in the view of the judges, a story which will be an inspiration to others. Details of past winners, with total weight-loss, are as follows:

1971   Jeannette Chappell, Stoke-on-Trent (6½ stone)
1972   Halina Smith, South Lancing (11 stone)
1973   Jeanette Edgar, Driffield, Yorks (10 stone)
1974   Brenda Smith, Rainham, Essex (5 stone)
1975   Marlene Johnson, Beverley (7 stone)
1976   Gail Ingham, Chester (6 stone)
1977   Helen Currie, Alloa, Clackmannanshire (7 stone)
1978   John and Linda Jenkins, Birmingham (11 stone)

'Before and after' – John and Linda Jenkins, joint winners of the Slimmer of the Year award lost just over 11st between them. Linda, 27, lost 4st to become 8st 12lb while John, 28, lost just over 7st to become 12st 12lb (*Press Association*)

SMOKING

National Pipesmoking Championships

The Pipe Club of Great Britain was launched in January 1970 to provide a national organisation for pipesmokers and a public relations medium on behalf of its subscribers – the major pipe and tobacco manufacturers. One of its first external activities was the promotion of a national pipesmoking competition. As known in some European countries, the object of the competition is for the smokers, given a measured quantity of tobacco and a number of matches, with a five-minute period for filling and a subsequent consecutive period of two minutes for lighting, to keep their pipes alight for the longest possible time, without refilling or relighting.

1971–72 R. M. Foulds, Nottingham – 107min 58sec
1972–73 R. M. Foulds, Nottingham – 121min 16sec
1973–74 B. M. Coles, Coventry – 111min 17sec
1974–75 Robert Locke, London – 145min 2 sec

1976–77 R. M. Foulds, Nottingham – 101min 22 sec (smaller capacity pipes were used in this competition)

Pipeman of the Year

The competition was first established in 1964 by the Briar Pipe Trade Association – which in 1978 changed its name to 'Pipesmokers' Council' – in association with *Tobacco Magazine*. Readers of *Tobacco Magazine* are presented with the names of several pipesmokers and invited to nominate one of these as 'Pipeman of the Year'.

The winner is invited to the Pipeman of the Year luncheon and is presented with the trophy, a pipe (not smoking) on a stand, on which his, and his predecessors' names are inscribed, which he keeps for one year. In addition he receives a replica of the trophy and a quantity of his favourite tobacco! Previous winning Pipemen:

1964	Rupert Davies
1965	Rt. Hon. Harold Wilson
1966	Andrew Cruickshank
1967	Warren Mitchell
1968	Peter Cushing
1969	Jack Hargreaves
1970	Eric Morecambe
1971	The Right Hon. The Lord Shinwell
1972	Not held

1973	Frank Muir
1974	Fred Trueman
1975	Campbell Adamson
1976	The Rt. Hon. Harold Wilson (Pipeman of the Decade)
1977	Brian Barnes
1978	Magnus Magnusson
1979	J. B. Priestley

SNOOKER (*See* Billiards and Snooker)

SNUFF

William Hill World Snuff Taking Championship

The William Hill World Snuff Taking Championship in progress

This took place at Wellington, Somerset, in February 1979 and nearly 200 competitors took part. The actual technicalities of this sport are a mystery to the uninitiated, but basically a small tin containing a measured amount of snuff is placed in front of each competitor, a time limit is enforced and the idea is to consume as much as possible within the time. Afterwards the amount left is measured accurately, subtracted from the original amount, the result being the score.

The winners were: Xavier Wenger (Ger) and Christina Strobel (Ger).

SOARING (*See* Gliding)

SOCCER (*See* Association Football)

SOFTBALL

World Championship

MEN First held in 1966.   1966 USA   1968 USA   1972 Canada   1976 Canada, USA and New Zealand

WOMEN   First held in 1965.   1965   Australia   1970   Japan   1974   Japan   1978   USA

SONGS

Britain's Song for Europe

An annual competition in which BBC television viewers vote for Britain's entry in the Euro-vision Song Contest.

1957   All, Patricia Bredin
1958   No entry
1959   Sing Little Birdie, Teddy Johnson and Pearl Carr
1960   Looking High, High, High, Bryan Johnson
1961   Are You Sure?, The Allisons
1962   Ring A Ding Girl, Ronnie Carroll
1963   Say Wonderful Things, Ronnie Carroll
1964   I Love the Little Things, Matt Monro
1965   I Belong, Kathy Kirby
1966   A Man Without Love, Kenneth McKellar
1967   Puppet on a String, Sandie Shaw
1968   Congratulations, Cliff Richard
1969   Boom-Bang-a-Bang, Lulu
1970   Knock, Knock, Who's There?, Mary Hopkins
1971   Jack in the Box, Clodagh Rodgers
1972   Beg, Steal or Borrow, The New Seekers
1973   Power to All Our Friends, Cliff Richard
1974   Long Live Love, Olivia Newton-John
1975   Let Me Be The One, The Shadows
1976   Save Your Kisses For Me, Brotherhood of Man
1977   Rock Bottom, Lynsey de Paul and Mike Moran
1978   The Bad Old Days, Co-Co
1979   Mary Ann, Black Lace

Olivia Newton-John singing Britain's entry 'Long Live Love' in the 1974 Eurovision Song Contest (BBC Copyright)

Eurovision Song Contest

An annual top award, the contest involves artists from over a dozen European countries, and attracts a huge television audience.

	Singer	Country	Song
1956	Lys Assia	Switzerland	Refrains
1957	Corry Brokken	Netherlands	Net Als Town
1958	André Claveau	France	Dors, Mon Amour
1959	Teddy Scholten	Netherlands	Een Beetje
1960	Jacqueline Boyer	France	Tom Pillibi
1961	Jean Claude Pascal	Luxembourg	Nous, Les Amoureux
1962	Isabelle Aubret	France	Un Premier Amour
1963	Grethe and Jørgen Ingmann	Denmark	Dansevise
1964	Gigliola Cinquetti	Italy	Non ho l'eta
1965	France Gall	Luxembourg	Poupee de Cire, Poupee de Son
1966	Udo Jurgens	Austria	Merci Cherie
1967	Sandie Shaw	United Kingdom	Puppet on a String
1968	Massiel	Spain	La, La, La
1969	(Four countries won – each with 18 points)		
	Salome	Spain	Viva Cantando
	Lulu	United Kingdom	Boom-Bang-a-Bang
	Lennie Kuhr	Holland	De Troubadour
	Frida Boccara	France	Un Jour, Un Enfant
1970	Dana	Ireland	All Kinds of Everything

1971	Severine	Monaco	Un Banc, Un Arbre, Une Rue
1972	Vicky Leandros	Luxembourg	Après Toi
1973	Anne Marie David	Luxembourg	Tu Te Reconnaitras
1974	Abba (Bjorn, Benny, Anna and Frida)	Sweden	Waterloo
1975	Teach-In	Netherlands	Ding Ding Dong
1976	Brotherhood of Man	United Kingdom	Save Your Kisses For Me
1977	Marie Myrian	France	L'oiseau et l'enfant
1978	Izhar Cohen and the Alphabeta	Israel	A Bi Ni Bi
1979	Milk and Honey	Israel	Hallelujah

SPEED SKATING (*See* Ice Skating, Roller Skating)

SPEEDWAY

World Championship

First held in 1936 at Wembley.

1936	Lionel Van Praag (Aus)	1957	Barry Briggs (NZ)	1968	Ivan Mauger (NZ)
1937	Jack Milne (USA)	1958	Barry Briggs (NZ)	1969	Ivan Mauger (NZ)
1938	Bluey Wilkinson (Aus)	1959	Ronnie Moore (NZ)	1970	Ivan Mauger (NZ)
1949	Tommy Price (Eng)	1960	Ove Fundin (Swe)	1971	Ole Olsen (Den)
1950	Freddie Williams (Wal)	1961	Ove Fundin (Swe)	1972	Ivan Mauger (NZ)
1951	Jack Young (Aus)	1962	Peter Craven (Eng)	1973	Jerzy Szczakiel (Pol)
1952	Jack Young (Aus)	1963	Ove Fundin (Swe)	1974	Anders Michanek (Swe)
1953	Freddie Williams (Wal)	1964	Barry Briggs (NZ)	1975	Ole Olsen (Den)
1954	Ronnie Moore (NZ)	1965	Bjorn Knutsson (Swe)	1976	Peter Collins (Eng)
1955	Peter Craven (Eng)	1966	Barry Briggs (NZ)	1977	Ivan Mauger (NZ)
1956	Ove Fundin (Swe)	1967	Ove Fundin (Swe)	1978	Ole Olsen (Den)

World Team Cup
First contested in 1960.

1960	Sweden	1966	Poland	1973	Great Britain
1961	Poland	1967	Sweden	1974	Great Britain
1962	Sweden	1968	Great Britain	1975	Great Britain
1963	Sweden	1969	Poland	1976	Australia
1964	Sweden	1970	Sweden	1977	Great Britain
1965	Poland	1971	Great Britain	1978	Denmark
		1972	Great Britain		

Speedway stars practising at Wembley. *Left to right:* **Ove Fundin, five times world champion; Ron How; Ronnie Moore, twice world champion and the youngest-ever finalist at 17 in 1950, and Aub Lawson, whose highest placing in nine world championships was third in 1958** (*Keystone Press*)

National League — British League

Introduced in 1932 the National League varied between all the English divisions. In 1960 the Provincial League was founded, and the British League was formed in 1965 as a merger of these two leagues.

National League champions							
1932	Wembley	1948	New Cross	1959	Wimbledon	1968	Coventry
1933	Belle Vue	1949	Wembley	1960	Wimbledon	1969	Poole
1934	Belle Vue	1950	Wembley	1961	Wimbledon	1970	Belle Vue
1935	Belle Vue	1951	Wembley	1962	Southampton	1971	Belle Vue
1936	Belle Vue	1952	Wembley	1963	Belle Vue	1972	Belle Vue
1937	West Ham	1953	Wembley	1964	Oxford	1973	Reading
1938	New Cross	1954	Wimbledon			1974	Exeter
1939	Belle Vue	1955	Southampton	**British League Champions**		1975	Ipswich
1946	Wembley	1956	Wimbledon	1965	West Ham	1976	Ipswich
1947	Wembley	1957	Swindon	1966	Halifax	1977	White City
		1958	Wimbledon	1967	Swansea	1978	Coventry

World Pairs Cup

First contested 1968.

1968	Sweden (Ove Fundin, Törbjorn Harrysson)	1974	Sweden (Anders Michanek, Soren Sjösten)
1969	New Zealand (Ivan Mauger, Bob Andrews)	1975	Sweden (Anders Michanek, Tommy Jansson)
1970	New Zealand (Ronnie Moore, Ivan Mauger)	1976	England (John Louis, Malcolm Simmons)
1971	Poland (Jerzy Szczakiel, Andrzej Wyglenda)	1977	England (Peter Collins, Malcolm Simmons)
1972	England (Ray Wilson, Terry Betts)	1978	England (Malcolm Simmons, Gordon Kennett)
1973	Sweden (Anders Michanek, Tommy Jansson)	1979	Denmark (Ole Olsen, Hans Neilsen)

SPIRITUALISM

Spiritualist of the Year

This award was instituted by *Psychic News* in 1966, and a gift commemorating it is presented at an annual dinner.

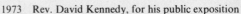

1966	Geraldine Cummins, automatic writing medium	1973	Rev. David Kennedy, for his public exposition
1967	Ena Twigg, medium for TV appearances	1974	Grace Cook, veteran medium
1968	Jessie Nason, medium for TV appearances	1975	George Chapman, healer
1969	Rosemary Brown, musical medium	1976	Leslie Flint, direct voice medium
1970	Gordon Higginson, president of the Spiritualists' National Union	1977	Coral Polge, psychic artist
1971	Ivy Northage, for her School for Mediums	1978	Doris Collins, medium
1972	Harry Edwards, the healer		Doris Stokes, medium

Rosemary Brown, musical medium, with spirit-dictated scores. She was the 1969 Spiritualist of the Year

SPORT

The BBC Sports Personality of the Year

Each year viewers of Grandstand and BBC television sports programmes cast their votes to find the year's outstanding sports personality. Winners since the competition began:

1954	Christopher Chataway (athletics)	1967	Henry Cooper (boxing)
1955	Gordon Pirie (athletics)	1968	David Hemery (athletics)
1956	Jim Laker (cricket)	1969	Ann Jones (tennis)
1957	Dai Rees (golf)	1970	Henry Cooper (boxing)
1958	Ian Black (swimming)	1971	Princess Anne (show jumping)
1959	John Surtees (motorcycling)	1972	Mary Peters (athletics)
1960	David Broome (show jumping)	1973	Jackie Stewart (motor racing)
1961	Stirling Moss (motor racing)	1974	Brendan Foster (athletics)
1962	Anita Lonsborough (swimming)	1975	David Steele (cricket)
1963	Dorothy Hyman (athletics)	1976	John Curry (ice-skating)
1964	Mary Rand (athletics)	1977	Virginia Wade (tennis)
1965	Tommy Simpson (cycling)	1978	Steve Ovett (athletics)
1966	Bobby Moore (football)		

The 'Daily Express'

SPORTSMAN OF THE YEAR

1946	Bruce Woodcock (boxing)	1962	Brian Phelps (diving)
1947	Denis Compton (cricket)	1963	Jim Clark (motor racing)
1948	Denis Compton (cricket)	1964	Robbie Brightwell (athletics)
1949	Reg Harris (cycling)	1965	Tommy Simpson (cycling)
1950	Reg Harris (cycling)	1966	Bobby Moore (soccer)
1951	Geoffrey Duke (motor cycling)	1967	Harvey Smith (show jumping)
1952	Len Hutton (cricket)	1968	Lester Piggott (horse racing)
1953	Gordon Pirie (athletics)	1969	Tony Jacklin (golf)
1954	Roger Bannister (athletics)	1970	Henry Cooper (boxing)
1955	Gordon Pirie (athletics)	1971	Jackie Stewart (motor racing)
1956	Chris Brasher (athletics)	1972	Gordon Banks (soccer)
1957	Derek Ibbotson (athletics)	1973	Jackie Stewart (motor racing)
1958	Ian Black (swimming)	1974	Willie John McBride (rugby union)
1959	John Surtees (motor cycling)	1975	David Steele (cricket)
1960	Don Thompson (walking)	1976	James Hunt (motor racing)
1961	Johnny Haynes (soccer)	1977	Geoff Boycott (cricket)
		1978	Steve Ovett (athletics)

SPORTSWOMAN OF THE YEAR

1952	Jeanette Altwegg (ice skating)	1966	Ann Jones (lawn tennis)
1953	Pat Smythe (show jumping)	1967	Beryl Burton (cycling)
1954	Pat Smythe (show jumping)	1968	Marion Coakes (show jumping)
1955	Pat Smythe (show jumping)	1969	Ann Jones (lawn tennis)
1956	Judy Grinham (swimming)	1970	Lillian Board (athletics)
1957	Diana Wilkinson (swimming)	1971	Princess Anne (equestrian three-day event)
1958	Judy Grinham (swimming)	1972	Mary Peters (athletics)
1959	Mary Bignal (athletics)	1973	Ann Moore (show jumping)
1960	Anita Lonsborough (swimming)	1974	Virginia Wade (lawn tennis)
1961	Angela Mortimer (lawn tennis)	1975	Virginia Wade (lawn tennis)
1962	Anita Lonsborough (swimming)	1976	Debbie Johnsey (equestrian three-day event)
1963	Dorothy Hyman (athletics)	1977	Virginia Wade (lawn tennis)
1964	Mary (Bignal) Rand (athletics)	1978	Sharron Davies (swimming)
1965	Marion Coakes (show jumping)		

The 'Daily Express' Sports Family of the Year

This is organised and televised by the BBC. Only one competition has been held so far – in 1978. The winners were the Brightwell family (Robbie Brightwell and Anne Brightwell (née Packer)).

Superstars

The first Superstars, a multi-sport contest between invited top competitors in different sports, was held in the USA in 1973 and won by the Pole Vaulter, Bob Seagren.

UK NATIONAL CHAMPIONSHIPS
1973   David Hemery (athletics – hurdler)
1974   John Conteh (boxing)
1975   UK title not contested, but David Hemery leading UK competitor in European Final
1976   David Hemery (athletics – hurdler)
1977   Tim Crooks (rowing)
1978   Brian Jacks (judo)

EUROPEAN CHAMPIONSHIPS
1975   Kjell Isaksson (Sweden, athletics – pole vault)
1976   Kjell Isaksson (Sweden, athletics – pole vault)
1977   Ties Kruize (Netherlands, hockey)
1978   Brian Jacks (GB, judo) and Ties Kruize (Netherlands, hockey)

WORLD CHAMPIONSHIPS
1977   Bob Seagren (USA, athletics – pole vault)
1978   Brian Budd (Canada, association football)
1979   Brian Budd (Canada, association football)

SQUASH RACKETS

World Open Championship

First held in 1976 at Wembley.

MEN
1976   Geoff Hunt (Aus)
1977   Geoff Hunt (Aus)
1978   Postponed

First held in 1976 in Australia.

WOMEN

	Individual	Team
1976	Heather McKay (Aus)	Australia
1979	Heather McKay (Aus)	Great Britain

World Amateur Championship

First held in 1967, it is contested every two years. Individual and team winners:

	Individual	Team		Individual	Team
1967	Geoff Hunt (Aus)	Australia	1975	Kevin Shawcross (Aus)	Great Britain
1969	Geoff Hunt (Aus)	Australia	1977	Maqsood Ahmed (Pak)	Pakistan
1971	Geoff Hunt (Aus)	Australia			
1973	Cameron Nancarrow (Aus)	Australia			

British Open Championship

First played in 1930, the British Open Championship in which both amateurs and professionals may compete was for years regarded as the unofficial world championship. Until 1947 the event was held on a challenge system with two-leg matches between the holder and his challenger. Held annually.

1930–31	Don Butcher (GB) (2)		1962	Mohibullah Khan (Pak)
1932–37	Abdel Fattah Amr Bey (Egy) (5)		1963–66	Abou Taleb (Egy) (3)
1938	James Dear (GB)		1967–68	Jonah Barrington (GB) (2)
1946–49	Mahmoud el Karim (Egy) (4)		1969	Geoff Hunt (Aus)
1950–55	Hashim Khan (Pak) (6)		1970–73	Jonah Barrington (GB) (4)
1956	Roshan Khan (Pak)		1974	Geoff Hunt (Aus)
1957	Hashim Khan (Pak)		1975	Qamar Zaman (Pak)
1958–61	Azam Khan (Pak) (4)		1976–79	Geoff Hunt (Aus) (4)

British Women's Open Championship
First held in 1922.

1922	Joyce Cave (GB)		1923	Nancy Cave (GB)
1922	Sylvia Huntsman (GB)		1924	Joyce Cave (GB)

1925–25 Cecily Fenwick (GB) (2)
1928   Joyce Cave (GB)
1929–30 Nancy Cave (GB)
1931   Cecily Fenwick (GB)
1932–34 Susan Noel (GB) (3)
1934–39 Margot Lumb (GB) (5)
1947–49 Joan Curry (GB) (3)
1950–58 Janet Morgan/Shardlow (GB) (10)
1960   Sheila Macintosh (GB)

1961   Fran Marshall (GB)
1962–77 Heather McKay (Aus) (16)
1978   Susan Newman/King (Aus)
1979   Barbara Wall (Aus)

Note that there have occasionally been two championships in the same year, and that in other cases a year is
missed. This is due to the championship being held in
December or January.

British Amateur Championship

First held in 1922 and contested annually. Winners since 1963:

1963–66 Aftab Jawaid (Pak) (4)
1967–69 Jonah Barrington (GB) (3)
1970   Geoff Hunt (Aus)
1971   Gogi Alauddin (Pak)
1972   Cameron Nancarrow (Aus)
1973–74 Mohibullah Khan (Pak) (2)

1975/6   Kevin Shawcross (Aus)
1976/7   Bruce Brownlee (NZ)
1977/8   Gamal Awad (Egy)
1978/9   Gamal Awad (Egy)
Most wins: 6   Abdel Fattah Amr Bey (Egy) 1931–33,
    1935–57

STEEPLECHASING (*See* Horse Racing)

SUNFLOWERS

Super Sunflower Competition

Held annually from 1971 to 1976, the national competition was organised by *Garden News*.
Winners and winning heights:

1971 Mrs A. Somerville Cowen, Battle, Sussex – 15ft
6 in (4.7m)
1972 Andrew Squires, Bitterne, Southampton – 16ft
6in (5m)
1973 Len Webb, South Harrow, Middlesex – 18ft 1½in
(5.5m)

1974 Edward Purver, Camberley, Surrey – 19ft 2in
(5.8m)
1975 Frank Kelland, Exeter, Devon – 21ft 6in (6.5m)
1976 Frank Kelland, Exeter, Devon – 23ft 6½in (7.2m)

SWIMMING

Olympic Games

Swimming events have been held at each Olympic Games since 1896, when three men's events
were included – 100, 500 and 1200 metres freestyle. Women's events were first included in
1912. Winners since 1948 have been:

MEN
100 Metres Freestyle
1948 Walter Ris (USA) 57.3
1952 Clarke Scholes (USA) 57.4
1956 Jon Henricks (Aus) 55.4
1960 John Devitt (Aus) 55.2
1964 Donald Schollander (USA) 53.4
1968 Michael Wenden (Aus) 52.2
1972 Mark Spitz (USA) 51.2
1976 Jim Montgomery (USA) 49.99

200 Metres Freestyle
1968 Michael Wenden (Aus) 1:55.2

1972 Mark Spitz (USA) 1:52.78
1976 Bruce Furniss (USA) 1:50.29

400 Metres Freestyle
1948 William Smith (USA) 4:41.0
1952 Jean Boiteaux (Fra) 4:30.7
1956 Murray Rose (Aus) 4:27.3
1960 Murray Rose (Aus) 4:18.3
1964 Donald Schollander (USA) 4:12.2
1968 Michael Burton (USA) 4:09.0
1972 Bradford Cooper (Aus) 4:00.27
1976 Brian Goodell (USA) 3:51.93

1500 Metres Freestyle
1948 James McLane (USA) 19:18.5
1952 Ford Konno (USA) 18:30.0
1956 Murray Rose (Aus) 17:58.9
1960 Jon Konrads (Aus) 17:19.6
1964 Robert Windle (Aus) 17:01.7
1968 Michael Burton (USA) 16:38.9
1972 Michael Burton (USA 15:52.58
1976 Brian Goodell (USA) 15:02.40

100 Metres Backstroke
1948 Allen Stack (USA) 1:06.4
1952 Yoshinobu Oyakawa (USA) 1:05.4
1956 David Thiele (Aus) 1:02.2
1960 David Thiele (Aus) 1:01.9
1968 Roland Matthes (GDR) 58.7
1972 Roland Matthes (GDR) 56.58
1976 John Naber (USA) 55.49

200 Metres Backstroke
1964 Jed Graef (USA) 2:10.3
1968 Roland Matthes (GDR) 2:09.6
1972 Roland Matthes (GDR) 2:02.82
1976 John Naber (USA) 1:59.19

100 Metres Butterfly
1968 Douglas Russell (USA) 55.9
1972 Mark Spitz (USA) 54.27
1976 Matt Vogel (USA) 54.35

200 Metres Butterfly
1956 William Yorzyk (USA) 2:19.3
1960 Michael Troy (USA) 2:12.8
1964 Kevin Berry (Aus) 2:06.6
1968 Carl Robie (USA) 2:08.7
1972 Mark Spitz (USA) 2:00.70
1976 Michael Bruner (USA) 1:59.23

100 Metres Breaststroke
1968 Donald McKenzie (USA) 1:07.7
1972 Nobutaka Taguchi (Jap) 1:04.94
1976 John Hencken (USA) 1:03.11

200 Metres Breaststroke
1948 Joseph Verdeur (USA) 2:39.3
1952 John Davies (Aus) 2:34.4
1956 Masura Furukawa (Jap) 2:34.7
1960 William Mulliken (USA) 2:37.4
1964 Ian O'Brien (Aus) 2:27.8
1968 Felipe Munoz (Mex) 2:28.7
1972 John Hencken (USA) 2:21.55
1976 David Wilkie (GB) 2:15.11

200 Metres Individual Medley
1968 Charles Hickcox (USA) 2:12.0
1972 Gunnar Larsson (Swe) 2:07.17

400 Metres Individual Medley
1964 Richard Roth (USA) 4:45.4
1968 Charles Hickcox (USA) 4:48.4
1972 Gunnar Larsson (Swe) 4:31.98
1976 Rod Strachan (USA) 4:23.68

4 × 100 Metres Freestyle Relay
1964 USA 3:33.2

1968 USA 3:31.7
1972 USA 3:26.42

4 × 200 Metres Freestyle Relay
1948 USA 8:46.0
1952 USA 8:31.1
1956 Australia 8:23.6
1960 USA 8:10.2
1964 USA 7:52.1
1968 USA 7:52.3
1972 USA 7:35.78
1976 USA 7:23.22

4 × 100 Metres Medley Relay
1960 USA 4:05.4
1964 USA 3:58.4
1968 USA 3:54.9
1972 USA 3:48.16
1976 USA 3:42.22

Springboard Diving
1948 Bruce Harlan (USA) 163.64
1952 David Browning (USA) 205.29
1956 Robert Clotworthy (USA) 159.56
1960 Gary Tobian (USA) 170.00
1964 Kenneth Sitzberger (USA) 159.90
1968 Bernard Wrightson (USA) 170.15
1972 Vladimir Vasin (USSR) 594.09
1976 Philip Boggs (USA) 619.05

Platform Diving (Highboard)
1948 Samuel Lee (USA) 130.05
1952 Samuel Lee (USA) 156.28
1956 Joaquin Capilla (Mex) 152.44
1960 Robert Webster (USA) 165.56
1964 Robert Webster (USA) 148.58
1968 Klaus Dibiasi (Ita) 164.18
1972 Klaus Dibiasi (Ita) 504.12
1976 Klaus Dibiasi (Ita) 600.51

WOMEN
100 Metres Freestyle
1948 Greta Andersen (Den) 1:06.3
1952 Katalin Szöke (Hun) 1:06.8
1956 Dawn Fraser (Aus) 1:02.0
1960 Dawn Fraser (Aus) 1:01.2
1964 Dawn Fraser (Aus) 59.5
1968 Jan Henne (USA) 1:00.0
1972 Sandra Neilson (USA) 58.59
1976 Kornelia Ender (GDR) 55.65

200 Metres Freestyle
1968 Debbie Meyer (USA) 2:10.5
1972 Shane Gould (Aus) 2:03.56
1976 Kornelia Ender (GDR) 1:59.25

400 Metres Freestyle
1948 Ann Curtis (USA) 5:17.8
1952 Valeria Gyenge (Hun) 5:12.1
1956 Lorraine Crapp (Aus) 4:54.6
1960 Christine von Saltza (USA) 4:50.6

Mark Spitz in 1972 when he won seven Olympic swimming Gold Medals to add to the two Gold, one Silver and one Bronze he won in 1968 (*Syndication International*)

800 Metres Freestyle
1968   Debbie Meyer (USA) 9:24.0
1972   Keena Rothhammer (USA) 8:53.68
1976   Petra Thuemer (GDR) 8:37.14

100 Metres Backstroke
1948   Karen Harup (Den) 1:14.4
1952   Joan Harrison (S. Af) 1:14.3
1956   Judy Grinham (GB) 1:12.9
1960   Lynn Burke (USA) 1:09.3
1964   Cathy Ferguson (USA) 1:07.7
1968   Kaye Hall (USA) 1:06.2
1972   Melissa Belote (USA) 1:05.78
1976   Ulrike Richter (GDR) 1:01.83

200 Metres Backstroke
1968   Lillian Watson (USA) 2:24.8
1972   Melissa Belote (USA) 2:19.19
1976   Ulrike Richter (GDR) 2:13.43

100 Metres Butterfly
1956   Shelley Mann (USA) 1:11.0
1960   Carolyn Schuler (USA) 1:09.5
1964   Sharon Stouder (USA) 1:04.7
1968   Lynette McClements (USA) 1:05.5
1972   Mayumi Aoki (Jap) 1:03.34
1976   Kornelia Ender (GDR) 1:00.13

200 Metres Butterfly
1968   Ada Kok (Hol) 2:24.7
1972   Karen Moe (USA) 2:15.57
1976   Andrea Pollack (GDR) 2:11.41

100 Metres Breaststroke
1968   Djurdica Bjedov (Yug) 1:15.8
1972   Catherine Carr (USA) 1:13.58
1976   Hannelore Anke (GDR) 1:11.16

200 Metres Breaststroke
1948   Petronella van Vliet (Hol) 2:57.2
1952   Eva Székely (Hun) 2:51.7
1956   Ursula Happe (Ger) 2:53.1
1960   Anita Lonsborough (GB) 2:49.5
1964   Galina Prozumenshchikova (USSR) 2:46.4
1968   Sharon Wichman (USA) 2:44.4
1972   Beverley Whitfield (Aus) 2:41.71
1976   Marina Koshevaia (USSR) 2:33.35

200 Metres Individual Medley
1968   Claudia Kolb (USA) 2:24.7
1972   Shane Gould (Aus) 2:23.07

400 Metres Individual Medley
1964   Donna de Varona (USA) 5:18.7
1968   Claudia Kolb (USA) 5:08.5
1972   Gail Neall (Aus) 5:02.97
1976   Ulrike Tauber (GDR) 4:42.77

4 × 100 Metres Freestyle Relay
1948   USA 4:29.2
1952   Hungary 4:24.4
1956   Australia 4:17.1
1960   USA 4:08.9
1964   USA 4:03.8
1968   USA 4:02.5
1972   USA 3:55.19
1976   USA 3:44.82

4 × 100 Metres Medley Relay
1960   USA 4:41.1
1964   USA 4:33.9
1968   USA 4:28.3
1972   USA 4:20.75
1976   GDR 4:07.95

Springboard Diving
1948   Victoria Draves (USA) 108.74
1952   Patricia McCormick (USA) 147.30
1956   Patricia McCormick (USA) 142.36
1960   Ingrid Krämer (Ger) 155.81
1964   Ingrid Engel (née Krämer) (Ger) 145.00
1968   Sue Gossick (USA) 150.77
1972   Micki King (USA) 450.03
1976   Jennifer Chandler (USA) 506.19

Platform Diving (Highboard)
1948   Victoria Draves (USA) 68.87
1952   Patricia McCormick (USA) 79.37
1956   Patricia McCormick (USA) 84.85
1960   Ingrid Krämer (Ger) 91.28
1964   Lesley Bush (USA) 99.80
1968   Milena Duchková (Cze) 109.59
1972   Ulrika Knape (Swe) 390.00
1976   Elena Vaytsekhovskaya (USSR) 406.59

World Championships
First held in Belgrade in 1973.

MEN

100 Metres Freestyle
1973 Jim Montgomery (USA) 51.70
1975 Andrew Coan (USA) 51.25
1978 David McCagg (USA) 50.24

200 Metres Freestyle
1973 Jim Montgomery (USA) 1:53.02
1975 Tim Shaw (USA) 1:51.04
1978 William Forrester (USA) 1:51.02

400 Metres Freestyle
1973 Rick DeMont (USA) 3:58.18
1975 Tim Shaw (USA) 3:54.88
1978 Vladimir Salnikov (USSR) 3:51.94

1500 Metres Freestyle
1973 Steve Holland (Aus) 15:31.85
1975 Tim Shaw (USA) 15:28.92
1978 Vladimir Salnikov (USSR) 15:03.99

100 Metres Backstroke
1973 Roland Matthes (GDR) 57.47
1975 Roland Matthes (GDR) 58.15
1978 Robert Jackson (USA) 56.36

200 Metres Backstroke
1973 Roland Matthes (GDR) 2:01.87
1975 Zoltan Verraszto (Hun) 2:05.05
1978 Jesse Vassallo (USA) 2:02.16

100 Metres Breaststroke
1973 John Hencken (USA) 1:04.02
1975 David Wilkie (GB) 1:04.26
1978 Walter Kusch (GDR) 1:03.56

200 Metres Breaststroke
1973 David Wilkie (GB) 2:19.28
1975 David Wilkie (GB) 2:18.23
1978 Nick Nevid (USA) 2:18.37

100 Metres Butterfly
1973 Bruce Robertson (Can) 55.69
1975 Greg Jagenburg (USA) 55.63
1978 Joseph Bottom (USA) 54.30

200 Metres Butterfly
1973 Robin Backhaus (USA) 2:03.32
1975 William Forrester (USA) 2:01.95
1978 Michael Bruner (USA) 1:59.38

200 Metres Individual Medley
1973 Gunnar Larsson (Swe) 2:08.36
1975 András Hargitay (Hun) 2:07.72
1978 Graham Smith (Can) 2:03.65

400 Metres Individual Medley
1973 András Hargitay (Hun) 4:31.11
1975 András Hargitay (Hun) 4:32.57
1978 Jesse Vassallo (USA) 4:20.05

4 × 100 Metres Freestyle Relay
1973 USA 3:27.18
1975 USA 3:24.85
1978 USA 3:19.74

4 × 200 Metres Freestyle Relay
1973 USA 7:33.22
1975 West Germany 7:39.44
1978 USA 7:20.82

4 × 100 Metres Medley Relay
1973 USA 3:49.49
1975 USA 3:49.00
1978 USA 3:44.63

Springboard Diving
1973 Phil Boggs (USA) 618.57
1975 Phil Boggs (USA) 597.12
1978 Phil Boggs (USA) 913.95

Platform Diving (Highboard)
1973 Klaus Dibiasi (Ita) 559.53
1975 Klaus Dibiasi (Ita) 547.98
1978 Greg Louganis (USA) 844.11

WOMEN

100 Metres Freestyle
1973 Kornelia Ender (GDR) 57.54
1975 Kornelia Ender (GDR) 56.50
1978 Barbara Krause (GDR) 55.68

200 Metres Freestyle
1973 Keena Rothhammer (USA) 2:04.99
1975 Shirley Babashoff (USA) 2:02.50
1978 Cynthia Woodhead (USA) 1:58.53

400 Metres Freestyle
1973 Heather Greenwood (USA) 4:20.28
1975 Shirley Babashoff (USA) 4:16.87
1978 Tracey Wickham (Aus) 4:06.28

800 Metres Freestyle
1973 Novella Calligaris (Ita) 8:52.97
1975 Jenny Turrall (Aus) 8:44.75
1978 Tracey Wickham (Aus) 8:24.94

100 Metres Backstroke
1973 Ulrike Richter (GDR) 1:05.42
1975 Ulrike Richter (GDR) 1:03.30
1978 Linda Jezek (USA) 1:02.55

200 Metres Backstroke
1973 Melissa Belote (USA) 2:20.52
1975 Birgit Treiber (GDR) 2:15.46
1978 Linda Jezek (USA) 2:11.93

100 Metres Breaststroke
1973 Renate Vogel (GDR) 1:13.74
1975 Hannelore Anke (GDR) 1:12.72
1978 Julia Bogdanova (USSR) 1:10.31

200 Metres Breaststroke
1973   Renate Vogel (GDR) 2:40.01
1975   Hannelore Anke (GDR) 2:37.25
1978   Lina Kachushite (USSR) 2:31.42

100 Metres Butterfly
1973   Kornelia Ender (GDR) 1:02.53
1975   Kornelia Ender (GDR) 1:01.24
1978   Mary-Joan Pennington (USA) 1:00.20

200 Metres Butterfly
1973   Rosemarie Kother (GDR) 2:13.76
1975   Rosemarie Kother (GDR) 2:13.82
1978   Tracy Caulkins (USA) 2:09.87

200 Metres Individual Medley
1973   Angela Hubner (GDR) 2:20.51
1975   Kathy Heddy (USA) 2:19.80
1978   Tracy Caulkins (USA) 2:14.07

400 Metres Individual Medley
1973   Gudrun Wegner (GDR) 4:57.31
1975   Ulrike Tauber (GDR) 4:52.76
1978   Tracy Caulkins (USA) 4:40.83

4 × 100 Metres Freestyle Relay
1973   GDR 3:52.45
1975   GDR 3:49.37
1978   USA 3:43.43

4 × 100 Metres Medley Relay
1973   GDR 4:16.84
1975   GDR 4:14.74
1978   USA 4:08.21

Springboard Diving
1973   Christine Kohler (GDR) 442.17
1975   Irina Kalinina (USSR) 489.81
1978   Irina Kalinina (USSR) 691.43

Platform Diving (Highboard)
1973   Ulrike Knape (Swe) 406.77
1975   Janet Ely (USA) 403.89
1978   Irina Kalinina (USSR) 412.71

Synchronised Swimming

	Solo	Duet	Team
1973	Teresa Andersen (USA) 120.460	USA	USA
1975	Gail Buzonas (USA) 133.083	USA	USA
1978	Helen Vanderburg (Can) 186.249	Canada	USA

European Cup

Team competitions for European nations' teams for both men and women were first held in 1969.

MEN

1969	GDR	1973	GDR	1976	USSR
1971	USSR	1975	USSR	1979	USSR

WOMEN

1969	GDR	1973	GDR	1976	USSR
1971	GDR	1975	GDR	1979	GDR

TABLE TENNIS

Swaythling Cup

The Men's Team World Championship for the Swaythling Cup was first held in 1927, and from then until 1957, with the exception of the war years it was contested annually; since then it has been held biennially.

1927–31	Hungary (5)	1949	Hungary	1965	China
1932	Czechoslovakia	1950–51	Czechoslovakia (2)	1967	Japan
1933–35	Hungary (3)	1952	Hungary	1969	Japan
1936	Austria	1953	England	1971	China
1937	USA	1954–57	Japan (4)	1973	Sweden
1938	Hungary	1959	Japan	1975	China
1939	Czechoslovakia	1961	China	1977	China
1947–48	Czechoslovakia (2)	1963	China	1979	Hungary

Corbillon Cup

The Women's Team World Championship for the Marcel Corbillon Cup was first held in the 1933–34 season, and like the Swaythling Cup was contested annually until 1957 and biennially since then.

1934	Germany	1938	Czechoslovakia	1949	USA
1935–36	Czechoslovakia (2)	1939	Germany	1950–51	Romania (2)
1937	USA	1947–48	England (2)	1952	Japan

1953	Romania	1961	Japan	1971	Japan
1954	Japan	1963	Japan	1973	South Korea
1955–56	Romania (2)	1965	China	1975	China
1957	Japan	1967	Japan	1977	China
1959	Japan	1969	USSR	1979	China

World Championships

First held in 1927. Singles winners have been:

MEN'S SINGLES

1927	Roland Jacobi (Hun)
1928	Zoltan Mechlovits (Hun)
1929	Fred Perry (GB)
1930	Viktor Barna (Hun)
1931	Miklos Szabados (Hun)
1932	Viktor Barna (Hun)
1933	Viktor Barna (Hun)
1934	Viktor Barna (Hun)
1935	Viktor Barna (Hun)
1936	Standa Kolar (Cze)
1937	Richard Bergmann (Aut)
1938	Bohumil Vana (Cze)
1939	Richard Bergmann (Aut)
1947	Bohumil Vana (Cze)
1948	Richard Bergmann (Eng)
1949	Johnny Leach (Eng)
1950	Richard Bergmann (Eng)
1951	Johnny Leach (Eng)
1952	Hiroji Satoh (Jap)
1953	Ferenc Sido (Hun)
1954	Ichiro Ogimura (Jap)
1955	Toshiaki Tanaka (Jap)
1956	Ichiro Ogimura (Jap)
1957	Toshiaki Tanaka (Jap)
1959	Jung Kuo-tuan (Chi)
1961	Chuang Tse-tung (Chi)
1963	Chuang Tse-tung (Chi)
1965	Chuang Tse-tung (Chi)
1967	Nobuhiko Hasegawa (Jap)
1969	Shigeo Ito (Jap)
1971	Stellan Bengtsson (Swe)
1973	Hsi En-ting (Chi)
1975	Istvan Jonyer (Hun)
1977	Mitsuru Kohno (Jap)
1979	Seiji Ono (Jap)

WOMEN'S SINGLES

1927–31	Maria Mednyanszky (Hun) (5)
1932–33	Anna Sipos (Hun) (2)
1934–35	Marie Kettnerova (Cze) (2)
1936	Ruth Aarons (USA)
1937	vacant (Ruth Aarons and Trude Pritzi finalists)
1938	Trude Pritzi (Aut)
1939	Vlasha Depetrisova (Cze)
1947–49	Gizi Farkas (Hun) (3)
1950–55	Angelica Rozeanu (Rom) (6)
1956	Tomi Okawa (Jap)
1957	Fujie Eguchi (Jap)
1959	Kimiyo Matsuzaki (Jap)
1961	Chiu Chung-hui (Chi)
1963	Kimiyo Matsuzaki (Jap)
1965	Naoko Fukazu (Jap)
1967	Sachiko Morisawa (Jap)

1969	Toshiko Kowada (Jap)
1971	Lin Hui-ching (Chi)
1973	Hu Yu-lan (Chi)
1975	Pak Yung Sun (NK)
1977	Pak Yung Sun (NK)
1979	Ke Hsin-ai (Chi)

MEN'S DOUBLES

Winners since 1965:

1965	Chung Tse-tung and Hsu Yin-sheng (Chi)
1967	Hans Alser and Kjell Johansson (Swe)
1969	Hans Alser and Kjell Johansson (Swe)
1971	Istvan Jonyer and Tibor Klampar (Hun)
1973	Stellan Bengtsson and Kjell Johansson (Swe)
1975	Gabor Gergely and Istvan Jonyer (Hun)
1977	Chen-shih Li and Liang Ke-liang (Chi)
1979	Dragutin Surbek and Anton Stipancic (Yug)

Most wins have been achieved by:
8 Viktor Barna (Hun): 6 with Miklos Szabados 1929–32, 1934–35, with Sandor Glancz in 1933 and with Richard Bergmann 1939

WOMEN'S DOUBLES

Winners since 1965:

1965	Cheng Min-chih and Lin Hui-ching (Chi)
1967	Saeko Hirota and Sachiko Morisawa (Jap)
1969	Svyetlana Grinberg and Zoya Rudnova (USSR)
1971	Cheng Min-chih and Lin Hui-ching (Chi)
1973	Maria Alexandru (Rom) and Miho Hamada (Jap)
1975	Maria Alexandru (Rom) and Shoko Takashima (Jap)
1977	Yong Ok Pak (NK) and Ying Yang (Chi)
1979	Chang Li and Chang Te-ying (Chi)

Most wins have been achieved by:
7 Maria Mednyanszky (Hun): 6 with Anna Sipos 1930–35, 1 with Erika Flamm 1928

MIXED DOUBLES

Winners since 1965:

1965	Koji Kimura and Masako Seki (Jap)
1967	Nobuhiko Hasegawa and Noriko Yamanaka (Jap)
1969	Nobuhiko Hasegawa and Yasuka Konno (Jap)
1971	Chang Shih-lin and Lin Hui-ching (Chi)
1973	Liang Ko-liang and Li Li (Chi)
1975	Stanislav Gomozkov and Anna Ferdman (USSR)
1977	Jacques Secretin and Claude Bergeret (Fra)
1979	Liang Ke-liang and Ke Hsin-ai (Chi)

Most wins have been achieved by:
6 Maria Mednyanszky (Hun): 3 with Miklos Szabados 1930–31, 1934, 2 with Zoltan Mechlovits 1927–28, 1 with Istvan Kelen 1933
5 Ferenc Sido (Hun): 3 with Gizi Farkas 1947, 1949–50, 2 with Angelica Rozeanu 1952–53

TELEVISION

Golden Rose of Montreux

The BBC entries for the most esteemed of television light entertainment awards.

1961   The Black and White Minstrel Show (Gold rose and Press Jury prize)
1962   Big Band Concert
1963   It's A Square World (Press prize)
1964   The Good Old Days
1965   The Benny Hill Show
1966   The World of Wooster
1967   Frost Over England (Gold rose, Int. Press prize and Special prize)
1968   The World of Charlie Drake
1969   Marty (Silver rose)

1970   Morecambe and Wise
1971   Monty Python's Flying Circus (Silver rose)
1972   The Goodies (Silver rose)
1973   The Dick Emery Show
1974   Some Mothers Do 'Ave 'Em
1975   The Goodies: The Movies (Silver rose)
1976   The Two Ronnies: The Picnic (Bronze rose)
1977   Shirley Bassey
1978   Dave Allen At Large (Silver rose)
1979   Fawlty Towers

Miscellaneous British Winners from 1977

The following is a selection of prizewinning British programmes and artists at various international festivals and in some other awards.

1977

International Film Festival of Culture and Psychiatry, San Antonio
Special citation to Out of the Darkness (Tyne Tees)

Club Mirror's Special Award to
Philip Jones (Thames), Controller of Light Entertainment

Imperial Relations Trust
Award to David Coulter, producer/director (LWT)

American TV Critics
Best Series Award to Upstairs Downstairs (LWT)

Monte Carlo International TV Festival
Best news reporting award for Norman Rees's coverage of the Cod War (ITN)

TV Times Awards
Most compulsive character: John Thaw, The Sweeney (Thames)
Funniest woman on TV: Yootha Joyce, George and Mildred (Thames)
Most popular female singer: Julie Covington, Rock Follies (Thames)
Best actor: Frank Finlay, Bouquet of Barbed Wire (LWT)
TV Hall of Fame: Noele Gordon, Crossroads (ATV)

US Christopher Awards
Spiders and Orangutans, Survival (Anglia), for affirmation of the highest values of the human spirit

Broadcasting Press Guild
Best Light Entertainment: The Muppet Show (ATV)

New York International Film and TV Festival
Gold Award to Children No More (Westward), and Award to The Collection (Granada)

1978

Broadcasting Press Guild
Most Original Contribution to TV: Looney Tunes, Rock Follies (Thames)
Best Drama Series: Hard Times (Granada)
Best Screen Performance: Geraldine James, Dummy (ATV)

Writer's Guild Pye Trophy
Best Written Comedy, Have a Happy Christmas (Yorks)

Radio Industries Club
ITV Personality of the Year 1977: Leonard Rossiter (Yorks)
Best ITV Programme: The Muppet Show (ATV)

Peabody Award in the US
Outstanding drama production: Upstairs Downstairs (LWT)

Sun Awards
Top ITV Series: The Sweeney (Thames)
Top Sports Personality: Dickie Davies
Top Factual Programme: World in Action (Granada)

Monte Carlo International Television Festival
Top Current Affairs Programme: Panorama (BBC) on how a private company was planning to launch spy satellites from a base in Central Africa.
Best news report: ITN, for a filmed report of an Ethiopian air attack on guerrilla forces in Eritrea which was first shown in 'News at 10'.
UNESCO award for the best play: A Special Kind of Loving (EMI), independent entry. It dealt with the problems of a mentally handicapped boy.

1978-79

Chicago International Film Festival
Gold Hugo for best documentary: The Search for Sandra Laing (ATV)

Trento International Festival
Gold Award: First Conquest of Everest without Oxygen (ATV)

Radio Industries Club
Newscaster of the Year: Anna Ford (ITN)

New York International Film and TV Festival
Gold Award, Clouds of Glory – Wordsworth and Coleridge (Granada): Silver Award, The Christians (Granada): Silver Award, Skilful Soccer with Jack Charlton (Tyne Tees)

Kermit and Robin from the Muppet Show which has won many awards, including Best Light Entertainment Production awarded by BAFTA in 1976

British Academy of Film and Television Arts Awards

Formerly the Society of Film and TV Arts and the Guild of Television Producers and Directors, the Academy gives Britain's most prestigious show business awards.

THE DESMOND DAVIS AWARD
1960   Richard Dimbleby
1961   Michael Barry
1962   Cecil McGivern
1963   Joan Kemp-Welch
1965   Humphrey Burton
1966   Alan Chivers
1967   Sydney Newman
1968   Ken Russell
1969   Richard Cawston
1970   David Attenborough
1971   Jeremy Isaacs
1972   Nigel Ryan
1973   James MacTaggart
1974   Denis Mitchell
1975   Jack Gold
1976   Bill Ward
1977   Norman Swallow
1978   Christopher Ralling

BEST DRAMA PRODUCTION
1954   Christian Simpson
1955   Gil Calder
1956   Joy Harrington
1957   *Play:* Rudolph Cartier
1958   *Play:* Silvio Narizzano
1959   *Play:* William Kotcheff
1960   *Play:* Peter Dews
1961   *Play:* Andrew Osborn
1962   *Play:* David Rose and Charles Jarrott
1963   *Play:* John Jacobs
        Series: Philip Mackie
1964   *Play:* Philip Saville
        Series: Rex Firkin

1965   *Play:* Cyril Coke and Peter Hammond
        Series: Philip Mackie and Silvio Narizzano
1966   *Play:* Kenneth Loach
        Series: Peter Graham Scott
1967   *Play:* Kenneth Loach
1968   Anthony Page, Parachute
1969   *Play:* Christopher Morahan, The Letter, and Nora You've Made Your Bed Now Lie on It
        Series: Verity Lambert, Somerset Maugham series
1970   Alan Bridges
1971   *Play:* Ted Kotcheff, Edna, The Inebriate Woman
        Series: John Hawkesworth, Upstairs Downstairs
1972   *Single Play:* Jack Gold
        Series: Derek Granger
1973   *Single Play:* Michael Apted
        Series: John Hawkesworth, Upstairs Downstairs
1974   *Single Play:* Jon Scoffield, Antony and Cleopatra
        Series: James Ormerod, South Riding
1975   *Single Play:* Alan Parker, The Evacuees
        Series: Cecil Clarke and John Gorrie, Edward the VII
1976   *Single Play:* Michael Tuchner, Bar Mitzvah Boy
        Series: Andrew Brown, Rock Follies
1977   *Single Play:* John Goldschmidt, Spend Spend Spend
        Series: Peter Goodchild and John Glenister, Marie Curie
1978   *Single Play:* David Hare, Licking Hitler
        Series: Andrew Brown and Waris Hussein, Edward and Mrs Simpson

BEST FACTUAL PRODUCTION
1957   Donald Baverstock and the Production Team of 'Tonight'
1958   The Production Team of 'Tonight'
1959   Denis Mitchell
1960   Michael Redington
        Current Affairs: 'Sportsview' Unit
1961   Tim Hewat
        Current Affairs: Bill Allenby
1962   Richard Cawston
1963   Peter Morley and Cyril Bennett
        Documentary: Anthony de Lotbiniere
1964   The Production Team of 'The World in Action'
        Documentary: Jack Gold
1965   Jeremy Isaacs and the Production Team of 'This Week'
        Documentary: Charles Squires
1966   The Production Team of '24 Hours'
        Documentary: Kevin Billington
1967   Desmond Wilcox and Bill Morton
        Documentary: Kevin Billington
1968   *Documentary:* Michael Darlow and Mike Wooller
        Current Affairs: Phillip Whitehead and Production Team
1969   *Documentary:* Paul Watson, A Year in the Life
        Current Affairs: ITN Production Team
1970   Adrian Cowell
1971   Jeremy Wallington and Production Team, World in Action
1972   *Single Programme:* Mick Rhodes
        Series: Peter Goodchild and Production Team
1973   *Single Programme:* Eric Davidson, Last Night Another Soldier . . .

Series: Gus MacDonald

1974 *Single Programme:* Frank Cvitanovich, Beauty, Bonny, Daisy, Violet, Grace, and Geoffrey Morton
Series: Peter Goodchild/Bruce Norman, Horizon

1975 *Single Programme:* John Willis, Johnny Go Home
Series: Brian Moser, Disappearing World

1976 *Single Programme:* John Purdie, The Rescue
Series: John Purdie/Roger Mills, Sailor

1977 *Documentary:* Tim King, Casualty
Series: Antony Thomas, The South African Experience

1978 *Documentary:* Adrian Cavell, The Opium War-lords
Series: Christopher Ralling, The Voyage of Charles Darwin

BEST LIGHT ENTERTAINMENT PRODUCTION
1957 Brian Tesler
1958 Joan Kemp-Welch
1959 Bill Ward
1960 James Gilbert
1961 George Inns
1962 Duncan Wood
1963 Colin Clews
1964 Francis Essex
Situation Comedy: Joe McGrath
1965 Joe McGrath
Situation Comedy: Michael Mills
1966 Ned Sherrin
Situation Comedy: Dick Clement
1967 James Gilbert
Situation Comedy: Michael Mills
1968 Dennis Main Wilson
1969 *Musical:* Yvonne Littlewood, Just Pet
Situation Comedy: Mark Stuart
1970 David Croft and Team
1971 John Robins and David Bell, The Benny Hill Show
1972 *Programme:* Ian McNaughton and Production Team
Situation Comedy: Graeme Muir
1973 *Programme:* David Bell
Situation Comedy: James Gilbert, Whatever Happened to the Likely Lads?
1974 *Programme:* David Bell
Situation Comedy: Sydney Lotterby
1975 *Programme:* Terry Hughes, Two Ronnies
Situation Comedy: John Howard Davies, Fawlty Towers
1976 *Programme:* The Muppet Show Production Team
Situation Comedy: Sydney Lotterby, Porridge
1977 *Programme:* Ernest Maxin, Morecambe and Wise Christmas Show
Situation Comedy: Ronnie Baxter, Rising Damp
1978 *Programme:* David Mallet, The Kenny Everett Video Show
Situation Comedy: Sydney Lotterby, Going Straight

BEST SPECIALISED PRODUCTION
1963 Margaret Dale
1964 Ned Sherrin
1965 Peter Watkins
1966 Ken Russell

1967 Basil Coleman
1968 Jack Gold
1969 Biddy Baxter, Edward Barnes and Rosemary Gill: Fred Burnley
1970 Christopher Burstall
1971 Norman Swallow
1972 *Programme:* Mai Zetterling and Team
Series: Michael Dibb
1973 *Programme:* Colin Nears
Series: Patrick Dowling
1974 *Programme:* Brian Gibson
Series: Humphrey Burton
1975 *Programme:* David Cobham
Series: Michael Latham
1976 *Programme:* David Hargreaves
Outside Broadcast Programme: F.A. Cup Final Production Team

SPECIAL AWARDS
1964 The Great War
1965 Joy Whitby
1966 BBC-ITV World Cup Consortium
1967 Donald Wilson and Team for the Forsyte Saga
David Nicholas and John Phillips for Home is the Sailor
1968 ITN's News at Ten
Bryan Cowgill, David Coleman and the Olympics Production Team
1969 Monty Python's Flying Circus
Michael Gill and Peter Montagnon
1970 Ronald Travers and Mark Shivas
1971 Jenny Barraclough

MOST ORIGINAL PROGRAMME
1978 Pennies from Heaven, produced by Kenith Trodd (BBC)

BEST ACTUALITY COVERAGE
1977 Antony Craxton
1978 The Open Golf Championship, produced by A. P. Wilkinson (BBC)

BEST ACTOR
1954 Paul Rogers
1955 Peter Cushing
1956 Michael Gough
1957 Michael Hordern
1958 Donald Pleasence
1959 Patrick McGoohan
1960 Lee Montague
1961 Rupert Davies
1962 Harry H. Corbett
1963 Alan Badel
1964 Patrick Wymark
1965 Alan Badel
1966 Warren Mitchell
1967 Eric Porter
1968 Roy Dotrice
1969 Edward Woodward, Callan
1970 Keith Michell
1971 John Le Mesurier, Traitor
1972 Anthony Hopkins
1973 Frank Finlay, Adventures of Don Quixote; The Death of Adolph Hitler; and Candide
1974 Peter Barkworth, Crown Matrimonial

Penelope Keith won a BAFTA Award, in 1976, for the Best Light Entertainment Performance in 'The Good Life'. Shown here (*left to right*) **in a scene from the programme are Felicity Kendal as Barbara, Richard Briers as Tom, Paul Eddington as Jerry, and Penelope Keith as Margo** (*BBC Copyright*)

1975	John Hurt, Naked Civil Servant
1976	Derek Jacobi, I Claudius
1977	Peter Barkworth, Professional Foul, The Country Party
1978	Edward Fox, Edward and Mrs Simpson

BEST ACTRESS
1954	Googie Withers
1955	Virginia McKenna
1956	Rosalie Crutchley
1958	Gwen Watford
1959	Catherine Lacey
1960	Billie Whitelaw
1961	Ruth Dunning
1962	Brenda Bruce
1963	Vivien Merchant
1964	Katherine Blake
1965	Gwen Watford
1966	Vanessa Redgrave
1967	Judi Dench
1968	Wendy Craig
1969	Margaret Tyzack, The First Churchills
1970	Annette Crosbie
1971	Patricia Hayes, Edna, The Inebriate Woman
1972	Billie Whitelaw
1973	Celia Johnson, Mrs Palfrey at the Claremont
1974	Lee Remick, Jennie
1975	Annette Crosbie, Edward the Seventh
1976	Sian Phillips, I Claudius; How Green Was My Valley
1977	Penelope Keith, Norman Conquests: Saving it from Albie
1978	Francesca Annis, Lillie

BEST LIGHT ENTERTAINMENT PERFORMANCE
1957	Tony Hancock
1958	Alan Melville
1959	Tony Hancock
1960	Stanley Baxter
1961	Eric Sykes
1962	Michael Bentine
1963	Morecambe and Wise
1964	Millicent Martin
1965	Peter Cook and Dudley Moore
1966	John Bird
1967	Alan Bennett
1968	Marty Feldman
1969	Eric Morecambe and Ernie Wise
1970	Eric Morecambe and Ernie Wise
1971	Ronnie Corbett and Ronnie Barker
1972	Eric Morecambe and Ernie Wise
1973	Eric Morecambe and Ernie Wise
1974	Stanley Baxter
1975	Ronnie Barker, Porridge
1976	Penelope Keith, The Good Life
1977	Ronnie Barker, Porridge
1978	Ronnie Barker, Going Straight and The Two Ronnies

THE RICHARD DIMBLEBY AWARD
1963	Bernard Braden
1964	Alan Whicker
1965	Malcolm Muggeridge
1966	Alastair Burnet
1967	David Frost
1968	Julian Pettifer
1969	Kenneth Clark
1970	Alastair Burnet
1971	Desmond Wilcox
1972	Alistair Cooke
1973	Jonathan Dimbleby
1974	Robin Day
1975	Robert Kee
1976	Frank Bough
1977	Alan Whicker
1978	David Bellamy

BEST SCRIPT
1954	Iaian McCormack
1955	Colin Morris
1956	Spike Milligan
1957	Colin Morris
1958	Colin Morris
	Ken Hughes
1959	Alan Simpson and Ray Galton
1960	Alun Owen
1961	Giles Cooper
1962	Troy Kennedy Martin
1963	Harold Pinter
1964	Ken Taylor
1965	Michael Mills and Richard Waring
1966	Dennis Potter
1967	John Hopkins
1968	Marty Feldman and Barry Took
1969	John Terraine
1970	Colin Welland
1971	Benny Hill
1975	Dick Clement, Ian La Frenais
1976	Jack Rosenthal
1977	Tom Stoppard, Professional Foul
1978	Dennis Potter, Pennies From Heaven

BEST DESIGN
1954	Michael Yates
1955	Bruce Angrave
1956	Reece Pemberton
1957	Stephen Taylor

1958	Stephen Bundy	1974	Lynda Beighton
1959	Clifford Hatts	1975	Jim Atkinson
1960	Frederick Pusey	1976	Mike Billing and Pam Meager
1961	Voytek	1978	A new set of ten awards for technical craft was introduced
1962	Eileen Diss		
1963	Richard Henry		

1958 Stephen Bundy
1959 Clifford Hatts
1960 Frederick Pusey
1961 Voytek
1962 Eileen Diss
1963 Richard Henry
1964 Richard Wilmot
1965 Eileen Diss
1966 Tony Abbott
1967 Julia Trevelyan Oman
1968 Roy Oxley
1969 Tony Abbott
1970 Peter Seddon
1971 The Rivals of Sherlock Holmes – Design Team
1972 Don Homfray
1973 Eileen Diss
1974 Bill McPherson
1975 Henry Graveney, Anthony Waller
1976 Tim Harvey
1977 Roy Stonehouse
1978 Alan Cameron and Martyn Hebert, Edward and Mrs Simpson

TECHNICAL CRAFT
1972 Alan Tyrer
1973 Alan Afrait

1974 Lynda Beighton
1975 Jim Atkinson
1976 Mike Billing and Pam Meager
1978 A new set of ten awards for technical craft was introduced

GENERAL
1968 Tom Moncrieff
1969 Terry Gilliam
1970 John Bloomfield
1971 News Teams, BBC and ITV in Ulster

SPECIAL AWARDS
Foreign Television Programme Award
1968 Czechoslovak Television Service
1969 Neil Armstrong and everybody associated with the first television pictures from the moon
1970 Not Awarded
1971 Marcel Ophuls
1972 Deutsche Olympische Zentrum
1973 Not Awarded
1974 Not Awarded
1975 Ingmar Bergman
1976 Peter Watkins
1977 No Award
1978 No Award

TENNIS (*See* Lawn Tennis, Real Tennis)

TENPIN BOWLING (*See* Bowling)

THEATRE

'Evening Standard' Drama Awards

Instituted in 1955 by the London *Evening Standard*, the awards aim to promote the arts in London. All major West End productions, writers, actors and actresses are eligible, and the winners are chosen by a panel of judges composed of critics from London newspapers.

BEST MUSICAL OF THE YEAR
1955 The Pyjama Game
1956 Cranks ('Best Musical Entertainment')
1957 No award
1958 West Side Story
1959 Make Me an Offer
1960 Fings Ain't Wot They Used T'Be
1961 Beyond the Fringe
1962 No award
1963 Oh What A Lovely War
1964 Little Me
1965 No award
1966 Funny Girl
1967 Sweet Charity
1968 Cabaret
1969 Promises, Promises
1970 No award
1971 No award
1972 Applause
1973 Rocky Horror Show
1974 John, Paul, George, Ringo and Bert

Ann-Marie Gwatkin as Annie, and Sandy, in a scene from 'Annie' which won the 1978 Best Musical of the Year *Evening Standard* **Drama Award** (*John Timbers*)

1975 A Little Night Music
1976 A Chorus Line
1977 Elvis
1978 Annie

BEST NEW PLAY OF THE YEAR
1955 Tiger at the Gates, J. Giraudoux
1956 Romanoff and Juliet, Peter Ustinov
1957 Summer of the Seventeenth Doll, Ray Lawler
1958 Cat on a Hot Tin Roof, Tennessee Williams
1959 The Long, the Short and the Tall, C. Shurr
1960 The Caretaker, Harold Pinter
1961 Becket, Jean Anouilh
1962 Caucasian Chalk Circle, B. Brecht
1963 Poor Bitos, Jean Anouilh
1964 Who's Afraid of Virginia Woolf, Edward Albee
1965 A Patriot for Me, John Osborne, and The Killing of Sister George, F. Marcus
1966 Loot, Joe Orton
1967 A Day in the Death of Joe Egg, Peter Nichols
1968 Hotel in Amsterdam, John Osborne
1969 National Health, Peter Nichols
1970 Home, David Storey
1971 Butley, Simon Gray
1972 Jumpers, Tom Stoppard
1973 Saturday, Sunday, Monday, Eduardo de Filippo
1974 Norman Conquests, Alan Ayckbourn
1975 Otherwise Engaged, Simon Gray
1976 Weapons of Happiness, Howard Brenton
1977 Just Between Ourselves, Alan Ayckbourn
1978 Night and Day, Tom Stoppard

BEST COMEDY OF THE YEAR (from 1970)
1970 The Philanthropist, Christopher Hampton
1971 Getting On, Alan Bennett
1972 Veterans, Charles Wood
1973 Absurd Person Singular, Alan Ayckbourn
1974 Travesties, Tom Stoppard
1975 Alphabetical Order, Michael Frayn
1976 Thoughts of Chairman Alf, Johnny Speight
1977 Privates on Parade, Peter Nicholls
1978 Gloo Joo, Michael Hastings

MOST PROMISING PLAYWRIGHT ('British', 1956–59)
1956 John Osborne
1957 Roger Bolt
1958 Peter Shaffer
1959 John Arden
      Arnold Walker
1960 J. P. Donleavy
1961 Gwyn Thomas
      Henry Livings
1962 David Rudkin
1963 Charles Wood
      James Saunders
1964 No award
1965 David Mercer
1966 David Halliwell
1967 Tom Stoppard
      David Storey
1968 No award
1969 Peter Barnes
1970 David Hare
      Heathcote Williams

1971 E. A. Whitehead
1972 Wilson John Haire
1973 David Williamson
1974 Mustapha Matura
1975 Stephen Poliakoff
1976 Stuart Parker
1977 Mary O'Malley
      James Robson
1978 John Byrne
      Brian Clark

BEST PERFORMANCE BY AN ACTOR IN THE YEAR
1955 Richard Burton
1956 Paul Schofield
1957 Laurence Olivier
1958 Sir Michael Redgrave
1959 Eric Porter
1960 Alec Guinness
      Rex Harrison
1961 Christopher Plummer
1962 Paul Schofield
1963 Michael Redgrave
1964 Nicol Williamson
1965 Ian Holm
1966 Albert Finney
1967 Lawrence Olivier
1968 Alec McCowen
1969 Nicol Williamson
1970 John Gielgud
      Ralph Richardson
1971 Alan Bates
1972 Lord Olivier
1973 Alec McCowen
1974 John Wood
1975 John Gielgud
1976 Albert Finney
1977 Donald Sinden
1978 Alan Howard

BEST PERFORMANCE BY AN ACTRESS IN THE YEAR
1955 Sian McKenna
1956 Peggy Ashcroft
1957 Brenda De Banzie
1958 Gwen Ffrangcon-Davies
1959 Flora Robson
1960 Dorothy Tutin
1961 Vanessa Redgrave
1962 Maggie Smith
1963 Joan Plowright
1964 Peggy Ashcroft
1965 Eileen Atkins
1966 Irene Worth
1967 Lila Kedrova
1968 Jill Bennett
1969 Rosemary Harris
1970 Maggie Smith
1971 Peggy Ashcroft
1972 Rachel Roberts
1973 Janet Suzman
1974 Claire Bloom
1975 Dorothy Tutin
1976 Janet Suzman
1977 Alison Steadman
1978 Kate Nelligan

Right: **Elaine Paige as Eva in 'Evita' won the award for the Performer of the Year in a Musical in 1978 given by the Society of West End Theatres** (*Zoe Dominic*)

Below: **A scene from the London Festival Ballet's 'Romeo and Juliet' which won the Outstanding Ballet Achievement, Society of West End Theatre Award in 1977** (*Anthony Crickman*)

Society of West End Theatre Awards

From 1976 the Society has presented its own theatre awards, similar to the United States' Tony Awards, at a ceremony which takes place at the Café Royal on the first Sunday in December each year. The Society's presidents have included John Gale, Sir Emile Littler, Stephen Mitchell, Toby Rowland, Peter Saunders, David Conville and Ian B. Albery.

MUSICAL OF THE YEAR
1976   Chorus Line
1977   Comedy of Errors
1978   Evita

PLAY OF THE YEAR
1976   Dear Daddy
1977   The Fire that Consumes
1978   Whose Life is it Anyway?

COMEDY
1976   Donkey's Years
1977   Privates on Parade
1978   Filumena

ACTOR OF THE YEAR (Revival)
1976   Alan Howard, Henry V/IV
1977   Ian McKellen, Pillars of the Community
1978   Alan Howard, Coriolanus

ACTOR OF THE YEAR (New Play)
1976   Paul Copley, King and Country
1977   Michael Bryant, State of Revolution
1978   Tom Conti, Whose Life is it Anyway?

BEST SUPPORTING ARTIST
1978   Margaret Courtenay, Separate Tables

BEST SUPPORTING ACTOR
1977   Nigel Hawthorne, Privates on Parade
1978   Robert Eddison, Twelfth Night

ACTRESS OF THE YEAR (Revival)
1976   Dorothy Tutin, A Month in the Country
1977   Judi Dench, Macbeth
1978   Dorothy Tutin, The Double Dealer

ACTRESS OF THE YEAR (New Play)
1976   Peggy Ashcroft, Old World
1977   Alison Fiske, Dusa Fish Stas And Vi
1978   Joan Plowright, Filumena

BEST SUPPORTING ACTRESS
1977   Mona Washbourne, Stevie
1978   Elizabeth Spriggs, Love Letters in Blue

PERFORMER OF THE YEAR IN A MUSICAL
1977   Anna Sharkey, Maggie
1978   Elaine Paige, Evita

DIRECTOR OF THE YEAR
1976   Jonathan Miller, The Three Sisters
1977   Clifford Williams, Wild Oats
1978   Terry Hands, Henry VI

DESIGNER OF THE YEAR
1976   Farrah, Henry V/IV
1977   John Napier, King Lear
1978   Ralph Koltai, Brand

COMEDY PERFORMANCE OF THE YEAR
1976   Penelope Keith, Donkey's Years
1977   Denis Quilley, Privates on Parade
1978   Ian McKellen, The Alchemist

OUTSTANDING OPERA ACHIEVEMENT
1977   Glyndebourne Festival, Don Giovanni
1978   English National Opera

OUTSTANDING OPERA PRODUCTION
1978   Lohengrin, Covent Garden

OUTSTANDING BALLET PRODUCTION
1978   A Month in the Country

OUTSTANDING BALLET ACHIEVEMENT
1977   London Festival Ballet's Romeo and Juliet
1978   Robert Cohan, London Contemporary Dance Theatre

SPECIAL AWARD
1976   Save London's Theatres Campaign

THREE-DAY EVENT (See Equestrian Events)

TOASTMASTERS

The Guild of Professional Toastmasters Best After Dinner Award

This was the idea of Ivor Spencer, President and Founder of the Guild, to give an incentive to speakers to improve the quality of their speeches. The Award has been won by the following people. After their names their reaction on hearing the news for the first time about their Award is mentioned.

1967   Lord Redcliffe-Maud, the former Master of University College Oxford, 'What an honour, you have made my day.'
1968   Sir Harold Wilson, former Prime Minister. Michael Halls, Sir Harold's private secretary, said 'Sir Harold said it is the nicest thing that's happened to him since he became Prime Minister.'
1969   Sheila Hancock, 'I can't believe it, please repeat it.'

1970   Alfred Marks, on hearing the news in his dressing room at the London Palladium, said 'It's about time.'
1971   Graham Hill. 'You couldn't have picked a better speaker. When can I make my speech?'
1972   Clement Freud. 'Thank you, I see you have got good taste.'
1973   Rachel Heyhoe. 'I am thrilled.'
1974   Tommy Trinder. 'You're kidding.'

1975 Marshal of the Royal Air Force Sir Arthur Harris. 'I am delighted to hear the news, and will be coming back especially from South Africa to receive the Award.'

1976 No Award.

1977 Commissioner Catherine Bramwell-Booth, 96-year-old grand-daughter of the Founder of the Salvation Army. 'I can't believe it. What odd bedfellows, myself as a non-drinker mixing with fellows who are involved all their lives with toasting and drinking. But I am absolutely thrilled and can't wait to make the speech at the Award Luncheon. God bless you.'

1978 No Award.

TOBOGGANING (*See* Bobsleigh and Tobogganing)

TOURISM

Come to Britain Trophy

The 'Come to Britain' Trophy was first offered by the British Tourist Authority in 1956 to stimulate interest in the provision of new services and amenities for visitors from overseas. The Trophy – Britain's 'Travel Oscar' is an award for tourist enterprise to the company, organisation, local authority or individual judged to have introduced the year's most outstanding new service, facility or amenity for overseas visitors. In addition there are two special awards, one for public enterprise, and one for private enterprise. Previous winners:

1956 Trust Houses Ltd (for modernisation within the hotel group)

1957 *Daily Telegraph* (for Son et Lumiere at Greenwich, London)

1958 'Talk of the Town' (for the 'Talk of the Town' theatre-restaurant in London)

1959 British Transport Commission (for various improvements and innovations in rail, hotel and catering services)

1960 Friends of Norwich Cathedral (for Son et Lumiere at Norwich Cathedral)

1961 Borough of Torquay (for the Princess Gardens Development Scheme)

1962 Chichester Festival Theatre Production Company Ltd (for the Chichester Festival Theatre in Sussex)

1963 Eastbourne Corporation (for the Congress Theatre and Conference Hall)

1964 Directors, Ulster Folk Museum (for the Ulster Folk Museum at Cultra Manor, Craigavad, Belfast)

1965 Isle of Man Harbour Board (for the Sea Terminal at Douglas)

1966 Brecon Beacons National Park Mountain Centre (for the Mountain Centre in mid-Wales)

1967 Aviemore Centre (for the Aviemore Centre in Inverness-shire)

1968 Anchor Hotels and Taverns Ltd (for the development of hotels throughout Britain; for the organisation of package tours; and for the introduction of 'Tourist Entertainment' houses)

1969 The Illuminating Engineering Society (for the installation in Trafalgar Square, London, of Britain's biggest ever floodlighting scheme)

1970 Visitor Centres Ltd (for the 'Landmark' visitor centre at Carrbridge, Inverness-shire)

1971 Medway Queen Co. Ltd (for the Medway Queen Leisure Park, Isle of Wight)

1972 Quarry Tours Ltd (for the Llechwedd Slate Caverns, Blaenau Ffestiniog, North Wales)

1973 Ironbridge Gorge Museum Trust (for the Ironbridge Gorge Museum, Shropshire)

1974 Welsh Canal Holiday Craft Ltd (for the Canal Exhibition Centre, Llangollen)

1975 National Railway Museum, York

1976 National Exhibition Centre, Birmingham

1977 Brighton Centre

1978 Brighton Marina

The National Railway Museum at York won the 1975 Come to Britain Trophy (*British Tourist Authority*)

TOYS

Toy of the Year

The National Association of Toy Retailers promotes this annual competition for manufacturers. It began in 1965. Winners:

1965	James Bond Aston Martin	1972	Plasticraft
1966	Action Man; Tiny Tears; Spirograph	1973	Master Mind (Game); Rotadraw
1967	Action Man	1974	Lego
1968	Sindy; Paint Wheels; Matchbox	1975	Lego
1969	Hot Wheels; Tippy Tombles; Airfix	1976	Peter Powell Kites
1970	Sindy; Corgi Rockets	1977	Playpeople
1971	Katie Kopycat	1978	Combine Harvester

TRACK AND FIELD   (See Athletics)

TRAMPOLINING

World Champions

World Championships were first held in 1964; there are Individual Championships for men and women and synchronised events for men and women. There is also a team event awarded on the basis of each nation's individual performances.

INDIVIDUAL CHAMPIONS

Men		Women	
1964	Danny Millman (USA)	1964	Judy Wills (USA)
1965	George Irwin (USA)	1965	Judy Wills (USA)
1966	Wayne Miller (USA)	1966	Judy Wills (USA)
1967	Dave Jacobs (USA)	1967	Judy Wills (USA)
1968	Dave Jacobs (USA)	1968	Judy Wills (USA)
1970	Wayne Miller (USA)	1970	Renee Ransom (USA)
1972	Paul Luxon (GB)	1972	Alexandra Nicholson (USA)
1974	Richard Tisson (Fra)	1974	Alexandra Nicholson (USA)
1976	Richard Tisson (Fra)	1976	Svetlana Levina (USSR)
1978	Tonisch (USSR)	1978	Tatiana Anisimova (USSR)

VEGETABLES

Giant Vegetable Competition

The competition was started by *Garden News* in 1960 and has been run annually since then. It was launched following the publication of one or two letters from readers claiming to have grown vegetables of record dimensions. This produced a chain reaction, with counter claims being made, and the then editor, John Bloom, thought that there was sufficient scope in this facet of gardening to warrant a competition. The first was so successful, in terms of both vegetable sizes and entry numbers, that it was decided to make it an annual competition.

There have always been odd classes at horticultural shows for giant vegetables, but always at a local level and the *Garden News* competition is open to all UK gardeners.

Garden News also instituted an 'Annual Giant League' competition for the largest specimens of vegetables and fruits grown in the British Isles. Thus many national records have been established, to serve as yardsticks for the future.

Mr Bishop, of Snailwell, Cambridgeshire, held the *Garden News* record for the largest vegetable marrow, weighing 60lb (27.2 *kg*), until 1977

VOLLEYBALL

Olympic Champions

First contested in 1964.

MEN		WOMEN	
1964	USSR	1964	Japan
1968	USSR	1968	USSR
1972	Japan	1972	USSR
1976	Poland	1976	Japan

World Champions

In addition to the Olympic Champions listed above.

MEN				WOMEN			
1949	USSR	1962	USSR	1952	USSR	1966	Japan
1952	USSR	1966	Czechoslovakia	1956	USSR	1970	USSR
1956	Czechoslovakia	1970	GDR	1960	USSR	1974	Japan
1960	USSR	1974	Poland	1962	Japan	1978	Cuba
		1978	USSR				

WALKING

Olympic Games: See Athletics section for Olympic winners.

Lugano Cup

The IAAF Walking Team Championship is contested annually by national teams for the Lugano Cup, which was first held at Lugano in 1961. Winners:

1961	Great Britain	1965	GDR	1970	GDR	1975	USSR
1963	Great Britain	1967	GDR	1973	GDR	1977	Mexico

Paul Nihill walking at London's Crystal Palace in 1970. He won a record 27 UK national walking titles (*E. D. Lacey*)

RWA Championships

The Race Walking Association hold annual English championships at 10 Miles, 20 000 Metres, 20 Miles and 50 000 Metres. In 1978 the 20 Miles was replaced by 30 000 Metres. Winners of most titles (in brackets the number of AAA titles won) are (AAA titles held at 2 Miles/3000 Metres, 7 Miles/10 000 Metres):

19 Paul Nihill (8); 9 Don Thompson (0); 9 Olly
Flynn (0); 8 Laurence Allen (0); 8 Harold Whitlock
(0); 7 Ken Matthews (10).
(*Note:* Roger Mills won 9 and Roland Hardy 8 AAA
titles)

Women's English Road Walking Championship

First held in 1933, winners of most titles:

8 Judy Farr: 1962–65, 1968, 1970, 1975–76
4 Joyce Heath: 1947–50, Betty Jenkins: 1967, 1969,
1971–72
Winner in 1977 and 1978 was Carol Tyson

WAR

Air Aces

The following lists set out the champion fighter pilots, with their tally of 'hits' in the two
World Wars.

FIRST WORLD WAR

The scores of above 50 victories from all nations are as
follows:

Manfred von Richthofen	Germany	80	Georges Guynemer	France	54
Rene Fonk	France	75	A. Beauchamp-Proctor	South Africa	54
Edward Mannock	Britain	73	D. M. MacLaren	Canada	54
William Bishop	Canada	72	Erich Loewenhardt	Germany	53
Ernst Udet	Germany	62	William Barker	Britain	52
Raymond Collishaw	Canada	62	P. Fullard	Britain	52
James McCudden	Britain	57	R. F. Dallas	Australia	51

SECOND WORLD WAR

The most successful fighter pilots of the Second World
War, by nationality, were:

Country of origin		Aircraft credited destroyed in combat
Australia	Wing Commander C. R. Caldwell	$28\frac{1}{2}$
Austria	Maj. Walter Nowotny	258
Belgium	Maj. Count Ivan Du Monceau de Bergendal	8
Bulgaria	Lieut. Stoyan Stoyanov	14
Canada	Flt.-Lieut. G. F. Beurling	$31\frac{1}{3}$
China	Col. Liu Chi-Sun	$11\frac{1}{3}$
Czechoslovakia	Second-Lieut. Rotnik Rezny	32
	Flt.-Lieut. K. Kuttelwascher	18
Denmark	Group Capt. K. Birksted	$10\frac{1}{2}$
Finland	Lmsti Eino Juutilainen	94
France	Capt. Marcel Albert	23
Germany	Maj. Erich Hartmann	352
Hungary	Second-Lieut. Dezso Szentgyorgyi	34
Italy	Magg. Adriano Visconti	26
	Capitano Franco Lucchini	26
Japan	Warrant Officer Hiroyoshi Nishizawa	87
Netherlands	Capt. C. Vlotman	4
New Zealand	Wing Commander C. F. Gray	27.7
Norway	Capt. Svein Heglund	$14\frac{1}{2}$
Poland	Wing Commander S. F. Skalski	21
Romania	Capt. Prince Constantine Cantacuzene	60
South Africa	Squadron Leader M. T. St J. Pattle	51 approx
UK	Group Captain J. E. Johnson	38

Country of origin		Aircraft credited destroyed in combat
USA	Maj. Richard I. Bong	40
USSR	Col. Ivan N. Kozhedub	62
Yugoslavia	Lieut. Cvitan Galic	36

WATER POLO

Olympic Champions

First contested in 1900 although the teams in 1900 and 1904 were club rather than national teams. Winners (men) since 1948:

1948	Italy	1964	Hungary
1952	Hungary	1968	Yugoslavia
1956	Hungary	1972	USSR
1960	Italy	1976	Hungary

World Champions

1973	Hungary
1975	USSR
1978	Italy

WATER SKIING

World Championships

The first World Championships were held at Juan Les Pins, France, in 1949. Championships are now contested biennially in three parts – Slalom, Tricks and Jumping, with a separate contest for the best overall performer. Overall Men's and Women's World Champions have been:

MEN

1949	Christian Jourdan (Fra) and Guy de Clercq (Bel)
1950	Dick Pope Jr (USA)
1953	Alfredo Mendoza (USA)
1955	Alfredo Mendoza (USA)
1957	Joe Cash (USA)
1959	Chuck Stearns (USA)
1961	Bruno Zaccardi (Ita)
1963	Billy Spencer (USA)
1965	Roland Hillier (USA)
1967	Mike Suyderhoud (USA)
1969	Mike Suyderhoud (USA)
1971	George Athans (Can)
1973	George Athans (Can)
1975	Carlos Suarez (Ven)
1977	Mike Hazelwood (GB)

WOMEN

1949	Willa Worthington (USA)
1950	Willa McGuire (née Worthington) (USA)
1953	Leah Marie Rawls (USA)
1955	Willa McGuire (USA)
1957	Marina Doria (Swi)
1959	Vickie Van Hook (USA)
1961	Sylvie Hulsemann (Lux)
1963	Jeanette Brown (USA)
1965	Liz Allan (USA)
1967	Jeanette Stewart-Wood (GB)
1969	Liz Allan (USA)
1971	Christy Weir (USA)
1973	Lisa St John (USA)
1975	Liz Shetter (née Allan) (USA)
1977	Cindy Todd (USA)

TEAM competition has been won by the USA for the 11 successive World Championships from 1957.

WEIGHTLIFTING

World and Olympic Champions

The first weightlifting World Championships were held in 1891 and weightlifting was included in the first modern Olympic Games in 1896.

From 1928 to 1972 the recognised lifts (all two-handed) were Clean and Press, Snatch, and Clean and Jerk. In 1972 the Clean and Press was dropped from the international programme. At the World Championships medals are awarded both for the individual lifts and for the aggregate total achieved in each weight category.

CHAMPIONS FOR AGGREGATE SINCE 1973
(* = Olympic champion) (with totals in kg)

Flyweight (52.0kg)
1973	Mohammad Nassiri (Irn)	240.0
1974	Mohammad Nassiri (Irn)	232.5
1975	Zigmunt Smalczerz (Pol)	237.5
1976*	Aleksandr Voronin (USSR)	242.5
1977	Aleksandr Voronin (USSR)	247.5
1978	Kanybek Osmonaliev (USSR)	240.0

Bantamweight (56.0kg)
1973	Atanas Kirov (USSR)	257.5
1974	Atanas Kirov (USSR)	255.0
1975	Atanas Kirov (Bul)	255.0
1976*	Norair Nurikyan (Bul)	262.5
1977	Jiro Hosotani (Jap)	252.5
1978	Daniel Nunez (Cub)	260.0

Featherweight (60.0kg)
1973	Dito Shanidze (USSR)	272.5
1974	Georgi Todorov (Bul)	280.0
1975	Georgi Todorov (Bul)	285.0
1976*	Nikolai Kolesnikov (USSR)	285.0
1977	Nikolai Kolesnikov (USSR)	280.0
1978	Nikolai Kolesnikov (USSR)	270.0

Lightweight (67.5kg)
1973	Muharbi Kirzhinov (USSR)	305.0
1974	Peter Korol (USSR)	305.0
1975	Peter Korol (USSR)	312.5
1976*	Peter Korol (USSR)	305.0
1977	Roberto Urrutia (Cub)	315.0
1978	Yanko Russev (Bul)	310.0

Middleweight (75.0kg)
1973	Nedelcho Kolev (Bul)	337.5
1974	Nedelcho Kolev (Bul)	335.0
1975	Peter Wenzel (GDR)	335.0
1976*	Jordan Mitkov (Bul)	335.0
1977	Yuriy Vardanian (USSR)	345.0
1978	Roberto Urrutia (Cub)	347.5

Light Heavyweight (82.5kg)
1973	Vladimir Rizhenkov (USSR)	350.0
1974	Trendafil Stojchev (Bul)	350.0
1975	Valeriy Shary (USSR)	357.5
1976*	Valeriy Shary (USSR)	365.0
1977	Gennadiy Bessonov (USSR)	352.5
1978	Yuriy Vardanian (USSR)	377.5

Middle Heavyweight (90.0kg)
1973	David Rigert (USSR)	365.0
1974	David Rigert (USSR)	387.5
1975	David Rigert (USSR)	377.5
1976*	David Rigert (USSR)	382.5
1977	Sergei Poltoratski (USSR)	375.0
1978	Rolf Milser (Ger)	377.5

Heavyweight 1 (100.0kg)
First held 1977.
1977	Anatoliy Kozlov (USSR)	367.5
1978	David Rigert (USSR)	390.0

Heavyweight 2 (110.0kg)
1973	Pavel Pervushin (USSR)	385.0
1974	Vladimir Ustyuzhin (USSR)	380.0
1975	Valentin Khristov (Bul)	417.5
1976*	Yuriy Zaitsev (USSR)	385.0
1977	Valentin Khristov (Bul)	405.0
1978	Yuriy Zaitsev (USSR)	402.5

Super Heavyweight (over 110kg)
1973	Vasiliy Alexeev (USSR)	402.5
1974	Vasiliy Alexeev (USSR)	425.0
1975	Vasiliy Alexeev (USSR)	427.5
1976*	Vasiliy Alexeev (USSR)	440.0
1977	Vasiliy Alexeev (USSR)	430.0
1978	Jurgen Heuser (GDR)	417.5

Most years as World or Olympic Champion (OG = Olympic Games)
8	Vasiliy Alexeev (USSR) 110.0 + : 1970–77 (inc. 2 OG)
8	John Davis (USA) 82.5: 1938; 82.5 + : 1946–52 (inc. 2 OG)
8	Tommy Kono (USA) 67.5: 1952 (OG); 75.0: 1953, 1957–59; 82.5: 1954–56 (inc. 1 OG)
7	Arkadiy Vorobyev (USSR) 82.5: 1953; 90.0: 1954–58, 1960 (inc. 2 OG)

WELLY HURLING

London Tournament

This event was held for the first time at the Tower of London on 8/9 September 1978. The winner received a golden mounted Wellington boot in recognition of setting a new world record with a distance of 173ft (52.7m). The event raised more than £3000 for charity.

The 1978 winner was Tony Rogers, Ship and Punchbowl, Warminster, Wiltshire.

WRESTLING

World Championships are held annually except in Olympic years at both Freestyle and Graeco-Roman style. Most World and Olympic titles have been won by:

8	Aleksandr Medved (USSR)	Freestyle Light-Heavy 1964*, 1966; Heavy 1967, 1968*; Super-Heavy 1969, 1970 1971, 1972*
6	Ali Aliev (USSR)	Freestyle Fly 1959, 1961, 1962; Bantam 1966, 1967, 1968*
6	Abdollah Movahed (Irn)	Freestyle Light 1965–70 (inc. 1968*)
6	Levan Tediashvili (USSR)	Freestyle Middle 1971, 1972*; Light-Heavy 1973–75, 1976*
5	Viktor Igumenov (USSR)	Graeco-Roman Welter 1966, 1967, 1969, 1970, 1971
5	Roman Rurua (USSR)	Graeco-Roman Feather 1966, 1967, 1968*, 1969, 1970
5	Valeriy Rezantyev (USSR)	Graeco-Roman Light-Heavy 1971, 1972*, 1973, 1974, 1976*
5	Nikolai Balboshin (USSR)	Graeco-Roman Heavy 1973, 1974, 1976*; Super-Heavy 1971, 1978

*Olympic champions

YACHTING

America's Cup

The America's Cup is an international challenge trophy, named after the schooner *America*, the winner of a race around the Isle of Wight in 1851. All the winning yachts listed here have come from the USA.

1870	*Magic*	1887	*Volunteer*	1920	*Resolute*	1964	*Constellation*
1871	*Columbia & Sappho*	1893	*Vigilant*	1930	*Enterprise*	1967	*Intrepid*
1876	*Madelaine*	1895	*Defender*	1934	*Rainbow*	1970	*Intrepid*
1881	*Mischief*	1899	*Columbia*	1937	*Ranger*	1974	*Courageous*
1885	*Puritan*	1901	*Columbia*	1958	*Columbia*	1977	*Courageous*
1886	*Mayflower*	1903	*Reliance*	1962	*Weatherly*		

Admiral's Cup

The Admiral's Cup is contested biennially by national 3-yacht teams. The competition comprises four races – a 200-mile Channel race, two inshore races held during Cowes Week, and finally the 605-mile Fastnet race from Cowes to the Fastnet Rock, off Southern Ireland, and back to Plymouth. First held 1957.

1957	Great Britain	1963	Great Britain	1969	USA	1975	Great Britain
1959	Great Britain	1965	Great Britain	1971	Great Britain	1977	Great Britain
1961	USA	1967	Australia	1973	W. Germany	1979	Australia

Olympic Games

The types of boat specified for Olympic competition have varied considerably over the years since 1900 when Yachting was first included in the Olympic Games. Individual winner of most Olympic titles:

4   Paul Elvstrom (Den) – *Firefly* 1948, *Finn* 1952, 1956, 1960

Singlehanded Trans-Atlantic Crossing Race

1960	*Gipsy Moth III* – Francis Chichester (GB) 40d 12hr 30min	1968	*Sir Thomas Lipton* – Geoffrey Williams (GB) 25d 20hr 33min
1962	*Gipsy Moth III* – Francis Chichester (GB) 33d 15hr 7min	1972	*Pen Duick IV* – Alain Colas (Fra) 20d 13hr 15min
1964	*Pen Duick II* – Eric Tabarly (Fra) 27d 3hr 56min	1976	*Pen Duick VI* – Eric Tabarly (Fra) 23d 20hr 12min

Whitbread Round the World Race

1973–74	Raymond Carlin, *Sayula II Mexico*	1977–78 Cornelius van Rietschoten, *Flyer Dutch*

INDEX